Operations Management and Productivity Techniques

Operations Management and Productivity Techniques

P.N. MUKHERJEE
Professor and Chairperson of
Total Quality Management and Supply Chain Management
and Head of Operations Management
Narsee Monjee Institute of Management Studies
Mumbai

T.T. KACHWALA
Professor of Operations Management and Decision Science
Narsee Monjee Institute of Management Studies
Mumbai

PHI Learning Private Limited

New Delhi - 110001
2009

Rs. 325.00

OPERATIONS MANAGEMENT AND PRODUCTIVITY TECHNIQUES
P.N. Mukherjee and T.T. Kachwala

ISBN-978-81-203-3602-5

The export rights of this book are vested solely with the publisher.

Published by Asoke K. Ghosh, PHI Learning Private Limited, M-97, Connaught Circus, New Delhi-110001 and Printed by Rajkamal Electric Press, B-35/9, G.T. Karnal Road Industrial Area, Delhi-110033.

CONTENTS

Preface .... *xv*

Chapter 1   OPERATIONS MANAGEMENT **1–30**

1.1   Introduction to Operations Management 1
1.2   Definition and Concept of Management 2
1.3   The Concept of Production and Operations Management 3
1.4   The Concept of Service Industry 4
1.5   Operations Management 5
1.6   The Operations Management Functions 7
1.7   Deming's P-D-C-A Cycle 8
1.8   Latest Trends in Operations Management 12
     1.8.1   The Process Approach 12
     1.8.2   ISO 9000:2000 13
     1.8.3   Statistical Process Control and Six Sigma Approach 14
1.9   Concept of Productivity 16
1.10 Managerial Roles and Skills 17
     1.10.1 Technical Skills 17
     1.10.2 Human Relations Skill 17
     1.10.3 Decision-Making Role/Entrepreneurship Skills 18
1.11 The Concept of Customer Satisfaction 19
     1.11.1 The Concept of Right Quality 20
     1.11.2 The Concept of Right Quantity 21
     1.11.3 The Concept of Right Time 21
     1.11.4 The Concept of Right Place 22
     1.11.5 The Concept of Right Price 22
1.12 The Importance of Return on Investment 23
1.13 The Functions of Contemporary Organization and Its Departments 26
Exercises 30

**Chapter 2   FACILITIES PLANNING—PLANT LOCATION, PLANT LAYOUT
               AND MATERIAL HANDLING** **31–60**

2.1   Types of Production 31
     2.1.1   Job or Project Production 32
     2.1.2   Batch Production 32

2.1.3 Mass Production 32
2.1.4 Continuous Production 33
2.2 Types of Manufacturing Processes 33
2.2.1 Assembling 34
2.2.2 Welding and Fabrication 34
2.2.3 Machining 34
2.2.4 Metal Forming 35
2.2.5 Forging 35
2.2.6 Casting 36
2.2.7 Plastic Forming 36
2.2.8 Chemical Processing 37
2.2.9 Heat Treatment and Plating 37
2.3 Hard Factors of Production 38
2.4 Soft Factors of Production 38
2.5 Plant Location 39
2.5.1 Important Factors for Plant Location 40
2.6 Plant Layout 43
2.6.1 Objectives of Plant Layout 44
2.6.2 Plant Layout Design Procedure 44
2.6.3 Planning, Designing and Implementation of Plant Layout 45
2.6.4 Computerized Relative Allocation of Facilities Technique (CRAFT) ... 46
2.6.5 Types of Plant Layout 47
2.7 Material Handling 55
2.7.1 Functional Activities 55
2.7.2 Fundamentals of Material Handling 56
2.7.3 Objectives of Material Handling 57
2.7.4 Stages of Material Handling 57
2.7.5 Material Handling Assessment 58
2.7.6 Factors for Selection of Equipments 58
2.7.7 Types of Material Handling Equipments 59
Exercises 60

Chapter 3 HOLISTIC MANAGEMENT PRACTICE FOR WORLD-CLASS PERFORMANCE AND LEADERSHIP 61–73

3.1 Introduction to Total Quality Management (TQM) 61
3.2 TQM with Reference to Indian Industries 62
3.3 Holistic Management Practice for World-Class Performance 64
3.3.1 Foundation 65
3.3.2 Infrastructure 67
3.3.3 Total Quality Management Process 70
3.3.4 The Result 71
Exercises 72

Chapter 4 QUALITY AND ITS DEFINITIONS, CONCEPTS AND FEATURES 74–125

4.1 Introduction 74
    4.1.1 Quality Concepts and Definitions... 76
    4.1.2 The Dimensions of Product Quality.. 78
    4.1.3 Vital Characteristics of Quality... 78
4.2 Evolution of Quality Management 80
4.3 Evolution of Total Quality Management Concept.................................... 81
4.4 TQM Leads to World-Class Management System 83
    4.4.1 Definition of Various Quality-Related Terms 85
    4.4.2 Definitions, Concepts and Features of "TQM"........................... 86
    4.4.3 The Eight Building Blocks of TQM 90
    4.4.4 Pre-requisites for the Success of 'TQM' 93
4.5 Cost of Quality.. 94
    4.5.1 Prevention Costs... 95
    4.5.2 Appraisal Costs... 96
    4.5.3 Internal Failure Costs... 96
    4.5.4 External Failure Costs... 96
4.6 '5' S of Housekeeping 96
4.7 Total Quality Management Pioneers 97
    4.7.1 Quality Contribution by Quality Gurus 98
4.8 Eleven TQM Steps to Become a World-Class Organization 102
4.9 ISO 9000:2000 Quality Mangement System 103
    4.9.1 Definition of ISO 9000:2000 104
    4.9.2 Purpose of the Quality Management System 104
    4.9.3 Evolution of ISO 9000 105
    4.9.4 Development of the Quality Management Systems 106
    4.9.5 The Present Versions of ISO 9001:2000 and ISO 9004:2000 are based on Eight Quality Management Principles Which Reflect the Best Management Practices 106
    4.9.6 ISO 9000 Expectations 109
    4.9.7 Details of ISO 9001:2000 Certification Standard 109
4.10 ISO 14001:1996 Environmental Management System 110
4.11 ISO/TS 16949:2002(E) (Earlier Specification QS 9000:1998)— 'QMS' for Automobile Industry.. 111
4.12 Quality Movements in Different Nations... 112
    4.12.1 The US Quality Revolution 112
    4.12.2 Quality Movement in Asian Countries.................................... 114
    4.12.3 Quality Movement in Japan 115
    4.12.4 Quality Movement in India 116
4.13 Why Do Some Quality Improvement Efforts Fail?............................... 120
    4.13.1 Reasons Why TQM Programme Fails....................................... 121
4.14 Future Challenges.. 123
4.15 Summary and Synthesis of Observations 124
Exercises.. 125

Chapter 5 STATISTICAL PROCESS CONTROL 126–153

5.1   Introduction to Statistical Process Control 126
5.2   Sampling 126
5.3   Frequency Distribution Curve, Bar Chart and Histogram 127
5.4   Inspection and Quality Control 129
5.5   Mean, Range, Standard Deviation and Variance 132
5.6   Continuous Sampling Inspection 133
     5.6.1   Single Sampling Plan 134
     5.6.2   Double Sampling Plan 135
     5.6.3   Multiple Sampling Plan 135
     5.6.4   Sequential Sampling Plan 136
5.7 $\bar{X}$ -Chart 136
5.8   R-Chart 137
5.9 p-Chart 140
5.10 c-Chart 142
5.11 Statistical Process Control 144
     5.11.1 Principle of Statistical Process Control 145
5.12 Dispersion and Process Capability 147
     5.12.1 Abnormal Distributions 148
5.13 Analysis of Process Out of Control 149
     5.13.1 Corrective Actions 149
5.14 The Causes of Process Variation 151
Exercises 152

Chapter 6 PRODUCTION PLANNING, CONTROL AND SCHEDULING 154–180

6.1   Demand Measurement and Sales Forecasting 154
6.2   Production Planning and Control 160
     6.2.1   Planning Phase 161
     6.2.2   Important Features of Production Planning and Control 164
     6.2.3   Strategies Used to Absorb Fluctuations in Demand 165
     6.2.4   Techniques for Absorbing Fluctuations in Demand 165
     6.2.5   Economic Batch Quantity (EBQ) 170
     6.2.6   Process Planning 171
6.3   Scheduling 172
     6.3.1   Objectives of Scheduling 173
     6.3.2   Types of Scheduling 174
     6.3.3   Factors Affecting Scheduling 174
     6.3.4   Scheduling and Loading Guidelines 175
     6.3.5   Scheduling Methodology 175
     6.3.6   Master Production Schedule (MPS) 178
Exercises 179

Chapter 7 PRODUCTIVITY IMPROVEMENT TECHNIQUES 181–197

7.1   Definition and Concept of Productivity 181
     7.1.1   Productivity and Performance 182
     7.1.2   Partial Productivity 182

7.1.3 Total Factor Productivity 183
7.1.4 Total Productivity 183
7.1.5 Applications of Productivity Technique 185
7.1.6 The American Productivity Centre Model 186
7.2 Total Productivity Model (TPM) 187
7.2.1 Salient Features of TPM 188
7.2.2 Causes of Poor Productivity 189
7.2.3 Sumanth's Five-Pronged Approach to Productivity Improvement 191
7.2.4 Implementation of Total Productivity Model 196
7.2.5 Limitations of the Total Productivity Model 197
Exercises 197

Chapter 8 WORK STUDY 198–216
8.1 Work Study 198
8.2 Application of Work Study 199
8.2.1 Advantages/Objectives of Work Study 199
8.3 Method Study 200
8.3.1 Objectives/Advantages of Method Study 200
8.3.2 Method Study Procedure 201
8.3.3 Flow Process Chart 201
8.3.4 Symbols for Drawing the Flow Process Chart 202
8.3.5 Flow Diagram 203
8.3.6 Operation Analysis 203
8.3.7 Material Type Flow Process Chart 205
8.3.8 Man Type Flow Process Chart 206
8.3.9 Machine Type Flow Process Chart 206
8.4 Motion Study 207
8.4.1 Analysis of Motion 207
8.4.2 Principles of Motion Economy 208
8.4.3 Therbligs 211
8.5 Time Study (Work Measurement) 212
8.5.1 Stop Watch Procedure for Collecting Time Study Data 213
8.5.2 Standard Time 214
8.5.3 Allowances 215
8.5.4 Standard Data 215
8.5.5 Time Study Form 216
Exercises 216

Chapter 9 WORLD-CLASS MANUFACTURING TECHNIQUE 217–243
9.1 Value Analysis (VA) and Value Engineering 217
9.1.1 Definition 217
9.1.2 Features of Value Analysis 217
9.1.3 Concept of Value 218
9.1.4 Steps in Value Analysis 218
9.1.5 Factors Influencing Product Design or Redesign 218

9.1.6 Methods of Value Analysis 220
9.1.7 Value Analysis—Areas of Improvement 222
9.1.8 Phases of Value Engineering 223
9.1.9 Darsiri Method 225
9.2 SMED (Single Minute Exchange of Dies) 226
9.2.1 Steps of SMED 227
9.2.2 Success Stories of SMED 228
9.2.3 Examples of SMED 228
9.2.4 Four Principles by Shingo for Achieving SMED 228
9.3 Total Productive Maintenance 229
9.3.1 Effects of Poor Maintenance 229
9.3.2 Causes of Machine Failures 229
9.3.3 Focus of Total Productive Maintenance 230
9.3.4 Features of Total Productive Maintenance 230
9.4 Benchmarking 232
9.4.1 Types of Benchmarking 232
9.4.2 Three Reasons for Benchmarking Competition 233
9.4.3 Elements of Benchmarking 234
9.4.4 Benchmarking Measurements 235
9.4.5 Process of Benchmarking 235
9.5 Business Process Re-engineering (BPR) 238
9.5.1 The Concept of Business Process Re-engineering 239
9.5.2 Implementation of Business Process Re-engineering 240
9.5.3 Case Study 242
Questions 243
Exercises 243

Chapter 10   SUPPLY CHAIN MANAGEMENT 244–267

10.1 Supply Chain Management 244
10.2 Logistics and Supply Chain Management 245
10.2.1 The Concept of Right Quality 245
10.2.2 The Concept of Right Quantity 246
10.2.3 The Concept of Right Place 246
10.2.4 The Concept of Time Utility 247
10.2.5 The Concept of Price Utility 247
10.3 Benefits of Supply Chain Management 248
10.4 Pre-requisites for Effective Supply Chain Management 249
10.5 Flow in the Supply Chain and Logistics Management 249
10.6 Logistics Management 250
10.7 Inventory Management 251
10.8 Dependent Demand and Independent Demand 252
10.9 Inventory Cost 252
10.9.1 Cost Associated with Materials 253
10.9.2 Eight Areas of Inventory Control System 254

10.10 Material Requirement Planning (MRP-I) 254
    10.10.1 Bill of Material (BOM) 255
    10.10.2 Inventory Status File 256
    10.10.3 Master Production Schedule 256
    10.10.4 MRP-I Package 257
10.11 Manufacturing Resource Planning (MRP-II) 257
10.12 Material Requirement Planning and Manufacturing
     Resource Planning (MRP-I & MRP-II) Combined 259
10.13 Distribution Requirement Planning (DRP) 259
10.14 Objectives of Supply Chain Management 260
10.15 Pre-requisites for the Success of MRP, DRP, and SCM 260
10.16 Just-in-Time (JIT) 261
    10.16.1 Core Japanese Practices of JIT 261
    10.16.2 JIT Enablers 262
    10.16.3 Just In Case Stock (JIC) 262
    10.16.4 Just-In-Time System 263
    10.16.5 JIT Purchasing 263
    10.16.6 Just-In-Time Production 264

Chapter 11 SERVICE QUALITY **268–314**

11.1 Preface on Quality Management Practices in Service Industries 268
11.2 Introduction to Quality Management Practices in Service Industries 270
11.3 Quality Management Practices in Service Industries in USA 272
    11.3.1 Surveys for Service Industries in USA 273
11.4 Quality Management Practices in Service Industries in Japan 274
11.5 Quality Management Practices in Service Industries in Asian Countries 274
11.6 Quality Management Practices in Service Industries in India 275
11.7 How Do We Define Service Sector? 282
11.8 Why is Service Sector Quality Control so Important? 284
    11.8.1 Why hasn't Quality Service Taken Hold? 284
    11.8.2 What is Service Quality? 285
    11.8.3 What is Total Quality Service? 286
    11.8.4 Does Quality Service Pay? 287
    11.8.5 Research Observations in USA in the Context
           'Does Quality Service Pay?' 287
    11.8.6 Importance of Customers in Service Quality 289
    11.8.7 Importance of Physical Environment in Service Quality 290
11.9 Categories of Service Quality Characteristics 292
11.10 Knowing the Customers 294
11.11 Difference between Goods and Services 296
11.12 Some Generalizations Regarding Service Sector 299
    11.12.1 Techniques for Determining Customer Needs 300
    11.12.2 Tools for Tracking and Measuring Customer Satisfaction 301
11.13 Effective Service Recovery 301
    11.13.1 Identifying Service Failures 304
    11.13.2 The Following are the Strategies for Recovering Successfully 305

11.14 Service Leadership Spells Profits 306
       11.14.1 Characteristics of Service Leaders 308
11.15 Factors Influencing Customer's Expectations 309
11.16 Service Quality (Customer's Perspective) 310
11.17 ISO 9001:2000 Quality Management Systems 312
11.18 Benchmarking 312
Exercises 313

Chapter 12   SERVICE QUALITY RESEARCH AND SUBJECT DEVELOPMENT 315–350

12.1   Research on Service Quality 315
12.2   Summary and Synthesis of Observations 329
12.3   Service Quality Management (From Customer's Point of View) 330
12.4   The Critical Dimensions of TQM (TQS) {From Management's Point of
       View or Service Provider's Point of View} as Defined in the Drawing 333
Exercises 337
Annexure 338

Chapter 13   THEORY OF CONSTRAINTS (TOC) 351–355

13.1   Introduction 351
13.2   *The Goal* by Dr. Eliyahu Goldratt Jeff Cox 351
13.3   Some Principles of Synchronous Production 352
       13.3.1 Empirical Observation One 352
       13.3.2 Empirical Observation Two 353
       13.3.3 Empirical Observation Three 353
13.4   The Drum–Buffer–Rope Mechanism 353
       13.4.1 The Drum 354
       13.4.2 The Buffer 354
       13.4.3 The Rope 355
Exercises 355

Chapter 14   BASIC INVENTORY CONCEPTS 356–370

14.1   Five Reasons for Holding Inventory 356
       14.1.1 Economies of Scale 356
       14.1.2 Balancing Supply and Demand 357
       14.1.3 Specialization 357
       14.1.4 Protection from Uncertainties 358
       14.1.5 A Buffer throughout the Supply Chain 358
14.2   Types of Inventory 360
       14.2.1 Cycle Stock 360
       14.2.2 In-Transit Inventories 361
       14.2.3 Safety or Buffer Stock 361
       14.2.4 Speculative Stock 363
       14.2.5 Seasonal Stock 364
       14.2.6 Dead Stock 364

14.3 Symptoms of Poor Inventory Management.. 364
14.4 Way to Reduce Inventory Levels 364
14.5 Improving Inventory Management 365
    14.5.1 ABC Analysis (Pareto Principle)—The 80/20 Rule 365
    14.5.2 Forecasting 367
    14.5.3 How ERP Systems Contribute to Improved Inventory Management 368
    14.5.4 Order Processing Systems 369
14.6 Summary 370
Exercises 370

Chapter 15 MANAGING MATERIAL FLOW **371–388**

15.1 Introduction 371
15.2 Scope of Materials Management Activities 372
    15.2.1 Purchasing and Procurement 374
    15.2.2 Production Control 374
    15.2.3 Inbound Logistics 375
    15.2.4 Warehousing and Storage 376
    15.2.5 Data and Information Systems 376
    15.2.6 Inventory Planning and Control 377
    15.2.7 Reverse Logistics 377
15.3 Forecasting 377
    15.3.1 Why Forecast? 377
    15.3.2 Types of Forecasts 378
    15.3.3 Forecasting Time Frames 378
15.4 Certifying Quality with ISO 9000 379
15.5 Total Quality Management (TQM) 379
    15.5.1 Difficulties in Implementing TQM 380
    15.5.2 Keys to TQM Success 380
15.6 Administration and Control of Materials Flow 382
15.7 Kanban and Just-In-Time Systems 383
    15.7.1 JIT 384
15.8 ERP Systems 387
15.9 The Logistics and Manufacturing Interface 387
15.10 Summary 388
Exercises 388

Chapter 16 FORECASTING METHODS **389–400**

16.1 Forecasting 389
16.2 Patterns in Time Series 389
16.3 Methods of Time Series 390
    16.3.1 Simple Average Method 391
    16.3.2 Moving Average 391
    16.3.3 Weighted Moving Average 392
    16.3.4 Exponential Smoothing 392
    16.3.5 Using Trend Projection in Forecasting 393

16.3.6 Seasonal Variation 394
16.3.7 Casual Regression 394
16.4 Qualitative Methods of Forecasting 395
Exercises 396
Exercise Problems 396

Chapter 17 INTRODUCTION TO OPERATIONS RESEARCH 401–406

17.1 The Historical Development 401
17.2 Nature and Significance of Operations Research 401
17.3 What is Operations Research? 402
17.4 What are Operations Research Techniques? 404
Exercises 406

References 407–409

Index 411–416

PREFACE

Outdated management theories and business principles are still practised in many business houses. This attitude needs to change with the changing business environment owing to liberalization and globalization processes started in the 1990s. However, we find that most of the conventional business houses still follow the outdated managerial practices. Today, the key factors recognized for survival and performance excellence of any industry are "Customer Satisfaction" and "Return On Investment (ROI)". This applies to both the manufacturing and the service sectors. Since the concerned managers do not necessarily appreciate these concepts in their correct perspective, industries after industries, both in the manufacturing and the service sectors, are suffering. Many industries, during the last two decades, have closed down their shutters, unable to cope with the international competition and the forces of globalization. Hence the pertinent question emerges—how to reverse this trend and survive in the current turbulent and challenging business environment?

The simple survival strategy is not adequate. Industries should aim for excellence in their performance to survive and prosper. In today's business environment, either you move ahead or you move out; the options are clear. The onslaught of foreign multinationals has been fast and impressive in every field of manufacturing—be it FMCG, automobiles, textiles or chemical industries. The liberalization and globalization era started in the 1990s, has swept much faster than the Indian industries could cope with. The management concepts and practices need to be upgraded to current international theories on management techniques. The current cases of business success of the globally renowned enterprises need to be looked into to redefine the emerging business strategies in a systematic and scientific manner.

With the rapidly changing business environment and the fast emerging international competition, the industries need to change their ways of functioning, redefine the management and the managerial roles as well as have clear-cut objectives and goals. The industries should evolve managerial style and functioning equivalent to world-class performance geared towards business excellence.

The recent overwhelming changes in the international business environment have made most of the conventional books on the subject redundant as they deal with the pre-globalization era. There is a dearth of comprehensive books covering all the aspects of modern-day operations management. Today, the students of engineering and management have to refer to a number of books and articles on the subject and still may be left in the lurch for want of information covering the entire syllabus. It is fervently hoped that this book will fulfil the need of the students in the area of operations management. The book also deals with the practical approaches to increase the productivity of an organization in a simple and definitive manner.

P.N. MUKHERJEE
T.T. KACHWALA

1

Operations Management

1.1 INTRODUCTION TO OPERATIONS MANAGEMENT

Outdated management theories and business principles are still taught in most of the management institutes. The curriculum needs to be updated to keep pace with the changes that have taken place in India and in the international business environment since the 1990s and into the new millennium as a result of liberalization and globalization. We find most of the conventional business houses still following the outdated managerial practices and definitions. Ninety per cent of the advertisements for job opportunities clearly insist on previous experience in the same function or department in the same or similar industry or industries. Students in the management institutes also aspire to specialize only in certain areas like marketing, finance, and HR and tend to turn a blind eye towards acquiring the basic knowledge in other areas.

The key factors for survival and performance excellence in any industry are *Customer Satisfaction* and *Return on Investment (ROI)*. This applies to both manufacturing and service sectors. Even though everybody talks about these things, hardly anybody understands the meaning in the correct perspective. The unfortunate result of this is many organizations, both in the manufacturing and service sectors, are closing down. The scenario is common in any industrial area in the country whether it is Peenya Industrial Area in Bangalore (once the largest industrial estate in Asia), the Wagle Industrial Estate in Thane near Mumbai (the second largest Industrial estate in Asia), the Bhosari Industrial Area in Pune, the Faridabad Industrial Area near Delhi in Haryana or Padi in Chennai. Seventy per cent of the industries have closed down their shutters, unable to face the international competition and the forces of globalization. Hence the pertinent question emerges—How to reverse the trend and survive in the current turbulent challenging business environment?

The simple survival strategy is not adequate. The industries should aim for excellence in their performance to survive and excel. In today's business environment, either you have to move ahead or you have to move out—the options are clear. The onslaught of the foreign multinationals has been fast and drastic in every field of manufacturing—be it FMCG, automobile, textile or chemical industries. The liberalization and globalization process took place in the '90s, much faster than the Indian industries could imagine and cope up with. The management thoughts and practices also needed to be upgraded to the latest international management theories, practices and techniques. The essence of current cases of business success of globally renowned enterprises has to be looked into in redefining the successful business strategies in a systematic and scientific manner.

With the overwhelming changes taking place in the business environment and the consequent intense international competition, the industries need to change their ways of functioning, redefine the management and managerial roles as well as have clear-cut objectives and goals integrated with the same intensity and functional unification of individual functions with the organizational goal. The industry should think today only of a managerial style and functioning equivalent to world-class performance oriented towards business excellence. After an intensive research in this direction, a simple holistic approach has to be adopted and conventional approach has to be replaced by a world-class performance orientation as described hereafter.

1.2 DEFINITION AND CONCEPT OF MANAGEMENT

In industrial and business circles, there is so much importance given to the concept of Management. However, if one asks practising managers from different levels to explain its meaning, there would be many explanations widely varying from one another. You come across various management activities like General Management, Purchase Management, Materials Management, Production Management, Operation Management, Marketing Management, Personnel Management, Human Resource Management, Maintenance Management, Logistics Management, Supply Chain Management and so on. With new challenges emerging with globalization and liberalization, the concept of management has undergone a sea change in its definition and interpretation. For each function, each individual differs widely in the understanding and interpretation of the concept of management. But they all agree on one common point, i.e. 'management is vital to running a business or for that matter any activity whatsoever successfully'. Let us get the fundamental concept of 'Management' clear before we proceed any further.

The universal conventional definition of 'management' is 'The Art and Science of getting things done from others'.

If we agree to this definition which is a century old, a basic question arises—what is the manager supposed to do? Is he supposed to get work done from others, but do nothing himself? It defies the fundamental principle of leadership wherein 'leaders' have to lead by example. It has been found that excellent organizations have a leader at the top who is also the role model for the rest of his team. This signifies that a successful manager also practises what he preaches to his team. Successful entrepreneurs like Bill Gates of Microsoft, Azim Premji of Wipro, Narayana Murthi of Infosys, Jamshedji Tata of the Tata Group and Dhirubhai Ambani of Reliance have been leaders as well as role models for their organizations and others. Many of them had no formal management education but they had one thing in common—extremely successful business management skills in which they were the role models who practised themselves every bit of what they preached about the business management to rest of their teams.

Now *'management' in its correct perspective can be defined as 'management is a continuous process of creating and maintaining an environment conducive for performance for a group of people working together towards attainment of a common objective or goal in time'.*

The definition can be elaborated as:

- Management is a process-oriented approach.
- Management is not a one-time activity.
- Management is the art and science of creating and maintaining an environment conducive for performance.
- Management is teamwork by a group of people bound by a common objective.
- The last two words 'in time' are extremely important. Every activity and every objective has a time element beyond which it becomes state and irrelevant.

For example, assume that you have consumed the least amount of resources for producing some goods and the quality is of the highest order. But it has to be ready by 10th of the month as per the 'letter of credit' delivery norms. Instead it got completed by the 20th day of the month. Here everything is fine but 'in time' element is not maintained. The result is zero as the delivery date has expired. The consignment becomes useless unless of course the customers agree to reopen the letter of credit extending the date which may be a remote possibility.

1.3 THE CONCEPT OF PRODUCTION AND OPERATIONS MANAGEMENT

The difference between Production Management and Operations Management is not yet clearly defined and explained by most of the management books. These two are distinctly different streams of the subject of management. Production management mainly deals with the manufacturing of any product, i.e. the conversion of raw material into finished goods. Production management is a relatively old concept of management. It is applicable only in manufacturing activity. Operations management is altogether a new management concept universally applicable in all functions including production, materials, human resources, marketing, logistics and supply chain management. Operations Management imparts knowledge as to how to handle any process in any function efficiently and effectively. A process or an operation has an input and an output (value added input) and the process itself consists of value addition through conversion. The Management of Operations involves the efficient and effective handling of the same wherein the value addition to input is maximum and the utilization of the resources is minimum aimed towards the maximization of customer satisfaction and Return on Investment. The concept of production management and operations management can be further elaborated in a simplistic manner by the explanation given hereafter.

If someone distributes a stainless steel sheet of 1 m × 1 m to a group of people in a lecture session and asks them to take it home, even if it is offered free of cost, the members of the group may not be interested. A 1 m × 1 m stainless steel sheet of odd size is difficult to carry home and is of no use to them. But by deploying men and machines if the same stainless steel sheet can be converted into 'utensils' and is offered to the group not free of cost but at an attractive discount of 25–30%, many members may be interested in these utensils now as they have value for them.

The example cited above is equally relevant to any 'manufacturing industry'. Production is a key activity in manufacturing industry.

Hence 'production' can be defined as 'value addition by conversion and/or transformation of input raw material into finished product with the deployment of men and machines and/or tools'.

If we elaborate this basic concept, we will come to the conclusion that:

- In a manufacturing industry, the input is the 'raw material' and output is 'value added raw material' or the 'finished product'.
- The finished product obviously has more value to the end-user than the raw material.
- Production leads to value addition to input raw material.
- The 'hard factors' of production are men, machines and materials.
- The 'soft factors' of production are management, money and technology.
- This 'value addition' process needs certain input resources like raw material, men, machines and/or tools.
- Each of these input resources costs money. Hence 'money' is another factor of production. However 'money' is considered a 'soft factor' of production.
- 'Management' teaches the process of adding maximum value by consumption of least amount of resources for attainment of the end objective.
- The cost of all these input resources added together constitutes the 'cost of value addition' to the input raw material.
- For an organization to survive, it must have the ability to create 'surplus' which can be explained as the value added minus the cost of value addition.

  For example, if Rs. 40 is the cost of raw material and another Rs. 30 is the cost of value addition, then Rs. 70 becomes the total cost of input resources. The product has to be sold at a price higher than Rs. 70 to create a surplus. If the customer is ready to pay Rs. 100 for the finished product, the value added is Rs. 100 – Rs. 40 = Rs. 60. The cost of value addition is Rs. 30. Hence the 'surplus' generated in this case is Rs. 60 – Rs. 30 = Rs. 30.
- The efficiency of an organization lies in its ability to create surplus.

1.4 THE CONCEPT OF SERVICE INDUSTRY

In the service industry, the input is the 'customer' and the output is the 'value added customers'. The process of value addition is also by conversion. The value addition to the customer should be more than the cost of value addition. This process should also be both efficient as well as effective, i.e. the entire process should follow a time schedule and as per the target. The efficiency of service sector is also its ability to create a surplus.

There were times till the 1980s when the contribution of the service sector to the nation's GDP was in single digit. Today, the service sector comprises more than one third of GDP for most nations in the world. The contribution of the service sector to national wealth is substantial.

The input of a management institute are the fresh graduate students. The management institute adds value to them by imparting management knowledge and converts them into management postgraduates whose market value with the industries is far more than those of fresh graduates. The input to a pleader is a litigated customer having a fear of either paying money or fine for economic offence or a client facing criminal proceedings for fear of being jailed. To retrieve himself from the litigation, he pays fees to the lawyer and the expected output is a litigation-free client. The input of a doctor is a sick human being and the output is a healthy human being.

While the word production is normally confined to the area of manufacturing, the concept of operation can be applied to any industrial sector—manufacturing or service sector and also to any function related to marketing, materials, human resource, etc.

1.5 OPERATIONS MANAGEMENT

Operations management is the management of a process or a sub-process consisting of a distinctive input and a well-defined process for value addition by conversion leading to a value added output. Operations management principles are uniformly applied to both the manufacturing and the service sectors. For the manufacturing industry, the input is the raw material and the output are the finished goods or products and the associated services (refer Figure 1.1). For the service sector, the input is the customer and the output is the value added customer. Here again operation is the process of adding value by conversion (refer Figure 1.2). In both the cases, the input resources are the men, machines, finance, management and technology. Operations management ensures that the process should be both efficient and effective and generate a surplus.

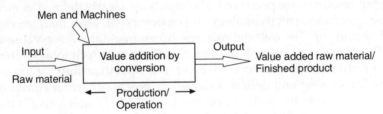

FIGURE 1.1 Value addition in manufacturing industry.

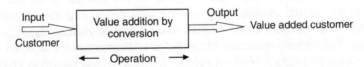

FIGURE 1.2 Value addition in service sector.

Hence *'Operations Management' can be defined as 'The operation of effectively and efficiently carrying out a business process or an activity which leads to accomplishment of the goal and/or objective normally related to an organization with the creation of maximum possible surplus in time'.*

This definition can be expanded for understanding as:

- Operations management is the management of a business process.
- The management of business process should be both effective and efficient.
- Effectiveness can be defined as the ability to achieve the target or rather the extent of nearness to the target.

- The concept of operations management has been introduced to the industry with the advent of 'CWQA' or company-wide quality assurance activity.
- 'Efficiency' can be defined as the ratio of the value of output to the value of the input resources consumed to reach the end objective with the least amount of resources. The efficiency of the process under focus should always be greater than one (>1) for the organization to survive and make a profit for growth and sustenance.
- 'Value added' is the value of the output minus the value of the input. 'The cost of value addition' is the value of consumed resources like men and machines for the purpose of value addition.
- 'Surplus' is the difference between the value added and the cost of value addition. For an organization to survive, the surplus should always be positive.
- The performance of a manager is measured by his/her ability to generate surplus in harmony with the organizational objective.
- For the management of any operation, there is always a goal or objective to be accomplished within a certain time frame.
- The concept of operations management can be equally and effectively applied to all functions including 'Production', 'Marketing', 'Finance', 'General Management', 'Human Resource Management', and also to both manufacturing and service sectors.

The final universal model of operations management is depicted in Figure 1.3, where the various input resources are portrayed. The inputs are clearly defined as men, machines, material, money, management, technology and environment. Men, machines and materials are the hard factors or the well-defined resources mandatory for value addition by conversion. The conversion process follows a well-defined technology. The technology enables the products and services to meet the specifications of performance in manufacturing/processing and defines a clear flow process chart for conversion which is the best alternative among the various options. Here the best alternative is that particular technology of conversion which satisfies the product feature requirements as well as the process requirements for conversion with the least consumption of input resources. The management ensures the optimum utilization of all the resources for the attainment of the business objective of maximizing the customer satisfaction and the return on investment in time. Finance to an organization is like blood to the human body which ensures effective circulation of various resources towards the attainment of the defined organizational objective. Environment plays a leading role in today's global business environment and international competition, shorter product life cycles, frequently changing political relationships between nations, constantly emerging threats from substitute products and technological innovations, etc. A systematic understanding of the political, social, economic and technological environment is mandatory for the survival and world-class performance of an organization. The most important aspect of the Operations Management is that it leads to the position of market leadership, all round performance excellence and multiplying return on investment with the same resources with no additional investment whatsoever.

The 1970s were the era of new innovations in products and services and belonged to the engineers. The 1980s belonged to marketing professionals whose job was to sensitize customers of the innovations of the 1970s and the 1980s and capitalize on the same to

MANAGEMENT

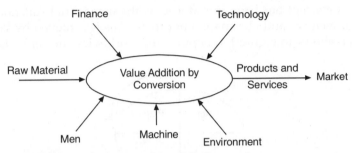

FIGURE 1.3 The universal model of operations management.

gain market leadership. The focus was basically on the product. The era between the end of the 1980s to the first two years of the 1990s were dominated by the financial managers who displaced the traditional Chartered Accountants who only kept details on inflow and outflow of the money and their auditing. The early 1990s to the beginning of the next millennium belonged to Information Technology professionals. Currently, Information Technology has been recognized as an enabler to all other functions without exception. Service industry was traditionally a single digit contributor to the GDP of most nations in the world. In the last two decades it has steadily jumped to a major contributor to the GDP of most of the nations in the world. In some of the world's leading economies, it is contributing nearly as much as the manufacturing sector. In this newly emerging dynamic environment, Operations Management is the latest field of management which enables an organization to have an all round performance excellence both in the manufacturing as well as in the service sector. It is therefore strongly felt that Operations Management will play a dominant and decisive role in the emerging business environment in the next decade.

1.6 THE OPERATIONS MANAGEMENT FUNCTIONS

Conventionally the managerial functions are Planning, Organizing, Staffing, Directing and Controlling. This managerial functions concept was discarded by the Japanese industry more than 50 years back. By mid-1970s and early 1980s the European, American and then the rest of the world's industry realised the flaws in the managerial function approach. The reasoning was simple. Can you ever draw a 'Plan' without an organization existing and without staff, i.e. without knowing the profile of the people going to execute the plan? It is just not possible. Therefore, organizing and staffing were recognized as the essential parts of 'planning' rather than as the subsets of planning. In fact, organizing and staffing are the necessary data inputs for effective planning. Next, if directing becomes a managerial function, then why not coordinating, leading and so on? These are all mental attributes. Hence they cannot be called managerial functions. However, 'Controlling' is a managerial function. Controlling is the periodical measurement to know whether the execution is proceeding as per plan and in case of any deviation to take corrective action.

The major departure from this conventional thinking regarding managerial function was followed by ISO 9000:2000 edition.

The process concept has been introduced as the managerial function with focus on continuous improvement and elimination of errors. This is achieved by Walter Shewart's P-D-C-A cycle (as shown in Figure 1.4) popularized worldwide further by Edward Deming.

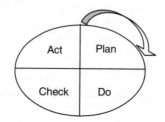

FIGURE 1.4 P-D-C-A Cycle.

1.7 DEMING'S P-D-C-A CYCLE

In P-D-C-A cycle **Planning** again plays the key role. It is often said that if you have one hour to cut down a tree, you must spend seven hours sharpening your axe. For a stage show of a few minutes, you have to rehearse for months together. Similarly, for an Olympic event of a few seconds, the athlete toils for years together. For any event to be successful, a lot of planning is required even if the actual event is only of a few minutes. Let us understand the concept of planning in the right perspective. Most of the industry does plan. But do they work out a complete 100% plan? Conventionally, the definition of planning is 'deciding the course of action in advance'. It is as simple as that. For some organizations, they are a bit advanced and they modify the definition by adding another phrase like **'planning is defining the course of action in advance and arrange resources for the same'**. You tend to agree that this is a good definition and settle down to carry out the actual work of planning.

Let us take an example. Your office is located in the suburb and you have to go to the centre of the city to attend a crucial meeting at 6:00 p.m., a simple activity. Now let us evaluate the number of alternatives for this simple work. Remember each alternative consumes resources in terms of money and takes some time for its execution. The alternatives could be:

- Travel in the company's air-conditioned car to the meeting.
- Since the time of meeting is in the evening, it may overshoot the driver's working hours, needing overtime.
- You may hire an A/C car for attending the meeting.
- You may walk down to the nearest railway station and catch a train nearest to the venue of the meeting and walk down to the place.
- You may take a local transport to the railway station where you get a faster train and get down at the nearest station without changing train or route and take a cab to reach the venue.

- You can take a cheap local transport to the outskirts of the city limits and then change over to a cab to reach the venue.
- You can take a local transport to a bus station and catch a direct bus to the venue.

Still, there are more alternatives for this simple work. But you will notice that each alternative involves different types of resources, costs, time elements, efforts and the associated comforts.

But what you actually do is: Take a hired air-conditioned tourist car from your factory and leave at 4:30 p.m. knowing that the drive time is one hour and you plan half an hour as a cushion. However, what actually happens is that you get stuck in the routine traffic jam of the evening hours on the outskirts of the city as all offices close around 5:00 to 5:30 p.m. You will reach the meeting point one hour late by 7:00 p.m. and by that time the person, whom you were supposed to meet, would have left his office. Hence next time you have a meeting in the town at the same time, you will probably catch a train to the nearest station and take a cab to the meeting place so that the failure of the earlier incidence is not repeated. It could also lead to consumption of the least amount of resources for realising the desired objective in time.

Hence definition of planning needs to be modified to make it perfect. Hence, **Planning can be defined as the 'decision-making process of choosing the best alternative leading to consumption of the least amount of resources giving you the maximum output towards the attainment of the end objective in time'.**

The maximum amount of effort, data and time are needed for working out Plan. The decision-making process of planning involves choosing the best alternative which satisfies all the musts and maximum number of wants with consuming the least amount of resources on a time-phased manner. Planning is the most important managerial function which ensures systematic efforts and approach to achieve the end result in time.

Once the plan is perfected, go ahead and execute it. Before the execution of the plan starts, an organization must ensure that all the resources are available as per plan. The resources must be of right quality and available in right quantity and at the right time, right place and right cost. The sequential flow process chart of the process of value addition at each stage should be charted out with well-defined resources and technology needed at each and every stage with the control points. The accomplishment of the plan as envisaged is the main objective of the action of 'do' or the execution.

However, as explained earlier, the execution may not be 100% identical to the plan. The next step is to **'Check'** for the concurrence of the execution with the plan by periodic measurement at the defined control points as stated above. If the execution of plan is proceeding exactly as per schedule, then hold on to the same charted outflow process chart or the route schedule. However, in case there are 'deviations' between the plan and your execution, then the organization should have incorporated a mechanism of back-up actions to rectify the deviation by taking suitable corrective action. This will put execution of the plan back on the right track.

Once you identify the deviations, check out the root cause of the deviation and **'Act'**, i.e. take corrective and preventive actions so that next time when you plan, you take precautions and do not repeat the same mistake. In future, when you plan, you will obviously not opt for the same plan but opt for a plan which will enable you to avoid the obstacles in the attainment of the end objective in time. Alternatives give you different courses of action that consume different resources and time for attaining the defined business plan.

Another feature is that the P-D-C-A is a cycle. Normally, the processes in an organization repeat cyclically and periodically every month, every week, etc. Normally the men, material and machines are more or less the same every month in the same organization.

Hence, the P-D-C-A cycle can be made more effective as illustrated in Figure 1.5.

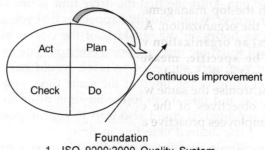

Foundation
1. ISO 9000:2000 Quality System
2. Employee involvement

FIGURE 1.5 An upgraded P-D-C-A cycle using continuous improvement.

An effective and improved P-D-C-A cycle can be modified in a manner that once a deviation or mistake has occurred, it does not repeat again. This will lead to a continuous process of refinement and error elimination on an ongoing process. The Japanese call it "Poka-Yoke" or mistake-proofing. However, it follows an elaborate complicated path. However, the objective is the same but the methodology is different. Here the objective is to simplify and synthesize all the healthy management practices under one continuous process so that it is simple to implement without any complicated management jargon and formalities.

Since the three basic hard factors of production—men, material and machines—are the same month after month and you keep on eliminating your mistakes and deviations every month and do not allow them to repeat, you are automatically on the path of continuous improvement. Today if you are measuring your errors in percentage, tomorrow the organization will measure the errors in part per million (p.p.m.), indicating a substantial drop in the number of errors.

However, to 'hold the gain', i.e. to ensure that the improvement does not drop to the original situation after sometime, the organization's functions should be sound enough to permanently absorb the improvement in their systems. The best system is to have a Quality Management System as per ISO 9001:2000. Every improvement should lead to updation of the operations manual by making relevant changes in procedure, work instructions and/or quality record so that change/improvement is implemented in the day-to-day working of the organization or its quality system. The ISO 9000:2000 quality management system not only ensures organizational stability by way of retaining the gains and maintaining the organizational performance, but it also creates an environment and approach for the continuous improvement in organizational performance.

Another important input to organizational health is the 'Total Employee Involvement'. Whatever you want to accomplish, unless the employees are involved in the process, nothing great can be achieved. All your best management practices can be grounded unless the employees wilfully cooperate to work for the attainment of the organization's goals and objectives. It is the quality and performance of the employees in the organization which differentiates a world-class organization and an ordinary organization with both operating in the same market with the same resources.

Hence fundamental to any good management practice is 'Total Employee Involvement' and it starts right with the top management. It is mandatory for the top management to declare the **'vision'** of the organization. **A 'vision' can be defined as the long-term goal (minimum 10–15 years) an organization wants to reach after a specified period of time. The 'vision' should be specific, measurable, attainable, realistic and time-bound (SMART).** The vision makes the people working in the organization clear about its goals and objectives and synchronise the same with individual goals and objectives. This ensures harmonization of the objectives of the employees with the organizational goals and objectives, makes the employees proactive and involves them leading to all round excellence in performance.

Mission **can be defined as the value system of an organization as to how the employees and the organization as a whole should conduct themselves to achieve the vision. Mission statement clearly indicates the means (ethical, legal, moral or otherwise) by which the employees working in an organization should accomplish their end objectives.** This will ensure attracting a certain kind of employees who believe in organizational values and principles. This assists in the goal integration of the employees and the employer enabling each other to give the best for the excellence of organizational performance.

The vision is normally broken up into annual goals and/or objectives of the organization.

To attain these goals and objectives, the organization must have a proper business plan. The business plan is an outcome of the development of a business strategy which is determined after a SWOT analysis.

SWOT analysis is done on two fronts:

- Assessment of the strengths and weaknesses of the organization vis-a-vis its competition. Here the competition implies the organizations manufacturing similar products and services as well as the substitute products and services. Here the organization should employ Michael Porter's theory of 'competitive advantage' to give customers that extra bit to differentiate the organization's products and services from the rest of the crowd. The strategy for the organization is to sensitize its customers about the strengths of its products and services and convince them to purchase them. On the other hand, the organization should overcome its weaknesses related to its products and services through proper research & development, product development, product innovation and customer training regarding the usage of the company's products and services, etc. The ultimate goal of the organization is to eliminate its weaknesses and if possible to convert the same into strengths.

- Assessment of the opportunities and threats vis-a-vis the environment. The environment analysis consists of the **PEST** analysis, i.e. the political, economical, social and technological environment existing as well as emerging in every potential market. The organizational objective is to develop a strategic action plan capitalizing on its strengths and opportunities and finding out the ways and means to convert the threats into opportunities through mergers, acquisitions or realignment of its facilities.

The outcome is an '**action plan**' for a world-class performance aiming to reach the top of the corporate ladder. The action plans are for the achievement of the annual targets, their periodic review for performance and taking corrective actions if needed to attain the end objective as stated above. The action plan and its execution involve the arrangement of resources, laying out the technical processes and the flow process chart, their periodic measurement and taking corrective actions in case of any deviation to ultimately achieve the quality objectives in the short run, and the vision in the long run.

1.8 LATEST TRENDS IN OPERATIONS MANAGEMENT

1.8.1 The Process Approach

The adoption of P-D-C-A cycle as a managerial function leads to the concept of Process Approach. In fact, the main improvisation in ISO 9000:2000 over the 1994 standard is a total shift from product approach to process approach. It is concluded that 'if the process is correct and within total control, the product cannot be defective'.

In fact, this process approach divides the entire business operations as an inter-linkage of processes. The ISO 9000:2000 clearly states that it promotes the adoption of a process approach.

A process can be defined as 'an activity needing resources and managed in order to transform an input into a value added output'.

In the interlinking of the process, the output of one process becomes the input for the next process.

'The application of a system of processes within an organization, together with the identification and interaction of these processes and their management can be referred to as 'Process Approach'.—ISO 9000:2000

Under the concept of the "Process Approach"—ISO 9000:2000 has defined in P-D-C-A (Plan-Do-Check-Act) approach all the four activities as follows:

- **Plan:** Establish the objectives and processes necessary to deliver results in accordance with the customer requirements and an organization's policies.
- **Do:** Implement the processes.
- **Check:** It has been defined as 'monitor and measure the processes and products against policies, objectives and requirements of the product and report the results'.
- **Act:** Take action to continually improve the process performance.

The P-D-C-A approach of managerial function has already been explained in detail earlier.

1.8.2 ISO 9000:2000

ISO 9000:2000 propagates a process-based approach of a Quality Management System as shown in the figure illustrating the process linkage in conjunction with the interpretation and manifestation of the four major clauses (see Figure 1.6).

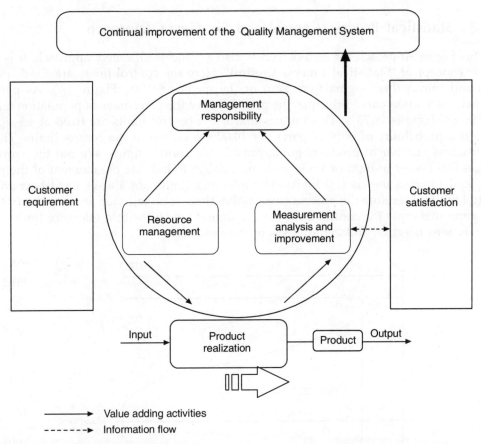

FIGURE 1.6   Model of process-based Quality Management System (ISO 9000:2000 Quality Management System model).

However, the standard clearly specifies the importance of customer satisfaction as the major objective of an organization in accordance with its policies.

The organization policy is the outcome of its business plan. The business plan is the output and interpretation of the organizational mission, vision, goals and objectives as explained earlier.

The process approach redefines the functions of the departments and the organization structure in a different perspective. It defines the purpose of the business as customer satisfaction and maximization of return on investment. With these two objectives being translated into measurable parameters, the rest of the business is broken up into inter-linkage of processes culminating in the attainment of the above two fixed end objectives.

At every stage of such process as mentioned above in there should be 'Value Addition'. At every process, continuous value addition and inter-linkage through a flow process chart ensures that the output of one process becomes the input of the next process. Hence it results in minimum confusion, evolution of clear guidelines and objectives leading to the wholehearted participation and involvement of the employees in their respective jobs.

1.8.3   Statistical Process Control and Six Sigma Approach

The Six Sigma Approach for zero-defects is also a 'Process-Oriented' approach. It is part of the concept of '**Statistical Process Control**'. Here the control limits are fixed on the plus and minus three sigma from zero or the mean line (see Figure 1.7). As per the normal distribution curve principle, the probability of the percentage of population falling within ±3 sigma is 99.73%. This implies that if the control limits are fixed at ±3 sigma, there is a probability of only 27 parts per 10,000 to go out of the control limits. This is a fairly less number of products going outside the control limits. We put the working signals like hooter or light or some such mechanism to indicate the moment of the parts that tend to cross the control limits. The tolerance limits are always fixed beyond the control limits. Therefore the process ensures that there is no rejection at any point of time. The parts that cross the control limit (i.e. ±3 sigma) are still within tolerance limits. This ensures zero rejection and zero-defects in the product.

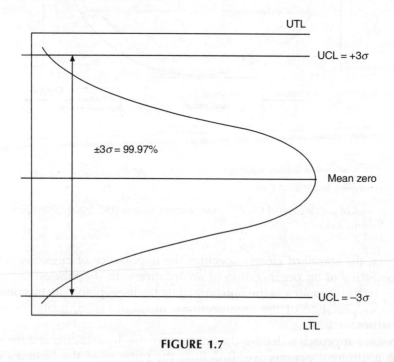

FIGURE 1.7

Hence it can be concluded that if **the process is under control, the product can never get rejected.**

$$\overline{X} = \frac{X_1 + X_2 + \ldots + X_n}{n}$$

$$\overline{R} = X_{max} - X_{min}$$

$$\sigma = \text{Standard Deviation} = \sqrt{\frac{(\overline{X} - X_1)^2 + (\overline{X} - X_2)^2 + \ldots + (\overline{X} - X_n)^2}{(n - 1)}}$$

(Denominator is '$n - 1$' for a sample lot and 'n' for the entire population).

Z = Variance = (Standard Deviation)^2

$$\text{Process capability } Cp = \frac{\text{Total tolerance}}{6\sigma} \geq 1.0$$

$$\text{Process capability factor } Cpk = \text{Minimum of } \frac{(UTL - zero) \text{ or } (zero - LTL)}{3\sigma} \geq 1.0$$

Ideally both the Cp and Cpk should be around 1.27 to 1.33 for good process capability. The Statistical Process Control ensures that the process is under control through periodic measure of the result and in case of deviation taking suitable remedial actions to ensure that the process is put back into the right track. This will ensure a self-renovating system producing products and services of zero defects and assured quality. The statistical process control ensures reliable performance of the products and services as per the customers' needs. The process also ensures that both the machines as well as the processes are capable of producing the products and services leading to total customer satisfaction. The process leads to the process and product standardization that finally results in improved and uniform performance. The statistical process control ensures fulfillment of the customers' expectations repeatedly and reliably.

The Six Sigma concept maintains the control limits at ±Six Sigma ensuring to keep the product performance practically perfect as per norms with 99.9996%. This implies that the probability of the product failure is 3.4 parts per million. The Six Sigma concept is an extension of the statistical process control. The Six Sigma was originally started at Motorola in 1979. Mikel Harry left Motorola in 1993 to join ABB in 1993. The Six Sigma effectiveness was proved in ABB with 68% reduction in defects and 30% in product costs. Mikel Harry and Richard Schroeder started Six Sigma academy in 1994. Jack Welch, the CEO of General Electric popularized the Six Sigma drive across the globe by implementing it strongly in all its divisions. Today, TCS, Wipro, Infosys and Patni Computer Systems, all practise Six Sigma due to their tie-up with General Electric. The Six Sigma has six defined goals as given below:

- To reduce variations.
- To reduce defects and rework.
- To improve yield/productivity.
- To enhance customer satisfaction.
- To improve the bottom line.
- To improve the top line.

The Six Sigma approach follows either DMAIC or the DMADV approach step-by-step. The steps in the DMAIC approach are as follows:

- Define: Determine the project to be undertaken, its objectives, scope, etc.
- Measure: Determine the Voice of the Customer (VOC), convert it into CTQ (critical to quality), obtain the data to quantify, and determine process performances.
- Analyze: Analyze the data to find out the root causes of defects.
- Improve: Intervene in the process to improve performance.
- Control: Implement a control system to maintain performance over time.

The DMADV approach is described step-by-step as:

- Define: Determine the project to be undertaken, its objective, scope, etc.
- Measure: Determine the Voice of the Customer (VOC), convert it into CTQ (critical to quality), obtain the data to quantify, determine process performances.
- Analyze: Analyze data to develop design concepts and produce a high-level design.
- Design: Develop detailed design, validate and implement the new design, integrate it with the existing system.
- Verify: Check the completed design and ensure its transition to the customer.

The Six Sigma approach follows the same main organizational objective as described earlier in the book as that of maximization of customer satisfaction and maximization of the Return on Investment. The Six Sigma incidentally has the same two business objectives. Six Sigma or Total Quality Management should be taken as a philosophy by the organization to transform the organization and change the employee's mindset. Six Sigma approach as a strategy ensures rapid growth of the organization. Six Sigma is also a tool to reduce costs, increase productivity, rejection, rework, etc.

1.9   CONCEPT OF PRODUCTIVITY

World class companies create *Surplus* through productive operations, i.e. the output is always more than the input of resources.

Productivity is defined as the ratio of output to input within a defined time period with due consideration for quality.

$$\text{Productivity} = \frac{\text{Output (within a defined time and good quality)}}{\text{Input}}$$

This formula can be elaborated as:

- Both the output and input should be quantified in tangible monetary terms for correct assessment.
- Productivity can be improved by
  (a) Increasing the output with the same input.
  (b) Increasing the output more than the increase in input.
  (c) Decreasing the input for the same output.
  (d) Increasing the output with decreasing the input.

- Productivity implies effectiveness and efficiency in individual and organizational performance. Here '**effectiveness**' means the achievement of the pre-set individual and organizational targets or the objectives whereas '**efficiency**' is the output–input ratio or the value addition to input resources minus the cost of value addition, i.e. surplus generated by a process or an organization as a whole.
- Managers should clearly know their goals and those of the organization to ascertain whether they are productive or not. It is therefore important for the organization to declare its mission, vision and annual objectives to chart out a clear unambiguous path without any confusion in the organization.

The concept of productivity is dealt with in detail in a separate chapter.

1.10 MANAGERIAL ROLES AND SKILLS

All managers have one objective, i.e. to create surplus. All managers need four types of skills to adapt themselves to their roles.

1.10.1 Technical Skills

Managers should have technical skills in terms of

(a) Knowledge about the product.
(b) Technical knowledge about the process.
(c) Technical knowledge about the usage of the product.
(d) Technical knowledge about the competency of the people to do this task in the team.

Technical skill is more required for the first line managers and supervisors. This enables them to understand the product and process to effectively guide and lead his team to carry out the assigned responsibility. This also enables a first line manager to lead his team by example or as such help the team in the maximization of the value addition at this juncture. Technical knowledge about the product, process and its usages increase product quality, better its applicability, enhance its life and customer satisfaction. It also brings down the cost of production and results in better utilization of men, machines and material.

However, as the manager goes up the ladder, the significance of his technical knowledge drops substantially. Technical knowledge as per modern management concept is required mostly at the operator's and supervisor's level. The need becomes lesser and lesser at the manager's level or up the hierarchy.

1.10.2 Human Relations Skill

Human relations skill is divided into two parts namely the communication skills of the recipient and the disseminator of information as well as presentation of departmental information and output to the rest of the organization. The second type of human relations skill is that of liasoning or interpersonal skill which is a key attribute for the enhancement of employees' morale and motivation.

Informational Role/Communication Skills

The managers represent the department or group of people reporting to them. Hence on behalf of the group he receives information and interaction about operations, processes, organizational policies, principles, etc. They have to pass the information effectively to their subordinates. The subordinates need help from the manager to understand and interpret their input information and get their doubts and queries cleared.

A manager also has to represent the department as its spokesperson at various meetings, forums, etc. It is said that most of the labour problems and unrests are due to lack of communication between the management and workmen. It is here that the manager's ability to perform the roles of the recipient, disseminator and spokesperson role becomes key to proper and healthy communication. All managers at all levels require good communication skills.

Inter-personal Role/Liasoning Skills

All the managers at all levels have to play the role of the head of the group of people they represent. He has to play not only the role of a leader but also has to act as a ceremonial head of the group.

The manager also plays the liasoning role in terms of getting the best deal for the people whom he represents as also to get the best productive output from the group of people reporting to him.

All the managers at all levels require these important inter-personal and liasoning skills to be successful managers.

1.10.3 Decision-Making Role/Entrepreneurship Skills

The manager has to have entrepreneurship skills wherein his ability to take timely and effective decisions becomes key to the business success. This attribute of decision making assumes a greater importance as the level of the manager becomes higher and higher. The main role of CEO or a General Manager is decision making on vital issues. The conceptual skills at the top are of vital importance (see Figure 1.8).

The managers have to act as entrepreneurs for their own departments. A manager has an objective or goal to accomplish. He has some resources, i.e. men, money, equipment and material at his disposal. These resources may not be adequate to accomplish the goal. Hence he has to play a negotiator role to optimize the resources to achieve the end result. He has to allocate the resources to the best and optimal use. In case of any disturbance in the execution of the plan or deviation, the manager has to handle the same efficiently to attain the end result.

On the whole, he has to act as an entrepreneur as if it is his own business where the key issue is to create a surplus by value addition on a consistent basis. He has to maximize the return on investment by enhancing the speed of business, minimizing consumption of resources and maintaining the value addition by transformation.

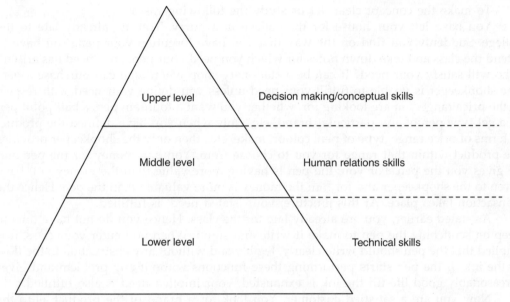

FIGURE 1.8 The importance of conceptual skills keeps them at the top of the skills pyramid.

1.11 THE CONCEPT OF CUSTOMER SATISFACTION

An organization survives because of its customers. An excellently managed technically sound organization with international certification may also go out of business due to lack of customer support. A business enterprise irrespective of whether in manufacturing or service sector has to have regular orders to keep its wheels running. In fact, it is the customers who at the end pay for the employees' salaries, meet all the organization's expenditure and create a surplus.

As another improvement, the ISO 9000:2000 standards incorporated customer focus as its key. Edward Deming, Philip Kotler and Dr. Joseph Juran have all insisted on one thing for success of a business enterprise—customer orientation or customer satisfaction.

"A customer is stated to be satisfied if his stated and implied needs are fulfilled."

Evidences of customer satisfaction are 'repurchase' repeat business and becoming a goodwill ambassador for the organization. The other evidences are the increase in the market share, addition of new customers and increase in the sales. The organization may also have a written assessment of its performance taking a rating from its customers.

Now let us understand the concept of customer satisfaction, i.e. the fulfillment of his stated and implied needs.

Stated need is normally the physical description and technical specification of a product. It is normally how the product is described in a 'Production Indent'.

The *'implied need'* is what the product is supposed to meet or perform whether it is mentioned or not. For example, a pen has to write, a car or a motorcycle has to run on the road and so on.

To make the concept clear, let us study the following cases:

You have left your house for the college in a hurry. You are already late to the college. Suddenly you find on the way that you have forgotten your pen. You have to attend the class and take down notes for which you need your pen. So a 'need has arisen'. Who will satisfy your need? It can be a stationery shop where you can purchase a pen. The shopkeeper is unable to fulfill your need unless you define your need with respect to the price range you are looking for, whether you want a fountain pen, a ball-point pen or a gel type pen of any particular brand, etc. Only when you have defined the product in terms of price range, type of pen, colour, make, etc., then only the shopkeeper provides the product within that range for you to choose from. You pay money for the pen and he gives you the pen. For you, the pen is having more value than the money you have given to the shopkeeper and for him the money is more valuable than the pen. Hence the transaction takes place. At this juncture, your 'stated need' is fulfilled.

As stated earlier, you are already late for the class. Hence you do not have time to keep on scratching the pen to make it write and so on. When you enter your class, it is implied that the pen should write clearly, legibly and without any obstruction to the flow of the ink. If the pen starts performing these functions without any problem and gives a reasonably good life till the ink is exhausted, your implied need is also fulfilled.

Now you are a satisfied customer. You look for a brand of the product as to the make and type so that next time you have a need, you will buy the same product.

We can now define customer satisfaction and state it as "a customer is satisfied if his stated and implied needs are fulfilled. Once he is satisfied, he will continue to buy the same product of the same brand unless influenced by external factors."

Here, the external factors could be better price, service, better technology, etc. Whatever may be the influence, a satisfied customer will always resist a change over to a new product.

Hence, customer satisfaction is a key factor in an organizational vision statement or quality policy. The modern concept is to orient the entire organizational activity towards fulfillment of the customer's stated and implied needs. The entire supply chain is defined and managed to fulfill the customer's needs.

A customer is fundamentally satisfied by the use of a product and the service associated with it while fulfilling the stated and implied needs.

With reference to the product, the quality and quantity are the predominant features a customer looks for. With reference to the service, the time utility, place utility and the price play a pivotal role in customer satisfaction wherein he looks at *Value for money*.

1.11.1 The Concept of Right Quality

Dr. Joseph Juran defines quality as fitness for use by the customer.

Philip B. Crossby defines that quality is the consistent conformance to requirement.

W. Edward Deming stated that quality is key to competitive advantage.

Quality is the ability of the product to meet the functional usage associated with it. It is interesting to know that a customer's perception about the quality varies along with the functional requirement. A product supposed to be of good quality for one purpose, can be considered as a product of bad quality for some other usage.

For example, a normal home floor and table cleaning liquid with nominal disinfectant power but of good fragrance could be a sought after product of good quality for day-to-day domestic use. The same product can be called of poor quality while used in the hospitals and operation theaters for lack of germicidal properties. Hence, the concept of quality is product-specific, usage-specific and customer-specific. However, it has some features in common under all circumstances, i.e. trouble-free performance, ease of handling and usage.

1.11.2 The Concept of Right Quantity

The concept of quantity is partly associated with product usage and partly with the service factor. For example, the same quantity of food served in a restaurant could be enough for a middle-aged man or woman on diet but it could be inadequate for a young sportsman.

The amount of soap and toiletries required by a domestic household, a medium-sized hotel and a large group of hotels, their buying habits as well as the concept of quantity are all different.

It is well known that the sales promotion campaign, quantity discount, packaging, transportation mode as well as the 'Distribution Requirement Planning (DRP)' depends largely on the concept of quantity.

Hence, customer satisfaction depends on the concept of providing goods and services of right quantity along with right quality. For example, initially when the beauty soap manufacturers offered a sales promotional scheme of one soap free on purchase of six soaps, it was a failure as the consumer's buying habit of beauty soap is maximum for a month, i.e., 3 or 4 for a normal household. Now most of the beauty soap manufacturers are offering the scheme of extra one soap on the purchase of two or three which are quite popular.

The daily wage earners and construction workers also need detergent powder or the shampoo. But they cannot afford to buy a shampoo bottle worth Rs. 50 or Rs. 100 at one time. The introduction of these products in pouches or swatches has created an additional market for manufacturers of these products which have grown to almost one third of the market. Hence the concept of right quantity is very important in customer satisfaction.

1.11.3 The Concept of Right Time

The concept of right time is very important in product usage and buying habit of the consumer. For example, when you are hungry you will be willing to eat even moderate quality of food in right quantity. If required you will make some compromises also in quality and quantity. If the same person is offered sound tasty good quality meal when his stomach is full, it will not appeal to him. In the month of January a normal person will not like to have ice-cream when the outside temperature is low. He will rather prefer a hot cup of tea. Hence the concept of right time of selling a product to a customer/consumer is when he needs it as well as he has the resource to buy the product and use it. The concept of right time is very important while providing customer satisfaction. The seasonal factor in terms of time always plays a role in the market place. Fans, refrigerators and air-conditioners sales are maximum during the summer season. The colour television sales peak before a world cup event in football or cricket. The clothes and white goods sales peak during Diwali and Dassera in India and during Christmas in Europe and America. Hence, the concept of right time is an extremely important aspect in marketing and customer satisfaction.

1.11.4 The Concept of Right Place

The product should be available at the right place where the demand exists. Most of the people who stay in the city are aware that the main/wholesale market is hardly a few kilometres away where goods are available at least 10%–20% cheaper than from your next door grocer or vegetable vendor. We still buy from the next door grocer or vegetable vendor at a price of 10%–20% more. This is the premium we pay for the place utility which saves our time and transportation cost. You are brand loyal to Coke and you are thirsty. If you do not get Coke in the nearby outlet, you won't travel a kilometre to get Coke. Rather you may settle down to buy the competing product, Pepsi.

To create place utility, the manufacturers develop a distribution network which is a powerful tool to make the product available where the demand exists. This **PDM or Physical Distribution Management** is a key factor in a company's market share and customer response.

For example, in an important metro city in India like Mumbai, Pepsi struggled to get its market share in spite of heavy advertisement because it could not create powerful distribution network and thereby the place utility. Dukes was a dominant brand in Mumbai with its powerful physical distribution management for many years. When Pepsi tied up with Dukes, it gained its market share and strengthened itself substantially. On the other hand, Coca-Cola had foreseen this factor and all along had this advantage due to taking over of Parle Soft Drinks Limited, manufacturer of a dominant soft drink brand Thums Up.

Procter and Gamble had an instant access to Indian market through its smart move of tying up with Godrej Soaps Ltd., having a wide distribution network to make the P&G product available at every possible retail outlet in the country thereby creating a place utility.

1.11.5 The Concept of Right Price

This concept is so obvious to understand that it needs little explanation. It can be redefined as *value for money*. Today, customers are technically knowledgeable and smart. They have a choice of global products and global pricing. All other factors like right quality, right quantity, right time and right place being the same, the right price plays a decisive role in affecting and influencing the decision of purchasing. Today, a product priced lower is no more considered an inferior product. Both products are compared by the customer and other things being equal, the product which is priced lower is still considered to be a better choice and the organization producing the product is considered to be more cost-efficient and competent in its operations management.

In industrial marketing, the customer is competent to technically assess and compare two products in terms of quality. Hence, there is no scope for paying higher for a particular brand. The product which is priced lower gets the order.

In consumer marketing, the concept of esteem value and brand may add value to the product. However, with the presence of so many brands and global competition and better product knowledge, the concept of esteem value giving a price advantage is gradually diminishing and a few years down the line, it may be an outdated concept.

Hence, the right price or the value for money is playing a lead role in customer satisfaction.

Hence, we can conclude that customer satisfaction is attained by satisfying his/her stated and implied needs. This is in intangible terms. When we translate this concept into tangible, definable and measurable terms, we can conclude that customer satisfaction is achieved by providing products and services of right quality, right quantity, at the right time, right place and at right price leading to fulfillment of the customer's stated and implied needs.

1.12 THE IMPORTANCE OF RETURN ON INVESTMENT

Customer satisfaction is the key to survival of an organization. But if we look from the point of view of management and investors/shareholders in an organization, their main objective is the return on investment (ROI).

If one keeps the money in fixed deposit, i.e. the safest form of investment and government securities, he earns around 7%–8%. If he takes slightly more risk and keeps the money in a private or co-operative bank, he may earn one per cent more. The next safest investment is gold which has both liquidity and lesser risk. The average annual increase in the price of gold is around 10%. The next opportunity for investment is in real estate. But the liquidity of the investment is gone and the return is not assured. The next option that offers the highest earning as well as risk is the share market. The risk is high and the possibility of gain is also equally high. The option which is most challenging, multifunctional, lucrative and serves individual as well as social objective is the entrepreneurship of starting an organization. The thumb rule is that it takes a new organization one or two years to reach its break even point and three to five years to recover the investment in an organization. This is why an individual invests in business fundamentally.

Hence the main objective of a businessman or the management of an organization is to maximize the return on investment. If this is not attractive, he will not invest in business. The return on investment depends on two factors, viz.

— The profit per transaction, and
— The number of times the working capital is turned round per annum.

Therefore,

ROI = Profit × Number of Working Capital Cycles per annum.

For understanding the concept of profit, let us first understand the importance of break-even point. For a businessman or an investor, the BEP or Break Even Point is the crucial point beyond which the firm starts making profit. The organization incurs two types of cost: fixed cost and variable cost (see Figure 1.9).

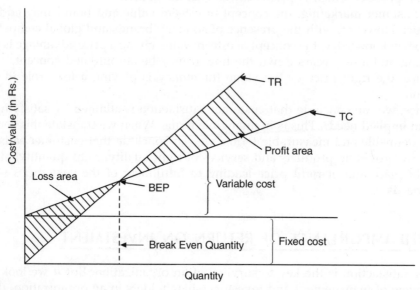

TR—Total Revenue/ Total Sales Value
TC—Total Cost
FC—Fixed Cost
VC—Variable Cost
BEP—Break Even Point

FIGURE 1.9 Break Even Point.

Variable cost is directly proportionate to a single unit being produced and is the cost of direct input resources like cost of material, man, running cost of machines like electricity, fuel, etc. Variable cost is incurred when the factory is in running condition.

Fixed cost is incurred even if a factory is closed. It consists of interest on loan, salary, plant maintainance cost, etc.

Contribution is the difference between the selling price (S.P) and the variable cost (V.C.).

$$\text{Contribution} = \text{S.P.} - \text{V.C.}$$

Below the Break Even Point, the business is in loss since the total contribution is not enough to cover the fixed cost.

At break even point the contribution becomes equal to fixed cost and it is a null balance point where the business makes neither loss nor profit.

Beyond the break even point, the contribution becomes equal to profit and the more the firm sells, the more is the profit. In other words, profit is equal to surplus generated by the business.

Now let us probe into the second concept of turning round of working capital cycle. The working capital is the capital invested in meeting the variable costs of the business. In accounting terms, working capital means the capital invested in stock, i.e. raw material,

W-I-P (work in progress) and finished goods, goods in transit, debtors and expenses during this period, i.e. wages, electricity, power and fuel cost, etc. The working capital cycle has important "Time Element". It starts with the receipt of order from customer and goes through the process of procuring material from the supplier, processing it and converting it into finished goods, dispatching to customer and ultimately recovering the money from the customer. The entire process duration is the working capital cycle time.

On completion of one working capital cycle, a firm earns one profit. Hence, if the firm completes two working capital cycles, it earns two profits. What it means is that if a firm's investment in the raw material is one month, WIP is one month, expenses one month, and debtors is two months for recovery, the total working capital cycle time is six months. Therefore, the turning round of working capital per annum is 2. The firm earns one profit per completion of working capital cycle. Hence in this case, the firm will earn two profits as its return on investment. In case the firm can compress its working capital cycle from four months to six months, it will turn round the working capital three times in a year. Hence, the 'return on investment' will be three times the profit. Hence,

ROI = Profit × Number of times turning round of working capital.

Here investment means total investment, i.e. capital + short term and long-term loans and advances.

To illustrate the concept of ROI further, let us analyze the case where manufacturing industry has certain goods in the stock. It has two customers, A and B. The customer 'A' agrees to allow the organization a profit margin of 20% with the payment terms as three months after the supply and acceptance of the goods. The customer A is a large organization. It takes up the processing of invoice for payment after three months and by the time the organization gets its cheque and realizes the payment, four months are over. The other customer B allows the organization a profit margin of only 5% (one-fourth of the profit compared to the first situation), but agrees to pay against delivery. The entire transaction of delivery of goods till realization of the payment is over in maximum five days including the week-ends. Which of these two situations is more beneficial to the organization as far as the return on investment is considered?

Obviously the dealing with the customer B is more beneficial. Let us analyze the case. Money is a scarce resource and every organization has a limitation of this resource. It therefore has the alternative uses and opportunity cost. In both the situations, let us assume that the customer places an order of Rs. 100,000. In the case of customer A, the organization keeps on supplying Rs. 100,000 worth of goods every month. At the end of the fourth month, he realizes Rs. 100,000 invoiced in the first month. Then onwards every month the organization gets Rs. 100,000 and earns a profit of Rs. 20000. The outstanding with customer A will be always Rs. 400,000. Hence the return on investment with the customer per month will be (20000/400000) × 100 = 5% only.

In the case of customer B, every five days the organization invoices the customer 'B' (or any other similar customer) Rs. 100,000 and realizes Rs. 5000. This way in 30 days or per month, the organization can complete 30/5 = 6 transactions. In every transaction he earns Rs. 5000. Hence, the organization earns Rs. 5000 × 6 = Rs. 30,000 per month on Rs. 100,000 investment, i.e. 30% per month. Hence, the return on investment is six times more beneficial in the case of customer B (30%) than in the case of customer A (only 5%).

Hence the current concept in business is the maximization of the return on investment and not only the profit. This concept is also known as increasing the **'throughput'** of the business. This also adds to liquidity and better cash flow management in any contemporary business organization.

1.13 THE FUNCTIONS OF CONTEMPORARY ORGANIZATION AND ITS DEPARTMENTS

It is now conclusively proved that for an organization to survive and prosper, it has clearly two major objectives:

- To maximize customer satisfaction
- To maximize the creation of surplus or rather maximize the return on investment

In most of the organizations, people follow strict departmental orientation and each department is a power centre by itself. An additional factor of departmental loyalty and departmental objective comes to play over and above the organizational objective and loyalty. More often than not, these two objectives clash with each other nullifying each other's effort and producing zero result.

In a typical monthly review meeting, the reason for not meeting the target will be discussed and each department representative, normally the department head, will give his explanation for non-performance. The marketing department would tell that they are the best marketing team in the world but they could not achieve the target as the product quality was much inferior compared to the competitors and/or the cost of production was too high to market the product competitively in the market. They will back up these statements with a number of field failures and customer complaints.

The production department people are equally smart. They will claim that they are the most competent and technically sound production department in the world. They are producing the product of world class quality and their cost of production is the lowest. They will back up this statement with in-house trial results against the world's best product. The report will show that the company's product is superior to even the world's best products. Their explanation will be that the marketing team is incompetent and not as capable as the competition. Hence, the reason for lower sales performance is pushed to the other side.

This meeting will last for hours together, but without any result. It is like two sides of the same railway track facing each other but never meeting at a common point. This could be called anything but teamwork. If one says 'yes', the other says 'no'. It leads to a situation where +1 and −1 make the result as zero. If the top CEO is very powerful, he may overrule by close supervision making the result at the most one plus one making it two.

The strong non-permeable departmental walls, individual departmental objectives and goals lead to non-sharing of ideas, stonewalling each other creating a situation of **converting departments into vertical chimneys** where all these non-productive waste of energy and gases go up in the air as in chimneys and of no use to the organization. The vertical chimney organizations are symbolic of strong power centres, autocratic working culture without goal integration of individual organizational goal, and cannot survive in today's highly competitive global environment. They are invariably the non-productive and non-performing outdated organizations struggling for survival (see Figure 1.10).

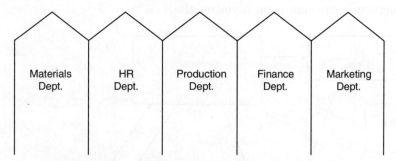

FIGURE 1.10 Vertical chimneys organizational structure.

The organizational goals and objectives thus get lost this way and these organizations waste their productive energy in in-fighting while the competition has a field day outside. The outlook of this type of organization tends to become negative and that of a loser or laggard rather than positive or that of a winner.

The functions of the departments and the organizational structure have to be reoriented to face the global competition as well as to survive and succeed in today's turbulent environment. The departmental walls should be thin and transparent mingling with each other in a continuous process wherein the output of one department becomes the input for another department. The department's objectives and goals are to be integrated with the organizational goals and objectives.

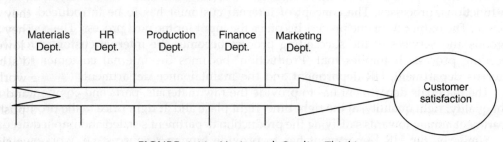

FIGURE 1.11 Horizontal Quality Thinking.

In horizontal quality thinking, departments supplement and complement one another producing the result by their individual as well as cumulative contribution by each one standing next to the other producing a result as one and one becomes eleven (1 + 1 = 11). The concept of *Internal customer* is introduced wherein one function becomes the internal customer for the other department. The marketing department becomes the internal customer for the production department which becomes the internal customer for the materials department (Figures 1.11 and 1.12).

$$
\begin{array}{ccc}
+\,1 & +1 & \\
-\,1 & +1 & 1+1 \\
\hline
0 & 2 & \text{eleven}
\end{array}
$$

As explained earlier, the organization as well as each department has only two major objectives:

- To maximize the customer satisfaction externally and internally
- To maximize the return on investment.

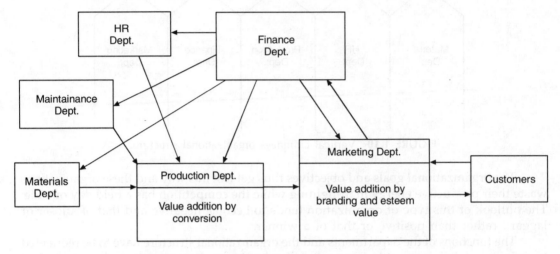

FIGURE 1.12 Functional Relationship of Departments.

To maximize customer satisfaction, the organization has to provide goods and services of right quality, right quantity, at the right time, right place and at right price.

The entire process of 'value addition by conversion' has to be broken up into sub-functions/processes. The concept of internal customer has to be introduced at this juncture. The output from one process becomes the input for the next process. The consumer of goods and services of the succeeding process becomes the internal customer for the preceding process. It implies that 'Production' becomes the internal customer for the materials department, HR department and the maintainance department.

The materials department has to provide the raw materials, parts and components of right quality, right quantity, at the right time, right place and at right price to the production department aiming towards satisfying the production department's stated and implied needs.

Similarly, the HR Department has to provide human resources, i.e. worker, staff, and managers of right quality, right quantity, at right time, right place and at right price to the production department who is an internal customer (see Figure 1.13).

The maintenance department has to provide machines and tools of right quality, right quantity, at the right time, right place and at right price to the production department (see Figure 1.13).

The marketing department is the internal customer for the production department and the production department has to provide products and services of right quality, right quantity, at the right time, right place and at right price to the marketing department.

Marketing department represents the organization and it has to provide products and services of right quality, right quantity, at right time, right place and at right price to external customers/consumers for their satisfaction.

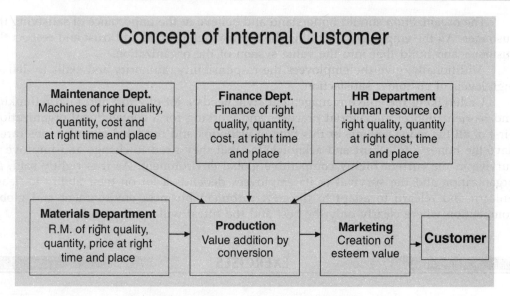

FIGURE 1.13 Departmental Functions.

The finance department has to arrange for money of right quality, right quantity, at the right time, right place and at right price. The finance department is a customer for marketing department since the latter has to get the payment for goods and services supplied and in turn provide these resources to respective departments.

The maximization of return on investment is principally concerned with reduction in cost of production. The profit can either be increased by an increase in selling price or by the reduction in cost of production. Due to the global competition and highly competitive marketing environment, the increase in selling price may drive a firm to go out of business.

Therefore, the second part of 'reduction in the cost of production' is the only way to increase profitability. The other areas where the firms are concentrating to enhance their return on investment are by proper logistics and supply chain management as well as debtor control and 'the faster turning round of working capital'. The minimum norm for a normal world class organization has to be minimum four or above turning rounds per annum. Certain good organizations have achieved turning round of working capital period to once in a month, i.e. 12 per annum.

Additionally, you should create a concept of 'listening post' in the organization. Under this concept, you should put personnel from the production department, HR department, materials department or the finance department at customer's end like a dealer shop or customer premises. These personnel from other functions should listen quietly to the customer/consumer without even letting them know of their identity. This 'listening post' concept is very effective in understanding the true feedback from customer/consumer without any bias or influence. This helps the entire organization understanding the customer's stated and implied needs.

Organizing a dealer meet in the factory, organizing customer visits to the factory and having interaction with factory personnel are also effective ways of understanding a customer's stated and implied needs.

The organization should understand and believe in the importance of satisfying the customer. All the employees including the top management should trust and respect the customer and build that into the value system of the organization.

Additionally, give the employees the responsibility, authority and skills to deliver high levels of customer satisfaction.

Undertaking the above management style needs a lot of effort and total rethinking and reorientation of managerial practices and working for a conventional organization. First of all the managements of this type of orthodox and outdated organizations rarely have the honesty to accept and acknowledge that they need to change and improve to survive in the current highly competitive global environment. As it is rightly said, an organization and the survival of its employees depends a lot on their ability to 'learn unlearn and relearn to adapt to the new turbulent business environment and global competition where clearly only the best and the fittest will survive and excel'.

EXERCISES

1. Define the latest concept of 'management'. Explain in detail the 'process approach' and how it is applicable to all the functional areas of an organization.

2. Explain the statement: 'Operation management is a key activity for achieving success in any business functions'.

3. Define 'Operations management'. How will you apply the concept of management for attaining both the 'effectiveness' and 'efficiency' in manufacturing as well as the service industry?

4. Explain Deming's P-D-C-A cycle and how it helps in continuous improvement?

5. What are the main business objectives to be fulfilled by an organization for its survival and performance excellence?

6. This chapter describes in detail 'the changing phase of management for survival in the current business environment'. Please discuss.

7. Explain 'Horizontal Quality Thinking' and the functional orientation of various departments.

8. Elaborate on the 'process approach'. How is it different from the product approach?

9. Design a contemporary modern organization for world class performance in the current global business environment.

2

Facilities Planning—Plant Location, Plant Layout and Material Handling

The earlier chapter has conclusively dealt with the concept of production and operations and its relevant details. It has also discussed the features of the manufacturing and service sectors and their working details and objectives. This chapter attempts to provide more details of the production activities to understand in detail the facilities planning and their relevant aspects. In this case, understanding the principal types of production activities and details of the manufacturing process are important for understanding the subject. The concept remains the same. The production and manufacturing process consists of the input as the raw material and/or components and the output is the value added raw material/component known as the products and services which are more valuable for the customer than the raw material. The production and manufacturing is the process of this value addition by conversion of raw material into finished product which should be both efficient and effective.

2.1 TYPES OF PRODUCTION

The production process converts the raw material into components which may be the intermediary stage components or the final products. The production methods are principally four types depending on the number of products being taken up for manufacturing at a time. Each type has its own unique features and procedures for conversion by value addition.

- Job or project production
- Batch production
- Mass production
- Continuous production

We are describing various types of production one-by-one, along with their features and detailed applications.

2.1.1 Job or Project Production

This represents a production method wherein you are normally doing a big project consuming substantial amount of resources and they normally are only one in number. The examples are construction of a bridge over a river, construction of a flyover, installation of a refinery, power plant, building a ship, etc.

Here the customers are heavily involved in the project right from the design stage and selection of the processes up to the execution and validation of the product produced. Every product needs a unique customer and may not repeat again. The duration of the completion of the project is fairly long. Managing the changing engineering orders and carrying out the modification is a major problem. Another problem is keeping track of all the activities and ensuring that they all contribute at the same time for smooth operation of the entire project in a time-bound manner. Time and quality are the two critical components of the project completion. The delay in completion of the project may lead to cost escalation and render it uneconomical for execution. The popular method of managing this kind of project is the implementation of the Critical Path Method and the Gantt Chart with the milestones. The resource balancing, crashing of the network, etc. are the common management techniques to expedite the project completion in time.

2.1.2 Batch Production

In a production system where products are taken in small numbers of 10, 20 or 30, in batches or in small groups, is known as batch production. An organization which has got a wide variety of products of small to moderate quantities in each type and fluctuating market demand are the unique characteristics of batch production.

Examples are the machine tools industry manufacturing components, die/mould making, educational institutes, computer software, etc. This normally involves a process type of plant layout. The components are machined or processed in batches to give economy in production as well as reduction in the manufacturing cost. This system is extremely flexible and leads to customization of the output. It needs close supervision and co-ordination of the activities. However, it leads to high per unit cost compared to mass production. Frequent changes in production make the production planning, control and scheduling more complex in batch production. Complete automation is not possible in batch production due to small quantities. Hence the machine tools used for batch production are of general purpose machines (GPMs) and the workforce has to be highly skilled to cope up with the variety of jobs they have to handle.

2.1.3 Mass Production

Mass Production System (MPS) is used while manufacturing standardized products in large quantities. This is popularly known as the Ford Production System conventionally. Products are primarily manufactured in 1000s normally for stock purpose from where they are sold to the customers. This needs a production system with dedicated equipments and SPMs as per the process of manufacturing follow a product layout. The mass production system normally involves automated, capital-intensive, highly repetitive, special purpose dedicated machineries, involving limited labour skills. The product flows from one end to the other. The examples for this are the production of soaps, detergents, consumer goods, food products, etc.

Mass production leads to the formation of work station auto-machine for material handling, statistical process control culminating in flow lines and assembling lines.

The main benefit of mass production is the economy of manufacturing, i.e. low per unit cost, better efficiency, simplest production planning and scheduling and negligible rejections. The main disadvantage is its inability to accommodate product design change or adaptability to changes in the demand or upgradation of the process of manufacturing.

This system has been modified to make it customer-oriented manufacturing system called the Flexible Manufacturing System (FMS) launched in the Toyota Motor Co. by the legendary Taichi Ohno. This is now a part and parcel of every world class manufacturing system. This manufacturing system is also known as the Toyota Production System or the "TPS". The production planning, control and scheduling system is customer-oriented. It reduces the machine set-up times to single digit minute and believes in frequent deliveries and smaller lot size production while maintaining large-scale production. Its objective is to provide the customer products and services of the right quality, in right quantity, at the right time, right place and at the least cost. The plant layout is also a hybrid between the product and process layout known as Group Technology.

2.1.4 Continuous Production

Continuous processes are followed for products like steel, polyester fibre, where the process of manufacturing is on a continuous basis wherein you cannot shut down the plant. In case you shut down the plant, restarting it is a herculean task. The result is production of highly standardized and high volume commodity products. The system is highly automated and the production is round-the-clock. The output is also continuous, consistent and repetitive. The other benefits are efficiency, ease of control and enormous capacity. It also makes the cost of production extremely competitive and quality highly standardized. This is feasible only for products with an extremely high and consistent demand with wide market coverage and demand. The disadvantages are plant obsolescence due to change in technology, limited variety of products, inability to adapt to changes and total rigidity. The technology cannot accommodate changes in product design as per the market demand or even the upgradation of the technology. Continuous production is currently pursued only in case of technology limitation for certain kind of products with mass consumption.

2.2 TYPES OF MANUFACTURING PROCESSES

While the types of the production details about the full production activity of value addition by conversion from the raw material/components to the final finished product. The manufacturing process elaborates on the various processes of conversion for value addition at the level of various sub-processes individually or jointly and provide the details about the value addition process by conversion in various ways of the individual items and components that go into the assembly producing the final product.

2.2.1 Assembling

This process involves processing individual components separately in-house or sourcing from outside. The parts are then assembled together to make either the sub-assemblies or the final product. Here the value addition objective is accomplished by simply joining or assembling two or more parts together which by itself can perform the end function or it can be part of the sub-assembly which along with other sub-assemblies forms the final product having a well-defined end use from the customers' point of view. The assembly process normally succeeds other manufacturing processes like machining, welding, etc.

In any collaboration, the process starts first with importing SKDs or Semi-Knocked Down sub-assemblies and assembling them one-by-one into final products. The components also can be sourced in completely knocked down condition (CKD). In this case, part of the components may be sourced indigenously or partly imported.

A car is an assembly of more than 5000 parts; a two-wheeler like a motor cycle is an assembly of more than 500 parts and so on. Most of the final products are produced by assembling individual components.

2.2.2 Welding and Fabrication

This process involves cutting the metal parts into suitable sizes as per design and joining them together either by welding (i.e. melting two metals and joining them) or riveting or fastening them by nuts and bolts.

In short, this process is quite popular in structured fabrication in the construction industry, the aircraft industry, body building of automobiles, buses, trucks etc. Welding could be of various types such as arc welding using an electrode or gas welding, submerged arc welding, inert gas welding, butt welding, etc. The metal pieces to be joined is heated by various means beyond their melting point or in a plastic stage in an inert atmosphere to avoid oxidization and then they are joined together by fusion of the metal to form one strong joint. Welding and fabrication is the fastest method of joining the metals in structural fabrication. A lot of technology is involved in this process that deals with the strength of the joint, its porosity, anti-corrosion treatment, making it leak proof for pipelines, durability and ease of the process itself and of course the overall cost of manufacturing.

2.2.3 Machining

By this process, the extra material is removed by a tool fixed on a machine. Either the tool could be stationary and the job is rotating as in a lathe machine or the job could be held stationary and the tool would be moving as in shaping or planning machine, milling machine or a surface grinder. There are machines wherein both the job and tools could be rotating as in a cylindrical grinding machine. The material could also be machined by new age technologies like spark erosion, wire cut electric discharge machine, laser technology or water jet machining.

To sum up, machining is a process of removing the extra material and giving shape and form to the job as desired. Automobile and machine shafts, gears, bearings, engine blocks, pistons, crankshafts, connecting rods are all produced by machining technology. The technology involves various processes like turning, shaping, grinding, milling, honing, lapping, etc. The machining process involves the critical measurement of the size, shape, tolerance and finish of the components. Various fits, finish and tolerances are specified as machining parameters for the machined components depending on their usage and application. The machining technology has been constantly upgraded in the past two decades from the conventional manually controlled machines to the automatic special purpose electrically controlled to electronically controlled machines to numerically controlled machines. The latest technology in machining is the computer integrated machining (CIM) which is a combination of CAD (computer aided design) and CAM (computer aided machining). This technology gives the benefit of reduction in set-up time, smaller lot size, better accuracy and better finish of the machined components with repeatability and zero defects.

2.2.4 Metal Forming

The thin sheets of metal from a fraction of a millimetre onwards in thickness are given various shapes and cut to various sizes by pressing in metallic heat treated hard dies fitted in presses operated mechanically, electrically or by hydraulic pressure. The metal sheets are given various shapes and forms in the lathes and power presses converting them into finished products like utensils, sheet metal parts and components like brackets, the body of a car, the fuel tank of motorcycle, the body of a scooter, the metal part of a wiper blade, etc.

The metal forming process is highly productive with high production rates, and capable of producing complex shapes and forms not feasible by machining. This process is capable of producing consistently the same size and shape with repeatability and low cost for mass production as the initial cost of die making is high and involves substantial time. The important metal forming processes are giving it a shape on a lathe like piercing, punching, bending, forming, drawing, etc.

2.2.5 Forging

Forging is a metal forming process where the metal blank is heated to plastic form in red hot condition and hammered between two parts of the die powered by a hydraulic or mechanical press leading to formation of the shape as per the void space in the die. The process is fast, accurate and cost-effective. It has the added advantage of giving shape to heavy and complicated parts like automobile crankshaft, connecting rod which cannot be processed by any other means. The accuracy of a forged part may not need further machining. The recent development in the forging industry is cold forging which reduces the stress during forging and produces more accurate components. The forging industry plays a leading role in the automobile components industry worldwide. This industry, like the machining sector, is going through constant upgradation of technology in terms of better productivity, higher product quality and process improvements. In India, this industry has attained a world-class status in performance excellence.

2.2.6 Casting

The steel with carbon percentage above 2.5% commonly known as cast iron, non-ferrous metals like aluminium, brass, gun metal, copper, zinc, lead, etc. are normally melted at their critical temperature and poured into a sand or metal mould to give it the shape of the void in the mould. Even the medium carbon steel is also manufactured by a similar process by high technology firms with special electrically controlled furnaces. The casting does not give a good finish and good dimensional controls. However, very intricate and difficult shapes like the automobile cylinder and engine body of both the two-wheeler and the four-wheeler are produced by the casting process. The casting process is fast, highly productive and cheap. Some advanced casting processes like investment casting, die casting, etc. can increase the finish and accuracy of the end product like what is seen in silver coins, the statues of Gods and Goddesses. The main problem in the casting process is the blow holes, i.e. the trapped air and gases in the molten metal while it gets solidified. The popular non-destructive testing methodology is by ultrasound testing.

Apart from metal casting, the most popular casting procedures are those used for the plastic parts and components manufacturing. Today's world is called the era of plastic or the plastic age. All plastic parts and products without exception are produced from the plastic granules melted in a heated chamber and then injected in a molten form into a plastic moulding die where the molten plastic solidifies at room temperature as per the shape of the void in the die. The product is then trimmed by a blade or scissors and finished into the final product. The process is fast, highly productive, cheap and mass produced. Various types of plastics are PVC, HDPE, ABS, etc. This type of manufacturing process is probably the largest industry in the manufacturing sector today. The technology pertaining to the product, process and raw material is continuously getting upgraded because of the special interest and attention paid by the world for this particular product category.

2.2.7 Plastic Forming

Plastic forming is a process of heating the material marginally to its plastic flow stage without melting and without any state or structural stage. This is employed in manufacturing the rubber components and products like vehicle tyres, engine mountings, suspension kits for automobiles, sewerage gaskets, water pipeline gaskets, window sealing gaskets, matting, etc. The rubber mixed with various chemicals is put into a heated metal mould and pressed in a hydraulic or mechanical press to enable it to flow in a plastic form inside the mould and take the shape of the mould cavity. The material gets cured during the process into a non-reversible condition with adequate tensile and compressive strengths to fulfill various functional requirements. The cured product from the die is taken out and the flash is removed by a blade or a scissor to produce the final product. Rubber is of various types like natural, nitrile, neoprene, SBR, silicon, viton, EPDM, etc. having different properties. The special properties of rubber are acid resistance, excellent sealing properties against gas, air, water, chemicals, etc. Its other properties include anti-vibration, anti-dumping, weather-resistant, etc. The technology pertaining to the manufacturing process, raw material properties and better product performance is undergoing constant upgradation. India has a strong global presence in this sector and the Indian rubber industry has reached a reasonable level of maturity in terms of quality, productivity, cost competitiveness and global presence.

2.2.8 Chemical Processing

Various chemicals and medicines are produced by chemical reaction among the input raw materials producing a new desirable compound which has a good market demand. The chemical reaction in which external heat is required to be supplied is called 'an endothermic reaction'. The chemical reaction which does not need external heat but generates heat is called 'exothermic reaction'. The exothermic reaction has to be controlled initially or else it may culminate into a 'runaway reaction' which is dangerous and may lead to violent explosion killing men and damaging property.

The chemical process is critically controlled in special containers where temperature, pressure and time duration of the process are critically monitored to arrive at the desired result. The output material is normally cleaned, filtered, crushed, purified and then used in the final refined form.

Examples of chemical processing products are medicines, soaps, detergents, various chemicals, synthetic fibres like polyesters, etc. The pharmaceutical industry has to maintain a high standard of technical and process sophistication, including cleanliness standards as per World Health Organization. All chemical processing firms have to maintain a very high level of safety standards. In India, this sector is lagging behind due to lack of research and technological development efforts. New formulations, new process technologies and product developments are mostly taking place abroad.

2.2.9 Heat Treatment and Plating

Even if it is a chemical process with supply of heat energy, no chemical reaction takes place. The physical properties of the constituent iron–carbon combination particles change giving different types of hardness in the heat treatment process. Heat treatment is followed only for the medium carbon steel with the percentage of carbon between minimum 0.3% and maximum 1.5%. Below 0.3%, the constituent elements are ferrite which do not respond to heat treatment process. Beyond 1.5%, as the carbon percentage approaches 2% to 2.5%, the carbon tends to get converted into graphite and it becomes cast iron.

In the soft-condition at room temperature, the constituent elements are ferrite, pearlite and cementite. All these are iron–carbon compounds of different crystalline structures, hardness and physical properties. When they are heated to the critical temperature range depending on carbon percentage for high speed steel, i.e. high carbon high chromium steel, the critical temperature is 1090°C to 1110°C. Pearlite and cementite get converted into 'austenite' at the critical temperature. Now, when you cool at a faster rate as in the air or oil (quenching oil), austenite gets converted into martensite. The conversion process starts at 200°C and stops at 180°C. Therefore in mar-quenching, the product is cooled between 180°C and 200°C in a salt solution known as 'mar quenching solution'. This enables the total conversion of austenite to martensite which is the desired material giving a hardness of 60 plus on the RC scale. This hardened material can be used for cutting steel, machining steel and other materials, as well as giving extended life for the shaft, gears, etc. by imparting better ware resistance.

Hence, heat treatment is a process used to impart high hardness (60–62 HRC) and wear resistance to carbon steels.

Electroplating is a similar process where the wear resistant and anti-corrosive metal gets deposited on the ordinary metal parts and components to give them special properties and protection. This is a chemical process similar to heat treatment that adds the special physical properties and chemical resistance to the base metal. This technology is employed to give better life to the dies and better shine to the end products by better finishing. It also builds anti-corrosive properties in utensils, automobile components, and decorative articles and gives better shine and finish to these components.

2.3   HARD FACTORS OF PRODUCTION

The tangible factors of production are known as the hard factors of production. Normally the hard factors of production are related to machines or the raw materials. The hard factors of production are enumerated hereunder for ready reference.

- The design of machines should be in the proper condition for the material to be processed as well as the jobs to be performed on the machine.
- Correct use of machines for the right job gives better productivity on the machine as well as better quality.
- There should be proper maintenance of machines to keep them in the running condition for production with minimum downtime.
- The raw materials should be as per the correct specifications to enable smooth processing on the machines.
- The wage bill and conversion cost should be comparable to the industry and if feasible it should be lower than the competition.
- The design of the products should be as per the organization's technical and manufacturing capability so as to attain the highest level of productivity and efficiency in manufacturing and the product quality should be as good as the best in the market.

2.4   SOFT FACTORS OF PRODUCTION

The soft factors of production are those related to the work force or the employees. Customer orientation and employees' involvement in the organizational working to create a healthy working environment resulting in products and services of the highest quality at the least cost. The soft factors of production are detailed below.

- Employee morale has a direct effect on the productivity of a firm, along with better quality of the product.

- Workers' participation in problem solving or quality improvement activities like Kaizen Gemba and Quality Circles produce the products and services of the highest quality at the least cost.
- Regular attendance of the workers brings in consistency in the productivity of an organization.
- Enhanced worker involvement increases profits for the organization by reduction in wastages and rejections.
- Fair wages and incentive schemes rewarding good performance act as an impetus for higher productivity.
- The self motivated work force gives the best all round performance in an organization.
- The work force should be innovative and solving their own problems and keep on continuously improving their performance.
- Good motivated work force develops world-class quality system in performance.

2.5 PLANT LOCATION

Plant locations were not planned in the earlier years of industrial development. It was more by default than by a well thought out plan. Historically, certain industries grew in certain areas due to a number of factors combined together. For example, Birmingham and the nearby areas got the maximum benefit of the industrial revolution and the industries were located there in a cluster. The same analogy applies currently to the Silicon Valley in the U.S.A. where the maximum number of I.T. companies are located.

Industry plays a lead role for the economic and social growth of a particular area by providing employment opportunities, enhancing the standards of living and purchasing power of the population in that particular area. This leads to the growth of the particular state and the nation as a whole. Hence the government is making an effort to develop industries across the country in rural areas as well as to foster uniform economic and industrial growth and reduce the pressure of transportation, sanitation and infrastructural facilities on the urban sector. This theory of planned location was first propagated by Lord Beveridge. The various Planning Commissions of the government of India emphasized the need for planned location of industries as a first step to develop the country on a regional consideration to reduce the stress on certain cities like Mumbai, Kolkata, Delhi and Chennai only. Various satellite towns like Bangalore, Hyderabad, Pune, Ahmedabad, Kanpur, Coimbatore, etc. also developed as a result of such efforts.

One of the first theories on plant location was given by Weber. He put his emphasis on the primary causes of plant location as the two principal factors of availability of raw material and transportation facility. He gave the law of transportation cost primarily based on two factors—distance and weight. Other factors like the types of materials, their specific gravity (lightness), topography of the route and mode of transportation were the other factors to be considered in the transportation cost which were overlooked by Weber. The secondary causes were classified as agglomerative factors which provide an advantage in production or marketing of a product due to the location advantage. The deglomerative factors gave advantages due to decentralization of the location. The only cause for the deviation of plant location was considered to be the availability of labour and the relevant labour cost. Let us now summarize the various factors to be considered for plant location in the contemporary business environment.

2.5.1 Important Factors for Plant Location

2.5.1.1 Historical factors

Historically certain industries are localized in a particular area. Those areas over time develop the core competence in manufacturing particular products most economically and with the highest quality due to unified sourcing of raw materials, availability of skilled labour for that industry segment, manufacturing units learning techniques from each other, continuous improvement in products and services due to healthy competition, etc. All these factors combined together make the industry in that area prosper. The classic examples are growth of leather chappals at Kolhapur, diamond industry in Surat, textile industry at Bhiwandi and Sholapur in Maharashtra and in Surat and Ahmedabad in Gujarat, steel industry in Birmingham, foundries in Kolhapur and Belgaum, the diesel engines at Rajkot, machine tool industry in Punjab, I.T. Industry in Silicon Valley of the USA, etc. are all examples of the growth of industry due to historical factors.

2.5.1.2 Raw material availability

The plant is located near the source of raw material whenever the input raw material is either an ore or mineral mined from a particular area or agricultural produce from the area. This is particularly true for industries whose conversion rate from raw material to the finished goods is quite low and the price of the raw material is less than half a US dollar internationally and in India less than Rs. 20 per kg. There are a number of examples to substantiate this fact.

The largest of the manufacturing industry, i.e. the steel industry, is mostly located in the eastern part of India. All the raw materials like hematite, i.e. iron ore having conversion rate to pig iron of more than 50%, coal which helps both in reducing iron oxide to iron as well as supplies the required heat and the limestone which acts as a catalyst are available in abundance in the Chota Nagpur region in the states of Jharkhand, Bihar and Orissa. Hence the bulk of the steel industries in India including 'Tata Iron and Steel Company Ltd. (TISCO)', all divisions of the 'Steel Authority of India (SAIL)' are located at Bokaro, Durgapur, Rourkela, Berhampur and Bhilai which are located in the above states.

For the food products-based industry, the world's one of the finest Champagne manufacturing plants is located near Nasik which is one of the largest growers of grapes in the world.

2.5.1.3 Proximity to the market

The proximity to the market is an important consideration in plant location so as to serve the customers better in an effective manner. This is particularly true of the SME (Small and Medium Enterprises) sector because proximity to the markets ensures better interaction with the customer, frequent deliveries, freshness of the product, reduction in transportation cost, small lot sizes and implementation of just-in-time purchasing principles. So, the location of a plant nearer to the market or the customer gives a decisive advantage to the products and/or services provider.

The examples for this type of plant location are automotive component manufacturers located in the Pune/Pimpri–Chinchwad industrial area, with a large number of automobile manufacturers like Tata Motors Ltd., Bajaj Auto Ltd., Bajaj Tempo Ltd., Kinetic Engineering Ltd. etc. Similarly, a large number of auto ancillaries are located in Delhi and its surrounding areas due to the location of the Maruti plant at Gurgaon and various divisions of Escorts around Delhi.

2.5.1.4 Transport facility

Historically, cities and towns have grown near the river banks, sea ports, highways and important railway junctions. Transportation management is an important part of logistics and supply chain management, etc. Transport cost is a very important factor for low cost products such as cement, salt, steel, etc. and needs to be managed properly. The location of a plant near a transportation hub, a port or a railway station ensures lower incoming raw material cost and lower transportation cost of the finished goods, and faster delivery for better customer service.

2.5.1.5 Power resource

One of the major negative factors in global competitiveness of the Indian industry is the high cost of electric power and its scarcity. Power cuts imposed by various state governments are detrimental to the growth and prosperity of the industry. The textile industry which is power intensive in India is facing fierce competition from China and Taiwan due to their low cost of electric power which is one-fourth of India's power cost. Apart from the above factor, the fact that there are no power cuts or fluctuations in power supply in China and Taiwan leads to higher productivity. Workers are never idle due to power cuts and no machine breakdowns due to power fluctuation.

2.5.1.6 Labour availability

One of the core competences of the Indian industries is the availability of cheap technical labour. This has led to fastest growth of the BPO and service sectors in India. The world's future centre of back offices, software development and service sector is going to be India, particularly in the NCR (National Capital Region), Mumbai, Hyderabad and Bangalore. The world's manufacturing sector is shifting to third world countries like China, India, etc. India has the distinctive advantage of an English-speaking populace. However, most of the multinationals which visited India to study the manufacturing sector had noticed low labour productivity wherein as a percentage of the selling price the cost of labour goes up even if per head count of the labour is cheaper. The study on labour productivity has shown that the European and American workers work for six and a half hour per shift but they are the most productive due multifunctional skills and could operate more than one machine at a time. The Japanese, Chinese, Taiwanese and Korean workers work for eight hours per shift whereas the Indians, Pakistanis, Bangladeshis, Sri Lankans, Thai and Vietnamese workers do not work more than three and half to four hours per shift. This is the reason why most of the manufacturing industries including some of the Indian organizations are shifting their manufacturing base to China whereas in the service sector India continues to dominate the market due to the availability of technically skilled manpower.

2.5.1.7 Cheapness of sites and services

A single large manufacturing unit brings with it a lot of employment opportunities by way of its own employees, the workers working in the ancillary units associated with the organization, as well as a host of other services the organization needs. This results in faster development of the area in particular and the state in general. Today, there is a competition among the Chief Ministers of different states in India to attract large industrial houses from India and abroad to their respective states by offering cheap sites and completion of all government formalities on a platter. The industry capitalizes on this factor to reduce its initial investment in plant sites and land procurement cost.

2.5.1.8 Availability of financial facilities

Every state has opened its own State Financial Corporation to sanction the initial capital requirement of a new industrial unit coming in that particular state at a competitive rate of interest as well as speedy sanction to enable the project to start at the earliest with minimum hassles. This easy availability of finance at relatively lower rates of interest is a major reason in deciding a plant location in a particular area.

2.5.1.9 Natural and climatic considerations

Natural and climatic consideration is critical for certain types of industries like agro-based industry. Software industry is mostly located in Pune and Bangalore due to favourable climatic conditions. The state of Orissa had initially attracted a lot of investment from various corporate sectors due to cheap sites and ample power availability. However, due to frequent cyclones every year and the related devastation of infrastructure has stopped this influx of industry into the state.

2.5.1.10 Personal factors

The promoter's background creates certain preferences regarding the location of a plant. The working comfort level with certain community of workers, past experience, family background all make important considerations for the plant location. A Gujarati businessman would prefer to set up an industry at Vapi in Maharashtra at Gujarat border in Gujarat rather than Talasari in Maharashtra.

2.5.1.11 Environmental factors and government incentives

The political, social, technological and economic factors have to be analyzed before setting up a plant in a particular location. The central or the state governments declare certain areas as industrially backward and give special incentives to the investors for setting up plants there. This incentive amount is given in the form of subsidy on capital investment, sales tax benefit, income tax benefit, excise duty relief for certain years from the year of setting up the plant. The extent of incentives given depends on the extent of backwardness of the area. Depending on the backwardness, the area is declared as 'A', 'B', 'C', or 'D' zone. There are no incentives for the 'A' zone as it is highly industrialized. For example, cities like Pune, Mumbai, Kolkatta, Chennai, etc. 'B' is a zone having some industries and declared as marginally backward whereas 'C' zone is more backward and 'D' zone is the industrially least developed area. The subsidy given is decided by the state or the central government. It is normally 35% for the 'D' zone, 25% for the 'C' zone and 15–20% for the 'B' zone limiting to a certain amount like a maximum of Rs. 20 lakhs. Certain Central government ruled union territories like Daman, Sylvassa and Diu have certain income tax and excise duty benefits. The new states of Uttaranchal and Himachal Pradesh have started giving excise duty and other tax benefits recently leading to an influx of pharmaceutical industries there.

Apart from the above environmental factors related to government subsidy, the industrial environment of industrial peace, cordial local people, positive political environment, infrastructural facilities, etc. play a leading role in deciding the plant location and the growth of industries in that particular area.

2.5.1.12 Strategic considerations

The industry may put up a plant in a foreign country with a large demand for its products and services to have the tag of 'Local Boy' which helps in getting the required market share. Many of the Indian industries are setting up small plants in the low cost European countries like Greece and the United Kingdom for just final assembly and distribution of products. They are sending these products in SKD condition. This is to have certain tax benefits and other relaxations as part of the agreement of trade among the 'European Union'. The USA suddenly withdrew India from the MFN status for the import of readymade garments a couple of years ago. A large portion of the Indian industry was dependent on exports to the USA. However, our neighbouring country Bangladesh continued to enjoy the benefit of MFN status for export of readymade garments enjoying certain critical duty and other benefits. These led to many Indian readymade garment manufacturers setting up their plants in low-cost Bangladesh and exporting garments from there enjoying these extra benefits and being competitive in the USA market. There could be many such strategic considerations for an organization to set up its plant in a specific location.

By and large it can be concluded that the plant location is a strategic business decision taking into consideration multiple factors as stated above. No particular single reason can be responsible for locating a plant at a particular place. The permutations and combinations of factors leading to a strategic and competitive business advantage normally decide the location of the plant anywhere in the world.

2.6 PLANT LAYOUT

We have seen in Chapter 1 that the basic objective of a manufacturing or the service sector is to add value by conversion to the input and the output is the value added input. This value addition takes place by successive conversion of the input raw material by deployment of the men and machines in the manufacturing sector and to the customer himself in the service industry. This is depicted in a flow process chart.

The plant layout is the arrangement of the machines and facilities like storage space, material handling equipment, etc. in a systematic scientific manner to attain maximum efficiency and effectiveness in the integrated use of the men and material along with the machines to attain the objective of the maximum value addition at the least cost.

The various reasons for the new plant layout or modifying it could be due to various factors like building a new plant, coming out with an expansion unit to meet the increase in the market demand or the modernization of the existing plant and facilities. The plant layout can also be reworked due to the product design change, product alteration or the introduction of a new product. The plant layout could be modified to accomplish realignment of machines or facilities for cost reduction, better working condition, reducing accidents better flow of men and material in line with the expansion or the diversification plan.

2.6.1 Objectives of Plant Layout

The objectives of plant layout are detailed below:

- The plant layout should be simple, easy to understand and implement.
- There should be minimum material handling and automation of material handling as far as possible.
- There should be adequate space for the movement of men and material.
- There should be minimum raw material and goods-in-process (G-I-P).
- There should be enough space for the storage of materials and manufacturing aids like jigs, fixtures, dies and moulds, etc.
- At the same time there should be no wastage of space.
- There should be better ergonomics in terms of adequate light, ventilation and temperature.
- The statutory and regulatory requirements as per provision of the factory act and the relevant facilities and norms should be adhered to. The specifications are standardized regarding the height of the roof, minimum distance of machines from the walls, etc., which are mandatory to be followed in the plant layout.
- The plant layout should take care of safety requirements like the provision of safety guards for all moving parts, provision of exit doors in case of emergency, provision of fire extinguishers near fire hazardous materials, etc. all these should be an integral part of the plant layout.
- The plant layout should avoid unnecessary capital investment and duplication of facilities and services as far as possible.
- The plant layout should lead to better labour motivation and utilization, better productivity and improved plant and machine utilization along with better quality of the finished products.
- The plant layout should have scope to accommodate further expansion plan in the near future.

2.6.2 Plant Layout Design Procedure

Once the objective of the plant layout is clear, the design of the plant layout follows with consideration on the factors of plant layout followed by the stages of planning and deciding on any particular type of plant layout for the optimum utilization of men, machines and materials.

The factors to be considered for plant layout are enumerated hereunder:

- The type, variety, quality and quantity of raw materials, work-in-process and finished goods.
- The technological specification at each stage and the process of conversion as depicted in a flow process chart.
- The type of machinery and manufacturing aids necessary for the conversion process as stated above.
- The human factor of skill level at each stage, the number of persons required, the safety requirements and their ergonomics.
- The statutory and regulatory requirements as per provisions of the factories act must be considered for the plant layout.
- The line balancing and waiting factor decides the space requirement for the material storage.
- The material handling system is an integral part of the plant layout. It is one of the major cost areas. It is decided based on the extent of automation required and associated cost, speed, volume to be handled and type of material.
- The change factors in terms of future expansion, product modification, product range, flexibility and versatility of the organization, its products and technology.
- Service factors for machines and men have to be provided for. The space for machine maintenance, safety requirements for men and machine, provision of canteen, urinals and toilets for workers, etc. is to be provided for in the plant layout.

2.6.3 Planning, Designing and Implementation of Plant Layout

After considering the factors for a plant layout and keeping in mind the objectives of plant layout, let us look into the process of actually planning and implementing the plant layout. Let us have a step-by-step approach for the same.

- Assess the customers' needs in terms of quality, quantity of the products and services along with the information as to where they are needed, when they are needed and the maximum price the customer is prepared to pay for the product and the associated service.
- Decide the location of the plant and the service centre.
- Determine the products and services to be produced as per the customers' needs as specified above.
- Decide the right technology and its details from the alternatives for the production of the product and service.
- Determine the process requirements.
- Decide the types of layout best suited for your organization, the product, process and volume of production, i.e. product layout, process layout, fixed position layout and group technology layout.
- Now prepare the route sheets, layout planning charts for conversion of raw materials into successive stages of conversion into finished products and services.

- Decide on the specific machineries, raw material and skill level as well as the number of operators needed for the manufacture of the products or services. Identify their sources and procurement strategies.
- Determine the work stations and their sequence of installation along with their paraphernalia of requirements and implement the same.
- Now design, draw and earmark the space making provision for the workstations with required services, storage space, etc.
- Provide for personal services like toilets, rest rooms, canteen, medical facilities, crèches, etc. in the plant layout.
- Arrange for other plant utilities like scrap yard, storage tank for fuels, office, generator rooms, maintenance room, tool room, etc.
- Determine the likely expansion in the near future as per the vision of the organization and make provision for the future expansion, product modification, alteration, etc.

2.6.4 Computerized Relative Allocation of Facilities Technique (CRAFT)

A number of computer software packages has been designed to facilitate good process layout by computer simulation and finding the best combination of men, machines and material at least cost. One such popular software package is '**Computerized Relative Allocation of Facilities Technique**' or '**CRAFT**'. CRAFT optimizes the exchange of positions between various departments to minimize the cost of material handling. CRAFT needs certain input data like load summary, existing and proposed layout, the distances between different locations and the space available. CRAFT tries to improve the relative placement of the departments with reference to the material handling cost. The Material handling cost between departments = Number of loads X Rectilinear distance between department centroids X Cost per unit distance. CRAFT makes improvements by exchanging pairs of departments relatively until no further cost reduction is possible. CRAFT is a heuristic programme and does not guarantee optimal solution. CRAFT is based on the starting condition. CRAFT assumes the variable path material handling equipment like the forklift trucks. When fixed path material handling equipment is employed like overhead cranes, CRAFT's applicability is greatly reduced. 'SPACECRAFT' is a modified version to handle multistory layout problems. In this case, the computer prints out the scaled layout pattern and the corresponding cost.

The other computer program for the plant layout are ALDEP (Automated Layout Design Planning), CORELAP (Computerized Relationship Layout Planning) and RMA (Richard Muther Associates). These programs works on the principle that two work areas should be near each other. All the computer programs for plant layout have tremendous limitations. It overemphasizes the material handling cost, ignoring the other aspects of plant layout. They all focus basically on process layout which has limited application. The practical plant layout is a combination of product and process layout or the group technology. All these computer programs for plant layout do not take into purview, the scope for future expansion and other future considerations of the product design change, etc. or the human relations and human psychology. Even if computerized plant layouts are applied to both the manufacturing and the service sectors, it is not found to be practically effective and popular in the industry.

Richard Muther developed a model for **closeness rating.** It helps in the analysis of relative importance of each combination of department pairs. This information is summarized into a grid as given in Figure 2.1.

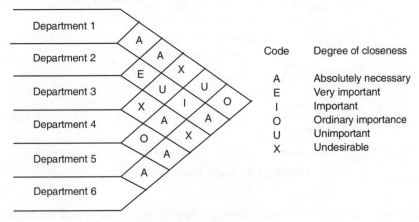

Code	Degree of closeness
A	Absolutely necessary
E	Very important
I	Important
O	Ordinary importance
U	Unimportant
X	Undesirable

FIGURE 2.1 Muther Grid.

Read the grid and the associated letters. The letters represent the importance of closeness for each department pairs. 'A' is the most important pair and 'X' is the undesirable pair. Muther suggests to use the same equipment and facilities and to share the same personnel or records. Then sequence the work flow and identify the similar work performance.

2.6.5 Types of Plant Layout

There are normally four types of plant layouts depending on the size and type of the job, the quantity to be produced, the technology used for production and the space available. The types of plant layout are as follows:

- Fixed Position Layout
- Product Layout
- Process Layout
- Normally practical layout is a combination of the above, known as group technology

2.6.5.1 Fixed position plant layout

The fixed position layout is deployed when the job involves one or two products of quite a large size where is quite cumbersome to move the job. Here the men, machines and manufacturing accessories are brought to the product location which are then assembled or used to produce the final product (see Figure 2.2). The example can be that of ship building, construction of a bridge or a flyover.

The fixed position layout is the arrangement and flow of men, machines, material and resources to the item being produced or serviced. This is decided by the complexity of the size and shape of the task being performed. It warrants the effective planning,

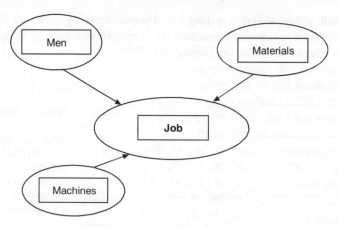

FIGURE 2.2 Fixed Position Layout.

scheduling, coordination and control of the productive activities aimed towards assembly or value addition of the individual as well as the composite product to complete the execution of the job at site.

In addition to manufacturing, the fixed position layout is also employed for the maintenance of items like a ship at the dockyard, assembly and manufacture of missiles, power plants, and large chemical processing plants.

2.6.5.2 Product or line layout

It is the sequential arrangement of facilities and equipments as per sequence of operations required for each unit of product or service offered. Successive units follow the same path (see Figure 2.3).

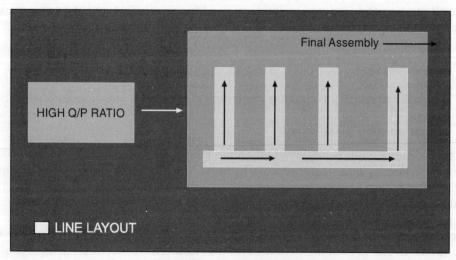

FIGURE 2.3 Line layout.

It is adopted when there is a large volume of production with a stable product design. Product layout is normally used for manufacturing and assembly operations. An example is that of the automobile industry. Since a machine is dedicated for each operation, there is a tendency to club maximum successive operations on a single machine, resulting in operation and finishing of the entire component. Hence, there is invariably a special purpose machine (SPM) designed for most of the workstations. This is feasible due to dedicated machines for each set of operations or a particular component which is normally produced on a large-scale and the sequence or the design of the product or the process does not change. This layout leads to highest productive utilization of the men, machines and materials. The entire system of material handling is normally automated and the intermediary products travel minimum distance. The entire process is standardized and the production planning and control process becomes simplified. This type of layout is highly productive, most cost-efficient and is an integral part of Ford's Mass Production System (MPS).

Due to globalization, liberalization and intense international competition, the product life cycle has shortened. The norm of the industry today is not single product or a product standardization, but product differentiation as per the need of the individual customer segment. This has led to the obsolescence of this type of plant layout as it cannot accommodate frequent changes in products or processes even if the products are of repetitive type for each type of product classification.

2.6.5.2.1 Advantages of product or line layout
- Material handling can be automated to reduce cost and time.
- Goods-in-process can be maintained at bare minimum.
- Space utilization is optimum.
- Planning, scheduling and control of operations are minimized as they are incorporated in the production line.
- The cost of the product is least under this type of plant layout.
- The utilization of men and machines is maximum.
- Productivity under this type of plant layout is the highest.
- This type of plant layout does not need highly skilled and costly work force due to high degree of automation and fool-proof system in place for the machine operation.

2.6.5.2.2 Disadvantages of product or line layout
- This type of plant layout lacks flexibility.
- Any change or modification in product design is difficult to accommodate.
- Duplication of costly special purpose equipment in different production lines may lead to higher investment.
- Any breakdown of the machine or equipment or any particular material shortage may lead to stoppage of the entire production which is costly.
- Repetitive task and high production rate may put stress on labour force.
- This type of plant layout cannot accommodate customer's urgencies.
- This type of plant layout is redundant compared to the current production management technique of Flexible Manufacturing System (FMS) or for the practice of Customer Relationship Management (CRM).

- This type of plant layout is uneconomical for a multi-product organization or the small lot production.
- Since the machines used for production are special purpose machines, any change in the product or process makes the machines obsolete as it cannot accommodate this flexibility.
- The product type of plant layout becomes obsolete with any major change in the technology of manufacturing, process or product design change.

2.6.5.3 Process or functional layout

It is an arrangement of facilities and equipment in groups according to functions. Different orders follow different paths due to flexibility needed for a large variety of products and services, low volume of orders with no standardization of components and parts (see Figure 2.4). When the product variety is large, and the quantity per product is low and the type of operation is unique for each type of product, the process layout is resorted to as an effective and efficient type of plant layout. Frequent changes in the setting of the machines involves a high degree of changes with low production volume. This is also known as the job shop type of production. The machines are general purpose machines or GPMs. This type of plant layout has total flexibility in terms of accommodating the variety of product design, small quantity in each product type, frequent machine setting and routing or process flexibility.

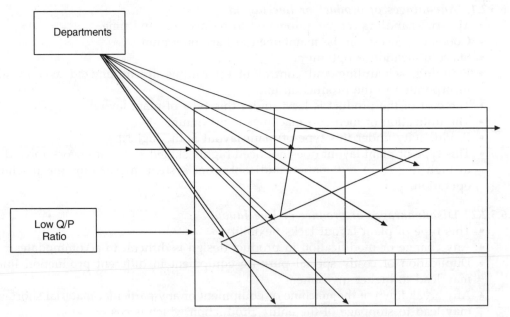

FIGURE 2.4 Process layout.

The danger of plant obsolescence is not there. The major flaw is that this process layout makes the cost of production very high for the repetitive type of jobs with large or moderate volumes as compared to the product type layout. This type of plant layout makes the movement of goods increase substantially and needs flexible material movement.

2.6.5.3.1 *Advantages of process or functional layout*
- General purpose machines are employed.
- No chance of obsolescence of machines or processes due to alteration/change in the product or process design.
- This type of plant layout incurs lower investment due to general purpose machines.
- Skilled workforce is needed due to a variety of jobs needing a variety of skills for processing. Hence workers have greater scope of skill development and job satisfaction.
- There is no disruption of production due to machine breakdown.
- There is a high utilization of men and machines.

2.5.5.3.2 *Disadvantages of process or functional layout*
- There is a high production cost per unit due to special set-up and frequent process adjustments.
- The variety of products also makes the cost of production go up further as there cannot be any standardization as a small number of units are processed per batch.
- There is process inventory due to a large variety of goods being processed simultaneously.
- The large variety of products and frequent movements to and from the departments leads to long processing time.
- The process layout requires costly and flexible material handling system as well as more space for the movement of material handling equipment.
- As products are not well-defined, automation is not possible. There is increased space requirement for travel routes and access to workstations.
- The production planning, scheduling and control process is complex.

2.6.5.4 Group technology

This is also popularly known as 'Cellular Manufacturing'. The group technology layout (Figure 2.5) is a hybrid between product layout and process layout. The group technology layout meets the needs of both automated factories and flexible manufacturing system. A product is the final assembly of individual parts and components in subsequent stages of value addition by conversion by way of machining, fabrication, etc. as explained at the beginning of this chapter or by assembly. The final product can be used by the end-user for its intended use. This is the level zero. We break the product into major sub-assemblies, sub-assemblies to individual parts and components till the parts or raw material is sourced from outside. This process is known as the *explosion* of the product into individual components and raw materials at various levels of zero, one, two, etc. These levels show the entry point of the part or the components and after entry how many times it will undergo conversion to be part of the final assembly. After this process, the parts are grouped together depending upon the similarity in the process of manufacturing. This is known as formation of *Groups by segregation*. The final process is adding up all the identical parts in the same group, together known as *aggregation*. This process of grouping the parts and components on the basis of similar processes of manufacturing is known as *explosion, segregation* and *aggregation*. The production of each individual group having

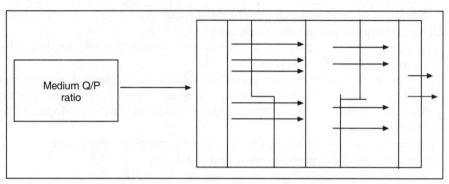

FIGURE 2.5 Group technology layout.

similar manufacturing process is accomplished by a group of machines arranged sequentially as per the process requirement. The production batch is small, but the layout of the machines of each group is similar to the line layout or the product layout. This is like a group of small plants separated on the basis of process differentiation, but combined together to form the main plant. This is part of the **'Flexible Manufacturing System (FMS)'**. The items handled under the *'Group Technology'* are the *'Dependent Demand Items'*. Dependent demand items are the items which are part of the final assembly or the final product.

These individual groups of items in a particular group are produced in a *cell* where the number of machines is laid as per the manufacturing technology of converting the raw materials into finished components or the sub-assembly. This is the reason why group technology is also known as *cellular manufacturing* where parts are grouped in sub-families on similarities of manufacturing functions. Each sub-family needs similar machines and similar processing. Group technology is suitable for large firms producing a wide variety of parts to moderate on high volumes. The processing required by each family can be performed within the cell where the machines are arranged to accommodate a common flow pattern for the parts of the family.

Group technology is thus a concept of organizing the manufacturing resources to increase productivity in the process focused small lot situations involving parts and products that are similar. The result is a group of small plants within a plant. Group technology is a hybrid between process layout and product layout.

For similar types of components, similar machines are grouped together in a process focused system, but the flow of the family of parts or products would be arranged in a line fashion. This grouped equipment can be arranged in a sequence that fits the various sizes and types very well.

Group technology concepts can include a computerized classification and codification system.

The coding system exploits the commonalities in the family of parts and products and can be coupled to Computer Aided Design, Computer Aided Manufacturing and integrating them together into Computer Integrated Manufacturing (CIM). CIM reduces the set-up time to bare minimum, usually to a few minutes reducing the pressure of lot sizes on the production and making it adapt to a small lot size production and frequent deliveries as per Just-In-Time as well as Flexible Manufacturing System.

2.6.5.4.1 Advantages of group technology: The group technology is the best form of plant layout. It has the combined benefit of both the product and process layout without their disadvantages. It thus makes the only and the best type of plant layout for a world-class manufacturing system. Group technology has the following advantages:

- Group technology combines the benefit of both the product and process layout.
- Group technology reduces work-in-process by production smoothing and line balancing. Small lot sizes also reduce the work-in-process and inventory in the system.
- Group technology reduces set-up time by the use of modernized computer integrated technology and individual similar jobs in the same group.
- Group technology reduces material handling cost by automation of the material handling system.
- Group technology leads to better scheduling.
- Group technology makes the optimum use of the input resources like men, machines and material.
- In a modernized plant, group technology is the only type of plant layout resorted to due to its adaptability to flexible manufacturing system, Just-In-Time manufacturing and Kanban system, etc.
- Group technology is the most efficient and effective form of the plant layout system.

2.6.5.4.2 Disadvantages of group technology: Group technology has hardly any disadvantages. However, a few can be looked into.

- There is difficulty in grouping into sub-families.
- In group technology, the flow analysis may be difficult.
- Sometimes group technology may need duplication of machine tools in separate cells which can be overcome by creating a technology centre within the GT Cell.

2.6.5.4.3 Types of group technology layout: There are three types of group technology layouts, giving it further adaptability to the "world class manufacturing system" and giving the best results. The features of all three different types of group technology layout are detailed below.

2.6.5.4.3.1 Group technology flow line: When the product families are closely related and quantity per product ratio is high, group technology flow line is applicable for the best result (Figure 2.6). Process routes have close relationship with each product being processed. Group technology flow line is line flow within a family. It gives advantages of both line layout, i.e. low process inventories and cycle time along with that of the functional layout, i.e. excellent equipment utilization and broader job design.

Group technology flow line gives the best benefit of the manufacturing system where close relationship with each product category exists in line with the processing route being followed for each individual product. Group technology flow line gives the highest productivity and production efficiency with the least cost of processing.

2.6.5.4.3.2 Group technology cell: Group technology cell concept is applied when processing flow for the families of parts are different (Figure 2.7). Here, neither the group technology

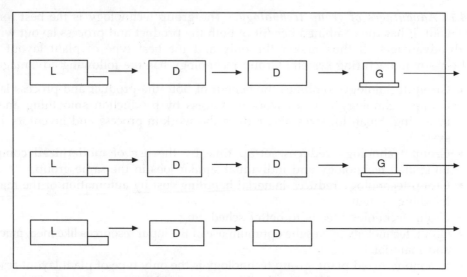

FIGURE 2.6 Group technology flow line.

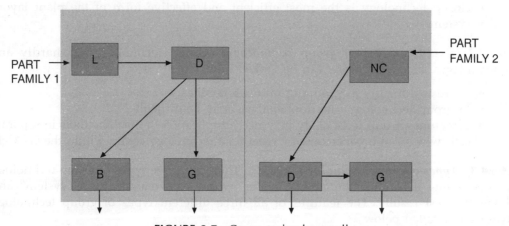

FIGURE 2.7 Group technology cell.

flow line nor the group technology centre concepts can be applied. For this kind of parts and components, all the operations for one or more of the families of parts are accomplished by a group technology cell that contains the alignment and presence of the necessary equipment needed to accomplish the necessary tasks. The group technology cell concept is then replicated to accommodate different families of parts. The group technology cell concept represents a compromise between the GT flow fine and GT centre.

The complexity and variety of the components accommodated in the group technology cell are more. The productivity and ease of control of group technology flow line are better than in the group technology cell.

2.6.5.4.3.3 Group technology centre: In the group technology centre concept, the groups with similar processing equipment are placed together as in the case of functional layout but the equipments are located in such a manner that a part family can be processed by the same equipment as far as possible. This is exactly similar to the group technology flow line plant layout but skips the line or the cell to avail of processing a costly and special machine which is not available in the cell or the line (Figure 2.8). The part may or may not come back to its original group or the line depending upon the stage of processing. This group technology layout mainly avoids duplication of costly machines having spare capacity to accommodate parts of the other group.

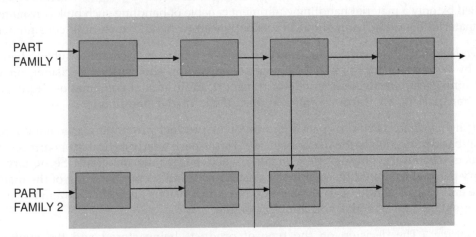

FIGURE 2.8 Group technology centre.

In the example above, the component from the sub-assembly Family 1 is quitting the line after processing in the third work station and joining the third machining centre in Family 2 to finish the operation on that particular part.

2.7 MATERIAL HANDLING

Material handling can be defined as 'the art and science of movement, storing and packaging of material in any form'.

It is the handling, storing of the raw materials, work-in-process and finished goods in primary, secondary and bulk packaging. Material handling is a non-value adding activity. It does not add any value to the end product but has the danger of damaging the product, delay in handling the product leading to inventory accumulation, pilferage and safety in handling the material if the material happens to be hazardous. The objective of material handling is either to minimize it or go for automation. On an average in a normal organization 10%–15% employees are involved in the material handling operation.

2.7.1 Functional Activities

The various functional activities of material handling are discussed one-by-one in brief:

Unit handling: Unit handling of a consignment depends on the weight of the consignment, the lightness of the unit, safety requirement as well as the shape of the unit. Depending on the above factors and repetitive nature of the unit to be handled, the material handling equipment and process are decided.

The international norms for unit that is to be manually handled should not have a weight more than 40 kgs, which can be handled comfortably by two people.

Bulk handling: Bulk handling means large consignment, heavy weight which needs to be handled by only a material handling equipment capable of handling such bulk consignment. The material handling team should be experienced to handle such bulk consignment.

Carrier handling: The carrier or transportation handling is a complex subject handled now by a separate logistics management department. The various decisions on time constraints, cost effectiveness, mode of transport, multi-modal combination, agreements with transporters, etc. form an integral part of the carrier handling.

Packaging handling: Primary packaging involves product promotion, merchandizing as well as basic protection to the material inside. This is particularly critical for pharmaceutical products, chemicals, photographic materials and hazardous materials. Secondary and tertiary packaging should be such that it ensures safe and secure handling of the material inside and ease of handling. It should also have dimensions and other parameters as per Incoterms, i.e. international norms of packaging.

Warehousing: The decision on the type of products being stored and the method of packaging the products decides the material handling equipments in the warehouses. The amount of products handled and their vertical stacking as well of location loading and unloading norms, location and methodology decide the type of material handling equipments to be installed and their flexibility, utilization and initial investment. This decision also depends on the nature of management and ownership of the warehouse in terms of whether the warehouse is owned by a company or a public warehouse or owned by the C&F agent.

Handling operation analysis: The process of material handling and the extent of handling can be depicted in a flow process chart with resource allocation. Then it can be critically analyzed for improvements and standardized to make the process of material handling cost-effective, efficient and least time-consuming.

2.7.2 Fundamentals of Material Handling

The fundamentals of the material handling process can be designed and standardized by answering the following five universal questions:

- *What is to be moved?* The properties of the material to be handled including specific gravity, lightness, volume, shape, chemical composition, inflammablity, being hazardous, etc.
- *When it is to be moved?* The time of material handling as well as the speed with which the material movement has to take place.

- *How much is to be moved?* The quantity of material to be handled and the manpower needed for loading and unloading of the material. The economics of right quantity handling is extremely important to control the cost of material.
- *What is the time of movement?* This is concerned with the lead time of movement of the material and its handling at a particular point for a particular consignment.
- *What is the suitable equipment for movement?* This is an important question to be answered depending upon the time available for material movement, the quantity of material to be handled, type of material and the budget available for the purchase or hire of the material handling equipment.

2.7.3 Objectives of Material Handling

- *Reduce cost by* reducing inventory, better space utilization and better productivity.
- *Reduce wastage by* control over in and out stock handling, avoiding climatic damage and providing flexibility.
- *Increase productivity by* better production control, increasing man-hour productivity, better workflows and machine efficiency.
- *Improve working conditions* by safe handling of material without spillage, no accidents, mechanized means of handling the material with least fatigue to the operators and workers.
- *Improve distribution by* better distribution, no damage, better storage during distribution and no material storage.
- *Low terminal time*—the material handling should involve the minimum time for the same.
- *Minimum amount of equipment required*—this will involve minimum cost of the equipment and minimum distance of travel of parts and components and will ensure bare minimum cost.

2.7.4 Stages of Material Handling

The following are the stages of material handling:

- *Unloading:* After the material reaches the factory from the supplier's end through transport, the material has to be unloaded safely and without any damage to the materials.
- *Movement to incoming goods store:* After unloading from the transporter's vehicle of the incoming materials, the same has to be moved to the incoming goods storage safely and securely. Here the material needs to be stacked or stored so that there is no damage during storage and the materials can be easily retrieved for dispatch to the production area as per the first in first out (FIFO) principle.
- *Movement to shopfloor:* As per the production indents requiring the materials for production purpose and value addition by conversion at various stages, the materials move from the incoming materials stores to the shopfloor from one machining or assembling centre to the next till the product gets converted into finished goods.
- *Movement to finished goods store:* After the product is finally produced, tested and ready for dispatch to the customer, it moves to the finished goods store

awaiting instructions from the dispatch/marketing departments to be dispatched to the customers.

- *Moving finished goods from store to transporters:* The finished goods need to be handled during dispatch to the transporters for onward delivery to the customers ensuring the safety and quality of the finished goods. Goods are dispatched from the finished goods stores as per the principles of FIFO or the customers' preferences.
- *Transporters to dealers/customers:* The transporters are now responsible for the timely delivery of the product safely and securely to the dealers and customers.

2.7.5 Material Handling Assessment

MHL is *Material Handling Labour to Total Labour ratio.*

$$\text{MHL} = \frac{\text{Material Handling Labour}}{\text{Total Labour}} \times 100$$

The industrial average for the material handling labour is about 10% for a good organization and maximum 15% for an average organization.

Movement to Operation ratio: This is a measure of productive operation movements, i.e. actions which add value to the raw material or component to transportation or material movement time and distance.

2.7.6 Factors for Selection of Equipments

The following factors are to be considered for selection of the right kind of material handling equipment:

- *Nature of material:* The physical state, fragility, sensitivity to temperature and light, leakage, safety, hazardous nature of material in terms of inflammability, chemical activity, etc. have to be assessed before selection of the right kind of material handling equipment.
- *Nature and volume of operation:* Nature of flow, process parameters, fumes, vapours, by-products, safety along with quantity of the material to be handled, etc. are the key points for consideration in selecting the material handling equipment.
- *Plant facilities:* Limitation of floor space, existing plant layout, structure of building and its rigidness for the overhead cranes, gangways for the movement of forklifts, condition of the floor, etc. are all to be considered for deciding the material handling equipment and its selection.
- *Cost:* Cost of equipment and payback period, cost benefit analysis, the economics of operations, cost of spares, annual maintenance cost, etc. are all to be considered in deciding the material handling equipment
- *Safety:* Prevention of breakage, pilferage, damage, accidents, corrosion, leakage of hazardous chemicals, inflammability of the material to be handled, etc. are all important considerations for the selection of the material handling equipment.

- *Engineering factors:* Floor condition, door, ceiling and aisle dimensions, structural strength. Power supply, maintenance facilities, etc. are to be considered for the selection of the material handling equipment.
- *Equipment reliability:* Maintenance-free performance, easy availability of spares, ease of maintenance, after sales service along with the past history of performance of the material handling equipment, etc. are important considerations for the selection of material handling equipment.

2.7.7 Types of Material Handling Equipments

There are various types of material handling equipment in use. They can be classified into two types. One set of material handling equipment is used inside the factory. The other type is used for bulk carriers outside the factory.

2.7.7.1 Internal material handling equipment

Conveyors: Conveyors are long continuous material handling equipment run by belt, chain, cable, roller, bucket, etc. Using conveyors is the safest, fast, efficient and convenient mode of material handling popularly used in automation in both the product layout as well in group technology. It is commonly seen in places like airports, power plants, etc. The conveyor could run for a few km also like in mines, cement and steel plants, etc.

Cranes: Cranes are the most popular material handling equipment starting from small mechanical device run by gear chain and ratchet to overhead crane to cranes mounted on vehicle. In the engineering and automobile industry, cranes are the most popular and versatile material handling equipment which do not occupy any space as they are mounted overhead, but run across the entire plant. The cranes are used to lift and carry medium to big loads. In sea ports, heavy duty cranes are used to load, carry and unload big and heavy consignments to and from the ships.

Elevators and hoists: Elevators and hoists are used mainly to lift the loads to a height. Elevators are common things at airports, malls for lifting men and goods between the floors. The hoists are commonly employed in the construction industry for carrying the construction material to the respective floors. Elevators and hoists are fixed position material handling equipments.

Positioning, weighing and controlling equipment: They are the manipulators, positioners, dampers, positioning tables and platforms, ramps, etc. for lifting the weights and materials between two defined points quickly and conveniently. Their application is use-specific and application-oriented.

Industrial vehicles: These material handling equipments are used for the transportation of materials within the plant. But they do not normally assist in loading and unloading the materials. These material handling equipment are forklifts, hand trucks, trailers, locomotives, etc. These industrial vehicles are flexible, quick and are versatile for carrying the material across the factory premises.

2.7.7.2 External material handling equipments

The external material handling equipments are usually transport carriers. This topic is dealt in detail under the subject of logistics and supply chain management as transportation management. The various external material handling equipments are as follows:

- *Railways:* The Indian railways are the second largest in the world and it is the most well-networked and the cheapest means of material transportation.
- *Marine carrier:* Most of the export consignments are handled by the marine carriers. This mode of transportation needs to be developed within India. The marine carriers are the cheapest and can carry large consignments. India has a lot of potential in this area as it is surrounded by sea on three sides and also has a number of large navigable rivers. The maintenance of waterways are extremely cheap and it will also help in flood reduction. It also reduces the dependence on transportation fuel in the country.
- *Animal carrier:* Animals are used for material handling in remote areas, in villages and jungles where the road is not well-developed.
- *Road transport:* Road transport is the most popular mode of transport in India and the world due to a well-developed road network, flexibility and approachability. This is the only way to provide door delivery. The vehicles are flexible mode of transport with various load carrying capacities as per the customer's requirement. This is the most popular method of external material handling.
- *Air transport:* This is the fastest, reliable, and convenient but the costliest mode of transport. The air transport is employed mainly for goods which have a high value to weight ratio or limited shelflife like food products, etc.
- *Pipelines:* Pipelines are popular material handling equipment for handling and transportation of liquids or gases. Petroleum, oils, water and gases are commonly transported through pipelines. Water is also handled and transported through pipelines.

EXERCISES

1. Explain the types of production and manufacturing processes. What are the hard and soft factors of production?
2. What are the factors to be considered for the plant location?
3. Define plant layout and explain the concept, reasons and different types of plant layout.
4. Explain the various types of plant layout design procedure: CRAFT, ALDEP, CORELQAP and Muther's Grid.
5. Explain in detail the various types of plant layout.
6. Write in detail about material handling equipment. What are the criteria for the selection of material handling equipment?

3

Holistic Management Practice for World-Class Performance and Leadership

3.1 INTRODUCTION TO TOTAL QUALITY MANAGEMENT (TQM)

India had been pursuing a closed-door shielded economy for a long time right through the fifties, the sixties up to late eighties. All through the fifties, sixties, seventies and eighties, Indian industry had a comfortable period due to 'Licence Raj', which in other words meant that the supply of a product in the market was always lower than the demand. This enabled even a junk product to have a customer. The industry followed a "push" strategy, i.e. produced products to maximize the utilization of the plant capacity and then look for the customer. The customer-orientation was totally missing leading to ever-widening gap between the customer's needs and products provided. The industry environment was stagnant with no innovation and no improvement in product, service, technology, modernization, etc. The socialist economic and labour policy, which the earlier governments followed, led to unproductive lethargic work force. The result was that India developed a conglomerate of private and public enterprises with outdated technology, lower productivity, poor product quality, and stagnant industry.

In the meantime Japanese industry followed the path and guidance of Dr. Juran and Mr. Edward Deming and followed the Total Quality Management principles and by mid-seventies became world leader in most of the industries and consumer product segment, e.g. Sony in consumer electronics, Toyota and Honda in the four-wheeler automobile sector, Honda and Yahama in the two-wheeler industry, Seiko, Citizen and Ricoh in the watch industry and Mitsubishi in heavy vehicles, etc.

Gradually the concept of TQM spread to most of the world's industries in Korea, Europe and the USA and it was accepted as a universal mantra for world-class performance and excelling in individual fields of operations. The concept of TQM became a way of life for most of the progressive industries around the world. The importance of product quality as well as associated services was universally accepted. The result was that while Japan had a revolutionary rate of growth in the sixties and seventies, the Europe, the USA and some of the Asian countries like China, Taiwan, and Korea had also similar fast pace of progressive production and growth in the late seventies and eighties.

When the floodgates of liberalization and globalization were opened in India in the early nineties, a wide gap existed between the products produced by the indian industry and products produced by the above-stated countries. The Indian industry with its lethargic working conditions just could not successfully face the global competition. The conventional Indian industries were unable to face this international competition which entered the country with globalization and liberalization.

The TQM principles started getting appreciated in the Indian industry as well. But its understanding was very little, particularly at the top management level. Industry tried to implement TQM principles in a loosely coordinated sporadic manner without involvement of the top management. Most of the management consultants emerged hardly understood the subject of TQM methods like SQC, JQI, Kaizen Quality Circles, etc were suggested in a tentative manner. Applying TQM without the involvement of top management gave minuscule benefits as the "holistic approach of TQM" was grossly missing. What was needed by the industry was acceptance and implementation of the TQM principles in totality. The Juran's Theory of TQM and Juran's Trilogy were hardly understood by the industry and it was reduced to the haphazard application of JQIP in areas selected at random. The result was obvious. Most of the existing Indian Industries could not face the stress and strain of globalization, liberalization and international competition and closed their shutters. Whereas a new group of Indian industries which practised TQM principles like customer focus, continuous improvement, employees empowerment, ISO9000 quality management system, quality planning, quality control and quality improvement, emerged as winners compared to others. Even many of the existing Indian industries which adopted and practised TQM principles, survived and gained success even in this challenging industrial environment.

3.2 TQM WITH REFERENCE TO INDIAN INDUSTRIES

During the sixties and seventies, in India, selling of goods from one state to another needed permits and licences. In the 1980s, the country as a whole got united from the point of view of trade and commerce and there was free trade without any inhibition within the country. With the collapse of the USSR and Eastern European Socialist and communist systems, the world became unipolar. This, coupled with information technology, led to a movement of globalization all over the world. The restrictions on the movement of foreign goods and services have been eased. With the opening up of economies as part of liberalization, international competition has entered the country. Everyday new steps in liberalization and globalization, like reduction of import duty, full convertibility of the rupee on trade account, abolition of licence Raj, signing agreements with WTO, are being taken and the market is becoming increasingly complex. The Indian industry has enjoyed monopoly for a long time. The market was essentialy a sellers' paradise. For simple items like a scooter or a car, the customer had to wait for years. The product quality was much below the international standard. Even for items of regular day-to-day use, such as soaps, detergents, kitchenware, electronic items, the options were limited and the products were of poor quality. Every substandard product also had a customer since government ensured that the demand is always more than the supply. Today the consumers have the entire world at their disposal. The latest designs and models of almost all the products are freely available, giving consumers a wider choice. Under the circumstances, only the best can survive.

Today, the Indian industry has learned to live in the 'Buyers Market' where **customer satisfaction** has become the key word. The customer is said to be satisfied when his/her stated and implied need gets fulfilled by the use of a product and associated services. The term **customer satisfaction** has changed the complexion of not only the Indian industry but also of the international Industry. The key to the success of the Japanese industry has been their orientation towards customer satisfaction. All these factors combined together have made it imperative for the Indian industry to adopt successful management practices to survive and compete globally.

With liberalization, signing of WTO and convertibility of the rupee, India became a part of the world market. Today's mantra for business success is **think globally but act locally.**

The key to customer satisfaction has to go beyond the concept of product quality or small "q". The big "Q" or the **Total Quality Management**. ISO 9000 is only a part of the Total Quality Management or TQM. ISO 9000 is an international standard on quality system aimed customer satisfaction. TQM, a part of which is ISO 9000, goes much beyond the quality control department or product quality and embraces in its fold all the functions, including marketing, production, materials, personnel and even finance.

In fact, under the TQM concept, the marketing department plays a critical role. As far as the organization is concerned, marketing becomes the internal customer for the organization and a channel of communication with the external customers or the actual customers. The production and operations department's function is "value addition by conversion" and all other departments support the operation. For each product, there were at least three to four dominant players in each country. Considering the fact that the impending implementation of WTO agreement round the corner and the fact that more than 120 countries have signed the agreement, three to four dominant players in each of these countries will be replaced by three to four dominant players internationally. In other words, three to four players out of 360 to 480 players are going to survive in each product category. Today, in the post-liberalization and globalization stage and there are only 3 to 4 dominant players in each category all over the world. In the globalized competition, only the best are going to survive. The TQM model for world leadership is the hypothesis of the author's research work. The TQM model is partly based on the Juran's theory of quality management process backed by *infrastructure* and a sound *foundation*. The model's title is 'The Holistic Management Practice for World-Class Performance'.

With my initial exposure to TQM, the all-embracing big 'Q' covering all functions influenced me. The subject interest grew further leading to reading of various books, theories and practices propagated by various management gurus like W. Edwards Deming, Armand V. Feigenbaum, Kaoru Ishikawa, Peter Drucker, Micheal Poter, Philip Crossby, Shiego Shingo, Micheal Hammer and Champy. The interest in this new avenue of world-class management systems and TQM grew further with reading more and more in this field. However, the greatest influence exerted on me was by Dr. Joseph M. Juran and his associates like Mr. Frank Gryna, Mr. A. Blanton Godfrey and so on. I have meticulously gone through most of the writings on the subject consisting of thousands of pages. Based on my theoretical knowledge and influenced by various writings on the subject, including case examples and backed up by over 20 years of industrial experience in senior positions like General Manager and Chief Executive Officer, the initial hypothesis model focused on TQM and the relevance of Dr. Juran's theory of quality planning, quality control and quality improvement. This was at the beginning of my research work.

As I went deeper into the subject and visited a good number of industries and participated as a leader of Juran quality improvement project, got involved in the working of various organizations as a consultant, and studied the cases in-depth, my thinking horizon widened further. There are many success stories of TQM but majority of them are cases. There are quite a lot of failure stories at the organization level. Hence TQM is not an all embracing solution to all ills and to face the current challenges from globalization and liberalization.

3.3   HOLISTIC MANAGEMENT PRACTICE FOR WORLD-CLASS PERFORMANCE

Holistic Management Practice for world-class performance is a three-step module of **Foundation, Infrastructure and Total Quality Management**. Each consists of further three subdivisions as stated in the following sub-sections (see Figure 3.1).

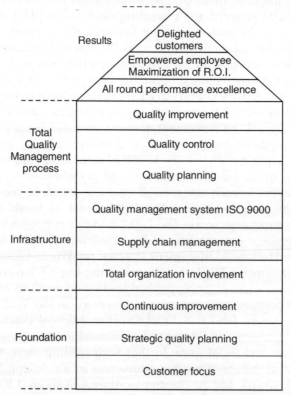

FIGURE 3.1   Dr. P.N. Mukherjee's theory of 'Holistic management practice for world-class performance and leadership'.

Foundation: Customer focus, continuous improvement and the strategic quality planning.

Infrastructure: Total organization involvement, logistics and supply chain management and quality management system.

Total Quality Management: Quality Planning, Quality Control and Quality Improvement.

The outcomes are delighted customers, empowered employees, higher return on investment and all round performance excellence.

3.3.1 Foundation

For establishing any system, first it needs a strong foundation. The foundation should be strong enough to hold the organization in turbulent times. Availability of sound infrastructure that supports consistent growth should be the basis of such foundation. Without the foundation, one can neither build an infrastructure nor an organization or a system.

The major mistake that has been committed by most of the organizations studied had no strong foundation. They jumped into implementing the TQM with a partially built infrastructure. This obviously has taken them nowhere. It is a common complaint that the company is an ISO 9000 certified company, yet it is not doing well. We have more than 50 or 100 JQIP to our credit, still we are struggling. There is an endless list of organizations who caught hold of just one or two isolated branches of TQM and thought they are doing fine. They have got some benefit out of it, but not enough to sustain during tough time.

Hence long before undertaking such fads of TQM or little understood fancy names like Kaizen Gemba, LSCM, Juran's Triology, TPM, BPR, ERP, etc., the foundation has to be laid down by an organization to understand and absorb such activities in the real sense so that they can derive benefits out of them. All their TQM activities are excellent and give tremendous benefits provided they are administered properly and at the right time and at the right place and tailored properly in the entire system of TQM. Without laying a proper foundation and infrastructure, these activities are just fancy names and a fad with industries.

Organizations with strong foundations practise customer orientation and **'customer focus'** in all their business activities. They also have a **'Sound Strategic Quality Planning'** that guides its growth plan on a long-term and short-term basis. They always believe in practising **'continuous improvement'** not only by their top managements but also by all its employees at every level. Only if the above three criteria are satisfied and practised, further support can be derived from them. The further progress of such organizational activities will ultimately lead to attainment of TQM and world-class performance.

A sound foundation has to be created as the first step of our journey for the world-class performance where the right form of mindset and attitude are built up all across the organization. This develops a strong inner strength that sees the organization through at all times apart from the obvious outcome of **customer focus** which makes an organization to survive in the present highly competitive environment, **continuous improvement** in all activities backed up by **Strategic Quality Planning** so that all parties concerned with the organization know where the organization wants to go, what are its value systems and what steps will enable the organization to reach there. There is a unified objective with all the concerned that they put in their effort and mind in accomplishing the organizational mission. Once their foundation is built up, the rest of the work becomes much simple. Without this foundation, nothing remarkable is achievable for the organization. The foundation creates the mental preparedness and one gets convinced as to why he should follow TQM and be the world-class organization. The foundation principle also tells where one stands and where he/she has to go. There is no universal rule for the time required for building this foundation. It is peculiar to the organization's present status, its size, the educational and training level of its employees, the number of units, the top management and business practices followed. The building of the foundation is extremely critical, may need a lot of patience and counselling. Building of the foundation is a total metamorphosis of the organization and attitudinal change from negative or neutral frame of mind to positive thinking and ultimately becoming pro-active as one can understand this transformation takes time. Continuous improvement, customer focus and the mental discipline to understand and follow strategic quality plan should enter into the 'habit' cycle. Once this is accomplished, we can certify that the organization is now ready to go to the second phase of infrastructure development. We shall now be elaborating on the three aspects of foundation building, i.e. customer focus, continuous improvement and strategic quality planning.

3.3.1.1 Customer focus

Customer focus is the fundamental requirement of an organization to survive. It is the customer who pays for the salary of the employees of an organization by paying for the products manufactured by the organization or the services provided by it. The customer is the engine, which pulls an organization. Hence customer focus and his satisfaction are the mandatory requirements for an establishment to survive in the present circumstances. The customer focus is created by Value Analysis, New Product Development, and Market Research to understand the customer's stated, implied and latent needs and by practising customer relationship management and mass customization if feasible. The process is identification and understanding the customer's stated and implied needs and developing the products and services which fulfill the same by way of right quality, right quantity, right place, right time and right price.

3.3.1.2 Continuous improvement

Continuous improvement lays the strong foundation for an organization aspiring to be world-class as continuous growth and improvement should be a way of life in such an organization. The adoption of Deming's P-D-C-A cycle (Plan-Do-Check-Act) in the day-to-day running of the organization leads to self-renovating institute continuously improving its performance by elimination of mistakes (Pokayoke). The implementation of the Kaizen culture of small improvements in day-to-day working in manufacturing, waste elimination, housekeeping, product features and customer satisfaction lead to an environment of continuous improvement which is a way of life. Organized quality improvement projects for converting weaknesses into strengths should be part of the day-to-day activity of the organization. Quality improvement or problem-solving teams like Kaizen Gemba, Quality Circle at the operator's level, Juran's Quality Improvement Projects (JQIP) at the middle level management and Quality Council at the top level management with ISO 9000:2000 Quality Management System forms an organization of continuously self-renovating culture. This organization always remains ahead of the competition and a leader in its class. Measuring the performance with the set standards, identifying the deviations and understanding the root cause of the deviations is the starting point of continuous improvement. The root causes of the deviations have to be removed by taking the preventive steps. This is the vital means for continuous improvement. The corrective steps are the temporary steps of continuous improvement.

3.3.1.3   Strategic quality planning

The **Strategic Quality Planning** gives direction values and guides an organization to a level of world-class performance and leadership. The strategic quality plan bridges the gap between where the organization is and where it wants to reach in the long run. The process starts with defining a mission and a vision statement. The mission defines the organizational value system. The vision is the long-term objective of the organization. The vision should be SMART, the acronym of specific, measurable, attainable, realistic and time-bound. The vision is broken into annual objectives or the short-term plans. The next process is to identify customers who will enable the organization to achieve its vision. A detailed market research is done to understand the customer's perception about the products and services leading to fulfillment of his/her needs, resulting in customer satisfaction. The strategic action plan is based on SWOT analysis which is the outcome of competitive analysis to assess the strength and weakness vis-à-vis competition and PEST Analysis (Political, Economic, Social and Technological environment) to ascertain the opportunities and threats. The strategic action plan consists of sensitizing customers about the strength of the organization inducing them to buy the organization's products and services, converting the organizational weaknesses into strengths through internal R&D with product improvements. It also consists of a strategy to capitalize on its strengths and convert the threats into opportunities by taking suitable action plan. The strategic action plan is implemented and reviewed annually to ensure proper implementation and continuous improvement as per the changing marketing or other environmental factors. The 'strategic action plan' is broken down function-wise and process-wise to enable the functional heads and individuals to know their targets and their precise roles to deliver results in tandem with the organizational requirements. This creates an environment of unification and integration of objectives among various processes, functions and individuals oriented towards the achievement of the end objectives.

3.3.2   Infrastructure

Infrastructure builds up a solid foundation which enables an organization to survive in this turbulent environment of globalization, liberalization and intense international competition. Infrastructure will enable an organization to face the competition on equal footing, hold the gains of continuous improvement, retain the existing customers and create a ladder for continuously going up in the performance level thriving for leadership in whatever area the organization chooses to be in. Infrastructure consists of Total Organizational Involvement (T.O.I), Logistics and Supply Chain Management and Quality Management System.

3.3.2.1 Total organizational involvement

Total organizational involvement includes a process of involving in the organization not only the employees and management but also the suppliers, customers and society as a whole. It goes much beyond the **TEI** or the Total Employee Involvement. The employee involvement is brought about by identification of their training needs, offering need-based training, working out a sound wage and remuneration system based on scientific Job Evaluation employing Time Study, Motion Study and Method Studies. It should recognize good performance and suitable reward system distinguishing performers and non-performers. The entire work force should be converted from a negative or neutral state of mind to a positive, active and ultimately a proactive state of mind. The top management should involve the heads into decision-making and effective implementation of decision by forming a Quality Council where all important decisions are taken. The members of the Quality Council are the heads of the functions with the CEO as the Chairman. The middle-level management is involved through participation in Quality Improvement and problem-solving teams like Value Analysis, Juran's Quality Improvement Projects (JQIP), suggestion scheme, empowerment and process orientation with its measurement of value addition. The operational level workforce is involved through quality improvement and problem solving teams in their work area through Quality Circle activities, Kaizen Gemba, suggestion scheme, total productive maintenance. The suppliers' capabilities are leveraged through their involvement in product and process development at their end, asking for their suggestions, organizing their factory visits and periodic need-based training programs.

The customers are involved in the organization through conducting market research on their perceptions on the products and services with respect to their quality, quantity, time, place and price, by organizing customers' or dealers' meets, etc. The entire process has to be properly planned, integrated and organized in a proper perspective to create effective Total Organizational Involvement.

3.3.2.2 Supply Chain Management (SCM)

Supply chain management involves integrating your supplier, customer and the entire business process into a single unified business process, oriented towards maximizing customer satisfaction and minimizing the inventory and lead time of processing a customer's order and the cost of such execution. Logistics and supply chain management involves fullfilling the demand and co-ordination of the same with the supplies. The first part involves the systematic management of dependant demand items that go into assembly of the finished product in Material Requirement Planning (MRP-I) from the suppliers-end to the organization. Then controlling and coordinating the entire process of conversion of incoming raw material and components into the finished product through the process of Manufacturing Resource Planning (MRP-II) and **Capacity Requirement Planning (CRP).** The final process in supply chain management consists of Distribution Requirement Planning (DRP) by arranging to deliver the finished products to the end users through the distribution channels so the end objective of providing the customers products and services of the right quality, in right quantity, right time, right place and right price is accomplished. This process leads to achieving the business objective of maximizing customer satisfaction as well as maximizing the return on investment.

This is the process of integrating the entire supply chain as per the demand in the market and fulfillment of the same. The process starts with the measurement of the demand in the market which pulls the entire system. The process is integrated from the customer's customer to the supplier's supplier with the organization at the centre of the entire planning system. What flows backward through the system is the information by way of demand and orders along with the money. The raw material, work in process and finished goods along with the information flow forward through the entire system. The integration of the entire system and all the activities take place through the backup of the online information technology consisting of the Enterprise Resource Planning–II along with the SRM or the Supplier Relationship Management at the back end at the supplier's end and CRM or the Customer Relationship Management at the front end at the customer's end. To ensure smooth and efficient operation of the entire supply chain, there should be adequate logistic support which has the five arms of the transportation management, warehouse management, material handling, packaging and information management. The integrated supply chain management, aided by logistics management, provides an efficient and effective management system for the attainment of the organization's end objective. The integrated supply chain management does not stop only at making the entire demand fulfillment activity effective and efficient but also makes use of the tremendous amount of data generated by the system. The data is first separated in terms of retaining the useful data from the organizational point of view and eliminating the junk data. This data separation is followed by the data synthesis, data integration along with the organizational objectives, and warehousing this data in an easily retrievable form. The Business Intelligence (BI) mines this data as per the business situation and supports the **DSS or the Decision Support System**. At the back end of suppliers, DSS and BI support the entire procurement or globalized sourcing, VMI or Vendor Managed Inventory and **CPRF**, i.e. Collaborative Procurement and Replenishment Function. At the front end it supports the accurate demand forecasting and Customer Relationship Management or **CRM**.

3.3.2.3 Quality Management System (QMS)

A Sound Quality Management System (QMS) like ISO 9000:2000 holds the organization together at all times. It creates root level strength in an organization from individual-oriented performance instead of from the team-oriented or the organization-oriented performance. The QMS creates a customer-oriented organization with process orientation and focus on continuous improvement. Every failure is analyzed to find out the root cause and take corrective and preventive action so that it is never repeated again. The QMS holds all the gains out of the improvements and does not allow the organization to slip back to the old inferior performance. The QMS creates an excellent infrastructure to retain the performance at its existing level and to continuously improve the same in accordance with the organizational objective and its value system defined in its vision and mission statement. It creates an environment in the organization where its customers as well as the employees are fully satisfied. It creates an infrastructure where both the business objectives of maximization of customer satisfaction and return on investment for the entrepreneur are assured.

3.3.3 Total Quality Management Process

After creating a sound foundation and strong infrastructure as stated above, the organization is now ready for the implementation of Total Quality Management to attain the best in its class or a world-class performance in whatever industry it is in. Here we are going to broadly base our theory similar to Dr. Juran's Triology of Quality Planning, Quality Control and Quality Improvement which has to be followed in totality and not in isolation or individually, to achieve the desired effective result. Total Quality Management establishes a **'World-Class Management System'** in an organization. Only when the foundation and the infrastructure are established, TQM can deliver the desired result, catapulting an organization to world class performance, enabling it to attain a leadership position as per its vision. Without establishing a sound foundation and a sound infrastructure, sporadic, directionless implementation of the TQM tools will not give the desired results of world-class performance excellence. It may give some benefit here and there but not enough to be a leader in its class. The TQM has three successive tools of Quality Planning, Quality Control and Quality Improvement which have to be integrated with proper coordination to achieve world-class performance.

3.3.3.1 The quality plan

An organization's mission defines its value system to attain its long-term strategic position or vision. The annual quality plan is drawn in line with the strategic quality plan. The quality plan benchmarks in all areas against the best and draws a quality plan for all functions, including operation/production, marketing, materials, human resources, technology and R&D, finance, etc. It defines the specific objective in each functional area in line with the overall business plan. Each milestone on the path to attain the respective objectives is well-defined on a time scale with details of the performance measures. The resources required to attain the quality plan are defined and arranged in advance to make it available just in time. The alternatives are analyzed and the best alternative for the achievement of the end objective in time is chosen. The one which satisfies all the musts and the maximum number of wants is chosen as the best course of action. It obviously consumes the least amount of resources to achieve the end objective in time. The quality plan gives a definite direction to the entire organization and integrates all its efforts without any wastage to achieve its individual as well as overall organizational objectives in time.

3.3.3.2 The quality control

The 'Quality Plan' is executed as per the laid out norms and guidelines. However, in spite of all efforts and precautions, deviations may take place leading to disruptions of the attainment of the end results. The quality control periodically measures the performance and identifies the deviations. It focuses more on the control of processes and produces periodic appraisal report on adherence or deviation from the quality plan at predetermined intervals and locations controlling the critical success factors. Quality control also rectifies and corrects these deviations found to put the process back on line with the expected result of the quality plan. It ensures that the performance of the organization remains at the specified level and does not deteriorate below it. Quality control activities also take care of the adherence to performance as per the plan.

3.3.3.3 The quality improvement

The quality council assesses the weaknesses of the organization, its products, services and input resources such as men, machines or material, as well as the impending threats to the organization. It also develops systematic measures of all the wastages and opportunities lost under the heading of the "Cost of Poor Quality (COQP)". The quality council then lists all these factors together and conducts a "Pareto Analysis" to prioritize the factor which if solved will give maximum benefit to the organization. The two factors to be considered for Juran Quality Improvement Project (JQIP) are the problems that are chronic in nature and under normal circumstances appear to be unsolvable. The organization takes up JQIP in these cases and converts the weaknesses into strengths, and threats into opportunities. The other objective could be to solve a major problem or a major wastage. The JQIP project team is cross-functional with representatives from each function and the leader is chosen from the most affected function. If the project is pertaining to increase in sales, the leader is head of the marketing and if the project is for product development, then the leader is normally the head of manufacturing or R&D. There are other quality improvement theories like quality circle, Kaizen Gemba, Deming's P-D-C-A cycle, Bottleneck Theory or Theory of Constraints or Kepner and Tregoe's Problem solving technique. Deming's P-D-C-A cycle also leads to continuous improvement in the day-to-day working of the organization. Quality improvement leads to improved performance of the organization and the world's best performance in the area of operation. Quality improvement leads to continuous improvement and elimination of problems and rapid rate of growth taking the organization to market leadership position and performance.

3.3.4 The Result

If this model is implemented step-by-step as indicated above, it will enable the organization to achieve its end objective, i.e. its vision or the long-term strategic position it is aiming to achieve. The implementation of this model will ensure the organization to attain total quality in every sphere of its working, i.e. attaining the ultimate in its performance which is the best in its class in the world which we have nomenclatured as the World-Class Performance and Leadership which is the sum total of a delighted customer, maximization of the return on investment, empowered employees and all round performance excellence.

3.3.4.1 Delighted customer

The identification and fulfillment of the customer's stated, implied and latent needs will lead to customer delightment leading to maximization of sales and revenue and will generate customer loyalty, support and a long-term enjoyable relationship between the customer and the organization.

3.3.4.2 Empowered employees

Total employee involvement will gradually lead to a situation where employees will progressively take more responsibility. This will develop a situation of employee empowerment leading to a relaxed, tension-free working environment where everyone is enjoying his/her work, having job satisfaction and ever-ready to give his/her best for the organization with practically zero labour turnover or labour conflict.

What differentiates a world-class organization from an ordinary one is its people and their involvement in the organizational activities.

3.3.4.3 Maximization of return on investment

An entrepreneur or a businessman goes into manufacturing or service sector basically because this is the only sector which promises him the highest return on investment than any other form of investment like fixed deposits, investment in gold or real estate or the share market with relatively lower risk. The maximization of the return on investment comes from the desired level of sales, lesser product failure and better market share. Dr. Juran has proved through his research work that top management is unilingual and understands only the language of money. The top management is also fully satisfied by this model as its objective of maximizing the organizational revenue is also achieved.

3.3.4.4 All round performance excellence

The model of holistic approach, if followed, will lead to all round excellence in performance due to reduction in wastages, rework, and external failures at customer's end or internal failures at final inspection or loss of order due to delayed delivery, etc. This saving is substantial. This will lead to committed delivery, zero defects, customer satisfaction, maximization of return on investment, increase in employee morale, excellent quality of products and services.

From the above analysis and validation of the model for the holistic management practice, it is now proved conclusively that the practice of the same leads an organization to the level of world-class performance and attainment of market leadership. The step-by-step approach of first building up the foundation by itself makes the organization strong, resilient and performance-oriented with a focused approach for attainment of its goal. Infrastructure enables the organization to give a consistent performance which will survive even bad times. Infrastructure is good enough to lead an organization to performance excellence. The foundation along with the infrastructure makes the organization so strong and result-oriented that its level of performance is retained and consolidated at all times and under any circumstances. This coupled with Total Quality Management approach of quality planning and quality improvement takes the organization to a new height of performance excellence beyond the reach of its competitors. This will accomplish world-class performance, delighted customers, empowered proactive employees, maximization on return on investment and all round performance excellence. All these features make the organization to be the best in its class and clearly a global leader in the relevant areas.

EXERCISES

1. Explain in detail the theory of 'holistic management practice for world class performance and leadership' in the current highly turbulent and competitive global business environment.

2. Design and apply the theory of 'holistic management practice for world-class performance and leadership' to the following industrial sectors:

   (a) Automobile car manufacturing unit.
   (b) Textile industry.
   (c) Pharmaceutical industry.
   (d) Two-wheeler manufacturing industry.
   (e) Computer hardware manufacturing industry.
   (f) Software development industry.
   (g) Travel and tourism industry.
   (h) Steel manufacturing industry.

4

Quality and Its Definitions, Concepts and Features

4.1 INTRODUCTION

Insistence on total quality as the fundamental business principle is becoming an indispensable practice in most of the present-day organizations. Now, managers are grappling with total quality to ensure a future for themselves and their companies. Ignoring quality jeopardizes their careers as well as the businesses they manage. During the last two decades, quality thrust in the form of TQM has come back to America (after the first thrust on SQC noticed during the World War II) as well as in European and Asian countries bringing great benefits in its wake.

The benefits of TQM programmes include greater competitive advantage and big financial savings by reducing the 'cost of quality' (the total business cost in achieving the desired quality), which is reflected in the costs of prevention, appraisal, internal failure, external failure, exceeding customer requirements and lost opportunities.

Although the industrial sector was the first to take advantage, total quality management has been found to be equally effective in the service industry—banking, insurance, hotels and restaurants, travel and holidays, health and the administration of public affairs. In fact, whenever an organization has a sequence of activities directed towards a defined end result, it has business processes, which can be analyzed and improved by TQM techniques.

Another outstanding feature of quality management of the last decade was the application of quantification of quality. The current belief is that every single attribute is quantifiable, anything that is quantified is measurable, anything that is measurable is monitorable, and anything that is monitorable is manageable. Hence, quality management is effective only when the quality parameter and standards are quantified.

In addition to marketing advantages and financial savings, TQM increases customer satisfaction which leads to customer goodwill, customer retention and additional business. They encourage the production of new products and services. They help to develop a more effective management focused on the right priorities. By empowering people, these

TQM programmes improve company morale and encourage genuine involvement in decision-making. They ultimately enhance a company's image (product image as well as overall image) and, in an uncertain world, attempt to assure a company's survival.

Total quality management is an approach to business, which looks critically at the products and services a company produces in relation to the processes it takes to create them and the people who do the work to make certain that the quality and quantity outputs fully satisfy the expected customer requirements. Internal customers (anyone who receives the intermediate goods and services of another within a company) are as important as the external customers or end-users of the goods or services because they create a chain of quality, which reaches out to the customer. The approach is called 'total' because it encompasses everything that happens in the company—all its processes, and the activities of all its employees at every level, all the time. It is a restless approach since it aims at continuous improvement, thus eliminating the waste and cost, and the strengthening of loyal relationships with suppliers and customers.

Although statistical quality control techniques, such as statistical process control (SPC) are used, the approach is more concerned with management than with specific techniques. There is an increased focus on quality than ever before because customers are becoming increasingly intolerant of poor service, late deliveries, unreliable goods, shoddy workmanship and the like. Customers are exerting control over the suppliers through buying from alternative sources. For example, the US customers for automobiles showed sharp preference for Japanese cars in the US automobile market. The reputation of Japanese car manufacturers, the reliability and 'value for money' of their cars posed a serious threat to their western competitors.

World-class companies put their efforts on quality, which has the biggest leverage to business prosperity. Quality is a double-edged sword, which has a Pincer Effect. It improves the sales revenue (top line), reduces costs (middle line), and increases profits (bottom line) simultaneously. Quality improvement results in customers perceiving superior value, making them buy more often and recommend to more customers. They are prepared to pay a decent price. Sales volume increases and sales revenue improves. Increases in volume improve productivity and push the costs further down. Simultaneously, quality improvement results in the first time right principle eliminating the wasteful costs of material scrap, re-work efforts, need for inspection and need for inventory (safety stock) and costs will go down. The human and machine efforts, which were wasted because of defects and further re-working, are now available to produce more products and services. That improves productivity and pushes the costs further down. This cycle results in more and more business, and more and more profits. Customers are happy, shareholders are happy, employees are happy, a sure win-for-all situation.

After tasting this success for some time, quality improvement becomes an intoxicating phenomenon. They move from one level to another: Percent levels to PPM (parts per million) levels, PPM levels to PPB (parts per billion) levels, PPB levels to zero defect levels. When defect levels go towards zero, the cycle times keep shrinking to unimaginably low levels: months becoming weeks, weeks becoming days, days becoming hours, hours becoming minutes, and minutes becoming seconds. A company set into this "improvement path" cannot go back. Companies getting into this cycle do not leave 'quality' to an unskilled manager. Quality management takes pride of place in the organization and the CEO himself leads the rest of the organization.

Take the case of a few companies, which are leaders in their industries like Motorola, HP and GE who have identified 'Quality Improvement' as the most critical strategic element to business. Although they maintain up-to-date technology, their success owes mainly to the priority they give to quality management. Motorola and GE have launched 'Six-Sigma' quality improvement programme as their strategic initiative. Whirlpool Corporation has launched a quality improvement programme through 'Cpk 2.0' initiative. We are quite familiar with the 'quality improvement' programme of Japanese companies under the guidance of Deming and Juran. Those companies used this single strategic weapon to establish not only business leadership in the chosen lines of businesses, they virtually took the battle into the turf of their masters, the U.S. and nearly surpassed them.

The purpose of the chapter is to demystify the topic and provide a concise, clear guide to total quality management.

4.1.1   Quality Concepts and Definitions

Traditional thinking would say that quality is conformance to specifications, that is, does the product do what it was designed to do? Some feel that this definition is the only meaningful definition of quality, because conformance is something that can be measured. However, according to Philip Crosby, that is precisely the reason we must define quality as "conformance to requirements" if we are to manage it. Thus, those who want to talk about quality of life must talk about that life in specific terms, such as desirable income, health, pollution control, political programmes and other factors that can be measured. When all criteria are defined and explained, then the measurement of quality of life is possible and practical.[1] Crosby makes a good point. By defining quality in terms of conformance, we avoid making unreasonable comparison. Is a Rolls Royce a better quality product than a Toyota Corolla? Not necessarily. Toyota may be a higher quality product relative to what it was designed to do. Conformance to specifications is based on a given design and the specifications defined for that design. Conformance to customer needs means that the design of the product is part of evaluation. Viewing quality in this broader way is both good and bad. It is good that it gets to the heart of the issue: quality is what the customer thinks it is. It is bad in that it makes it difficult to measure quality and then difficult to improve it. In a nutshell, conformance to requirements means that the design, aesthetics, etc. are a part of evaluation.[2]

Conventionally 'quality' has been associated with a 'product'. A mark like ISI for technical product and 'Agmark' for food products are considered to be symbols of good quality. However, with globalization, emergence of intense international competition and market transformation from the sellers' to the buyers' market has led to a situation where the same product features may not be acceptable to the entire user segment. Hence, quality has also become user-segment-specific. A product which is of good quality for a certain user-segment, may be of bad quality for another user-segment under similar or different conditions of use.

Dr. Juran, the most acclaimed management and quality 'Guru' of 20th century has defined: quality is fitness for use.

Philip Crosby, another leading exponent of TQM has defined: **quality is conformance to requirement**.

ISO 9000:2000, the International Standard on Quality Management System has defined: **'Quality is the degree to which a set of inherent characteristics fulfill requirements'**.

To sum up all the contemporary definitions:

'Quality can be defined as the totality of the features or states of the products and/ or services that satisfy the stated and implied needs of the customer'.

This definition brings out a uniform universally applicable definition of quality for both the manufacturing and the service sector. This definition also makes it amply clear that quality is the outcome of well-planned and researched combination of the features of the products and services, along with the conditions of usage. Quality has become a complex and key aspect of current business management and success of an organization. With the evolution of contemporary management theories and creative work done by world-class companies in the challenging global business environment, the paradigm of organizational success has shifted from other functions to quality. Hence quality is the key parameter for business success as defined by Edward Deming who states that leadership in quality decides market leadership.

Quality has many facets as described hereafter:

(i) Meeting or exceeding customer requirements now and in the future. This means that the product or service performs better than the way the customers expect, resulting in customer delight.

(ii) Quality is the integrity in delivering what a customer has a legitimate right to expect in view of what was promised at the time of the agreement or purchase.

(iii) The quality of a product or service is a customer's perception of the degree to which the product or service meets his or her expectation.

(iv) Quality is meeting or exceeding customer's expectations.

(v) Quality is the single most important force, leading to organizational success and, company, growth in the national and international markets.

(vi) Quality is a measure of how closely a good or service conforms to the predefined standards or specifications.

(vii) Quality is everyone's concern, it is job one.

(viii) Quality can be described as doing the right thing, doing it the right way, doing it at the right time, doing it right the first time and doing it right every time.

(ix) Quality is a critical factor in strategic performance.

(x) Quality is what is in the eye of the customer.

(xi) Quality is a basic customer's decision factor for an explosively growing number of products and services today.

(xii) Quality is in its essence a way of managing an organization.

(xiii) Quality is what the customers want; it is not what the company.

(xiv) Quality has become the most powerful corporate change agent of our time and perhaps the single most important managerial demand facing many companies today.

(xv) Quality means meeting customer's (agreed) requirements, formal and informal, and stated and implied, first time and every time at the lowest cost.

(xvi) Quality requires continuous improvement.

(xvii) Quality is a means to an end.

(xviii) Quality includes the totality of features and characteristics of a product or service that bears on its ability to satisfy the stated or implied needs. (Adopted by the American Society)

4.1.2 The Dimensions of Product Quality[3]

- *Performance:* How well the product or service performs the customer's intended use. For example, the speed of a laser printer.
- *Features:* The special characteristics that appeal to customers. For example, power steering and central locking system in an automobile.
- *Reliability:* The ability of a product to perform a specified level of performance for a defined period of time.
- *Serviceability:* The speed, cost and convenience of repairs and maintenance.
- *Appearances:* The effect on human senses such as the look, feel, taste, smell, or sound.
- *Customer service:* The treatment received by customers before, during and after the sale.
- *Safety:* How well the product protects users before, during and after use.
- *Durability:* The length of time or amount of use before the product or service needs to be repaired or replaced.

4.1.3 Vital Characteristics of Quality

In brief, we can sum up the vital characteristics of 'quality' as:

4.1.3.1 Satisfies Three 'F's—Fit, Form and Function

This is a conventional and orthodox definition of 'quality' which is basically confined to a product satisfying the need for the required dimensions, fitment, required form and aesthetics. The product should also be able to fulfill the functions desired to be performed by the product. This definition is more product-focused and does not include the services under its paradigm.

4.1.3.2 Fitness for use

According to Dr. Juran, a product or service is considered to be of good quality if it is fit enough for the intended use, i.e. it can be used satisfactorily. A product or service need not be perfect. In spite of other drawbacks, if the product or service satisfies the end use conditions, it is said to be having a good quality.

4.1.3.3 Fitness for purpose

The product or service should serve the purpose for which it is used. If the product is used efficiently, but it does not serve the purpose for which it is intended to be used, it is not supposed to be having good quality. It is like the old story that if you give a wood cutter an axe made out of gold instead of steel, it is of bad quality since it does not fit his purpose. He needs a strong axe, only made of steel, to cut the wood. Therefore, a product or service should serve the purpose if it is to be of good quality.

4.1.3.4 Totality of features and characteristics

An organization striving to excel in business as well as in the field of quality must offer the product and service together as a complete package so that the customer is not required to look beyond the organization. This also needs a detailed research to find out the customer's requirements and to translate them into design and development of the products and services to give shape to the totality of features and characteristics.

4.1.3.5 Conformance to requirements

This definition of 'quality' is given by Philip Crosby. Here the requirements may go beyond the customer's stated needs. The customer himself/herself may not be fully aware of his/her needs or the customer may not be aware that such a kind of product or service exists which is better suited to fulfill his/her requirements. True quality is achieved when a customer's requirements are exactly investigated and understood by an organization and the products and services are offered accordingly.

4.1.3.6 Quality satisfies the stated and implied needs

Stated needs are the needs which the customer specifies for procurement of the goods or services. They are the physical parameters or the tangible description of the product or the service. Thus are of the purchase indents in an organization. Implied needs are the associated functions the product is supposed to perform irrespective of whether it is stated or not. The stated need is you may need a pen with certain specifications and in a certain price range. The implied need is that the 'pen' should be able to write clearly, legibly and smoothly till the time the ink gets exhausted. The quality goal is achieved by an organization if it makes efforts to understand a consumer's stated needs as well as his implied or latent needs correctly and it offers products and services in accordance with the same. In case this can be achieved, the customer who is going to use the product or the service is bound to be satisfied or delighted.

4.1.3.7 Customer satisfaction

The buzz word in today's marketing management or Total Quality Management is the customer's satisfaction. A customer is satisfied when his stated and implied needs are fulfilled. Here the need could go much beyond the product or service to enter areas like aesthetics, time of delivery, place of delivery, life, the way a sales transaction is handled, etc. The true definition of quality emerges only and mainly from customer satisfaction.

Customer satisfaction can be achieved through the fulfillment of the stated and implied needs of the customer by the use of the products and/or services offered by the organization.

The effect of the customer satisfaction is continued brand loyalty, repurchase of the products and services as well as the customer acting as an opinion leader in the market for the organization. To satisfy a customer, it is extremely important for the organization to understand what the customer actually needs. The need could be partially understood by the customer who is in a position to state and define the same whereas a part of the need may be the dormant or a latent need which he may not be in a position to state or define. Both the needs should be understood, defined and suitable steps like addition of product features, etc. has to be undertaken to satisfy both the stated and the implied needs. Then only the customer satisfaction is possible. It is this customer-orientation that has made the Japanese industries secure world leadership in their respective fields of operation. The evidence of customer satisfaction or its measure should be obtained periodically by market surveys, market share, percentage of customer coming back for repurchase of the product or the service, periodic customer satisfaction and need assessment surveys and measure of percentage return of goods or the rejection.

The required quality values for customer satisfaction have to be embedded in the organizational culture. A concept of internal customer can be imbibed into an organization. By this system, the marketing department becomes the customer for the manufacturing department who in turn becomes the customer for the materials or the human resources department. There can be a periodic training programme conducted in this regard to "understand, trust, believe the customer and respect them" and built in the culture of the organization. The organization can develop formal and informal listening post to stay in touch with the customer and can ensure all-level employees participation.

Having accepted and implemented the required quality in an organization, the next step would be to institutionalize it, i.e. develop a "quality management system" which will ensure that the organization is in a position not only to retain the quality at the desired level but also to continuously improve it and bring it at the level that is considered to be the best in the trade. The best way to remain firm in the path of quality is to make the organization's intensions clear to its employees, customers and the society at large. In this direction, getting a third party audit of the 'quality management system' as per a well-known international standard and an international quality body like ANSI-USA or UKAS-United Kingdom would like to help the organization to achieve its quality goal. Hence a certification as ISO 9000:2000 for the organization's quality management system definitely helps to establish and reconfirm its business leadership through the well-accepted and time-tested path of quality and customer satisfaction.

4.2   EVOLUTION OF QUALITY MANAGEMENT

Over a period of time quality management has changed. Its reactive approach of finding and correcting defects in products manufactured has changed to a 'pro-active' approach of focusing on preventing defects from recurring altogether.

In the early 1900s, F.W. Taylor, the 'Father of Scientific Management', emphasized on quality by including product inspection and gauging in his list of fundamental areas of manufacturing management. G.S. Radford's contributions were notions of involving quality consideration early in the product design stage and linking together high quality, increased productivity and lower costs. In 1924, Shewart introduced statistical control charts to monitor production. In 1930, Dodge & Romig introduced tables for acceptance sampling.

In 1950, quality movement evolved into quality assurance. World War II caused a dramatic increase in emphasis on quality control. Soon after, US universities started training engineers in the industries in the use of statistical sampling techniques and professional quality organizations, such as the American Society for Quality Control started emerging in the US. W. Edwards Deming introduced Statistical Quality Control (SQC) methods to Japanese manufacturers to help them to rebuild their manufacturing base and to enable them to compete in the world markets. In 1950, Joseph Juran began his 'cost of quality' approach, emphasizing accurate and complete identification and measurement of costs of quality.

Mid 1950s, Armand Fiegen Baum proposed total quality control, which enlarged the focus of quality control from manufacturing to include product design and incoming raw material. In the 1960s, the concept of 'zero defects' gained favour. Philip Crosby, who was the champion of the zero defects concept, focused on employee motivation and awareness.

In 1970, quality assurance methods were used in services such as government operations, healthcare, banking, etc. In the late 1970s, there was a dramatic shift from quality assurance to a strategic approach to quality. This new strategic approach closely linked quality to productivity and profits. In addition, this approach placed greater emphasis on consumer satisfaction and involved all levels of management as well as workers in a continuing effort to increase quality.

From 1980 onwards, interest in quality grew at an unprecedented rate. Companies applied Total Quality Management and Company Wide Quality as a major part of business strategy.

4.3 EVOLUTION OF TOTAL QUALITY MANAGEMENT CONCEPT

Althrough the fifties, sixties, seventies and eighties, Indian industries had a comfortable period due to Licence Raj, which in other words, meant that the supply of products in the market was always lower than the demand. This enabled even a junk product to have a customer. The industries followed a *push strategy*, i.e. producing products to optimize the plant capacity and then looking for a customer. The customer orientation was totally missing, leading to an ever-widening gap between the customer needs and the performance of the products provided. The industrial environment was stagnant with no innovation and no improvement in products, services, technology, modernization, etc. The socialist labour and economic policies that successive governments followed until 1990 led to unproductive, lethargic work force. The result was that India developed a conglomerate of private and public enterprises with outdated technology, lower productivity, poor product quality, and stagnant industry.

At the same time, Japanese industries followed the path and guidance of Dr. Juran and Edward Deming and followed the Total Quality Management principles and by the mid-1970s became world leader in most of the industries and consumer products segment, e.g. Sony in consumer electronics, Toyota and Honda in the four-wheeler automobile sector, Honda and Yahama in the two-wheeler industry, Seiko, Citizen and Ricoh in the watch industry and Mitsubishi in heavy vehicles, etc. Pioneering work in TQM was also done by Taichi Ohno who implemented the famous Just-In-Time manufacturing or the Kanban and Toyota Production System (TPS). There were other Japanese management gurus like Matsushita, Sheigo Shingo, Ishikawa and recently Masaaki Imai who contributed substantially to the field of TQM.

Gradually the concept of TQM spread to most of the world's industries in Korea, Europe and the USA and it was accepted as a universal mantra for world-class performance and excelling in individual fields of operation. The concepts of big Q overlook small q and TQM became a way of life for most of the progressive companies in the world. The importance of product quality as well as its associated services was universally accepted. The result was that while Japan had a revolutionary rate of growth in the sixties and the seventies, Europe, USA and some of the Asian countries like China, Taiwan, and Korea had similar fast pace of progressive production and growth in the seventies and the eighties.

In the 1970s, a General Electric task force studied consumer perceptions of the quality of various GE product lines. Lines with relatively poor reputation for quality were found to de-emphasize the customer's viewpoint, regard quality as synonymous with tight tolerance and conformance to company defined specifications, tie quality objectives to manufacturing flow, express quality objectives as the number of defects per unit, and use formal quality control system only in manufacturing. In contrast, product lines that received customer praise were found to emphasize satisfying the customer expectations, determine customer needs through market research, use customer-based quality performance measures and have formalized quality control systems in place for all business functions, not solely for manufacturing. The task force concluded quality must not be viewed solely as a technical discipline, but rather as a managerial discipline. That is, quality issues permeate all aspects of a business enterprise: design, marketing, manufacturing, human resources management, supplier relations and financial management, to name just a few.

Total quality is a people-focused management system that aims at continued increase in customer satisfaction at continually lower real cost. TQM is a 'total system approach' and an integral part of high-level strategy. It works horizontally across functions and departments, involves all the employees, top to bottom and extends backward and forward to include the supply chain and the customer chain. TQM stresses learning and adaptation to continual change as keys to organizational success. Total quality includes systems, methods and tools. The systems permit change but the philosophy remains the same. The core principles of total quality explained below are: A focus on the customer, participation and team work, employee involvement and empowerment, continuous improvement and learning, ownership and elements of self-management.

When the floodgates of liberalization and globalization were opened in India in the early nineties, a wide gap existed between the products produced by the Indian industries and those by the above-stated countries. The Indian industry was caught unawares. Because of the lethargic working culture settled over the years, the Indian industries could not successfully face the global competition. The conventional Indian Industries were unable to face this international competition which entered in the country after globalization and liberalization.

The TQM principles started gaining priority in the Indian industry as well. But concepts are still not well-understood and effectively implemented by the managements in the industries. Industries tried to implement TQM principles in a loosely coordinated manner without committment of the top management. A new branch of management consultants emerged who hardly understood the subject of TQM and in bits and pieces. Methods like SQC, JQI, Kaizen, quality circle, etc. were being used without studying the needs and suitability. This bits and pieces practice of TQM without the involvement of top management gave little benefit as a "holistic approach of TQM" was grossly missing. What was needed by the industry was acceptance and implementation of the TQM principles in totality. The Juran's theory of TQM and Juran's Triology were hardly understood by the industry and it led to the sporadic adoption of JQIP in areas selected at random. The result was obvious, most of the existing Indian industries could not face the stress and strain of globalization, liberalization and international competition and closed their shutters. Whereas a new group of Indian industries like the TVS Group, Wipro, Infosys, Reliance Industries, PCS, etc. who practised TQM principles like customer focus, continuous improvement, employees empowerment, statistical process control like Six-Sigma, ISO 9000 Quality Management System, Quality Planning, Quality Control and Quality Improvement emerged as winners compared to others. Among the existing Indian industries who adopted and practiced TQM principles like the Mahindra group, Tata group, L&T group, the Kumarmangalam Birla group survived and gained success even in this challenging industrial environment.

4.4   TQM LEADS TO WORLD-CLASS MANAGEMENT SYSTEM

With the current globalization and liberalization, organizations have no options but to face international competition. They have to 'think globally but act locally'. Everyday new steps in liberalization like reduction of import duty, full convertibility of rupee on trade account, abolition of licence raj, signing of WTO agreement, the market is becoming increasingly complex. The Indian industry has been enjoying monopoly for a long time. The market was a sellers' market. For simple items like a scooter or a car, the customer had to wait for years. The product quality was much below the international standards. Even for items of regular day-to-day use like soaps, detergents, kitchenware, electronic items, the options were limited and that of a poor quality. Every substandard product also had a customer since government ensured that the demand is always more than the supply. Today the consumers have the entire world at their disposal. The latest designs and models of almost all the products are freely available, giving consumers a wider choice. Under the circumstances, only the Best can survive.

Today the Indian industry has learned to live in the "Buyers Market" where customer satisfaction has become the key word.

Customer satisfaction is a state in which customer needs, wants and expectations are met and exceeded resulting in repurchase and continued loyalty. In otehr words, the customer is said to be satisfied when his/her stated and implied needs get fulfilled by the use of the product and the associated services.

The term **customer satisfaction** has changed the whole complexion of not only the Indian industry but also of the world industrial scenario. The key to the success of Japanese industry has been their orientation towards customer satisfaction. All these factors combined together have made it imperative for the Indian industry to adopt successful management practices like TQM to survive and compete globally. The best part of it is that the TQM practices multiply profitability, productivity and efficiency leading to excellence in every field of business without any investment.

The key to customer satisfaction has to go beyond the concept of product quality or small "q". For customer satisfaction is the adoption of the big "Q" or the Total Quality Management. ISO 9000 is only a part of the Total Quality Management or TQM. ISO 9000 is an international standard on Quality Management System aimed at customer satisfaction. TQM, a part of which is ISO 9000 goes much beyond quality control department or product quality and embraces in its fold all the functions including marketing, production, materials, personnel and even finance (see Figure 4.1).

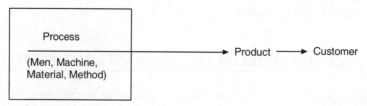

Q = Total Quality
q = Product Quality

TQM = Orientation towards process and company wide performance excellence in all functions involving everybody

FIGURE 4.1 The role of employee in ensuring customer satisfaction and realizing the organisational vision as a part of TQM.

In fact under the TQM theory, the marketing department assumes a critical function where the TQM activity begins and ends. As far as the organization is concerned, marketing becomes the internal customer for the organization and a channel of communication with the external customer or the actual customer. Operation/Production department's function is "Value addition by conversion" and all other departments function is to support the operation.

TQM redefined management as 'The process of designing and maintaining an environment conducive for performance for a group of people working together for the attainment of the common objective in time. The word "total quality" encompasses the totality of the entire business operation.

The basic objective of an organization or a manager is to create a surplus. The business operation ought to be productive both in terms of efficiency—output should be more than the input and effectiveness—nearness to the goal or objective.

Here planning is not merely budgeting but an elaborate 'Quality Plan' which selects the best alternative for attainment of the end objective in time with least consumption of resources. The next step is to execute the plan, i.e. 'do it'. However, in actual situation, there is a deviation between what you plan and what you do. Hence, the next logical step is to check the deviation and then analyze its root cause and then take corrective action so that any mistake once committed should never be repeated again. As every month it is the same organization, same product, same machine setup, managerial function is an ongoing process or a cycle. Every time you analyze the root cause of the deviation and take corrective action in the next plan so that the mistake once committed is never repeated again. Therefore in an organization, if the deviations today are expressed in % (percentage), after some time the deviations will reduce to part per million (ppm). The entire organization will be on the path of continuous improvement. The entire system should be backed up by a sound quality management system which allows the improvements to be sustained on a long-term basis. This quality system is nothing but the ISO 9000:2000 quality system, which are defines the entire management system, resource allocation, marketing, design and development, purchasing, production, housekeeping, quality assurance, inventory management, training and after sales service process-oriented P-D-C-A cycle approach externally maximizes 'customer satisfaction' and internally for the organization generates the highest possible return on investment. These two factors combined together lead not only to market leadership but also ultimately the attainment of the global business Leadership.

The departmental orientation of vertical chimney type organization is replaced by *Horizontal Quality Thinking* where the entire organization is oriented towards attainment of a common objective or goal. The departmental boundaries are thin in the current organizational structure. The ultimate objective of a world-class organization is 'customer satisfaction' leading to its business success and market leadership position. Its objective is to maximize customer satisfaction by providing the right quality of product in and right quantity, at the right place, the right time and at the right price. The same concept is brought towards the function of the internal department supplementing and complementing the production or rather the operation function. Hence the function of the materials department is to provide right quality of material, in right quantity, at right place, at right time and right price. The human resource department provides the right quality of manpower, in the right quantity, at the right time, the right place and at the least cost. Same is applicable to the finance function of providing the right quantity of finance, of the right quality, at the right time, the right place and the right price. This attainment of "customer satisfaction" with optimization of input resources will not only ensure cost competitiveness and market leadership but also enable the organization to maximize its Return on Investment.

Here the concept of the **Internal Customer** can be effectively introduced to increase accountability, better efficiency, effectiveness and measurement of **Value Addition** at each stage or function or department towards fulfillment of the overall objective of the organization, i.e. measured in terms of market leadership, customer satisfaction, profitability and return on investment. Thus marketing becomes the internal customer for the manufacturing or the factory, the manufacturing becomes internal customer for the materials or the human resources department.

4.4.1 Definition of Various Quality-Related Terms

The various quality-related terms are defined as per the universally accepted ISO 9000:2000 standard.

Quality: Ability of a complete set of realized inherent characteristics of a product, system or process to fulfill requirements.

Quality Policy: The overall intensions and directions of an organization are related to quality as formally expressed by the top management.

Quality Management: Coordinated activities to direct and control an organization.

Quality System: A set of interrelated or interacting elements.

Quality Planning: Part of QMS focused on setting quality objectives and specifying the necessary operational processes and related resources to fulfill the quality objectives.

Quality Management System: A management system is to direct and control an organization with regard to quality.

Quality Objective: Something sought, or aimed for, related to quality. Objectives should be specific, measurable and quantifiable.

Quality Control: Part of QMS focused on fulfilling quality requirements.

Quality Assurance: Part of QMS focused on providing confidence that quality requirements will be fulfilled.

Customer Satisfaction: A customer's opinion of the degree to which a transaction has met the customer's needs and expectations.

Top Management: A person or group of people who direct and control an organization at the highest level.

Quality Improvement: Part of quality management focused on increasing the ability to fulfill quality requirements, i.e. effectiveness and efficiency of QMS.

Effectiveness: A measure of the extent to which planned activities are realized and planned results achieved.

Efficiency: Relationship between the result achieved and the resources used.

Document: Information and its support medium, Examples: record, specification, drawing, report, standard (medium can be paper, magnetic, electronic or optical computer disc, photograph or master sample, or a combination thereof).

Quality Record: Document stating results achieved or providing evidence of the activities performed.

4.4.2 Definitions, Concepts and Features of "TQM"

The study of TQM is certainly not new. The development, application, and assessment of TQM techniques by scholars, consultants and managers in the production and operations research fields has been underway for the last six decades. A small sampling of such work includes works by quality leaders Crosby (1979, 1989), Deming (1952), Ishikawa (1985), Juran (1989), Mizuno (1988), and Suzaki (1987) and research conducted by Ernst and Young, American Quality Foundation (1992), Feigenbaum (1991), Garvin (1988), Jaikumar (1989), and Kantor and Zangwill (1993).

The term TQM has been commonly used to denote a system of managing for total quality. While a precise definition of TQM remains elusive, it can be said that quality, customers and continuous improvement are the key themes of this new paradigm.

TQM is an approach to improve flexibility and effectiveness of a business as a whole. It addresses the bottom line of an organization. The most important component of TQM is the people, who need GRAPES (Growth, Recognition, Achievement, Participation, Esteem and Self-Actualization). Its second component contains quality improvement tools and techniques like statistical process control, benchmarking, and Six Sigma, etc. Third ingredient of TQM is systems. ISO 9001:2000 on quality management system is an example.[28]

Oakland (1992) defined TQM as:[29] "A comprehensive approach to improving competitiveness and flexibility through planning, organizing and understanding each activity and involving everyone at each level. TQM ensures that management adopts a strategic overview of quality and focuses on prevention rather than inspection".

Sinclair, D. and Zairi, M. (1996) state that TQM is:[30] "A positive attempt by the organizations concerned to improve structural, infra-structural, attitudinal, behavioural and methodological ways of delivering to the end-customer, with emphasis on: consistency, improvement in quality, competitive enhancements, all with the aim of satisfying or delighting the end-customer".

Milliken Industries Ltd., U.K. (Jeanes, 1990) defines it as:[31] A total operational philosophy which covers every aspect or everything we do.

British Telecom (Kelly Simon, Lloyd Joana and McCormic, 1991) elaborates TQM as:[32]

Total: Everyone is involved.

Quality: Meeting customers' (agreed) requirements at lowest cost, first time, and every time.

Management: It is owned and led by the management team top-down.

TQM is a total, company-wide effort through full involvement of the entire workforce with focus on continuous improvement to achieve customer satisfaction. TQM is both a comprehensive managerial philosophy and a collection of tools and approaches for its implementation. While the concept of TQM has been around for some time, A.V. Feigenbaum recognized the importance of a comprehensive approach to quality in the 1950s and coined the term total quality control.

According to Feigenbaum, total quality control is defined as: "An effective system for integrating the quality development, quality maintenance and quality improvement efforts of the various groups in an organization so as to enable marketing, engineering, production and service at the most economical levels which allow for full customer satisfaction". The Japanese adopted Feigenbaum's concept and renamed it company-wide quality control (CWQC). Wayne S. Reiker listed the following five aspects of total quality control practised in Japan:

(i) Quality emphasis extends through market analysis, design and customer service rather than only the production stages of making a product.

(ii) Quality emphasis is directed towards operations in every department from executives to the clerical level.

(iii) Quality is the responsibility of the individual and the workgroup, not some other group such as inspection.

(iv) There are two types of quality characteristics as viewed by customers: those that satisfy and those that motivate. Only the latter are strongly related to repeat sales and a "quality" image.

(v) The first customer for a part or piece of information is usually the next department in the production process (i.e. the internal customer).

According to Wruck and Jensen[33], "TQM is a new organizing technology that is science-based, non-hierarchical, and non-market-oriented. It improves productivity by encouraging the use of science in decision-making and discouraging counter-productive defensive behaviour. It also encourages effective creation and use of specific knowledge throughout the organization."

At the heart of TQM is the conviction that it is possible to achieve defect-free work most of the time. This assertion is phrased in various ways like do it right the first time, work smarter and work for zero defects. The idea is to strive for perfection in the work, the way an archer aims for the bull's eye on a target. One may not always achieve the target, but the 'mindset' to strive for perfect work is important. "It's better [in this sense] to aim at perfection and miss than it is to aim at imperfection and hit it," said Thomas J. Watson, the founder of IBM. The first time right or zero defects emphasize on prevention, and the diligent use of measurement, process controls and the data-driven elimination of waste and error. It serves as a goal for continuous improvement. Prevention is the aim of all quality assurance. Through planned and systematic actions such as documentation of work processes, or cost of quality audits, quality assurance prevents quality problems.

The TQM approach has been given a variety of names in the last decade, with most major companies have launched full-scale quality programmes. A few of them are the following: Leadership Through Quality (Xerox); Quality the ICL Way (ICL); Quality Service Program (Nat West); Total Quality Culture (Texas Instruments); Total Quality Excellence (Ford); Quality Focus on the Business Process (IBM); Quality Enhancement Strategy (National Semiconductors); Six-Sigma at Motorola; Perfect Design Quality at Intel; Total Quality Control at Hewlett-Packard.

To move to TQM, the greatest challenge an organization faces is resistance to change. A paradigm shift in mindset is therefore considered vital. Evidently, the faster an organization adapts to TQM culture, the better are its prospects towards attaining world-class manufacturer's status. TQM is definitely the order of the millennium. Focus on stated and implied needs of stakeholders for both products as well as service quality is needed. However, it should always be kept in mind that quality is like a rolling stone. It is a Herculean task to take it up and attain a world-class manufacturer's status. But it slides down very fast unless continually monitored by the top management with a missionary zeal. Continual improvement must be a way of life.

TQM is all about prevention. As Phillip B. Crosby said: The purpose of it (quality management) is to set up a system and management discipline that prevents defects from happening in the company's performance cycle. To accomplish this, you have to act now on situations, which may cause problems, some time from now. Act now for reward later.[34]

The seven underlying principles of TQM[35] are: Strive for quality in all things; take the customer needs as the criteria for quality, improve the process or system by which products are produced; quality improvement is continuous, never ending activity; worker involvement is essential; ground decisions and actions in knowledge; and encourage teamwork and cooperation.

Total quality demands new styles of managing and an entirely new set of skills. These styles include the following characteristics: thinking in terms of systems: defining customer requirements; planning for quality improvement with each customer; dealing with customer dissatisfaction; ensuring ongoing quality efforts; developing a life-long learning style; team building; encouraging openness; creating climates of trust and eliminating fear; listening and providing feedback; leading and participating in group meetings; solving problems with data; clarifying goals and resolving conflicts; delegating and coaching; implementing change; and making continuous improvement a way of life.

The major axioms of TQM[36] are commitments to quality, extensive use of scientific tools and techniques, total involvement in the quality undertaking (universal responsibility), continuous improvement.

Total Quality Management can be defined as 'an organized scientific approach towards continuous improvement in quality involving everyone in the organization covering every function aimed towards total customer satisfaction'.

Therefore the goals of TQM are:

- **Customer delightment/satisfaction in totality:** The TQM concept originated when the Japanese redefined quality as a customer-related or user-related concept than a product-related concept. It is the customer who runs the wheel of an organization. This implies the very existence of an organization depends on its customers. The organization can only survive and excel when it is producing products and services fulfilling the customers' stated and implied needs leading to his/her satisfaction. The vital factor to an organization's performance excellence is its ability to be user-friendly and develop as close a relationship with the customer as possible.
- **Continuous improvement:** The best organizations in the world are not keeping quiet, but growing at a good pace. Juran clearly states that an organization with a revolutionary growth rate can only reach and sustain the global leadership. Deming's principle of P-D-C-A cycle is heavily oriented towards growth and continuous improvement. Change for the better at a revolutionary pace is the ideal business mantra for business excellence in the current highly competitive environment.
- **Total employee involvement and empowerment:** The difference between winners and losers is not the machine or raw materials but the difference between the motivational levels of their employees. The employee involvement and their proactiveness can only create an environment for performance excellence of each and every individual leading to an all-round business leadership.
- **Optimization of resources:** In today's competitive world, the market forces decide the price. Unless an organization's cost of production of products and/or services are low, the organization cannot survive. This is where the Japanese concept of controlling "Muda" and methodology of reduction of 'cost of poor quality' by Dr. Juran's methodology plays a vital role in world-class performance of organization.
- **Do it right the first time:** To fulfill the requirement of customer satisfaction of providing products and services of the right quality, in the right quantity, at the right time, place and the least price depends only on the concept of do it right the first time because in the current competitive world nobody is going to give you the chance a second time. An organization has to capitalize on the opportunity first time itself if it has to survive and excel.

The importance of TQM is not only to the goods, products and services produced by industries, but also to the industries themselves and ultimately to the society in general. Edward Deming and Joseph Juran are seen as the main forces in converting non-significant, low profile Japanese companies of the fifties and the sixties into world leaders in their respective fields of operations by the end of the seventies and the eighties. These are the two management gurus who made the world realize the key to business leadership is the management of quality on all aspects of business operations and not merely to the product quality. Joseph Juran was the first to publish the book "Quality Control Handbook" way back in 1949 that sold over 3,50,000 copies. Juran, along with Edward Deming, has started a silent revolution all over the world—The quality revolution. This has led to a remarkable growth in the importance of quality to society. Today's industrial society provides its citizens with the marvelous benefit of technology. The continuity of this very life style depends on the quality of goods and services available. Today, the survival of an organization depends on its ability to satisfy its customers. The customer satisfaction is derived from the fulfillment of his need by using the products and services. Quality as defined by Dr. Juran as fitness for use. Hence, quality plays the lead role in customer satisfaction. TQM embraced the paradigm of quality for not only products but also services. Hence quality became a prime organization-wide-activity.

TQM is a long-enduring journey of infinite length. The TQM has a bottom-up approach at the operational level. To implement TQM, an organization has to move the ideas to each employee, but should not try to force strategies but try to change people's mindset. TQM is a people's process. Hence everybody in the organization should be oriented towards the common goal of maximization of the customer satisfaction as well as the attainment of the organizational vision (see Figure 4.1). The organization should always challenge the 'business as usual' attitude and develop a self-renovating business organization with focus on continuous improvement.

"The attainment of the desired quality required commitment and participation of all members in an organisation whereas responsibility of quality management belongs to the top management".

4.4.3   The Eight Building Blocks of TQM

The internationally recognized building blocks of the TQM can now be summed up into eight building blocks detailed as follows (see Figure 4.2):

(a) Act always in line with the customer's needs by understanding his/her stated and implied needs by supplying the products and services as per the same. This will lead to achieving the customers' satisfaction and ultimately the market leadership. The very objective of an organization's existence depends on the customers who are the only source of income for the organization. The customer consumes the products and services generated by the organization and in turn pay for the same, thereby becoming the only revenue generating agency which fulfills the organization's all expenses as well as the profit. Unless the organization fulfills the customers' needs leading to customer satisfaction and repeat purchase, the organization will not survive in the current global intense competitive environment.

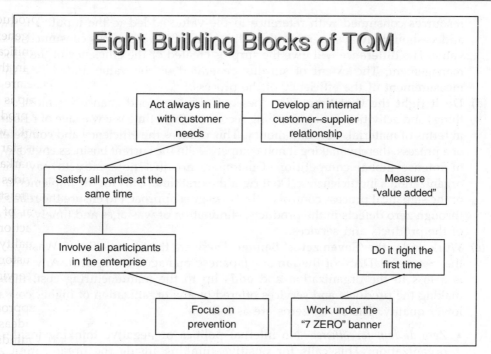

Eight Building Blocks of TQM

Act always in line with customer needs

Develop an internal customer–supplier relationship

Satisfy all parties at the same time

Measure "value added"

Involve all participants in the enterprise

Do it right the first time

Focus on prevention

Work under the "7 ZERO" banner

FIGURE 4.2 The eight building blocks of TQM.

(b) **Develop an internal customer supplier relationship** as explained in the first chapter in detail. The processes or functions in the organization are all aligned in such a manner that the output of one process or function is input to the next process or function, thereby the succeeding process/function becomes the customer for the preceding process/function and the customer has to be satisfied. Hence the customer is for the entire organization, the marketing department becomes the internal customer to the production department which, in turn, becomes the internal customer for the materials, maintenance and human resource department. While the organization has to supply the products and services of the right quality, in right quantity at the right time, at the right place and at the right cost for the maximization of the customer's satisfaction, the materials department has to supply the 'raw material' of the right quality, in right quantity at the right time, at the right place and at the right cost to the production department which is internal customer to the materials department. Similarly, the human resource department has to supply the 'human resource' of the right quality, in the right quantity at the right time, the right place and at the right cost and the maintenance department has to supply the 'machines' of the right quality, in right quantity at the right time, at the right place and at the right cost to the production department. This creates an organization where the functions supplement and complement each other for the maximization of the performance efficiency and excellence.

(c) **Measure the value added** to the process or the sub-process under you. Measure both the value added to the input and the cost of value addition, i.e. cost of the resources consumed with reference to the value added to the input. The value added should always be more than the value of the resources consumed to add value. The difference will give the surplus created or the efficiency of the process management. The extent of surplus generated or the value added is a direct measurement of the efficiency of the process.

(d) **Do it right the first time.** Life does not give a second chance for most of the things and activities. Doing anything second or third time is a wastage of resources in terms of material, time and money. This reduces the efficiency and competency of a process, thereby making it non-competitive in the current business environment of intense global competition. Customers are just not ready to pay for an organization's inefficiencies. 'Do it right the first time' calls for the implementation of the statistical process control or the Six-Sigma approach to ensure the reliability through zero defects in the products, elimination of wastages and timely delivery of the products and services.

(e) **Work under the 'Seven zeros' Banner.** These are the famous 'Seven Wastages' or the 'Seven MUDAS' of the famous Japanese management system. Any wastage is a loss to the organization and adds up to the manufacturing cost, thereby making the products and services offered by the organization of higher cost and lower quality. The seven zeros are as follows:

- *Zero disdain for others:* No internal politics or negative thinking inside the organization. This calls for positive thinking inside the organization and appreciating each other's work.
- *Zero stock or inventory:* Inventory is a non-value added activity and leads to blockage of money and useful resources apart from inventory related risks and costs.
- *Zero delay:* Zero delay in response to fulfillment of a customer's order or response to a query or unnecessary waiting of machines or goods for further processing is also a form of wastage.
- *Zero paper:* Every transaction like release of a purchase order, indent, inspection report, etc. is on a real-time basis by sharing of information network wherein the paper work is minimum.
- *Zero downtime:* It pertains to the absence of any breakdown of machines thereby no loss of production due to stoppage of machines for maintenance. This objective is achieved by the practice of 'total productive maintenance' or preventive maintenance activities in an organization.
- *Zero defect:* It is achieved by following the 'statistical process control' with the help of the control limits and control mechanism which do not allow a defective product to be produced an organization.
- *Zero accident:* The safety mechanism should be so perfect that an organization should have no accidents whatsoever by guarding the moving parts.

(f) **Focus on Prevention.** Prevent the repetition of mistakes. Any failure or mistake has to be analyzed to find out the root cause and take suitable corrective and preventive actions so that the mistake or the failure never repeats.

(g) **Involve all the participants in the organization.** TQM advocates involvement of not only its employees, but also an organization's suppliers, vendors as well as its customers.

(h) **Satisfy all parties at the same time.** An organization should endeavour to satisfy not only its employees, suppliers and customers, but also the environment, its shareholders, society and the country at large.

These eight techniques are practised together in a cycle for the implementation of TQM. The objective is to attain a performance level of the highest order for each and every employee as well as the suppliers so that the organization attains the market leadership. The 12 TQM steps, along with these eight building blocks, can take an organization to an invincible position in industry standards. This will enable the organization to attain the market leadership position globally as well as implement a world-class management system.

4.4.4   Pre-requisites for the Success of 'TQM'

- *Committment at the Top:*   For TQM to be successful, only the involvement of the employees is not enough. The commitment should come from the top management. The top management must declare the organizational vision, mission and quality policy. The top management should arrange for the resources for fulfillment of the objective. The top management must motivate the entire staff to make the TQM implementation successful.
- *Organisation for quality:*   The organization for implementation and success of TQM should create a quality council at the highest level to decide and implement all the vital decisions. The quality council members are the heads of the various functions and the chairman of the quality council is the CEO of the organization. The organization should have different quality improvement teams at different levels for the implementation of TQM activities and problem solving.
- *Strategic direction:*   The strategic direction consists of formulating a long range plan known as the 'vision' and a value system for the organization known as the 'mission', along with the annual business plans formulated after 'SWOT' analysis and formulation of function-wise strategic action plan. This is extremely important and explained in detail in the 12 steps to implement a world-class management system.
- *Customer orientation:*   As explained in detail in the first chapter, the main objective of an organization for its survival and performance excellence is maximization of customer satisfaction and the return on investment. The first objective of customer satisfaction can only be achieved by customer-orientation, understanding the customer's stated and implied needs and developing user-friendly customer-oriented products and services. It is the customers who run the wheels of an organization.
- *Need-based education and training:*   TQM is a new concept which changes the working of an organization totally. To adapt to these new concepts and techniques, an extensive as well as intensive education and training are a must to make the TQM system work. Even otherwise, the TQM system warrants continual improvement at all levels, thereby needs constant upgradation of the skill level of all its employees which can only happen by continuous education and training.
- *Total involvement of employees:*   Depending on the work environment and work culture, people contribute differently for the attainment of the organizational

objectives. A negative person will not do any value addition even if he is capable of doing so. Similarly, a neutral person has to do his bare minimum. The positive and active employees will contribute positively for the attainment of the organizational goal. The proactive person will not only perform par excellence himself but also help others to achieve the organizational goal.

- *Supportive culture:* The TQM system will expect support from the various functions as well as from the suppliers of the organization. The concept of internal customer develops into a supportive culture for performance excellence with each supplementing and complementing the other.
- *Teamwork:* TQM focuses on a teamwork for performance excellence. The horizontal quality thinking with common objective of maximization of customer satisfaction and return on investment is based totally on a cohesive teamwork mobilizing the entire resources for the achievement of the organizational goal. The importance and significance of teamwork is also explained in the first chapter.
- *Prevention-based systems:* TQM makes the prevention-based system compulsory so that a mistake once committed is never repeated. Whether the working is as per Deming's P-D-C-A cycle or ISO 9000:2000 quality management system or various problem-solving techniques like quality circle or Kaizen Gemba, the fundamental principle of all these systems is formulation of a prevention-based system. For any failure or mistake, the prevention-based system finds out the root cause for the same and takes a corrective and preventive system so that the mistake or the failure is not repeated.
- *Recognition and reward system:* TQM system is based on the principle of rewarding the performers after their identification and training and educating the non-performers to upgrade their skill level. A non-performer after improvement can stake his claim for recognition and reward. TQM tools like Kaizen Gemba, quality circle, etc. believe in rewarding a contributing person.

4.5 COST OF QUALITY

The TQM system must include methods and procedures to determine and evaluate the impact the cost of quality or the cost of poor quality (COPQ) has on the profitability of an organization. Here the cost of quality is a measure of the level of quality the organization wants to maintain and the associated cost of the same, whereas the cost of poor quality or COPQ is a measure of all the nine wastages as listed under the subject of 'Muda' or wastages.

The purpose of the cost of quality reporting system is to provide the management with a tool to identify the improvement areas. In the initial stage, the external failure and rejection are high. As the inspection system gets effectively implemented, the external failure gets eliminated at the cost of increase in the internal failure. As the quality management system matures further, the appraisal and preventive steps are taken. The moment the root causes of the failures and the people responsible for the same are identified, the failure rate comes down considerably after taking the corrective measures. This is the point where the total cost of poor quality and overall failure rate take a fast dip within a short time. The external and internal failures gradually become zero as also the appraisal cost starts coming down. The root causes of the failures are identified and the corrective and preventive actions are taken. Hence, as the system matures, the preventive cost goes up and it should ideally be the only cost.

The above facts can be graphically depicted as illustrated in Figure 4.3 as the distribution of quality cost on a time-scale as the total quality management system matures.

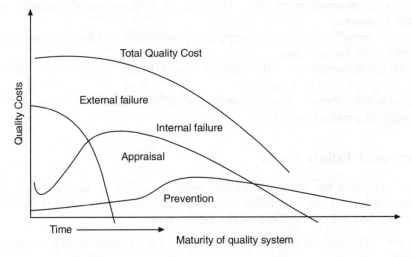

FIGURE 4.3 Distribution of quality costs on a time-scale as the TQM matures.

The cost of quality is the cost that is incurred because of poor quality. Two broad categories of quality costs, prevention and appraisal, are incurred because poor quality may exist. Those products that do not conform to quality standards often cause an organization to incur failure costs. Depending on the point at which quality problems are identified, failure costs are often classified as internal or external.

4.5.1 Prevention Costs

Prevention costs are those incurred to prevent poor quality products from being produced. The following are some components:

(i) *Quality planning:* Costs of preparing an overall plan, numerous specialized plans, quality manuals, and procedures.

(ii) *New-product review:* Cost of reviewing or preparing quality specifications for new products, evaluation of new designs, preparing of tests and experimental programmes, evaluating vendors and marketing studies to determine customers' quality requirements.

(iii) *Training:* Cost of developing and conducting training programmes.

(iv) *Process planning:* Costs of designing and developing process control devices.

(v) *Quality data:* Cost of collecting data, data analysis, reporting.

(vi) *Improvement projects:* Cost of planned failure investigations aimed at chronic quality problems.

4.5.2 Appraisal Costs

Appraisal costs are an outcome of activities undertaken to prevent poor quality services from being processed beyond a point at which they become nonconforming to the standards and cannot be delivered to customers. The following are some of the components:

(i) *Incoming materials inspection:* The cost of determining the quality of incoming raw materials.

(ii) *Process inspection:* All tests, sampling procedures and inspections done while the product is being made.

(iii) *Final goods inspection:* All inspections or tests conducted on the finished product in the plant or the field.

(iv) *Quality laboratories:* The cost of operating laboratories to inspect materials at all stages of production.

4.5.3 Internal Failure Costs

Internal failure costs are those associated with materials or services that fail to meet quality standards and are identified before the product or service is delivered to the customer. The following are some of the components:

(i) *Scrap:* The cost of labour and material of a product, which cannot be used or sold.

(ii) *Rework:* The cost of redoing a product, which can be made to conform.

(iii) *Downgrading:* Cost in terms of selling the product at less than full value due to quality problems.

(iv) *Retest:* Cost of inspection and tests after rework.

(v) *Downtime:* Cost of idle facilities and people due to quality failures.

4.5.4 External Failure Costs

External failure costs are those incurred due to poor-quality products delivered to customers. The following are some of the components:

(i) *Warranty:* The cost of refunds, repairing or replacing products on warranty.

(ii) *Returned merchandise:* Merchandise which is returned to the seller due to poor quality.

(iii) *Complaints:* The cost of settling customer complaints due to poor quality.

(iv) *Allowances:* Cost of concessions made to customers due to substandard quality.

4.6 '5' S OF HOUSEKEEPING

Housekeeping is given a lot of importance in the TQM system. It reduces wastages of time and improves the efficiency and effectiveness of the work. Improper housekeeping may lead to accidents, dull working environment and other work-related problems. The five 'S' of housekeeping are:

SEIRI—Orderliness: The orderliness of the manufacturing aids, arrangement of raw materials near the machine, keeping the files and drawings in order make the working faster, effective and efficient without wastage of effort, time and material.

SEISO—Clarity: The clarity of work process, flow process charts, arrangement of raw material, finished goods and intermediary services make the work place more efficient and effective.

SEITON—Tidiness: Tidiness ensures adequate space for machines and the movement of men. Tidiness prevents undesired mixing of different materials and product identification becomes easy. The chances of rejection and rework get minimized.

SEIKETSU—Cleanliness: It is said that cleanliness is next to godliness. Cleanliness of the shopfloor and the office are mandatory for a good working environment, good product quality and elimination of accidents. This is also important to put up a decent appearance of the organization before guests and visitors.

SHITSUKE—Shitsuke recommends the practice of all the four housekeeping practices together to enhance the effectiveness of the housekeeping practice. This talks about self discipline in implementing the good housekeeping practices.

4.7 TOTAL QUALITY MANAGEMENT PIONEERS

Total quality management has emerged as a powerful technique worldwide over the last five decades. This is also known as the world-class management system. The contribution made by it is shortlisted below its highlighting main contributions in the field of TQM.

Walter Shewart:
- Founder of P-D-C-A cycle
- Originator of statistical procss control at A&T Bells Lab in 1930

W. Edward Deming:
- Led quality revolution in Japan, post-World War II
- Quality is a key competitive advantage
- Deming quality award by Japan is the most prestigious quality award
- Deming's 14 points for excellence

Joseph M. Juran:
- Led quality revolution in Japan post-World War II
- He defined quality as fitness for use by customer
- Juran's triology of quality planning, quality control and quality improvement
- Started Juran's institute in USA
- Introduced cost of poor quality

Philip B. Crosby:
- Started Crosby quality college
- Created the concept of "zero defect"
- Defined quality as conformance to requirment

Taiichi Ohno:
- Formulated the flexible manufacturing system (FMS)
- Father of the just-in-time and Kanban system of manufacturing
- Father of "TPS" or Toyota Production System

Sheigo Shingo:
- Originator of 'single minute exchange of dies'
- Introduced the concept of modular manufacturing

Kaoru Ishikawa:
- Originator of fish-bone or the cause and effect diagram

Masaaki Imai:
- Popularized the Kaizan concept of continuous improvement

E. Goldrat:
- Theory of constraints.

All of them advocated that 'involvement of top management' for successful TQM implementation.

4.7.1 Quality Contribution By Quality Gurus

W. Edward Deming: Deming defined quality as 'continuous improvement'. He said, "If I had to reduce my message to managers to just a few words, I would say it all had to do with reducing variation". The central problem of management in all its aspects, including planning, procurement, manufacturing, research, sales, personnel, accounting, and law, is to understand better the meaning of variation, and extract the information contained in variation. (Guidance from questions and pronouncements of Lloyd S. Nelson, Director of Statistical Methods for the Nashua Corporation)[4]. Deming believed that quality and productivity always increased as variability decreased. Deming's approach to quality built on Shewart's work and aimed at understanding the causes of two types of variation:

Uncontrolled variation: That is due to assignable or special causes. For example, change of operation, procedures or raw materials and breakages are all outside influences on a process, which interrupt its normal pattern of operation.

Controlled variation: This is due to non-assignable, chance, random or common causes. All of these causes are due to the process itself, its design and installation.

Thus quality improvement for Deming must begin with an accurate identification of the two types of variation. If one finds a great deal of deviation from the normal operation of a system due to special causes, it is quite impossible to evaluate those changes the management might make in the system attempting to improve it. 'Process capability' in these circumstances loses its meaning. Once the special causes of variation have been eliminated and only common causes are left, quality improvement can come about only by management reworking or redesigning the system. If a manager wrongly identifies the cause of the variation, getting one type of cause mixed up with another, the action taken by the manager to improve things can, in fact, make them worse.

Deming has been a critic of quality efforts in the United States, attributing most of the problems to the system, and saying that managers are responsible for it. Support of top management is not sufficient. It is not enough that top management commit themselves for life to quality and productivity. They must know what it is that they are committed to. That is what they must do. These obligations cannot be delegated. Support is not enough: action is required.

Deming has evolved 14 major points for improving quality, which are summarized below[5]. The 14 points for management are the basis for transformation of the American industry. It will not suffice merely to solve problems, big or small. Adoption and action on the 14 points are a signal that the management intends to stay in business and aims to protect investors and jobs. Such a system formed the basis for lessons of the top management in Japan in 1950, and in subsequent years. The 14 points apply anywhere, to small organizations as well as to large ones, to the service industry as well as to manufacturing. They also apply to a division within a company.

1. Create constancy of purpose towards improvement of products and services, with the aim to become competitive and to stay in business, and to provide jobs.
2. Adopt a new philosophy. We are in a new economic age. Western management must wake up to the challenge, must learn their responsibilities, and take on leadership for change.
3. Stop depending on inspections to achieve quality. Eliminate the need for inspection on a mass basis by building quality into the product in the first place.
4. End the practice of awarding business on the basis of price tag. Instead, minimize the total cost. Move towards a single supplier for any one item, on a long-term relationship of loyalty and trust.
5. Improve constantly and forever the system of production and service, to improve quality and productivity, and thus constantly decrease costs.
6. Introduce the practice of training on the job.
7. Promote progressive leadership. The aim of supervision should be to help people, machines and gadgets to do a better job. The management, workers and the whole system should be supervised through a proactive approach to achieve total quality.
8. Drive out fear so that everyone may work effectively for the company.
9. Bridge the barriers between departments. People in research, design, sales, and production must work as a team to foresee problems of production and in use that may be encountered with the product or service.
10. Eliminate slogans, exhortations, and targets for the workforce asking for zero defects and new levels of productivity. Such exhortations only create adverse relationships, as the bulk of the causes of low quality and low productivity belong to the system and thus lie beyond the power of the work force.

11. Eliminate work standards (quotas) on the factory floor, substitute leadership; eliminate management by objective and by numbers and numerical goals. Goals are necessary for everybody, but numerical goals set for other people, without a road-map to reach the goal, will be counter-productive.
12. Remove barriers that rob the hourly worker of his right to the pride of workmanship. The responsibility of supervisors must be changed from sheer numbers to quality. Remove barriers that rob people in management and in engineering of their right to the pride of workmanship. This means, inter alias, abolishment of the annual or merit rating and of management by objective.
13. Institute a vigorous programme of education and self-improvement.
14. Put everybody in the company to work to accomplish the transformation. The transformation is everybody's job.

Joseph M. Juran: Juran defined quality as 'fit for use'. Juran believes that quality happens only through projects—the quality improvement projects established in every part of the company. Addressing the Rank Xerox 1985 Mitcheldean Quality Convention, Juran outlined his basic approach which matched exactly what Xerox had been doing—the Juran trilogy—quality planning, quality control, and quality improvement. He outlined his basic approach as, first set up a quality council, and next identify projects, the more, the better. "There is no such thing as improvement, in general", he said, "It all takes place project by project and in no other way." Perhaps Juran is open to criticism here, implying as he does, that virtually all quality improvement is achieved through a project-by-project method. In reality, projects are only part, however important, of a TQM process. Juran opines that quality does not happen by accident. It must be planned.

Juran developed a nine-point quality planning road-map. Sequence of his steps are as follows:

1. Identify who are our customers. The customer is one on whom the product has an impact.
2. Determine the needs of these customers. The needs of the customers are enormous and vary from customer to customer.
3. Translate the customer needs into manufacturing needs.
4. Develop a product that can respond to these needs.
5. Optimize the product features so as to improve the needs of the manufacturer as well as the customer. Here the goal is to meet customer needs and minimize production cost.
6. Develop a process which is able to produce the product.
7. Optimize the process.
8. Prove that the process can produce the product under operating conditions.
9. Transfer the process to the operating forces which include: Process specification, procedures, on-the-job training, formal training course, and prior participation.

Kaoru Ishikawa: Kaoru Ishikawa defined: "quality is the most economical, the most useful and always satisfactory to the consumer". Kaoru Ishikawa argued that the American management style whereby 'management manages and people do' could not be grafted on to Japanese work practices. He suggested a blend of the best of techniques, such as the American flow-line production techniques, and Japanese practices be fused with traditional European craftsmanship. He developed the idea of bringing craftsmanship back to groups rather than to individuals.

Ishikawa's 'fishbone' diagram, which bears his name as the Ishikawa diagram, was invented in 1943 as a management problem-solving tool. Quality improvement teams use it worldwide.

Ishikawa's quality circles were first piloted at the Nippon Telegraph and Cable Company in 1962. By 1978 there were one million quality circles with 10 million employees mostly in manufacturing. Today there are two million quality circles involving 20 million members and extending into the service sectors of Japan. In his book *"What is Total Quality Control?"*[6] Ishikawa said that seven basic tools were 'indispensable for quality control'. These are Pareto analysis, fishbone diagrams, stratification, tally charts, histograms, scatter diagrams and control charts. With these tools, Ishikawa argued, managers and staff could tackle and solve the quality problems facing them.

Philip Crosby: Philip B. Crosby defined quality as "conformance to requirements". In his book *Quality is free; The Art of Making Quality Certain*, Crosby says, "Quality is free, it's not a gift. What costs money are the poor quality things—all the outcomes as a result of not doing jobs right the first time."[7]

Crosby lists four essentials of quality management, which he calls 'the absolutes':

1. Quality is defined as conformance to requirements, not as goodness.
2. Quality is achieved by prevention not by appraisal.
3. The quality performance standard is zero defects (a concept he invented in the 1960s when he worked for the Martin company on missile projects) and is best known for no acceptable quality levels.
4. Quality is measured by the price of non-conformance, not by indexes.

Philip Crosby's 14 Steps for Quality Improvement Programme[8]

Step One:	Management commitment
Step Two:	Quality improvement team
Step Three:	Quality measurement
Step Four:	Cost of quality evaluation
Step Five:	Quality awareness
Step Six:	Corrective action
Step Seven:	Establish an ad hoc committee for the zero defects programme
Step Eight:	Supervisor training
Step Nine:	Zero defects day
Step Ten:	Goal setting
Step Eleven:	Error cause removal
Step Twelve:	Recognition
Step Thirteen:	Quality councils
Step Fourteen:	Do it over again

4.8 ELEVEN TQM STEPS TO BECOME A WORLD-CLASS ORGANIZATION

Having understood the various aspects of total quality management now, let us sum up the overall concept and convert it into the practical application to make the organization a "World-Class Organization".

TQM overview: TQM is people's process and involvement of the top management is a must for its success. Hence the entire organization must have a review of TQM and accept to implement it in right earnest. This assurance for total commitment is mandatory for the TQM implementation to start.

Set Mission: The organization should define its value system for every employee to follow. Total adherence and commitment to its value system known as 'Mission', is the vital first step towards the attainment of the world-class management system.

Identify Customers: The third step is to identify customers who respect the value system and who have the potential to make the organization reach the world-class status by way of quantity and quality.

Identify Customer's Needs: Break up the product into attributes and classify the attributes into 'musts' and 'wants' or 'vital few' and 'trivial many' according to the customers' perceptions collected during the market survey. The 'vital few' or the 'musts' attributes decide the customers' preference for buying a particular product. The product which performs the best on these attributes in the market invariably becomes the market leader. For example, the outcome of various workshops conducted by the undersigned in this respect and market survey, the 'musts' or the 'vital few' attributes of a colour television is the picture quality and the sound. For a pen it is the ability of the pen to write legibly and clearly during its entire life.

Define Critical Processes & Measures: These 'musts' or 'vital few' attributes are the outcomes of certain processes and their control to ensure consistent production of these attributes. These processes are defined as the critical processes, and control points for these processes are the measures. The input raw material for these processes, the machineries required for their conversion and the process itself should not be less than the world's best. For the same examples, the picture quality of a colour television depends on the quality and flatness of the picture tube and the electronic parts used for the receipt of the picture and the sound signals, their demodulation, synthesis, amplification and reproduction on the picture tube and the speakers. For sound system, the quality of the magnet used in the speaker, the shape of the speaker for resonance and permutation and combination of the sound waves for the reproduction of the required quality of sound are the examples of controlling the quality of the critical processes to have the best performance on the key attributes, as the best in its class to have the required market share and product performance.

Set Organizational Vision: Now the product performance is defined as the best as per customers' requirement. This is now based on customers' feedback on the product performance and validation by the chosen group of customers. Now the long-term goal or the objective as to where the organization wants to position itself after 15–20 years is defined as the 'vision' statement which should be 'SMART', i.e. specific, measurable, attainable, realistic and time-bound.

Develop Strategic Plan (10–20 yrs): After all these steps are over, then perform a SWOT analysis. This means the strengths and weaknesses assessment vis-à-vis the competitors and assessment of the opportunities and threats vis-à-vis the environment under different environmental conditions of 'PEST' analysis, i.e. political, economic, social and technological. Develop the strategic plan sensitizing your customers about the positive points and inside the factory develop product attributes to convert the weaknesses into strengths. The strategic plan should also try to capitalise on the opportunities and try to convert the threats into strengths. This is a long-term strategic plan to achieve the organizational vision.

Develop Annual Plan for Breakthrough: The next step in the total quality management is to break up the long-term strategic plan into the annual business plan for breakthrough. This annual business plan should further generate the marketing plan and financial plan followed by the production plan. This is further followed by the individual plans of other functions in the organization. But all these plans are integrated into the business plan.

Revise Roles and Responsibilities: Here we are looking for a world-class performance excellence from all the employees without exception. Hence the employee's individual assessment and core competencies are to be decided and suitable training and education needs to be provided to overcome the deficiencies. Once this is done, the organization has to be reoriented and the role and responsibilities have to be redefined and revised to attain this world-class management system and related performance.

Form "Quality Council" to set change strategy: An individual can make mistakes when he takes a decision in isolation. The task of world-class performance excellence is a tough job to be accomplished. Hence it needs a more composite organizational structure. Normally total quality management organization forms a 'quality council' consisting of all the functional heads and chaired by the CEO or the Managing Director. This apex body takes initiative to implement the change in strategy.

Annual Review: Now the periodic or the annual measurement of performance is carried out to find if the performance is going as per the business plan for the year or not. In case there is a deviation or shortfall, corrective actions are taken to put the business plan back on the track. This feedback is given for correction in the performance as also to keep the organization abreast of the emerging opportunities.

4.9 ISO 9000:2000 QUALITY MANGEMENT SYSTEM

ISO 9000:2000 is a world-class quality management system giving the certified organization, the status of a world-class organization. It defines the quality chapter-by-chapter and verse-by-verse. In the current globalized and liberalized era, the ISO 9000:2000 certification has become mandatory for entry into the global as well as the local markets and getting the firm registered with a reputed organization (see Figure 4.4).

Due to different standards existing in various countries, a need was felt to have one unified standard to facilitate international trade. This was the first organizational standard in quality management consistent in terminology as well as content for the international trade ISO 9000 standards had a great impact on international trade and quality systems implementation by organizations worldwide. The standard has been adopted as national standard by more than 120 countries. This is applied through a wide range of industry, economic, service and government regulatory areas. The ISO 9000 standard deals with the management system set by an organization to design, produce, deliver and support their products. The standard applied to all generic product categories: hardware, software, processed materials, etc.

4.9.1 Definition of ISO 9000:2000

The ISO 9000 standard defines the formal quality management system necessary to assure that the technical, administrative and human factors affecting the quality of an organization's products or services are under control.

Further this formal system must be implemented such that its effectiveness can be demonstrated to the organization's management, to the customers of the organization and to an independent third party for the purpose of verification and certification.

4.9.2 Purpose of the Quality Management System

The purpose of the quality management system is to enhance customer satisfaction through effective application of system. The entire organization should be customer-oriented and continuously assessing the customer's stated and implied needs. Based on this feedback, the organization is generating products and services, leading to continual customer satisfaction. The quality management system also includes the processes for continual improvement. The QMS also results in the maximization of return on investment along with total employee involvement.

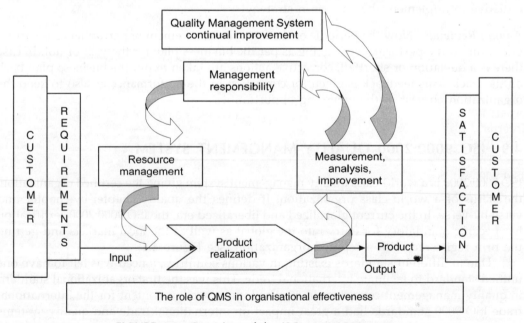

FIGURE 4.4 Overview of the ISO 9000:2000 system

The QMS follows a process orientation with Deming's P-D-C-A cycle. The organization must have a main process for value addition by conversion and break it up into linkages of sub-processes. At every stage, the system measures the input, output, the value addition and efficiency and effectiveness of the process management with quantitative measurement of the effectiveness in terms of generation of surplus as per schedule.

ISO 9000:2000 edition gives a fundamental quality management system for an organization. The earlier standard ISO 9000 series was first introduced in 1987 and revised in 1994 and was focused on quality assurance system and consisted of standards—ISO 9000, 9001, 9002, 9003, 9004. The current revision published in December 2000, consists of only three standards, i.e. ISO 9000:2000; ISO 9000:2000—Quality Management System—Fundamentals and Vocabulary; and ISO 9001:2000 Certification Standard for quality management systems with a process approach in design, development, production, installation and servicing. It is a provision for certification with a single exclusion limited to requirement within the clause 7.0 product realization where such exclusion does not affect the organization's ability or responsibility to provide quality product and must meet customer and applicable regulatory requirements.

ISO 9004:2000 gives guidance on a wider range of objectives of a quality management system than does ISO 9001, particularly for continual improvement of an organization's overall performance.

The main improvisation that has been done in ISO 9000:2000 edition compared to the 1994 edition is that the 2000 edition introduced a process approach to business and organizational working than the product approach; while the 1994 edition was more of a quality assurance system, the 2000 edition is a quality management system. The ISO 9000 family does not deal with any technical specification for a product and is complementary to any technical specifications, standards or regulations applicable to the organization's product or its services. The standards in ISO 9000 family are produced and maintained by technical committee 176 of the international standards organization (ISO). The first meeting of ISO/TCI 176 was held in 1980. ISO 8402, the vocabulary standard, was introduced in 1986 and the initial ISO 9000 was published in 1987.

4.9.3 Evolution of ISO 9000

Apart from ISO 8402, 9000, 9001 and 9004, the other members of the ISO 9000 family of international standard are as follows:

ISO 19011 guidelines on quality and environmental audition.

The shift from quality assurance standards, i.e. ISO 9000 to 9003:1994 to the latest ISO 9000 and 9001 standard 2000 is on quality management system. The difference can be summarized as follows:

Quality Management	*Quality Assurance*
1. Achievement of quality related results.	1. Demonstration of achievement of requirements of quality.
2. Motivated by stakeholders both internal, i.e. management and external, i.e. customer.	2. Motivated by stakeholders, external to the organisation, mainly customers.

Quality Management	Quality Assurance
3. Process-oriented	3. Product-oriented
4. Goal is satisfying all the stakeholders	4. Goal is satisfying customers
5. Superior overall performance is the intended result.	5. Confidence in the organizations is the intended result.
6. Scope covers all activities that impact the total business result of the organization.	6. Scope covers activities that directly impact product results.
7. Continuous improvement is mandatory	7. Continuous improvement is not mandatory.

4.9.4 Development of the Quality Management Systems

ISO 9000 system has become mandatory and popular all over the world due to the phenomenon of 'globalization'. The total management approach in the standard leads an organization first to understand and analyze the customers' needs and expectations, keeping in mind the customer requirements, as well as the requirements of all other stakeholders, including the management. It establishes the quality policy and quality objective of the organization. It then defines the products and services which are acceptable to the customer as well as in line with the attainment of the quality objectives. The system then should have a sound quality control, i.e. measurement of the effectiveness of the processes should be done on a periodic on-going basis. Then establish a documented quality management system to attain the quality objectives. Then measure the effectiveness of the processes towards attaining quality objectives. After measurement analyze and review the effectiveness and efficiency of the processes, find out deviation and take corrective and preventive actions for continuous improvement and complete the feedback loop by giving this feedback to the beginning of the quality management system (see Figure 4.5).

The overall objective of this quality management system is prevention rather than detection, and continual improvement of the system and therefore the continual improvement of the product and/or service supplied which results in customer satisfaction.

4.9.5 The Present Versions of ISO 9001:2000 and ISO 9004:2000 are Based on Eight Quality Management Principles which Reflect the Best Management Practices

The current ISO 9000:2000 family has consolidated 20 standards of the 1994 edition to be replaced by four:

- ISO 9000 : Quality management systems—Fundamentals and vocabulary
- ISO 9001 : Quality management systems—Requirements
- ISO 9004 : Quality management systems—Guidance for performance improvement
- ISO 19011 : Guidelines for auditing quality and environmental management systems.

The new ISO 9000:2000 is based on eight total quality management principles as detailed below:

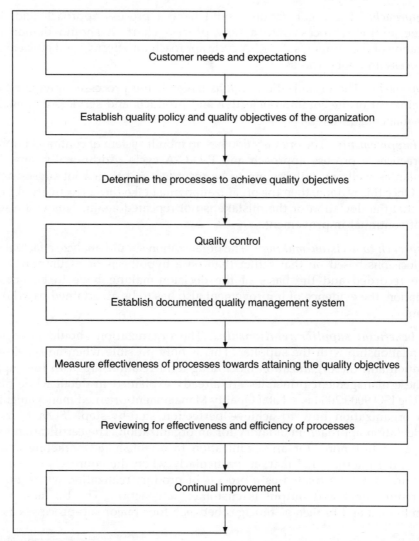

FIGURE 4.5 The popular ISO 9000 is based on prevention and continual improvement of the quality system.

Customer focus: the organization should have obtained the feedback on its products and services from the customers and must have the inclination of satisfying the customers and should be customer-oriented.

Leadership: An organization should aim for the leadership position either globally or in a particular segment.

Involvement of people: The organization should practise 'TEI' or total employee involvement towards the attainment of the organizational quality policy and quality goals as defined in the manual.

Process approach: The organization should have a process approach and depict its entire value addition process into a flow process chart. It should demonstrate the implementation of the Deming's P-D-C-A cycle approach for effective and efficient handling of each process and sub-process.

System approach: The organization should have all the processes integrated together for the attainment of the common objective and products and services culminating into a sound management system.

Continual improvement: The organization has an inbuilt system of continual improvement when it practices a process approach and P-D-C-A cycle. Additionally, any deviation from the plan as well any failures are to be recorded and their root causes have to be found out. Once this is done, then the organization must take the corrective and preventive actions so that the deviation or the mistake is not repeated again. This will also lead to a system of continual improvement.

Factual approach to decision-making: The organization should analyze a factual situation and take decisions based on that rather than on a hypothesis or assumption. The facts have to be recorded and the basis of the decision-making have to be noted. After implementation, the evidence of improvement also has to be ascertained based on factual information.

Mutually beneficial supplier relationship: The organization should have mutually beneficial relationship with the supplier. This is only possible when he is selected after due evaluation and the organization has a long-term relationship with the supplier.

All these management principles are already explained in detail while discussing the TQM. The ISO 9000:2000 is a Total Quality Management-oriented management system. It tells an organization how to achieve perfection step-by-step. ISO9000 makes the process-orientation approach mandatory for an organization. The certification by a third party is a good testimony for an organization to establish its marketing and quality credibility in the international market, particularly when the country's image does not sell. The entire system is treated as a process of product realization where the input is customer requirement and output is customer satisfaction. The business process is further subdivided and broken as linkages between four major sub-processes as detailed below:

- **Management responsibility** to declare vision, quality objectives, mission and review the process continuously for improvement.
- **Resources allocation** of men and infrastructure for product realization.
- **The product realization** itself involves customer's requirement assessment, material procurement, design and development, manufacturing, testing, etc.
- **The Measurement, Analysis and Improvement** of all these processes to ensure the eight management principles of customer focus, leadership, continual improvement, factual approach to decision-making, mutually beneficial supplier relationship and involvement of the people. The other two principles of the process approach and system approach are in-built in the quality management system.

4.9.6 ISO 9000 Expectations

- Is the organization's quality system adequate?
- Does the organization follow its quality system?
- Is there a process orientation in the organizational activities?
- Is there a platform for holding the gain and for continuous improvement?
- Does the organization audit itself?
- Is there evidence of documented quality system audits with evidence of resulting corrective action?
- Are management reviews of the quality system conducted and acted upon?

4.9.7 Details of ISO 9001:2000 Certification Standard

- Clause 1 : Scope
- Clause 2 : Normative References
- Clause 3 : Terms and Definitions

The main requirement of ISO 9001:2000 is:

Quality System Requirement: The organization shall establish, document, implement and maintain a quality management system and improve its effectiveness. The clause also talks about identification, implementation and control of processes, documentation requirements in terms of a 'quality manual' consisting of flow process charts, operating procedures, work instructions and quality records. The clause also deliberates on procedures to control the documents and records and their retention time with the specified authorities and responsibilities.

Management Responsibility: Clause 5 defines the management's responsibility and commitment. The organization shall establish, document, implement and maintain a quality management system and improve its effectiveness.

Resource Management: The organization shall determine and provide resources needed for implementing, maintaining and continuously improving the effectiveness of QMS and enhancing customer satisfaction by meeting customer requirements. The resources to be managed are in terms of human resources, infrastructure and work environment.

Product Realization: The organization shall plan and develop a process for product realization in line with quality objectives and allocate resources for the same. It should have specific criteria for product acceptance and will have recorded evidence for the same. The clause addresses customer-related processes, design and development, purchasing, production and servicing as well as control of monitoring and measuring instruments.

Measurement Analysis and Improvement: The organization shall plan and implement the monitoring, measurement, analysis and improvement processes needed to ensure conformity and continuous improvement of the product as well as the QMS. The clause focuses on monitoring and measurement of process, product, customer satisfaction and internal audit; along with control of non-conforming product. The clause also deliberates on analysis of data for continual improvement by taking corrective and preventive actions.

Hence ISO 9000:2000 becomes an excellent starting platform for an organization to not only start a world-class management system but also to implement and sustain it in the face of intense global competition.

To an ordinary employee ISO 9000 quality management system unfolds the mystery of quality and TQM phrase-by-phrase. The ISO standard is simple, clear and a step-by-step approach of implementing the quality management system.

ISO 9000 is the bare minimum requirement for attainment of TQM and the first step towards it. The latest addition ISO 9000:2000 breaks up the entire business into certain basic fundamental process. ISO 9000 system implementation ensures proper implementation and an organized approach towards the conduct of a business enterprise. It ensures consistency in performance, in terms of products and services offered by the organization. It guarantees minimum assured world-class performance by an organization. The ISO 9000 registration has become a mandatory requirement for exporting to Europe and America as well as most of the reputed organizations. ISO 9000 ensures a structure for holding the gains as well as for continuous improvement. It also audits for involvement of top management, education and training to all employees, process control and customer satisfaction as part of the total quality system.

The current ISO 9000:2000 edition puts additional focus on continuous improvement, apart from customer satisfaction. The achievement of this is professed by the international standard organization by switching over to process-orientation from product-orientation. This advancement is bound to strengthen the infrastructure by a more sound, effective and efficient quality management system. To an ordinary employee, ISO 9000 quality management system unfolds the mystery of quality and TQM phrase-by-phrase. The ISO standard is simple, clear and step-by-step approach of implementing the quality management system.

4.10 ISO 14001:1996 ENVIRONMENTAL MANAGEMENT SYSTEM

The ISO 14001:1996 is a part of the quality management system of an organization pertaining to environment management. All the organizations have to control the impact of their activities, products and services on the environment. Most governments in different countries have stipulated stringent regulations to protect the environment as part of the worldwide concern for the protection of the environment and control of pollution is increasing. The organizations have to undertake environmental reviews and audits to assess their environmental performance and ensure that the same is as per the legal as well as the company's environmental policy requirements. To achieve this, the organizations must have a structured management system integrated with the overall management system of the organizations.

This international standard on the environmental management system specifies the requirements of an effective environmental management system applicable and adaptable uniformly to all types and sizes of organizations. The basis of the approach is shown in Figure 4.6.

The environmental management system should have commitment from all levels and functions and establish convincing evidence of conformance to the environmental policies, objectives and procedures. The overall aim of this environmental management

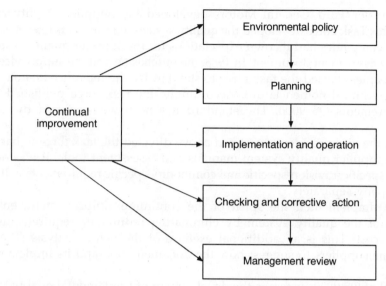

FIGURE 4.6   ISO 14001:1996 is that part of the quality management system which pertain to environment management.

system is to protect the environment and prevent pollution in balance with the socio-economic needs. The environmental management system may address many of the requirements concurrently or revisited at any time. The environmental management system encompasses a full range of issues, including those with strategic, competitive or the key survival issues.

The complementary standard for detailed and further guidance on the environmental management system is the ISO 14004:1996, environmental management systems—general guidelines on principles, systems and supporting techniques. The ISO 14001:1996 environmental management system is a certification standard.

4.11   ISO/TS 16949:2002(E) (EARLIER SPECIFICATION QS 9000:1998)— 'QMS' FOR AUTOMOBILE INDUSTRY

There is another popular Quality Management System (QMS) known as QS 9000 which is a derivative of the ISO 9000:1994 standard. This was first brought out in August, 1994 followed by the second edition in February, 1995 and the third edition was brought out, in March, 1998. This Quality Management System standard is typically applicable to the suppliers of the automobile industry. The QMS is divided into two sections. The first section is typically the ISO 9000-based requirements. The second section is the 'customer-specific requirement'. In the second section, the specific requirements of the three major automobile manufacturers of the world that is Chrysler, Ford and General Motors are given in detail. At the end of the standard, a passing reference is made to the reference standard of the other global automobile manufacturers like Mack Trucks, Navister, Paccar, Toyota—Australia, Mitsubishi Motors—Austrialia and Volvo standards.

The Chrysler/Ford/General Motors developed the Supplier Quality requirement Task Force. This Task Force developed the quality system requirements QS 9000. Previously, each of these companies had its own expectations for the supplier quality system and the corresponding assessment document. In 1988, the purchasing and the supply vice-presidents of these companies charted the task force to standardize the reference manuals, reporting formats and technical nomenclature. Accordingly, the task force published the quality system requirements QS 9000. The standard has been well-received by the supplier community.

In 1992, the vice-presidents as stated above directed the task force to harmonize the fundamental supplier quality system manuals and assessment tools. It was decided that the company-specific, division-specific and commodity-specific requirements will be handled by each company separately.

QS 9000 implemented the spirit of the continuous improvement, enhanced the performance of the quality system by eliminating redundant requirements and thus reducing the cost. This is an additional exercise of the value analysis. The task force encourages the suppliers to suggest how the documentation and its implementation can be improved.

The goal of QS 9000 system is the development of fundamental quality systems that provide for continuous improvement, defect prevention and the reduction of variation and waste in the supply chain.

The QS 9000 defines the fundamental quality system expectations of the Chrysler, Ford, General Motors, Truck manufacturers and other subscribing companies for the internal and external suppliers of production and service parts and materials. These companies are committed to working with their suppliers to ensure customer satisfaction, beginning with conformance to the quality requirements, and continuing with reduction of variation and waste to benefit the final customer, the supply base and themselves.

The quality management standard QS 9000:1998 was revised, keeping in mind the requirement of ISO 9000:2000 quality management system standard into a revised quality management system standard ISO/TS 16949-2002(E). This quality management system standard specification defines the requirement of a quality management systems for the particular requirements for the application of ISO 9001:2000 for automotive production and the relevant service part organizations. ISO/TS 16949:2002 was prepared by the International Automotive Task Force (IATF) and Japan Automobile Manufacturers Association, Inc. (JAMA) with support from ISO/TC 176—a technical committee formed by International Standards Organization for quality management and quality assurance as well as the technical committee for formation of the ISO 9001:2000 standard.

4.12 QUALITY MOVEMENTS IN DIFFERENT NATIONS

4.12.1 The US Quality Revolution

During the 1970s, increased global competition and the appearance of high quality products in the market led the US consumers to consider their purchasing decisions more carefully. Consumers became more apt than ever before; to compare, evaluate and choose products critically for total value—quality, price and serviceability. Government safety regulations, product recalls mandated by consumer product safety commissions and rapid increases in product-liability judgments have changed the society's attitude from 'let the buyer beware' to 'Let the producer beware'. Quality excellence became recognized as a key to worldwide competitiveness and was heavily promoted throughout the industry. The US companies focused not only on improving internal operation but also on satisfying external customers.

One of the most influential individuals in the US quality revolution was W. Edward Deming. He played a key role in the development of Japanese quality and in the transformation of the Japanese industry three decades earlier. Soon, the US companies started seeking his help and his leadership and experience helped many US companies, such as Ford Motor Company, General Motors and Procter & Gamble to revolutionize their approach to quality.

As business and industry began to focus on quality, the US government recognized that quality is critical to the nation's economy. It is not surprising that GM, Ford and Chrysler were among the first US companies to take on TQM in a massive way returning to a clear customer focus and the time when 'made in USA' was a badge of quality.

In the late 1970s, quality circles blossomed on the American scene and by the mid-1980s, 90% of the *Fortune* 500 companies had quality circle programmes. But for most companies, it was just a fad that soon faded when it became clear that they could not conjure up the quick fix solutions that most firms were looking for. In the U.S., a QC is normally organized as a formal staff organization, whereas a QC in Japan is an informal group of workers. A manager in Japan serves as an advisor or a consultant. In the U.S., a production manager, appoints facilitators for quality of work life, employee involvement, employee participation, and quality circles, and at the end all of which disintegrate. A good place to start a quality circle in America is with the management. For example, purchasing managers need to follow through the production lines, the materials that they purchase. This would call for quality circles consisting of purchasing, production, research, engineering design, and sales. Many companies already have a quality circle in management but never thought of them as quality circles. Quality circles composed of supervisors and inspectors are excellent, and will be spontaneous with a little encouragement.[9] Too often in the USA, quality circle programmes became something the top told the middle, to do, to the bottom of the organization. They lacked solid company-wide support.

Today companies realize that total quality means a sweeping renewal of a firm's entire culture, a complete change in a company's philosophy, and an unwavering commitment to continuous improvement. Apart from aerospace and agriculture where the United States competes mightily, there are few markets where the United States holds its own in international trade. Poor quality in products and services became the number one brake on the nation's productivity and competitiveness in global markets. The car makers discovered this in the early 1980s when they realized that Americans were not buying Japanese cars just because they were cheaper, but because of their superior quality. The US car makers are now closing the gap. Semiconductor manufacturers lost the market to the Japanese for the computer memory chips in the late 1970s and have yet to win it back, although they have improved their quality.

In 1985, NASA announced an Excellence Award for Quality and Productivity. The Act of Congress established the Malcolm Baldridge National Quality Award in 1987. Today, quality management and control is recognized as the foundation of business competitiveness and is proactively integrated with all business practices.

A study that asked managers of manufacturing firms in the USA to define quality, produced the following different responses: perfection, consistency, eliminating waste, speed of delivery, compliance with policies and procedures, providing a good, usable product, doing it right the first time, delighting or pleasing customers, total customer service and satisfaction.[10]

4.12.2 Quality Movement in Asian Countries

The time sequence for the diffusion of quality management technology across Asia can be identified as follows: Quality control circles started in the 1960s. These were followed by Total Quality Control (late 1970s), Total Quality Management (late 1980s), ISO 9000 (1992), and world class practices (after 1995)[11].

Summary of the evolution of quality management practices among the Asian countries

1960s to 1980s	Industrialization, import substitution and exports drive product quality standards, which were initially the key focus in the industrialization programme. Formation of productivity groupings and government agencies overseeing quality was initiated by the Asian Productivity Organization (APO).
1980s	Formation of QCCs progressed under the productivity councils. Use of improvement tools and techniques, short-term improvements and productivity improvements company-wide. QC, TQC and TQM started being used.
1990s	Early 1990s: Widespread use of TQM techniques and philosophy. ISO 9000 certification was seen to be necessary for exports, especially to Europe. Adoption of ISO standards.
	Mid to late 1990s: SQM or service quality was emphasized. Resurgence of TQM with modifications in techniques, with better results.
	Second half of 1990s: ISO 14000 was adopted due to environment concerns by consumers because of rapid industrialization and denudation of environment with urban development and conversion of semi-urban areas for industrialization.
	National Quality Awards were instituted to recognize achievers and to encourage further quality improvements.
	Companies try to achieve better results by adopting business re-engineering and business process re-engineering as new ideas.
	Late 1990s: World-class and global best practices were adopted. The concept and the practice were more widespread.

Sources: Quazi and Chan (1999); Hammer and Champy (1993); Author's (Chan) management consulting experience from 1983 to 1989.

4.12.3 Quality Movement in Japan

Japan has few natural resources and high population density. From this background, it has been an overriding national priority after World War II to create industrial products of superior quality and export them to foreign countries. Quality initiatives formally started with Civil Communication Services (CCS) course mainly for top executives of communication equipment manufacturers in autumn 1949.[12]

In 1950, through the efforts of Dr. Edward Deming, the Statistical Quality Control (SQC) approach was introduced in Japan and was taken up enthusiastically by engineers and plant managers as well as top management of industries. A large number of engineers were trained in SQC techniques. In 1951, the Deming Prize was instituted to promote company-wide quality control in manufacturing industry. By 1960, in the course of 10 years or so, the proportion of industrial firms using SQC and the associated methods had become larger than those in the USA or in any other country of the world. The result was a spectacular improvement in quality, coupled with an appreciable reduction in the cost of production which made it possible for Japan to enter the world market on competitive terms and become a major exporting country in a very short time. Training of SQC personnel is essential but not enough. Japan has shown that it is necessary and possible to make SQC a truly management movement.

Dr. K. Ishikawa of the Tokyo University also contributed significantly to the quality movement in Japan. Because of the colossal scale of organization of educational and promotional programmes and also the involvement of the general public on a large-scale, QC has developed and is gaining strength in Japan more than in any other country of the world and is bringing about continual improvement of quality and lowering the cost of Japanese goods in both the domestic and export markets.

Masaaki Imai, the author of the successful book *Gemba Kaizen*, advocated the importance of corporate culture that governs how people do their jobs, improve quality, reduce costs and meet customer requirements. Imai in his book explained a common sense, low-cost approach to management, to reassert the importance of the shopfloor in bringing about continual improvement in an organization.

Japanese enterprises do not appear to be organizations that maximize profits for the benefit of stockholders. Capital is obtained through bank loans, with fixed rates of return. With no shareholders to please, Japanese firms are free to operate on behalf of another constituency—their workers. "Large businesses are run primarily for the employees who, in traditional legal terms, are the beneficial owners," Peter Drucker has observed. Since the workers are the beneficiaries of what would otherwise be profits, labour–management trust comes naturally.[13]

Yoshibazu Tsudo talked about corrective action for successful implementation. The two types of corrective actions are temporary and permanent. An example of temporary corrective actions is repairing the product but permanent corrective action involves taking action to prevent the recurrence of defect and focuses on the process. The permanent corrective actions, together with small improvements, can result in major improvements to the health of the company.

As a result of these initiatives, the economic growth in Japan has increased substantially and the national product doubled in 7 to 8 years. From 1950 to 1970, in the course of 20 years of quality movement in Japan, the per capita income had increased roughly by four times. During the same period, the per capita national income in India increased by less than 20 per cent.

4.12.4 Quality Movement in India

Quality has been a tradition in India and monuments, relics, handicrafts, gems, jewellery and craftsmanship have woven quality into our heritage. While quality was a way of managing business in the US and Japan in the 1950s, it was not so in India. Prof. Mahalanobis started the quality movement long back with the establishment of the Indian Statistical Institute at Calcutta in the early 1930s. He was instrumental in setting up SQC units in industrial centres during the 1960s–1970s. Prof. Sundari Vaswani head of the statistics division at Ahmedabad Textile Industries Research Association (ATIRA founded by Vikram Sarabhai) started the QC movement and advocated quality practices for the textile industry in Ahmedabad. The quality movement was consolidated in the 1980s in the Indian industries to bring about a synergy of resources by the pioneering efforts of Confederation of Indian Industry (CII).

Walter Shewart, the father of statistical quality control, visited India for a short period of three months during 1947–48, and initiated the SQC movement through visits to factories, personal discussions and lectures. Dr. Edward Deming who taught the Japanese the means of applying the Plan-Do-Check-Act cycle (known as Deming Cycle) came to India in the early 1950s. The formal launch of the TQM movement in the US in the early 1980s triggered a movement for quality in India and in 1982 the quality control circle was born. Among some of the first companies launching the quality control circles were public sector undertakings—Bharat Electronics and Bharat Heavy Electricals Limited. CII provided a focus and an impetus to the quality movement by forming the TQM division in 1987. By then, the focus had shifted from quality circles to quality management. The Quality Circle Forum in India (QCFI) consolidated the movement on quality circles. Prof. Ishikawa, founder of quality movement in Japan was invited by CII to come to India to address the Indian industry in 1986. CII set up the TQM division with the help of 21 companies who agreed to support the cause by pooling in the resources and pledging to start the journey of TQM. The chief executives of these companies formed the National Committee on Quality, which brought into focus the need to build awareness.

The year 1987 brought the ISO 9000 standards into reality and visible strategies emerged from the European market to set a global trend towards standardizing and certifying quality systems. Since, the European market was a big market for the Indian industry; CII organized training courses for ISO 9000 in 1989. Two years later, in 1991, the first company in India got certified to ISO 9000. From there onwards, the movement has gathered momentum and today more than 500 companies have secured ISO 9000 certification. The new industrial policy, introduced in 1991, set the direction for competitive and market economy (eighth five-year Plan, 1992–97). P. Chidambaram said in the early 90s 'All the traditional competitive advantages that India has will shrink. It will only be the quality factor that will constantly expand.' (*Business Today*, 1995).

Indian quality journey has come a long way during the past decade. A critical study shows that it has gone through many meaningful transformations. Quality, as a part of business strategy, is getting increasingly accepted by enlightened large corporates. Further, they are setting significant quality trends for the nation. Global competition is fierce and ruthless. The inefficient ones are being washed out, quite often without any trace. Though India was thrown open to global competition in the early 1990s, the first few years of the decade have been essentially a period of learning and that, of course, corrections. Since then, the Indian industry is visibly looking forward to being competitive globally. During the early 1990s, India's quality ranking was dismal. On global benchmarking of TQM practices, India ranked 38 in a sample of 41. It was worse on customer-orientation, having been ranked 40 out of a sample size of 41. These findings were so distressing that, corporate India had very little to cheer about. A quality revolution was, therefore, essential even for its sheer survival, leave alone growth.

Many organizations in India, are yet to build and nurture quality culture. Awareness of change drives organizations towards quality. To make it happen throughout, an organization and later to institutionalizing the same, it is essential that 'Commitment to Quality' should be the organizational motto. Organizational quality commitment is an outcome of individual quality commitment, which can come about only through effective quality education and training at all levels.

There is no better teacher than necessity. Indians, by nature, do not stand up to face challenges unless forced. They react to 'crisis' and that is what liberalization is. It is now or never. We have a few Indian examples already, look at Reliance, BPL, Ranbaxy, and TVS Suzuki. What is required of most Indian companies are guts to stand up, courage to launch quality programmes, and single-minded approach to act. The message is very clear. If they avail this opportunity and commence a 'world-class journey', the sky will be the limit. If they allow this opportunity to slip, most of them will not remain in business for long.

The TQM movement today encompasses not only engineering industries, but also servicing and information technology industries. Today, TQM has become a thrust area in quality movement as it was realized that through ISO 9000 certification alone companies cannot become world-class or competitive. Sharing experiences and building each other's strengths became essential ingredients towards the "idealization of TQM". The companies practising TQM have implemented some common features, such as "people's movement" (through quality control circles, quality improvement teams, suggestion schemes, Kaizen and JIT), quality assurance systems (ISO 9000), vendor development, statistical process control, and other tools and techniques, such as quality function deployment, reliability and design of experiments.

The future thrust of the quality movement in India would be in the following areas:

(i) Application research where we need to understand what has to be done within the context in which it needs to be done. This requires a deep understanding and will be possible through synergy of industry and academics.

(ii) Grooming of facilitators through local people being trained as facilitators of TQM/ISO 9000 in every organization willing to implement TQM.

(iii) Experience sharing to understand the means to get organizational performance through TQM.

(iv) ISO 9000 certification for small-scale industries that are exporters or potential exporters.

(v) Environmental protection, safety and consumer protection by the industrial organizations through highly focused effort on quality enhancement.

4.12.4.1 Some Indian examples practising quality management compiled from magazines/journals

(1) **Narmada Chematur Petrochemicals Ltd.** in Gujarat has made 921 modifications to their plant and machinery (imported from Sweden) for the first time anywhere in the world and raised their productivity and quality levels considerably.[14]

(2) **MICO Bosch Group,** at their plant in Nasik, has quality benchmarks for customer complaints and their principals in Germany are so impressed with the increase in output and productivity that a decision has been taken to shift all the manufacturing operations from Brazil and Turkey to Nasik, India[15]

(3) **The Electrical & Electronics Division of L&T** is a leader in its range of products. Right from its inception in the early '60s, this division has focused and used quality as a vehicle to remain a market leader. To reach its goals, the division is using every quality principle and method in the quality toolbox. A few such quality tools include ISO 9001, ISO 14001 standard, OHSAS 18001 standard, NABL accreditation, JIT practices, value-engineering, the Capability Maturity Model (CMM), Enterprise Resource Planning (ERP), Product Lifecycle Management, and now Six-Sigma approach and Design for Six-Sigma. The division has already implemented the TQM principles from the year 1992. This has provided a platform to successfully launch many changes in management initiatives. L&T has been training its engineers in the area of quality practices to acquire expertise. This is because the division has a passion that anything which is new in quality and excellence should be adopted. It has over 30 leading assessors internally from various cross-functional areas, in addition to a number of internal auditors it has. This signifies the importance the division gives to quality and the belief it has in internalizing good practices so as to be able to implement it effectively. Many of its current quality efforts are based on Six-Sigma. Continual improvement being the motto, it should be supported by sound systems and indepth understanding by one and all. Training such a large cross-section of employees helps in understanding the system and its effective implementation.[16]

(4) **Quality at Amara Raja Batteries Ltd.** starts from the design stage itself. To ensure everything goes well first a design FMEA (Failure Mode Effect and Analysis) is done, then at the process stage Process FMEA is carried out. After this and before the product is made, an Advanced Product Quality Planning (APQP) is carried out.[17]

(5) **Rashtriya Ispat Nigam Ltd.** TQM programme followed the following four phases: Creating quality awareness, formation of cross-functional—quality action teams; creating a value employee index, and exposing workmen, i.e. employee involvement through quality circles and suggestion scheme. The TQM programme suffered stagnation due to the following reasons: the non-executive of the non-works (finance, HR, etc) departments were a bit skeptical about TQM programme, employees not empowered enough to participate in decision-making, practicing without commitment and involvement from employee's side, and organizational hierarchies.[18]

(6) **Nalco.** Various dimensions of TQM at Nalco include: Defining customer expectations and translating them into realistic organizational goals and objectives, managing projects and processes to consistently improve and redesign systems, processes, and practices in order to ensure error prevention; conducting root-cause analysis to identify the real causes of organizational problems; and planning and realizing continuous improvement, using, developing and empowering human resources. TQM department supervises the overall functioning of the quality circles and quality improvement projects. QCs are considered as powerful TQM tools. Barriers to QIP activities were: Selected projects were not linked to strategic business units; absence of clear goals and objectives of team members; irregular meetings and actions; lack of trained facilitations and bypassing of processes; non-involvement of senior executives of TQM departments; rush to accomplishment; little focus on implementation of recommendations; lack of follow up; and monitoring and process measurement systems.[19]

(7) **Lucas-TVS Limited.** Quality initiatives have been taken since 1992. A person, who produces is entrusted with the tasks of ensuring quality, streamlining of quality assurance practices; educating work-force involves: stressing the importance of quality systems, maintaining quality control charts, using visual displays, and following the work instructions and procedures.[20]

(8) **Sundaram Clayton Limited.** SCL is the flagship company of the TVS group. Their core principles are quality, reliability and service. They are the winners of the prestigious Deming Prize, which stands for the highest recognition. The Deming Prize testifies the "comprehensive evaluation of implementation of quality initiatives based on a 10 parameter framework" (the 10 parameters are top management leadership, TQM framework, quality assurance systems, management systems, human resource management, effective utilization of information, TQM concepts and values, scientific methods, organizational powers, and contribution to realization of corporate objectives).

The following is the three-step implementation route:

Step 1: Introduce and expose the whole organization to the best in the world and their practices. This will help to create an interest among the employees.
Step 2: Train and adopt new practices, i.e. empowerment of employees and this will help to arouse a desire. Employees are the wealth of an organization and it pays to invest time and efforts in them for the future.
Step 3: Set goals to the organization (such as winning the Deming prize) to motivate the employees towards action.
Step 4: Make TQM the culture of the organization and sustain the interest and focus on quality by raising the benchmarks and goals on a continuous basis.[21]

(9) **Amtrex Appliances Limited**[22]. They initiated a TQM programme in 1996, following the recommendations by Eicher Consultancy Services. Prior to the TQM programme, the company had a Zero-Defect-Machine (ZDM) initiative. It used to test machines at the customer-end for quality. Based on certain sequence of checks, an air-conditioner was certified to be ZDM (if it passed all checks). From a mere 18 per cent ZDM in 1992-93, the company improved to over 90 per cent ZDM by 1995. However, the company felt that the ZDM was more reactive than proactive

and did not fundamentally improve the quality of the manufacturing process. It viewed TQM as the way to reach 100% ZDM, while ensuring that defects that were identified were completely eliminated at the manufacturing stage itself. As a result of the TQM programme, both productivity and quality levels increased. The rejection rate of components declined from 20–25% levels to near zero levels. Compressor failure rate in the field, reduced from 3.5% to 0.1%. Compressor inventory levels were fewer than three days' production requirements, down from 10–15 days (the compressor formed 45% of the air-conditioner cost).

Of late, we have shining examples[23] like Tata Steel, the winner of CII Exim award for the year 2000, becoming a world-class low cost steel producer in three to four years, with top-driven focus. The TVS group in South, made India proud by some of its units meeting the stringent Deming Prize standards. Reliance is another example for achieving world-class standards in its operations. We have several service functions like HDFC, with world-class quality operations, which are increasingly competing to be in the good books of every single customer. More importantly, they are quickly responding to the market requirements and are constantly re-engineering their operations to be ahead of competition. The Indian IT industry is a shining example here, not only for its business results, but also for the way they were responding to global needs and fast-changing market requirements. The leading ones have moved well beyond customer satisfaction and customer delight, and are constantly looking for ways and means to innovatively add value to customers. More importantly, they are getting increasingly customer-centric.

A look at the models to achieve excellence, which are being practised internally, by major Indian business houses: Tatas have their own business excellence model to annually recognize the best companies of the group. Similarly, the A.V. Birla group has their own internal Chairman's Awards for Manufacturing Excellence. RPG Group instituted the RPG annual quality awards to recognize the best companies moving towards business excellence, separately for manufacturing companies and for the service stream. Most other large businesses are applying for one of the three prominent national awards for excellence, namely CII EXIM, IMC Ramakrishna Bajaj and Rajiv Gandhi awards, the latter instituted by the Indian government.

All these models, apart from encouraging healthy competition, are helping Indian organizations to measure themselves against global levels.

4.13 WHY DO SOME QUALITY IMPROVEMENT EFFORTS FAIL?

According to a study carried out on the companies who initiated quality improvement efforts, one-third of the companies obtained significant results, another one-third obtained moderate results, and the remainder one-third were dissatisfied with the results. The reasons why implementation fails are as follows:

- Managers focus on short term financial results.
- Excessive focus on financial results tends to destroy the underlying quality system as lay-offs are encountered or training is slashed to improve short-term financial results.

- Managers instinctively blame the employees instead of themselves for quality failures inspite of the fact that only managers can change the underlying system that causes quality problems rather than employees.
- Managers believe in tradeoffs. They believe that quality cannot be achieved without sacrificing the schedule or the costs.
- Managers interfere with true teamwork. Either they do not really delegate decision-making to the team or they continue to reward individual performance over team performance.
- Some firms have very poor procedures and processes and yet fail to realize how this affects quality. Intelligent employees or good management cannot compensate for a bad system.

4.13.1 Reasons Why TQM Programme Fails

Juran (1993, 1994) notes that the seeds of failure in quality management both for manufacturing and service industry are: Management ineptitude on quality issues, preoccupation with imports, quality lacks the necessary priority, no appropriate measures, laissez-faire attitude, misguided leadership, unbalanced relations between headquarters and divisions.

Organisations often do not understand their quality needs and fail to study and select the right method. For example, a study by Ernst & Young and the American Quality Foundation (1992) (although presenting no formal evidence on TQM's effectiveness) argues that firms often adopt inappropriate and ineffective quality practices. Even preliminary consideration illustrates why implementing TQM is difficult. In addition to a large and continuing investment in employee training, it requires major changes in the organizational rules. And because the components of TQM are interdependent, problems in implementing one or more components can cripple the effectiveness of the entire programme.

Because quality management is process-oriented, it is difficult to gain a strong understanding of how it works without examples or case studies. An analogy can be made to the legal process. The memorization of laws, regulations, and judicial procedures does not provide a satisfactory understanding of the legal process; it is also necessary to study the details of their application to specific cases. For this reason, where relevant, one must draw on examples from the firms they have studied.

The relatively frequent occurrence of failed or badly performed implementation processes is a problematic phenomenon, which negatively affects organizations, irrespective of size, in their development towards business excellence and ultimately survival in a competitive environment. The most common causes for the failure of TQM programme (based on research studies) appear to be the following: Lack of commitment from the top management, focusing on specific techniques rather than on the system, not obtaining employee buy-in and participation, stopping the programmes after initiating training session, expecting immediate results, instead of a long-term payoff, forcing the organization to adopt methods that are not productive or compatible with its production systems and personnel.

In the case study[38], "Sundaram Clayton-Winning the Deming Prize"; the following major reasons for TQM failure have been identified: Lack of customer awareness, no relation to business strategy, lack of compatibility, lack of communication, and lack of integration.

In the research paper "Total Quality Management and Organizational Change" **Dr Treasa Hayes**[39] reports that disappointingly high failure rates have been quoted for TQM initiatives, indicating that attempts to bring TQM to full fruition in an organization can be problematic. An appreciation of the causes underpinning resistance to change and methods to seek their resolution should provide the insights regarding the best practice in bringing about new initiatives in undertakings, including TQM.

In the research paper[40], and Total Quality Management Implementation Model For Indian Industries, Raju, R. and Dr. Balasubramanian, N. report that to successfully implement TQM in Indian industries, culture change is considered very important. Chakraborthi (1997) observes that implementing TQM in India is tough because of the following cultural and social problems:

(i) Lack of shared vision and common understanding on quality.
(ii) Poor commitment across levels.
(iii) Inadequate methods of convincing members.
(iv) Insufficient mechanisms to overcome the hurdles of implementation.
(v) No understanding on how difficult it is to bring about change in attitudes.

Singh, A. (1991)[41] found that quality comes mainly from people, as a result of attitudes and values and not by technology alone. As TQM promises change in organizational culture, it is advocated that unless the TQM drive aims at attitudinal change, discarding stereotype beliefs and promoting conducive leadership styles, it may not be feasible to introduce it.

Umesh, Bushi, M. and K. Vizayakumar (2000)[42] conducted a field study in India and collected the opinions of the experts on TQM as follows:

1. TQM appears to be attractive, but deploying the concepts in India is difficult as it takes a very long time, to be fully ingrained in an organizational culture and the management, being result-driven, loses faith on the concept quite quickly. Thus, there is a lack of continued commitment to the TQM philosophy and practice.
2. Top management is not clear about the very purpose of TQM.
3. One of the prime reasons for failure is the lack of clearly defined and prioritized vision-based goals.
4. Management expects significant results in monetary gains within a year of its implementation, whereas the benefits of TQM implementation at such an early phase are intangible.
5. There is marginal/no improvement in the culture of working, productivity and the business prospects after the implementation.
6. Unless our society becomes quality-conscious, TQM/ISO will be only a bandwagon (in Japan, quality started from society and came to industry). As long as quality does not become a way of life (unless the entire society adopts it), TQM will only be in books.

7. Lack of faith, mutual trust and confidence has led to TQM failure.
8. Unless there is profit-orientation in terms of contribution to society, the essence of TQM cannot be nourished.
9. For another decade or more, the success story of TQM in Indian industries will be far from truth.

From the above discussions, it is understood that, the implementation of TQM in Indian industries requires basic fundamental cultural change. Unless the basic resistance factors are isolated and addressed, it is difficult for TQM to succeed in the Indian context.

4.14 FUTURE CHALLENGES

The world has moved from single owner to multinationals and now into a single global economic village, with barriers of trade from one country to another gradually breaking down. Within countries, a number of customer needs, values, ethics and norms have undergone changes. With customer wants, options and alternatives gaining priority, the market has shifted from a sellers to a buyers market. There is rapid industrialization all over the world. This has resulted in free availability of goods and services. Marketers have to, therefore, make efforts to sell their products and services.

India today stands in the community of nations as one of the agro-industrial giants, having a sound base of mechanized agriculture alongside with advanced manufacturing capabilities, in some areas, of world standards. If one looks at the last six decades of development in India, what India has achieved is primarily because of planned strategies. It is the five-year plans, which have transformed India within a period of five decades and positional it among the first ten industrialized nations of the world. Though, the basic management education system in India has retained its characteristics of knowledge-based pursuit; it is through planned strategies that it has taken strides to provide both the manpower as well as the expertise for the techno–economic transformation.

However, as the country enters the era of industrial and economic revolution assisted by computers and artificial intelligence, the demand for skilled and trained manpower as well as the need for technology innovation in quality management have thrown up new challenges. Cognizance has to be taken of the global developments in international business environment. The global quality-consciousness, coupled with the free economy drive, has compelled all nations of the world, especially the developing countries, such as India, to identify the areas in which substantial changes have to be made both in orientation as well as in the inputs and the work environment.

Even in the developed nations like the USA, companies still struggle to integrate quality into their management efforts. Quality movement has resulted in many successes, but also in many failures. This does not mean that we should be skeptical of quality management initiatives because failures were mainly because of poor management, not the soundness of principles. Therefore, rather than being discouraged by the failure, we should learn lessons from it and be better prepared for the future.

Quality management cannot be separated from other departments and followed in isolation. Quality has to be everywhere, integrated into all aspects of a successful organization. Quality professionals, meanwhile, need the business and functional skills in design, manufacturing and marketing to contribute to their organization's long-term success. Embracing quality at every level is the only way to compete successfully in the digital age.

4.15 SUMMARY AND SYNTHESIS OF OBSERVATIONS

This chapter has been general in coverage of quality management concepts. It covers manufacturing and services, in large and small organizations. It addresses definition and concept of quality, definition and concepts of TQM, principles and axioms of TQM, and other aspects of quality management. The literature sources are textbooks on TQM both international and Indian editions, research papers and both international and Indian journals. The detailed references are given at the end of the text.

An Artistic presentation of Letters 'A to Z' in Relation to Quality:[25]

- A – Ability of a product to satisfy implied/stated needs of customer.
- B – Basic customer decision factor for buying products/services.
- C – Conformance to specifications.
- D – Doing it right first time.
- E – Everyone's job, management's responsibility.
- F – Fitness for use.
- G – Good job done.
- H – Having focus on customer's needs.
- I – I know it, when I see it.
- J – Job security today.
- K – Kaizen or continuous improvement.
- L – Less expensive than alternatives.
- M – Matter of survival and moving target in a competitive market
- N – Never ending quest for improvement.
- O – Orientation to customer satisfaction.
- P – Philosophy of doing the right thing in the right way, right on time and right every time.
- Q – Quality of design, quality of conformance.
- R – Rendering good service.
- S – Single most important force leading to organizational success.
- T – Totality of all features of products/services.
- U – Universal goods sought by all.
- V – Variability reduction and value addition.
- W – Way of managing the organization.
- X – 'X' ray for detection of defects.
- Y – Your expectations fulfilled, yield improvement.
- Z – Zero defects.

EXERCISES

1. Define and explain "Quality" and the various terms related to quality.

2. Explain the important dimensions of product quality.

3. Explain Deming's 14 points for improving quality.

4. Explain Juran's nine-point quality planning road-map.

5. Explain the term "most economical, most useful and always satisfactory to the consumer" defined by Kaoru Ishikawa.

6. Explain Philip Crosby's 14 steps for quality improvement.

7. Briefly explain the evolution of quality management with specific reference to the USA, Asian countries and Japan.

8. Discuss the quality movement in India.

9. What are the different types of costs of quality?

10. Define 'The Total Quality Management'. Elaborate on the concepts and features of TQM.

11. Explain the eight building blocks of TQM.

12. What are the pre-requisites for the success of TQM?

13. What steps will you follow to make a world-class organization in the following sectors?
    (a) A food processing industry.
    (b) An automobile component manufacturer.
    (c) A pharmaceutical industry.
    (d) A software development company.

14. Explain in detail the importance of a 'Quality Management System' and its contribution in creating a world-class organization.

15. Define ISO 9000:2000 and the significance of various standards associated with it. Explain its underlying principle. Interpret and elaborate on its various clauses and its relevance to effective and efficient operation of an organization.

16. Explain in brief the ISO 14000:1996 and QS 9000 Quality Management System and its significance.

17. Elaborate on the reasons why some of the TQM programmes fail to obtain the desired results.

18. Explain how TQM has helped industries across the globe in attaining world-class performance.

5

Statistical Process Control

5.1 INTRODUCTION TO STATISTICAL PROCESS CONTROL

Statistical process control is an extremely important element of TQM or the world-class management system. Statistics believes in the probability theory that inspection or measurement of a few samples is indicative of the whole lot produced. This is called statistical sampling inspection of the products. The shifting of the control paradigm from product to process has also shifted the focus from sampling inspection to statistical process control. The first of the statistical process control was Walter Shewart of the Bell Laboratories. However, it was popularized all over the world due to its usefulness and was extensively used by both Edward Deming and Dr. Joseph Juran. The statistical process control focuses on the control of process rather than on the product. The philosophy of the statistical process control is that if the process is under control, i.e. the process capability figure 'Cp' and the process capability factor 'Cpk' are more than one and preferably around 1.27 to 1.33, it is impossible for this process to produce a defective product. This is already explained partially in Chapter 1. However, the fundamental theory of the statistical process control will be built up and elaborated in detail in this chapter.

5.2 SAMPLING

Sampling means drawing a certain percentage of components for inspection from a large size batch. The philosophy of sampling is that it represents the whole lot. By inspecting a sample lot, we can ascertain the probability of the whole lot being accepted, that is if the lot is good or bad. This is the fundamental principle of statistical quality control. Let us take an example to elaborate the concept.

EXAMPLE 5.1
Assume that a batch contains 5000 castings out of which 100 are defective. A sample of five pins is drawn for inspection.

The probability of the casting being defective

$$= \frac{100}{5000} = 0.02 \text{ or } 2\%$$

The probability for the second, third and fourth pins to be defective lies between

$\frac{100}{4999}$ and $\frac{99}{4999}$; $\frac{100}{4998}$ and $\frac{98}{4998}$; and $\frac{100}{4997}$ and $\frac{97}{4997}$ respectively. All these probability values do not differ much from each other. It is more or less constant over the sample drawn. Hence, the probability of drawing a defective casting from a large lot is constant for all the components of the small sample drawn.

Let 'p' be the probability of a component being defective, and q is the probability of a component being non-defective.

Taking the above example

$$p = \frac{100}{5000} = 0.02 \text{ and } q = (1 - 0.02) = 0.98$$

and

$$p + q = 1$$

Please note that $p(0) = q^n = (0.98)^5 = 0.904$

From the above, it can be concluded that the probability of drawing a non-defective casting is 0.904. It implies that if the random sample of five castings is drawn from the lot of 5000 on separate occasions, a non-defective pin will be found $5000 \times 0.904 = 4520$ times.

5.3 FREQUENCY DISTRIBUTION CURVE, BAR CHART AND HISTOGRAM

EXAMPLE 5.2
Forty components were manufactured on a machine and their diameters in mm were measured. The frequency distribution table indicates the tabulation of the dimensions measured in the following Table 5.1.

TABLE 5.1 Frequency distribution table

Dimension (diametre, mm)	Tabulation	Frequency
5.1	I	1
5.2	IIII	4
5.3	IIII IIII	10
5.4	IIII IIII IIII III	18
5.5	IIII IIII	10
5.6	IIII	5
5.7	II	2

The approximate normal distribution curve shows a common pattern of distribution. Depending upon the type of object being measured, there is a pattern of distribution which indicates the way in which a dimension varies.

Figure 5.1 shows a normal curve can be divided into two halves about the mean size, i.e. $\dfrac{5.0 + 5.6}{2} = 5.3$.

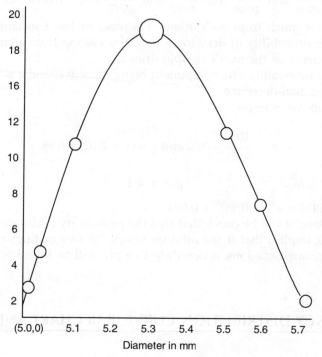

FIGURE 5.1 Frequency distribution curve.

There are approximately an equal number of items smaller and larger than the mean size on either side of the normal distribution. The normal distribution curve is also a frequency distribution curve. The curve is a reverse bell mouth curve with the population distributed around the mean line almost uniformly.

Figure 5.2 shows a bar chart prepared from the data given in the frequency distribution Table 5.1. A bar chart makes use of the bars. The height of each bar is proportional to the frequency of the particular measured dimension. This is a pictorial presentation of the concentration of the population on various strata chosen on the scale.

Figure 5.3 shows a histogram which is another way of presenting the frequency distribution graphically. Histogram makes use of constant width bars.

The histogram is the most popular and effective representation in which a data is presented for suitable analysis of a statistical purpose. It helps in stratifying the data in certain groups according to the need and depicted accordingly to highlight the particular strata which is occurring for the maximum number of times. In the advanced management

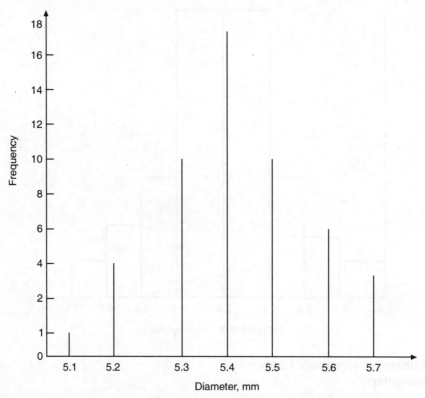

FIGURE 5.2 Bar chart.

tools like the 'Pareto Analysis', the frequencies of occurrence of an event in various strata are represented as a histogram in the order of their frequencies of happening. The stratum which has the maximum number of occurrences is placed on the extreme left side, followed by the next one and so on. This enables the frequencies to be added up on a different graph on a scale of hundred and shows the percentage of their occurrences individually and collectively.

5.4 INSPECTION AND QUALITY CONTROL

Various patterns of the normal distribution curves are shown in Figure 5.5 and such patterns get generated under different circumstances as explained hereunder:

1. Normal distribution:
   (a) Symmetrical
       – Producing items within tolerances.
       – Producing items not within tolerances.
   (b) Skewed
   (c) Leptokurtic
   (d) Platykurtic

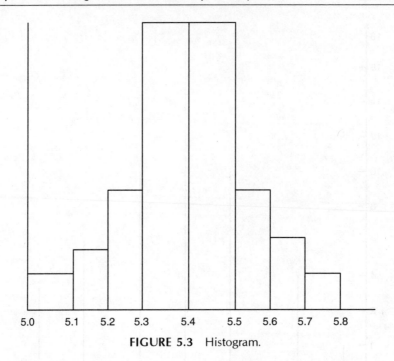

FIGURE 5.3 Histogram.

2. Multimodal acceptable limits
3. Triangular

1. (a) *Symmetrical:* The normal distribution curve shown in Figure 5.4 depicts a stable process, producing components within the tolerance limit.

   The other normal distribution curve shown in Figure 5.5 is of a process which is stable but is not able to produce items within tolerances.

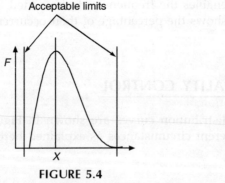

FIGURE 5.4

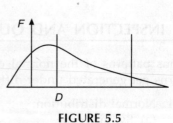

FIGURE 5.5

   (b) *Skewed:* This normal distribution curve shown in Figure 5.6 is inclined more to one side. It shows that there are more over-sized products than mean-sized or under-sized.

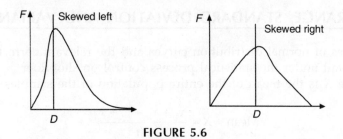

FIGURE 5.6

(c) *Leptokurtic:* It has a peak higher than a normal curve. Refer Figure 5.7.
(d) *Platykurtic:* It has a peak lower than a normal curve. Refer Figure 5.8.

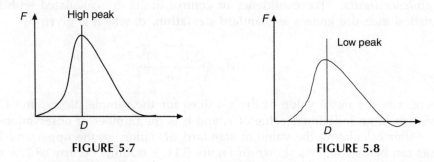

FIGURE 5.7   **FIGURE 5.8**

2. *Multi-modal:* It has two or more peaks. Such a distribution pattern indicates that either the products made on different machines have got mixed up or the process is not stable. Refer Figure 5.9.

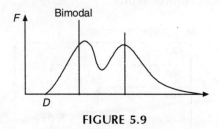

FIGURE 5.9

3. *Triangular:* This distribution pattern is the result of a defective process or machine whose parameters are changing in one direction with the passage of time. Refer Figure 5.10.

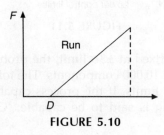

FIGURE 5.10

5.5   MEAN, RANGE, STANDARD DEVIATION AND VARIANCE

The various types of normal distribution curves and the relevant corrective actions are dealt later in detail under the statistical process control on shopfloor.

Mean value X is the mean of the entire population of the samples taken.

$$\text{Mean} = \overline{X} = \frac{x_1 + x_2 + \dots + x_n}{n}$$

The range R is the difference between the x max and x min.

$$R = x\ \text{max} - x\ \text{min}$$

Confidence limits: The confidence or control limits are calculated with the help of a statistical measure known as **standard deviation, σ,** which is given by

$$\sigma = \sqrt{\frac{\Sigma (x - \overline{x})^2}{n}}$$

where, x is the mean value of the x values for the sample pieces, and $(\overline{x} - x)$ is the deviation of an individual value of x, and n is the number of observations.

After calculating the value of standard deviation, σ, the upper and lower control limits can be decided. As shown in Figure 5.11, $\pm \sigma$ limits occupy 68.27% of the area of the normal distribution curve. It indicates that one is 68.27% (UCL) confident that a random observation will fall in this area. Similarly, $\pm 2\sigma$ and $\pm 3\sigma$ limits occupy 95.45% and 99.73% area of the normal curve and possess confidence levels of 95.45% and 99.73%. For plotting control charts in statistical process control, generally 3σ limits are selected and they (LCL) are termed as control limits.

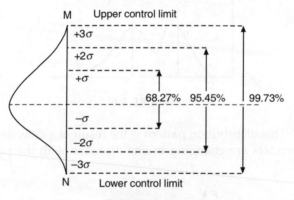

FIGURE 5.11

When the control limit is fixed at $\pm 3\sigma$ limit, the probability of a component falling outside the control limit is 23 in 10,000 components. The tolerance limit of the component is normally beyond the control limits. If the process capability figure 'Cp' is more than 1, the process of manufacturing is said to be capable. 'Cpk' or the process capability factor is an indication of the extent the process is uniformly distributed around the mean. Hence for a process to be capable, the 'Cpk' has also to be more than 1.

The above formulae of the standard deviation hold good when the readings given indicate the whole population of the items measured. This implies that 'n' is the population.

In case of sampling inspection, where n denotes the number of samples taken, the formula for the standard deviation is modified and the denominator becomes $n - 1$.

$$\sigma = \sqrt{\frac{\sum (x - \bar{x})^2}{(n - 1)}}$$

EXAMPLE 5.3

The dimension for shafts being machined on a lathe machine are as follows: 8.2, 8.3, 8.3, 8.5, 8.5, 8.4, 8.0, 8.2, 8.3, 8.3. Calculate the mean, range and the standard deviation.

Solution: There are 10 samples taken

$$\text{The mean } \bar{X} = \frac{8.2 + 8.3 + ... + 8.3}{10} = \frac{83}{10} = 8.3$$

The range $\bar{R}$ = R max. – R min. = 8.5 – 8.0 = 0.5.

Since the readings noted are for the entire population,

$$\text{The standard deviation } \sigma = \frac{(8.3 - 8.2) + (8.3 - 8.3) + ... + (8.3 - 8.3)}{10}$$

$$= \sqrt{(0.02)} = 0.14$$

Analysis of Variance: Variance is the square of standard deviation,

$$\text{Variance} = \sigma^2$$

The analysis of variance is a useful technique in the field of experimental statistics. Moreover, the analysis can be used for analyzing the results of enquiries conducted in the fields of industrial engineering, agriculture, etc. Normally there are variances between different treatments and variances between the samples having same treatment.

5.6 CONTINUOUS SAMPLING INSPECTION

In this system, the existing inspection results help us to decide whether to go for sampling inspection or 100% inspection for inspecting the next lot of items.

The principle of statistical sampling inspection is that the sample represents the whole lot and what is normally true for the sample lot is true for the entire lot. For a highly reliable process, a single sampling plan of inspection is okay. However, depending on the confidence level of the company, it may decide to go for double sampling or multiple sampling. If the multiple sampling plan also shows an extremely bad result, the company may decide to go for 100% inspection till the process of manufacturing improves and the results show more reliability. Once the organization regains its confidence level, it may revert back to the statistical sampling plan.

5.6.1   Single Sampling Plan

Under the single sampling plan, a lot is accepted or rejected on the basis of a single sample drawn from that lot. This is the normal procedure of conducting a statistical process control for an organization with a reasonably good performance level.

First, a single sample of size n, i.e. of n component parts are drawn. The sample size may either be calculated or found from tables or decided as per the company's norms.

Then inspect the sample lot and find the number of defective components in the lot. If the defective pieces are less than the 'Accepted Quality Level (AQL)' of acceptance number c, the lot is accepted. If the defective pieces exceed the acceptance number c, the lot is rejected.

In case the lot is rejected, each and every piece of the main lot size is inspected by 100% inspection or by resorting to the double sampling plan. Now either replace or salvage and correct the defective parts.

Determination of Sample Size from the table: The sample size is determined depending on the main lot size as shown in Table 5.2. Depending on the criticality of usage of the products and services, the organization decides the allowable per cent defective and the sample size is determined based on those criteria also.

TABLE 5.2   Determining a sample size

Lot size	Sample size	Allowable per cent defective				
		1	2	3	4	5
		C	C	C	C	C
Up to 499	75	1	2	3	4	5
500–799	115	2	3	4	6	8
800–1299	150	3	4	5	8	10
1300–3199	225	4	5	8	11	14
3200–7999	300	5	7	10	14	18
8000–21999	450	6	9	14	20	26

For a lot size of 850 and allowable per cent defective 3%, the table gives a sample size of 150 and the acceptance number 'C' is 5.

This means from the lot containing 850 parts, pick up 150 parts at random, inspect them and find out the number of defective pieces. If defective pieces are up to 5, accept the lot; if their number is 6, 7, 8 or more, reject the lot.

The characteristic of the single sampling plan is easy to design, explain and administer. It is the only practical type of sampling plan under the conveyor production system when only one sample can be selected.

Single sampling plan involves a lower cost of training and supervising employees. It accurately estimates the lot quality. It is more economical than double sampling plan when the lots have their % defectives closer to the AQL.

Single sampling plan involves a bigger sample size than the double sampling plan. It is simpler and involves lesser record keeping than the double and multiple sampling plans. A single sampling plan provides maximum information concerning the lot quality because each sample can be plotted on the control chart.

5.6.2 Double Sampling Plan

If it is not possible to decide the fate of the lot on the basis of the first sample, a second sample is drawn out of the same lot and the decision whether to accept or reject the lot is taken on the basis of the combined results of the first and the second samples.

Double sampling plan procedure: Both the sample lots are drawn as per the laid out norms from the full lot to be inspected. The C_1 and C_2 are the acceptance numbers for the first sample size and the second sample size and $C_2 > C_1$.

Inspect a sample of size 'n' from the first lot and find out the defective parts if any. Now count defective parts k_1.

There could be three situations:

(a) If $k_1 > C_2$, then reject the lot.
(b) If $k_1 \leq C_1$, then accept the lot.
(c) If $C_1 < k_1 \leq C_2$, then draw another sample of size n_2. The total sample size is now $n_1 + n_2$, inspect and the effective parts are now $K_1 + K_2$. If $(K_1 + K_2) > C_2$, then reject the lot, and if $(K_1 + K_2) \leq C_2$, then accept the lot.

The double sampling plan is more expensive than the single sampling plan.

The double sampling plan involves less inspection than the single sampling plan.

The double sampling plan gives a second chance to a lot before rejecting it.

The double sampling plan consumes more inspection time, more costly, needs more record keeping and has more overheads than a single sampling plan.

It does not give as accurate estimation of the lot quality as the single sampling plan. When the levels of confidence on the manufacturing process and the level of quality of the finished product are lower, the double sampling plan is recommended to reduce the rejection level.

5.6.3 Multiple Sampling Plan

A multiple sampling plan accepts or rejects a lot upon the results obtained from several sample lots of components drawn from the main lot under inspection.

The multiple sampling plan procedure consists of inspecting the first sample lot and count the number of defects found in the sample lot. If this number of defective components is small, then accept the main lot.

If there are quite a large number of defective pieces, then reject the lot.

If the number of defective parts is on the borderline and no conclusive decision can be taken, then draw and inspect the second sample. If the number of defects in the first and the second samples combined together is very small, then also accept the main lot under inspection.

If the number of defects in the first and the second samples combined together is large, then also reject the main lot.

If the number of defects in the first and the second samples combined together is on the borderline and no decision can be taken, then draw and inspect the third sample. Count the number of defective pieces in all the three samples combined together, (a) if it is small accept the lot, or (b) if it is quite large, then reject the lot, or (c) if it is on the borderline and no decision can be taken then draw and inspect a fourth sample and so on.

The multiple sampling plan involves smaller first samples than single or double sampling plans. A multiple sampling plan is comparatively difficult to design and explain, and expensive to implement. The multiple sampling plan has higher overhead cost, more record keeping and less effective in improving the quality standard. It unnecessarily gives too much flexibility for accepting the lot and increases the inspection time and cost substantially. The multiple sampling plan is resorted to when the confidence level pertaining to the products and services is extremely low.

5.6.4 Sequential Sampling Plan

The sequential sampling plan is a plan which undertakes the item-by-item analysis and acceptance of the main lot. It is a plan in which the sample size is increased by one component at a time till the sample size becomes large enough and contains an adequate number of defective pieces to decide rationally whether to accept the lot or to reject it.

It is easy to design, but more expensive to execute than a comparable multisampling plan since the steps are more complex to take a decision.

Since sample size is increased one-by-one at a time, the sample results are analyzed much faster than a single or double sampling plan. In sequential sampling plan, the sampling costs are the least but the overhead costs are the maximum.

5.7 X̄-CHART

The X̄-chart is the most popular and widely used control chart in the industry. It is the most powerful statistical process control tool. In an organization, everyday a number of sample lots are picked up from the process as per laid down norms. The mean of each such sample lot is calculated. The norm could be one sample lot of 10 pieces per shift of working. This individual means are added together, say for a week; and the mean of all the sample lots mean is taken during the week. This is the mean of all the sample lots means. This is $\bar{X}$. Now the upper and lower control limits are calculated after ascertaining the mean range $\bar{R}$ and multiplying by the constant A_2.

Normally both the $\bar{X}$- and the R-charts are used together for the statistical process control exercise.

The $\overline{X}$-chart shows the changes in the process average and is affected by changes in the process variability. It helps in identifying the process variables by establishing a cause and effect relationship. It is a chart for the measure of central tendency. It shows erratic or cyclic shifts in the process like Run, Trend, etc. It detects steady progress changes like tool wear.

This is the most commonly used variables chart and used along with the R-chart.

The $\overline{X}$-chart tells when to leave the process alone and when to rectify the causes leading to variation.

The $\overline{X}$-chart helps in controlling the quality of incoming material, work-in-process and finished goods and it is a very important tool of the statistical process control and the statistical quality control.

$\overline{X}$ and R-charts when used together form a powerful instrument for diagnosing quality problems, taking corrective and preventive actions and for the process control also.

5.8 R-CHART

Along with the $\overline{X}$-chart, the R-chart is the most popular and widely used control chart in the industry. It is one of the most powerful statistical process control tools and shows the dispersion of the process. In an organization, everyday a number of sample lots are picked up from the process as per the laid down norms. Along with the mean, the range of each such sample lot is calculated. The norm could be one sample lot of 10 pieces per shift of working. These individual ranges are added together, say for a week, and the mean of all the sample lots' mean taken as the mean R during the week. This is the mean of all the sample lot means the mean line of the R-chart.

Now the upper and the lower control limits are calculated after ascertaining the mean range R and multiplying by the constants D_3 & D_4.

Normally both the $\overline{X}$ and the R charts are used together for the statistical process control exercise.

The R-chart shows the dispersion or the spread of the process and is affected by changes in process variability.

Plotting of $\overline{X}$ and R Charts

EXAMPLE 5.4
A good number of samples of items coming out of the machine are collected at random at different intervals of times and their quality characteristics (say diameter or length, etc.) are measured.

For each sample, the mean value and range are found out. For example, if a sample contains five items, whose diameters are $d_1, d_2, d_3, d_4,$ and d_5, the sample average

$\overline{X} = (d_1 + d_2 + d_3 + d_4 + d_5)/5$ and, Range
R = Maximum diameter – Minimum diameter.

A number of samples are selected and their average values and range are tabulated. The following example will explain the procedure to plot $\bar{X}$ and R-charts.

Sample No. (Sample size 5)	$\bar{X}$	R
1	6.5	2
2	7.0	3
3	8.0	3
4	8.5	2
5	8.0	3
	$\Sigma \bar{X} = 38.0$	$\Sigma R = 13$

$\bar{X} = \Sigma X / \text{No. of samples}$
$\bar{R} = \Sigma R / \text{No. of samples}$

Therefore,
$$\bar{\bar{X}} = \frac{38}{5} = 7.6$$

For $\bar{X}$ chart $\bar{R} = \dfrac{13}{5} = 2.6$

Upper Control Limit (UCL) = $\bar{\bar{X}} + A_2 \bar{R}$
Lower Control Limit (LCL) = $\bar{\bar{X}} - A_2 \bar{R}$

For R Chart:
Upper Control Limit (UCL) = $D_4 \bar{R}$
Lower Control Limit (LCL) = $D_3 \bar{R}$

The values of various factors (like A_2, D_4 and D_3) based on normal distribution can be found from the following Table 5.3.

TABLE 5.3 Finding various factors like A_2, D_4 and D_3 based on normal distribution

Sample size (Number of items in a sample)	A_2 Limit average	D_3 Range lower limit	D_4 Range upper limit
2	1.88	0	3.27
3	1.02	0	2.57
4	0.73	0	2.28
5	0.58	0	2.11
6	0.48	0	2.00
8	0.37	0.1	1.86
10	0.31	0.2	1.78
12	0.27	0.28	1.72

Sample size in this problem is 5, therefore,

$$A_2 = 0.58, D_3 = 0 \text{ and } D_4 = 2.11$$

Thus, for $\bar{X}$ chart:

UCL $= 7.6 + (0.58 \times 2.6)$

   $= 7.6 + 1.51 = 9.11$

LCL $= 7.6 - (0.58 \times 2.6)$

   $= 6.09$

and for R chart:

UCL $= 2.11 \times 2.6 = 5.48$

LCL $= D_3 \times R = 0 \times R = 0$

These control limits are marked on a graph paper on either side of the mean value (line). When X and R values are plotted on the graph and jointed (as shown in Figures 5.12 and 5.13), we get the control chart of $\bar{X}$-chart and R-chart.

Both the $\bar{X}$-chart and the R-chart show that the process is under control.

$\bar{X}$ -chart

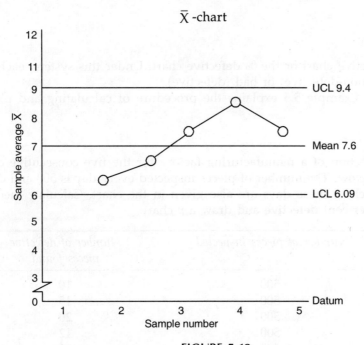

FIGURE 5.12

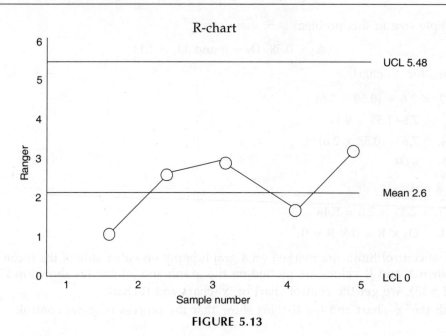

FIGURE 5.13

5.9 p-CHART

It is a fraction defective chart or the % defective chart. Under this system, each item is classified as good (non-defective) or bad (defective).

The following Example 5.5 explains the procedure of calculating and plotting a p-chart.

EXAMPLE 5.5

The results of inspection of a manufacturing factory for the five consecutive days are given in the table below. The number of pieces inspected every day is 500 and defective pieces found on each of these days are also given in the chart. Calculate the fraction defective and the per cent defective and draw a p-chart.

Date	Number of pieces inspected	Number of defective pieces found
July 11	500	10
July 12	500	15
July 13	500	20
July 14	500	12
July 15	500	13
Total number of days = 5	2500	70

Solution:

Date	Number of pieces inspected (a)	Number of defective pieces found (b)	Fraction defective $P = (b)/(a)$	% defective 100 p
July 11	500	10	0.02	2.0
July 12	500	15	0.03	3.0
July 13	500	20	0.04	4.0
July 14	500	12	0.024	2.4
July 15	500	13	0.026	2.6
Total number of days = 5	2500	70		

Upper Control Limit, (UCL) $= \bar{p} + 3 \times \sqrt{\dfrac{\bar{p}(1 - \bar{p})}{N}}$

Lower Control Limit, (LCL) $= \bar{p} - 3 \times \sqrt{\dfrac{\bar{p}(1 - \bar{p})}{n}}$

where

$$\bar{p} = \frac{\text{Total number of defective pieces found}}{\text{Total number of pieces inspected}}$$

$$\bar{p} = \frac{70}{2500} = 0.028 \tag{1}$$

and n = number of pieces inspected every day = 500

Therefore,

$$\sqrt{\frac{\bar{p}(1 - \bar{p})}{n}} = \sqrt{\frac{0.028 \times (1 - 0.028)}{500}}$$

$$= \sqrt{\frac{0.028 \times 0.9720}{500}}$$

$$= 0.007$$

and

$$3 \times \sqrt{\frac{\bar{p}(1 - \bar{p})}{n}} = 0.007 \times 3 = 0.021 \tag{2}$$

From Eqs. (1) and (2),

Therefore the UCL = 0.028 + 0.021 = 0.049

and the LCL = 0.028 − 0.021 = 0.007

Now let us draw the *p*-chart. Please refer Figure 5.14.

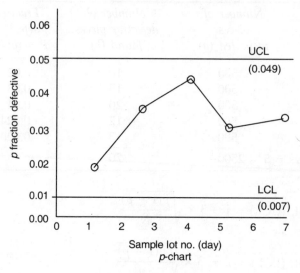

FIGURE 5.14

The *p*-chart is plotted first by calculating the fraction defective and then the control limits. The process is said to be in control if the fraction defective values fall within the control limits. In case the process is out of control, an investigation has to be undertaken to find out the root cause and suitable corrective and preventive actions should be taken.

5.10   *c*-CHART

It is the control chart in which the number of defects in a piece or a sample lot are ascertained, noted down and then plotted to scale on a graph paper.

The objective is to control the number of defects observed per unit or per sample. Normally, the sample size is taken as constant for the *c*-chart.

The *c*-chart is used where the average number of defects noted are much less than the number of defects which is likely to occur if everything possible that can go wrong actually goes wrong.

Whereas *p*-chart considers the number of defective pieces in a given sample lot size, the *c*-chart takes into account the number of defects in each defective piece or in a given sample. A defective piece may contain more than one defect.

For example, an automobile shaft may be defective on account of:

(a) Diameter of the shaft oversize.
(b) The shaft may have surface cracks.
(c) The shaft may be oval in shape due to faulty machining.
(d) The run out of the shaft may be outside tolerance.

The *c*-chart is preferred for large and complex parts like automobile crankshaft for a car, LCV or a truck, it has more than 100 simple and relative dimensions.

c-chart is plotted in the same manner as p-chart, except that the control limits are based on Poisson distribution which describes more appropriately the distribution of defects. This chart is used to control the overall quality of a component. The objective is to find out if the fluctuations in product quality level are due to chance cause alone or it is men, machine or process-related. It can be used for the variable sample size also, but calculating control limits for each sample is rather cumbersome.

EXAMPLE 5.6

Ten automobile transmission shafts were inspected in detail. Each of the components was observed to have a certain number of defects as given below. Draw a c-chart.

Transmission Shaft No.	No. of Defects
1	3
2	6
3	4
4	5
5	4
6	3
7	5
8	4
9	2
10	4
Total sample = 10	Total defects = 40

Solution:

Therefore, $\bar{c} = \dfrac{40}{10} = 4.0$

and

$$UCL = \bar{c} + 3\sqrt{\bar{c}}$$

$$LCL = \bar{c} - 3\sqrt{\bar{c}}$$

or $UCL = 4.0 + 3\sqrt{4.0} = 4.0 + 3 \times 2 = 10.0$

and LCL $= 4 - 6 = -2.0$.

Since the number of defects cannot be negative, let us take the LCL as zero.

The value of c, control limits and the number of defects per casting are plotted on the graph paper. Please refer to Figure 5.15. It is concluded that since all the values of c lie within the control limits, the process is under control.

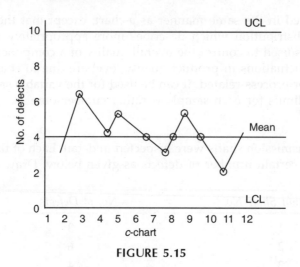

FIGURE 5.15

5.11 STATISTICAL PROCESS CONTROL

The statistical process control is a management technique and a "Reliability Engineering Tool" to control the reliability of a manufacturing process through regular sampling and statistical analysis.

The statistical process control focuses its attention on measuring the product output from a process at regular intervals and evaluates the process performance from this output. The entire process of the statistical process control, right from the sensing to the collection of data, analyzing the same and taking suitable corrective actions to putting the process back into its original desirable track is achieved by the **'computer-aided statistical process control system'**.

The computer-aided gauging automation for the process control of the manufacturing system is integrated through the Program Logic Controller (PLC) of the Computer Integrated Manufacturing (CIM) makes the process error-free and actually achieves an integrated manufacturing and quality control system known as autonomation where it is impossible to produce a defective product. In this computer aided statistical process control system, the attainment of 'Zero Defect' becomes automatic.

If the output is within the control limits, the computer only keeps track of the data generated and monitors them and gives simple statistical analysis like what is the population of components checked, how many are OK, how many are on the border line of dimension, how many are outside the control limit, etc. The computer further analyses the data and determines the mean, range, standard deviation and the control charts. In case some deviation occurs in one of the dimensions, the gauging system as well as the computer sense the deviation through the sensors and activate a warning system like an electric hooter or a revolving red light on the top of the machine indicating that the process has started producing defective parts and it warrants immediate attention. The system simultaneously stops the manufacturing process to prevent it from producing defective parts. Now the supervisor/machine operator resets or adjusts the machine or corrects the defect by manual corrections and restarts the machines after ensuring removal of the deviation. This can be automatically done by the machine itself provided it is integrated with the quality control system or with the automated gauging system.

A sensor can be a mechanical device like a dial gauge or a pneumatic or air plug used for internal diameter measurement. Similarly an air caliper or an air ring gauge for the external diameter measurement. The sensor can be an electronic probe mounted on a suitably designed fixture for the measurement of the external or internal diameters. Out of the three most accurate is the pneumatic sensors. The output from the sensor can be displayed on a mechanical gauge like a dial gauge, an air gauge unit or an electronic gauging unit. The mechanical and air gauge units can only display the readings. The electronic display unit can directly read the mechanical and electronic sensors and indirectly through a converter converting the pneumatic signal into an electronic signal. In case the electronic unit senses the signal in analog units of micro current or voltages, the signal needs to be converted, through an analogue to digital signal (A/D) converter, into a digital signal. The electronic display unit displays the reading on a linear scale or in absolute digital units. At the same time, the data output is connected to a computer to do a complete analysis of the data, its interpretation, and suitable process correction to ensure zero defect output from the system.

5.11.1 Principle of Statistical Process Control

The entire **Computer Aided Quality System** for the **Reliability Engineering** or the **Statistical Process Control System** is explained schematically in Figure 5.16.

Figure 5.17 is an actual printout of such Computer Aided Manufacturing system integrated with the quality known as **automation** in the modern latest manufacturing technique developed in line with the **TOYOTA Manufacturing System** followed by the Japanese industries.

The formulas used to calculate the summary statistics are in-built in the computer program. The system can also draw the 'Control Charts'.

A1 Histogram Statistics
Histogram Summary Statistics

Histogram c01				ENT
n				418
min[177]				4.9877
max [333]				5.0111
Ave				4.99987
SD				0.00352
−3s				4.98931
+3s				5.01043
Cp	0.95		Cpk	0.94
Rej	Wrj	Acp	Wrk	Rwk
0%	8%	85%	7%	0
= 7	T	A	T	
	3	V	3	

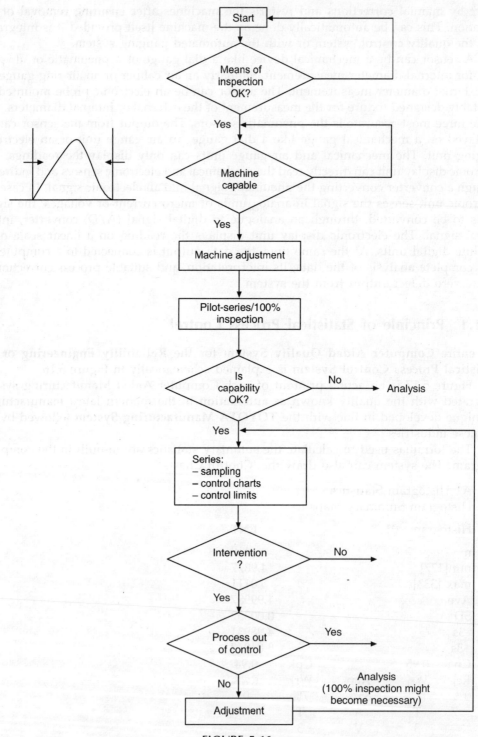

FIGURE 5.16

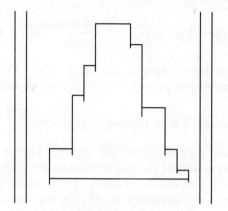

FIGURE 5.17

5.12   DISPERSION AND PROCESS CAPABILITY

Before discussing in detail the dispersion or process capability, let us get certain basic terms of the statistical process control system well defined.

The dispersion curve is depicted in Figure 5.18.

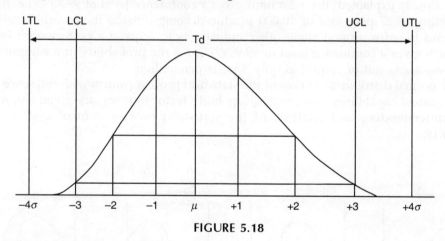

FIGURE 5.18

LCL = Lower Control Limit
LTL = Upper Tolerance Limit
UCL = Upper Control Limit
LCL = Lower Control Limit
Td = Total Tolerance
$\mu \approx \bar{X}$ = mean value of the samples
R = Range. It is the difference between the maximum and the minimum values. It shows the dispersion or the spread.
σ = Estimated standard deviation.

Process Capability Index 'Cp' $= \dfrac{Td}{6\sigma} = \dfrac{\text{Total tolerance}}{6\sigma} \geq 1.0$

For a process to be declared capable, the value of the Cp should be more than or equal to 1. The ideal figure of the process capability is between 1.27 and 1.33.

Process capability factor 'Cpk' $=$ minimum between $\dfrac{UTL - X}{3\sigma}$ or $\dfrac{X - LTL}{3\sigma} \geq 1.0$

This is also known as "process capability index". This is the measurement of the central tendency of the dispersion of the population or the components being measured. The central line mean of the process or product specification, should coincide with the components being produced on the machine. If it is the same, the values of 'Cp' and 'Cpk' will be the same. In case the 'Cp' is more than or equal to one and the 'Cpk' is less than one, the situation indicates that the process is capable but the process of manufacturing or the machine needs adjustment or setting to put the process back around the mean.

Normally the control limits are put on the $\pm 3\sigma$ limits. The upper control limit is put on the $+3\sigma$ limit and the lower control limit is put on the -3σ limit. Normally, the tolerance limit, specified on the product, part or the component, is more than this limit. Hence, the upper tolerance limit should be beyond $+3\sigma$ limit and the lower tolerance limit should be beyond the -3σ limit for the process to be capable.

As already explained, the $\pm 3\sigma$ limit gives a confidence level of 99.73%, i.e. there is a probability of 27 parts out of 10,000 produced being outside the control limits. The latest trend in software and some other industry is to achieve a performance level of $\pm 6\sigma$ which gives a confidence level of 99.99997%, i.e. the probability of a component or the process going out of control is only 3 parts per million.

The normal distribution curves of the statistical process control with reference to the various process capabilities and process capability factor indexes, are given below for a better understanding and analysis of the statistical process control system. Refer Figure 5.19.

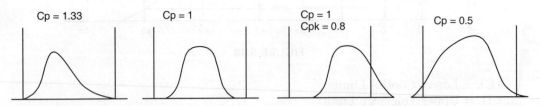

Cp = 1.33   Cp = 1   Cp = 1
                                                Cpk = 0.8   Cp = 0.5

FIGURE 5.19   Normal distribution curves of statistical process control with reference to the various process capabilities and process capability factor indexes.

5.12.1   Abnormal Distributions

This has been already explained in detail in the beginning of this chapter. The examples are given once more with specific figures of skew and kurtosis. Please refer to Figure 5.20.

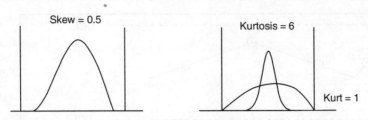

Ideal figure for skewness is = 0±0.4 and for kurtosis is = 3±1

FIGURE 5.20 Examples for skew and kurtosis normal distribution.

The normality test depends in fact on the lot size and should be done whenever the standard deviation is used.

Now let us discuss some typical cases of analysis of the control charts and the recommended corrective actions to be taken. Some typical control charts and their analyses below.

5.13 ANALYSIS OF PROCESS OUT OF CONTROL

5.13.1 Corrective Actions

For rectifying the process deviations and shifts from the normal distribution curve, the three steps to be taken are given below. Let us first discuss the various situations as depicted in Figure 5.21.

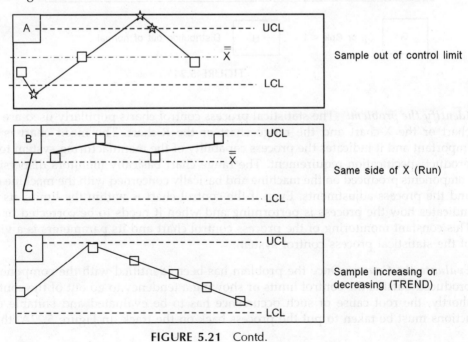

FIGURE 5.21 Contd.

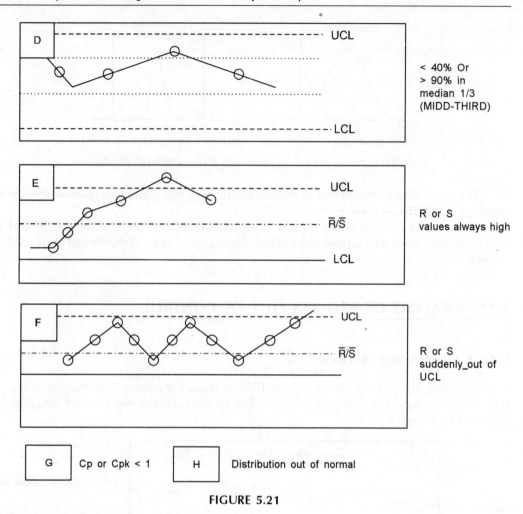

FIGURE 5.21

Identify the problem: The statistical process control charts popularly used are the mean chart or the X-chart and the range chart or the R-chart. The mean chart is the most important and it indicates the process capability of the manufacturing system to meet the product specification requirement. The range chart basically monitors dispersion of the components produced on the machine and basically concerned with the machine capability and the process adjustments. Even if the control chart is within the limits, its tendency indicates how the process is performing and when it needs to be corrected or adjusted. This constant monitoring of the process control chart and its parameters is a vital aspect of the statistical process control system.

Evaluate the Cause: Once the problem has been identified with the components being produced outside the control limits or showing a tendency to go out of the control limits shortly, the root cause of such occurrence has to be evaluated and suitable corrective actions must be taken to put the process back on the track. In Figure 5.22A, the process capability for manufacturing the component is not there. A radical redesign of the component or the process is necessary. The immediate action is to revert back to 100% inspection.

In Figure 5.22B, the process capability for manufacturing the component is there. However, it needs process adjustment or resetting of the machine around the mean or shortly the parts produced may be outside the control limits. This tendency of process being one side of the mean is known as Run.

In Figure 5.22C, the process capability and machine capability for manufacturing the component is there. This is a common type of 'Trend' chart where the tool gets worn out as it machines the components. As the tool gets worn out, the component dimension changes slowly in one direction. The external diameter of the component gradually increases for outer diameter machining as the tool gets worn out. The tool needs to be re-sharpened and reset as the corrective action.

Figure 5.22D shows that the process capability and machine capability for manufacturing the component is much above the laid out standard.

Figure 5.22E is an advanced case of Figure 5.22B where the parts produced have gone beyond the control limit. The corrective action is the same as stipulated in Figure 5.22B.

Figure 5.22F shows the process suddenly going out of control. This is due to the sudden tool breakage or machine failure.

The cases in Figures 'G' and 'H' show that both the process capability and the machine capability are not there. 100% inspection may be necessary.

Take corrective and preventive actions: Once the control charts show that either the process has gone out of control or has the tendency to go out of control even if it is still under the control limits, the operator has to intervene and call for an official in-charge. The process should be stopped to prevent it from producing any defective parts or components. Then suitable corrective and preventive actions should be taken as suggested in the earlier point to eliminate the root cause and put the process back into its original setting so that consistency in product performance and zero defect are achieved.

5.14 THE CAUSES OF PROCESS VARIATION

Tool: Process variation can occur due to the selection of wrong tool, excessive tool wear, lesser tool strength, etc.

Machine: Process variation can occur due to bearing wear, or due to clearances between the moving parts, thereby producing erratic and inconsistent dimensions. It can also happen due to worn out machine parts.

Material: Process variation can occur due to lack of homogeneity in the material with sudden spots of dimensional or hardness variation, leading to excessive load on the machine as well as cutting tools used for machining. Use of a material different from the specified one will need total change in the processing parameters or the desired results cannot be achieved.

Operator: Process variation can occur due to variations in operator's skill, his training level, eyesight, physical health, habits like drinking, etc. and other human factors. Every processing needs certain amount of operator skill and this is an important process variable.

Process: Process variation can occur due to the method of doing a job or variation in the process itself. A job can be machined on a lathe, shaping, milling or pantograph machines. Depending on the speed, feed, depth of cut and the type of machine used, the process of value addition will be different which will be typical of a certain process and may not be acceptable under all circumstances.

Maintenance: The process variation can occur due to inadequate or improper maintenance leading to faulty machine operation. Lack of lubrication, regular checking and tightening of the V-Belt tension, routine replacement of bearings will all lead to variations in the setting and process performance. This will produce faulty and defective products.

Environment: Process variations can occur due to fluctuations in environmental factors like variation in the power supply leading to lower power output in the machine. This will lead to overloading of the machine and burning of the electric motors, poor finish of the component, overloading of the tool and the machine leading to their failure. This may also lead to the vibrations in components. The temperature variation may lead to dimensional deviation if the accuracy is measured in microns.

EXERCISES

1. Explain the 'probability theory' and fundamental logic behind the statistical measurement.

2. Explain the concept of 'normal distribution curve, mean, range, standard deviation and variance'. Give the relevant formulae.

3. Explain in detail 'statistical sampling techniques—single sampling, double sampling, multiple sampling, sequential sampling'.

4. Explain the concept of control charts: p-chart, c-chart, X-chart and R-chart, etc.

5. Define the 'statistical process control'. Explain the principle of working of the statistical process control system. Explain the concepts of process capability and process capability factor.

6. Elaborate on the methodology of analyzing the 'SPC charts' that is reliability analysis of the process or the process output and undertaking corrective and preventive actions.

7. Explain the computer-aided quality management system and how it ensures 'zero defect' in the output of products.

8. 25 components were manufactured on a machine and their diameters in mm are measured and given below:

   10.2, 10.3, 10.2, 10.3, 10.4, 10.2, 10.3, 10.2, 10.3, 10.4, 10.2, 10.5, 10.1, 10.3, 10.5, 10.2, 10.4, 10.3, 10.1, 10.3, 10.2, 10.5, 10.3, 10.4, 10.1.

   Draw the frequency distribution table, frequency distribution curve, bar chart and histogram.

9. The dimensions of a shaft being machined on a lathe machine are as follows: 6.2, 6.3, 6.3, 6.5, 6.5, 6.4, 6.0, 6.2, 6.3, 6.3, 6.4, 6.1, 6.0, 6.3, 6.2. Calculate the mean, range and standard deviation.

10. A number of samples are selected and their average values and range are tabulated below:

Sample lot No.	Mean ($\overline{X}$)	Range (R)
A	8.0	2.5
B	8.5	2.0
C	8.0	3.0
D	9.0	2.5
E	10.0	3.5
F	7.0	2.0
G	8.0	3.0
H	8.5	3.0
I	9.0	2.5
J	8.0	3.0

Calculate the mean, range and standard deviation. Draw the $\overline{X}$-chart and the R-chart. If the tolerance limit specified for the mean dimension is given as ±2.0, calculate the process capability figure 'Cp' and process capability factor 'Cpk'.

11. A manufacturing factory's inspection results for six consecutive days are given in the table below. The number of pieces inspected everyday is 700 and the defective pieces found on each of these days are also given in the chart. Calculate the fraction defective and the per cent defective and draw a p-chart.

Date	Number of pieces inspected	Number of defective pieces found
June 5	700	12
June 6	700	15
June 7	700	18
June 8	700	20
June 9	700	16
June 10	700	13

6

Production Planning, Control and Scheduling

6.1 DEMAND MEASUREMENT AND SALES FORECASTING

The accuracy and effectiveness of production planning depends largely on the accuracy of sales forecasting and achievement of the sales target. Production will follow the sales order booking and products are manufactured accordingly. If the order booking is more than the anticipated sales forecasting, there will be a short-supply in the market creating a situation where the loyal customer may switch over to use a competitor's product due to non-availability of the company's products in the market. In case the market needs less than the number of products produced due to wrong sales forecast, there will be inventory piling up leading to blockage of fund in inventory as well as the danger of product obsolescence in case the product lies in the stock for a long time. Hence the accuracy of the sales forecast and demand measurement are vital factors for the management of business.

The conventional practice of the time series analysis, sales forecast based on the past-data and on the judgment of individuals, have become redundant in today's global and highly competitive environment. The shorter product life cycle, frequent product innovations and changes in technology related to the processes as well as the product, make sales forecasting an extremely challenging proposition. It totally depends on the market feedback and accurate assessment of the current business environment. A strategic action plan based on the above factors is the only answer for an accurate sales forecast.

Let us first define and understand the concept of market demand. "Market demand for a product is the total volume needed by a defined customer group in a particular geographical area within a specified period, normally a month or a year, in a defined competition in a defined marketing environment under a well-defined marketing plan".

The above definition makes it clear that sales forecasting is a critical management task considering so many variables to be defined after accurate collection of data and its analysis. The variables are as follows:

- Product range
- Product application
- Substitute product including emerging products
- Market segment in terms of customer profile
- Demographic market segment
- Time period
- Marketing environment
- Marketing programme

The market is three-dimensional in terms of **Product level. Space level and Time level.** The demand measurement has to take into consideration the precisely defined quadrant of demand measurement. The PRODUCT level has six dimensions: Product item, Product form, Product line, company sales, industry sales and total sales. The SPACE level has five dimensions: a particular customer, customers in a territory, customers in a region, in India or at the whole world level. The TIME level has three components of short term, medium term and long term. This makes the total quadrant to be individually assessed for demand measurement by the organization $6 \times 5 \times 3 = 90$. This is quite a lot of preparatory work for accuracy in sales forecasting.

The organization has to define the level of the market. Out of the total population of 100%, only 10% could be the potential market. If we extend this potential market to a scale of hundred, the available market may not be more than 40 and the served market may only be 20. The penetrated market by the organization may only be 10. This means that the organization's penetrated market could be only 1% of the targeted population.

The sales forecast for the next year or the current year will depend a lot on the Product Life Cycle (PLC) (see Figure 6.1). If the product is at the introduction or the growth stage, the market is likely to grow whereas if the product is at maturity or decline stage, the market is likely to shrink.

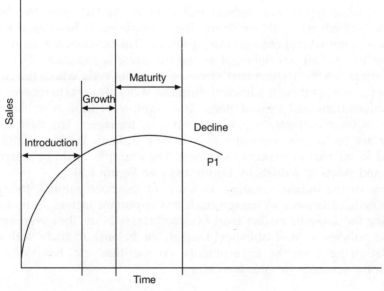

FIGURE 6.1 Product Life Cycle (PLC).

The organization should practise **Demand Technology Cycle** by which when one product reaches the maturity stage, a modified or innovated or an altogether new product as per market demand has to be introduced so that the organization does not die with the death of the product (see Figure 6.2). This practice of updating the existing products by product innovation and adding contemporary features, along with the practice of demand technology cycle, is practised by all the world-class organizations like Maruti Suzuki Motor Corp. Ltd., Colgate Palmolive Ltd., Hindustan Lever Ltd., etc.

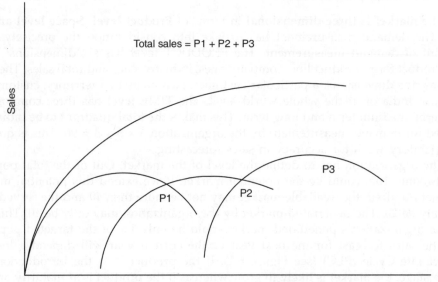

FIGURE 6.2 Demand Technology Cycle.

PLC is of three types—fad, fashion and style. In the fad cycle, the demand for a product rises suddenly and falls suddenly. The example could be sales of *Rakhis* during *Raksha bandhan* or the sales of crackers during Diwali. The fad does not allow the recovery of investment in product development as the life cycle is too short. The organization should concentrate on the fashion part of the product life cycle where the customers are ready to adapt as well as there is sufficient duration of the life cycle to recover investments in product innovations and upgradations. The example of fashion is like 'Bell-bottom Pants' in the 1970s or currently wearing of blings by teenagers. The third one, the style cycle should not be touched normally as it is very difficult to change and it lasts for centuries and forms part of a country's culture. The example, could be wearing of *dhotis* by villagers and pants and shirts by Europeans (see Figure 6.3).

The state of the Indian economy, in terms of monsoon rainfall, foodgrain stock, industrial growth, inflation and foreign trade are important factors, to be kept in mind while assessing the domestic market apart from political stability, the government's foreign and domestic policies. In case of export market, the balance of trade with a particular country, relation between the governments, competition, etc, has to be taken into consideration for accuracy in sales forecasting.

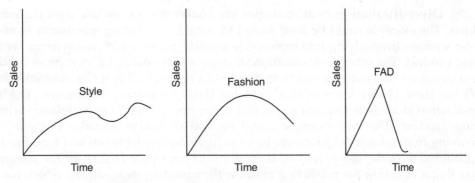

FIGURE 6.3 Style, Fashion and Fad Life Cycles.

The demand for a product increases with marketing effort during prosperity as compared to during recession. If the organization wants to maintain its sales at the same level during recession, it has to put in additional marketing effort to increase its market share.

The final factor to be considered for sales forecasting is the organization's growth strategy. There is only $3 \times 3 = 9$ growth strategy (as shown in Figure 6.4). The **intensive** growth strategies are **Market Penetration, Market Development and Product Development**. Market penetration means increasing the market share in the same market with the same products. Market development means expanding to new markets with the same product range and adding to the existing business. Product development is developing a product range depending on the market segment. For example, Hindustan Levers Ltd. introduced new varieties of detergent powders like 'Wheel', 'Rin', 'Surf' and 'Surf Excel' depending on the market segment based on the income in the same geographical market segment.

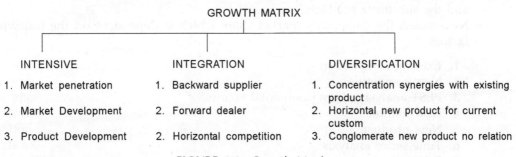

FIGURE 6.4 Growth Matrix.

The **integrative** growth strategies are **Backward** or **Forward** or **Horizontal**. Backward integration growth strategy is practiced by The Reliance Industries Ltd. in expanding into the processing of raw materials and input to the parent industry. The forward integration growth strategy is putting up its own showroom for direct selling to the customers like Bata Shoe Co. Ltd. or opening the franchisee outlets. The horizontal integration growth strategy is practised by Blow Plast Ltd. manufacturer of VIP brand moulded luggage manufacturer taking over a competitor like 'Safari' or 'Aristocrat' brand moulded luggage manufacturer or the Rahejas for the automotive battery manufacturer Chloride India Ltd. (Exide Battery) taking over a competitor Standard Batteries Ltd.

The **Diversification** growth strategies are **concentric**, i.e. in line with the existing products. The example could be Bajaj Auto Ltd. which is a leading manufacturer of two-wheeler scooters diversifying into motorcycle manufacturing which has synergy with the existing product. The other diversification strategy is **Horizontal**, i.e. new product for the current customer. The example can be that of TELCO going for Light Commercial Vehicles (LCV) for their Heavy Commercial Vehicles (HCV) transport customers. The third diversification strategy is **Conglomerate** that is the new product has no relation with the existing product. The best example could be that of Indian Tobacco Company Ltd. diversifying from tobacco/cigarettes to hotel industry to vegetable oils and food products.

Coupled with the above factors, there are four important factors for the company's market share: equating the marketing effort with marketing expenditure, which has two components—carrying forward effects of the past marketing expenditure or the marketing effort and the geographical focus in terms of allocation of expenditure for the marketing effort. The second important factor is the synergistic effect of the product mix and the marketing mix. The third and the fourth important factors for the company's market share are the marketing effectiveness and the marketing elasticity.

Now let us define sales forecast. A company **Sales Forecast** is the expected level of the company sales based on a chosen marketing plan and an assessed marketing environment.

Sales Budget is a conservative estimate of expected volume of sales and is used primarily for making current purchasing, production and cash flow decisions.

Sales Forecast and Sales Budget: The steps in sales forecasting (see Figure 6.5) are detailed below:

- Assess the total market potential which is the sum of the area sales potential.
- Find out the actual industry sales which are the sum of sales of all the competitors and the substitute products.
- Now assess the company's market share which is dependent on the following factors:

    1. Existing competition
    2. New competition
    3. PEST analysis of environmental factors
    4. New market
    5. New product
    6. Time series analysis
    7. Substitute products
    8. Marketing program
    9. Marketing effort/expenditure
    10. Percentage industry growth
    11. Product range expansion
    12. Company's growth strategy

- Taking into consideration the above factors, work out the company sales forecast which is the sum of area sales forecasts.

TOTAL MARKET POTENTIAL
Q= N.Q.P.
↓
AREA MARKET POTENTIAL
↓
ACTUAL INDUSTRY SALES
(Add up all Market Shares)
↓
COMPANY MARKET SHARE

NEW COMPETITION ⟶ | ⟵ ENVIRONMENT
NEW MARKET ⟶ | ⟵ MARKETING PROGRESS
NEW PRODUCTION ⟶ | ⟵ MARKETING EXPENDITURE
TIME SERIES ANALYSIS ⟶ | ⟵ % INDUSTRY GROWTH
NEW SUBSTITUTE PRODUCTION ⟶ | ⟵ % COMPANY'S GROWTH
| ⟵ PRODUCTION/RANGE EXPANSION

COMPANY SALES FORECAST/AREA SALES FORECAST
↓
COMPANY SALES BUDGET/
AREA SALES BUDGET
SUGGESTED 80% OF SALES FORECAST
↓
BIFURCATE INTO PRODUCTION/ITEMWISE/PERSONWISE
SALES QUOTA

FIGURE 6.5 Steps in sales forecasting.

- As a thumb rule, the sales budget is normally kept at 80% of the sales forecast. break up the sales budget into area-wise sales budget.
- The final step is the bifurcation of the sales budget into product-wise, item-wise, and personnel-wise sales quotas.

This is actually the correct and practical methodology to arrive at the accurate sales forecast. However, for information sake, there is a need to discuss the conventional ways of sales forecasting. The approaches to sales forecasting are mainly three types. However, more than one method of sales forecasting can be used. The three principal methods (as shown in Figure 6.6) for sales forecasting are detailed below:

(1) Judgemental: The judgemental method of sales forecasting is basically a subjective way of sales forecasting. The judgment could be that of an individual normally the CEO or the Management Director or could be the joint decision arrived at by a committee comprising the branch managers and heads of functions and chaired by either the marketing head or the CEO. The judgement could be fact-based comprising the feedback from the market survey, opinion of the market experts, known as the Delphi method. Ultimately, all the sales forecasting ends with the final decision taken based on judgement after considering all the data and the relevant analyses. The judgemental method of sales forecasting can be either hunch-based or past performance based or based on past data analysis and reasoning.

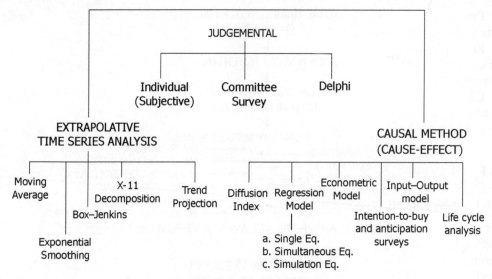

FIGURE 6.6 Approaches to Forecasting.

(2) *Time Series Analysis:* This method of sales forecasting is based on the past data of sales performance and extrapolating it to the future. There are various ways of smoothing the past data and applying them to the future trends. Sales forecasting under this methodology could be the simple trend projection, moving average, exponential smoothing, Box–Jenkins or the X-11 decomposition. This method was quite popular in the past. Currently, it has become redundant due to shorter product life cycle, globalization, frequent product innovation, intense international competition and fast change in technology as these factors lead to a situation where the past is not likely to repeat in the future. The current competition, market situation and the speed of product development and innovation are mind-boggling and taking place at a tremendous speed never seen hitherto.

(3) *Causal Method:* This sales forecasting methodology is a combination of the past data on the various causes or reasons affecting the sales performance. This sales forecasting methodology is also known as the cause and effect methodology.

The various methodologies adopted are diffusion index, econometric model, life cycle analysis, intension to buy and anticipation surveys, input–output model and regression analysis. The regression analysis could be a single equation, simultaneous equation or a simulation equation. This sales forecasting methodology is sensitive to the market situation as it can separately measure the effect of variation of individual causes on the final sales performance. Most of the current software packages for sales forecasting follow this methodology.

6.2 PRODUCTION PLANNING AND CONTROL

The accuracy of Production Planning and Control depends a lot on the accuracy of sales forecasting or demand measurement. Production planning and control takes the figure of sales from the sales budget which is normally 80% of the sales forecast. Let us now define production planning and control.

Production is value addition by transformation of input raw material into finished goods known as **Product**.

Planning is the decision-making process to achieve the end objective by choosing the best alternative which consumes the least amount of input resources and gives the maximum output.

Control ensures that the planned production is constantly monitored and maintained and any deviation is avoided.

A *Production and Planning System* has the following functions to perform:

6.2.1 Planning Phase

6.2.1.1 Prior planning

Prior planning activity mainly consists of data collection and arranging for various inputs for effective production planning and control system. The accuracy of the production planning and control system depends on the accuracy and correctness of the activities in the prior planning. There are broadly three major activities in prior planning namely the sales forecasting, order writing and design data.

(A) *Sales forecasting:* The importance and the relevance of sales forecasting in the production planning and control activity as well as in the successful working of the organization is already explained in the beginning of this chapter. Sales forecasting estimates the type, quantity and quality of the future order. Production planning and control data is taken from the sales budget which is normally lower than the sales forecast by 20%.

If the sales forecast is higher than the actual sales, there will be piling of inventory leading to the blockage of capital and other inventory-related risks, like product obsolescence, warehousing cost, pilferage, damage, deterioration, insurance and other costs. This will disturb an organization's liquidity and create disturbance in its functioning. On the other hand, if the demand is more than the sales forecasting, there will be shortage in the market for the organizations' products and services, leading its loyal customers' to try out the competitor's product. These loyal customers may permanently switch over to the competitors with the organization losing the opportunity of earning the profit on the sale if the product was available in the stock. The accuracy and efficiency of production planning and control depends mainly on sales forecasting.

(B) *Order writing:* The workstations in an organization are well-defined with its capability, capacity, manpower and other resources needed. The sales branches have defined branch managers and sales personnel territory-wise. The order writing gives authority to one or more persons to undertake a particular job as per the schedule defined in the production planning and control system.

(C) *Product design:* Sales forecasting and production planning and control decide the product-mix, product range and the item details. The master schedule of production and bills of material gives the details of a number of items needed to meet the market demand as per the given product-mix in the production planning and control planning sheet. The product design should have the entire flow process chart of conversion, processing and assembling of the various parts into the final assembly. The product design should also collect information regarding specifications, bill of materials, drawings, etc. The quality, quantity and other technical information should be available at the right time and the right place for the ease of execution of production planning and control.

6.2.1.2 Active planning

This is where the active process of the production planning and control starts with active planning. It plans and arranges for all the technical information regarding the process of conversion of the raw materials and components to finished products as per the production planning and control with the least consumption of resources. Active planning also plans and arranges for all the resources at the least cost at the right time, right place, of right quality and right quantity.

(A) *Process planning and routing:* Process planning is designing and finding the most optimum and economic way of doing the work. Process planning decides where and how the work will be done. It consists of planning and organizing the raw materials and components, tools and manufacturing aids needed for the smooth production, loading and scheduling of the machines and the scheduling of the operations. Process planning finds and works out the most economical and effective way of converting the raw material and components into the finished product in the least time. The process planning also finds the route of conversion and assembly into the final product.

(B) *Material control:* It involves determining the requirement of raw materials and components in terms of both quality and quantity, as well as the sources of material in terms of right price and to be made available at the right time and at the right place. The production planning and control system should instill a control mechanism of the material at every stage. Normally the suppliers and vendors are rated and approved for each component. There are normally two suppliers for each component. The one who is more reliable in terms of consistency in quality as well as delivery is rated as a superior supplier and given 70% of the requirement and the other vendor is 30%. The parent organization ensures that the processes of manufacturing at the supplier's end are under control. This is verified by routine visits of its quality control engineers to the vendor's organization.

(C) *Tools and Manufacturing Aids Control:* The production planning and control activity decides the manufacturing process and it facilitates the availability of the right kind of tools and manufacturing aids of the right quality and price at the right place and the right time. The right kind of machining tool for a particular machining process decides the productivity of the manufacturing process. Similarly, the right kind of jigs and fixtures reduce the manufacturing cycle time substantially. The dies and moulds needed for the non-ferrous and ferrous metal casting, rubber and plastic industry, forging industry are important manufacturing aids which decide the quality of the end products as well as the productivity and economics of production. These are the key factors for production planning and control. The production planning and control activity monitors the above tools and manufacturing aids for their availability, accuracy and timely maintenance and designs a control system for the same.

(D) *Loading:* An important integral part of the production planning and control system is the systematic distribution of work to workstations, production lines and their proper balancing so that there is neither idle time on the workstations nor there is piling of inventory. The proper deployment of the manpower, machinery and raw material with line balancing of the resources is the crux of an efficient and effective production planning and control system. In the **Just-In-Time** manufacturing system, the **Kanban Card system** is a production planning and control loading system. Loading is an important aspect of the production planning and control system which authorizes taking up a job for processing or assembling after making arrangements for all the necessary resources for the same.

(E) *Scheduling:*   Scheduling is the time phase of the loading. Scheduling production planning and control gives the details of what is to be taken up for manufacturing and in what sequence the work will be done. It determines the starting as well the finishing time of the respective jobs, the gap and sequence between the jobs. The scheduling in production planning and control also decides the inter-linkages between various processes and ensures that the gap between the subsequent processes and the inventory accumulation on the shopfloor is bare minimum.

6.2.1.3   Action phase

This is the most important aspect of production planning and control. This is the action phase of production planning and control where the manufacturing activity takes place as per the plan. This is the practical implementation of production planning and control. The action phase constitutes two principal parts of execution and dispatching of products produced to the customers via the finished goods store and the distribution network.

(A) *Execution:*   This is the transition phase from planning phase to action phase in production planning and control. In this phase, the team members and workers are instructed to start the actual work and execute it as per the laid down plan. Before the execution phase starts, all the resources have to be arranged in terms of men, machines, material and manufacturing aids of the right quality, of the right quantity, at the right time, at the right place and at the optimum cost in the production planning and control system. Once the execution process starts, the production should flow smoothly without any interruption or piling up of goods-in-process. The execution phase in production planning and control should ensure that the final finished product is of the right quality and available in the right quantity as per the customer's requirement. The execution phase of the production planning and control should ensure that there is no gap or deviation between the planning and execution.

(B) *Dispatching:*   In this phase of production planning and control, the product manufactured as described above is dispatched to the finished goods store for storage, segregation and safely packed for onward dispatch to the customer's end through the distribution channel so as to satisfy the four 'P's of marketing leading to customer satisfaction. Dispatching in the production planning and control system creates the time and place utility associated with the product. The dispatching system also affects the pricing of the product for low-cost products.

6.2.1.4   Control phase

Planning in the production planning and control system ensures that the system has in-built periodic monitoring system at the critical well-defined points known as the control points. The control phase of the production planning and control system runs concurrently with the action phase. The control phase has two distinctive phases of progress reporting and in case of deviations taking the corrective actions. The two phases of the production planning and control system are explained below.

(A) *Progress reporting:* The production planning and control system incorporates an in-built mechanism in every plan to collect the data regarding the progress of the job. This data is collected on a predetermined interval and the same is compared with the pre-set level of performance in terms of performance as well as the time and resources consumed as laid down in the plan. Whether the execution is proceeding as per the plan or not is the main job of the progress reporting. The progress reporting phase of the production planning and control system not only measures the progress of execution as per the plan, but also notices the non-adherence of certain activities to the plan or the deviations. The progress reporting process records such exceptions and reports the same to the relevant authorities for necessary action.

(B) *Corrective action:* Once the deviations or the changes from the plan are noticed, the root cause of the problem is identified. Once the root cause is identified, the corrective action is resorted to in production planning and control. When it is found that the actual performance deviates from the planned performance, suitable steps of *correction, expedition, replanning or rescheduling* are taken in terms of resources allocation, time element, work order and purchase order. A suitable preventive action will enable the cause of the deviation to be permanently eradicated.

6.2.2   Important Features of Production Planning and Control

- The analysis of the causes of deviation of performance from the plan and the effectiveness of the corrective steps taken will provide good lessons which can be used in future planning. This *feedback* leads to a state of continual improvement in performance of the production planning and control activity and leads to perfection.
- For continuous mass production having a product type of plant layout, the production planning and control activity is relatively simple. In case of batch or job production with a process type plant layout, the production planning and control activity is fairly complex and needs more experience, closer monitoring and continuous upgradation to be effective.
- Accurate *Sales Forecasting* is a preamble to successful production planning and control activity. For accurate sales forecasting, the process has to start with demand measurement, market potential, product life cycle, demand technology cycle, marketing strategy, environmental factors, consumer behaviour, growth strategy, substitute products, market recession and prosperity, etc. The methodologies of sales forecasting are judgemental, time series analysis, exponential smoothing, regression analysis, etc.
- To make production planning and control activity effective, certain strategies need to be drawn to absorb the fluctuation in demand. The deployment of the right kind of technique for absorbing fluctuations in demand is the key factor to the success of the production planning and control function.

6.2.3 Strategies Used to Absorb Fluctuations in Demand

- If the demand increases, the extra load can be shifted to subcontractors and ancillaries.
- Inventory levels should be adjusted to absorb seasonal fluctuations in demand.
- During off-peak period, the industry can shift to other types of products which can be produced from the same plant and machinery. For example, the fan manufacturers in eastern Uttar Pradesh switch over to the manufacturing of agricultural motor pumps during winter months. The demand for fans is at the lowest in winter and the demand for agricultural motor pumps is at the highest due to shortage of water during winter. The machines and technology for manufacturing both the items are identical.
- The work force can be divided into own workforce and that of the contractor's. The work force can be increased or decreased to meet the product and market demands.
- Fluctuations in demand can also be met by varying the working hours, i.e. under-time or over-time.
- Increasing or decreasing the prices or launching a sales promotional scheme will lead to sudden spurt in demand and sale of the product.
- Pending orders and orders with delayed delivery schedule can be taken up during the lean period.

6.2.4 Techniques for Absorbing Fluctuations in Demand

The major challenge in production planning and control activity is how to handle the fluctuations in demand. We have already discussed the various ways to handle the same. Let us understand a few techniques to handle the fluctuations in demand.

6.2.4.1 Graphic technique

The graphic technique is a simple way of data presentation to a scale. The graphic technique is a simple *static* technique and shows clearly the fluctuations in the production demand. The graphic technique does not generate a solution by itself.

It compares different alternative plans and by itself does not generate an optimum plan. It works as an optimum balance between uniform production per month irrespective of market demand and/or adjusting labour force, subcontracting to outside agencies to match with the fluctuating market demand keeping a bare minimum in plant capacity.

Normally an organization has about 12–15% of its work force deployed for material handling. The material handling work does not require any special training or skill. Whatever bare minimum training is needed, it can be imparted in a day or two. During the peak period all the organization's trained employees are deployed on the workstations and contractor's men are put on the material handling job. During the off peak period, the company's employees are retained and they do the material handling job and the contractor's men are terminated.

The company's own workforce can also plan their annual leaves with the off-peak period. The rainy season is a slack season for most of the industry whereas the workers from the local area need leave during this period to do their farming activities. Both can be synchronized so that need for the workers get balanced with the market demand.

Month	Market demand	Cumulative demand	Average per quarter
April	450	450	
May	500	950	
June	600	1550	517
July	400	1950	
August	450	2400	
September	700	3100	517
October	800	3900	
November	800	4700	
December	700	5400	767
January	820	6220	
February	800	7020	
March	900	7920	840
Average Sales	660		

Let us assume that the average production per worker is 10 units per month. The average inventory carrying cost per unit is Rs. 100. The average monthly sales are 517 units per month for the first six months and 803 units for the next six months with an average monthly sales estimate of 660 units per month for the entire year.

PLAN 1: The Plan 1 will go for an average monthly production of 660 units per month needing 66 workers. Let us review the situation under Plan 1.

Month	Market demand	Production	Inventory
April	450	660	+210
May	500	660	+370
June	600	660	+430
July	400	660	+690
August	450	660	+900
September	700	660	+860
October	800	660	+720
November	800	660	+580
December	700	660	+540
January	820	660	+380
February	800	660	+240
March	900	660	+0
Average sales	660		Total = 5920

The inventory carrying cost will be Rs. 5,92,000 under Plan 1.

PLAN 2: The Plan 2 will go for an average monthly production of 520 units per month needing 52 workers for the first six months and will go for an average monthly production of 800 units per month needing 80 workers for the first six months and let us review the situation under Plan 1.

Month	Market demand	Production	Inventory
April	450	520	+70
May	500	520	+90
June	600	520	+10
July	400	520	+130
August	450	520	+200
September	700	520	+20
October	800	800	+20
November	800	800	+20
December	700	800	+120
January	820	800	+100
February	800	800	+100
March	900	800	+0
Average sales	660		Total = 880

The inventory carrying cost will be Rs. 88,000 under Plan 2. The savings in the inventory carrying cost will be Rs. 5,04,000 under Plan 2, i.e. 85% reduction in the inventory carrying cost. The company has permanent workers as compared to the required 66 in the earlier case. This will lead to the reduction in the permanent liability cost of 14 workers, i.e. 21% reduction. The balance 28 workers can be hired from the labour contractor as discussed earlier for the peak season between October to March next year. This can be further reduced by asking your permanent workers to plan their annual leave during the lean season. Many organizations have their lean season during the monsoon. The workers with agricultural background also need holidays during monsoon season. This can be worked out for mutual benefit (see Figures 6.7 and 6.8).

6.2.4.2 Linear programming method

The linear programming method of balancing the sales estimate with the production and line balancing between various options of workstations, vendors, etc. are a comprehensive scientific method of handling the fluctuation of the demand most effectively. It can be worked out by simple or complex linear programming equation or by the North-West corner method which gives a simplified, easily understandable and effective method of balancing the supply and demand to meet the customer's requirement in time.

Both the simplex and the distribution models can be employed for aggregate planning in which the demands are also specified as aggregated demand. After ascertaining the aggregate level, a model is developed to carry out the plan.

The model considers various requirements like over-time, slackness, inventory, back-orders, and sub-contracting as also the feasibility and economic assessment of loading the

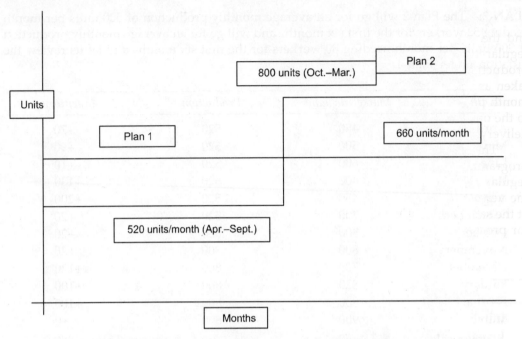

FIGURE 6.7 A descriptive view of graphic technique.

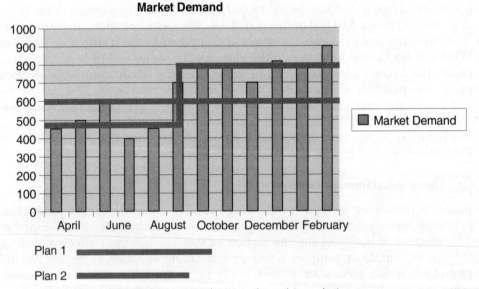

FIGURE 6.8 Actual view of graphic technique.

jobs between the various workstations. The distribution matrix takes into consideration the sales requirements along with the capacities—normal and overtime, individually as well as collectively loading and scheduling the flow pattern of the jobs, scope of sub-contracting, etc.

'X' is taken as the regular time production cost/unit in the workstation 1 as Rs. 100 and the overtime production cost on the workstation 1 is Rs. 115. 'Y' is taken as the regular time production cost/unit in the workstation 2 as Rs. 110 and the overtime production cost on the workstation 2 is Rs. 125. The inventory carrying cost/unit 'c' is taken as Rs. 10 per unit per month and the back order cost/unit is added as Rs. 5 per month per unit. All the costs are added to the matrix as shown. The subcontracting cost to the outside vendor is Rs. 120 in normal course and Rs. 140 in urgency with committed delivery.

The distribution matrix is solved by the North-West corner method of linear programming. The solution matrix will show the number of units to be produced on regular production, in over-time on either of the workstations 1 and/or 2 as well as at the vendor's end and in three different months to minimize the cost of production and at the same time meet the delivery schedule. The top right hand side corner gives the cost for processing in each quadrant.

SALES

	Month 1	Month 2	Month 3	Capacity
Initial	10	20	30	
Inventory	50			50
Workstation 1	100	100	110	
Regular	100	100		200
Production				
Workstation 1		115	125	
Overtime		40		40
Production				
Workstation 2		110	120	
Regular		60	60	120
Production				
Workstation 2		125	125	
Overtime			40	40
Production				
Vendors			120	
			100	100
Demand	150	200	200	550 \ 550

Distribution matrix with capacity, demand and cost values

Total Cost = (50 × 10) + (100 × 100) + (100 × 100) + (40 × 115) + (60 × 110) + (60 × 120) + (40 × 125) + (100 × 120)

= Rs. 60,900

Unit cost = Rs. 60900/550 = Rs. 110.73.

6.2.5 Economic Batch Quantity (EBQ)

The setup time plays a lead role in the manufacturing industry as large amounts of productive time was lost due to change in the components to be machined. Each such change warranted re-setting the machine for the new component. This setting time was a major component of the cost of various manufacturing processes, like machining, forging, casting of ferrous and non-ferrous materials; and rubber and plastic moulding, etc. To set off the machine setting cost and to minimize it, an effort is made to manufacture a large number of components in one batch. The batch quantity which is the most economical to produce is known as *Economic Batch Quantity.*

There are two types of *costs:*

(a) The cost which **increases** with the batch size is normally known as the Inventory Carrying Cost or (ICC). This consists of the cost of the working capital requirement for material and labour, the cost of handling and storage of the material, the insurance and tax charges as well as the interest cost on the capital investment. In the current business environment with intensive international competition, there is a great danger of product obsolescence.

(b) The costs which **decrease** with batch sizes are the cost per unit of setting up machines, the cost of paper work like process sheets, shop orders and cost of production planning and control activity.

Cost (a) and cost (b) are plotted graphically and the total cost curve is drawn by adding these costs.

Economic Batch Quantity (EBQ) is the quantity at which the total cost is minimum and at this point, the cost (a) and cost (b) curves intersect each other (see Figure 6.9). However, this concept of economic batch quantity has become obsolete now due to the reduction in the setting time for machining by deployment of technologies like group

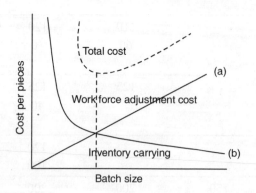

Assume:
Q is economic batch quantity
D is annual requirements
S is preparation and set-up cost, each time a new batch is taken up

FIGURE 6.9   Graphic representation of Economic Batch Quantity.

technology, computer integrated machining technology and techniques like single minute exchange of dies, etc. which made small lot sizes and frequent deliveries possible. Mathematically, EBQ can be determined as follows:

Inventory carrying cost $= I$

Cost per unit $= C$

Average inventory $a = Q/2$

Value of average inventory $= (Q/2) \times C$

Cost of carrying inventory $= (Q/2) \times C \times I = QCI/2$ (a)

No. of set-ups in a year $= D/Q$

Cost of set-ups $= (D/Q) \times S = DS/Q$ (b)

Total Cost $T = a + b = QCI/2 + DS/Q$

For T to be minimum, put $dT/dQ = 0$

$dT/dQ = CI/2 - DS/Q^2 = 0,$

$Q = \sqrt{2DS/CI}$

EXAMPLE 6.1

Find economic batch quantity using the data given below:

Set-up cost = Rs. 20 per set-up. Annual requirement of parts = 1000
Inventory carrying cost = 10% of value, i.e. 1 and cost per part = Rs. 2.

Solution: E.B.Q. $= \sqrt{2DS/CI} = \sqrt{2 \times 1000 \times 20/2 \times 0.1}$

$= 447$ parts.

By rounding off E.B.Q. = 500.

Hence the economic number of batches per year is $1000/500 = 2$.

6.2.6 Process Planning

Process planning can be defined as the preparation of a detailed work plan for the conversion of raw materials into finished product through successive stages of conversion as per the manufacturing technology and the flow process chart.

After deciding which product to manufacture, the process of manufacturing as well as the technology is ascertained. The process of manufacturing and sequence of stages of conversion, including the arrangement of resources and their optimum utilization have to be planned.

Process planning develops a broad plan of manufacturing for the components or the number of components needed to assemble a product. This is developed based on input drawings and specifications and the number of products to be produced is determined on the basis of sales forecast.

Process planning is determining the most economical method of performing an operation or activity. Process planning involves not only arrangement of men, machines and material but also making the provision of correct manufacturing aids, cutting tools for machining, dies and moulds and spares, as well as their most economical and optimum usage. Process planning has to take into purview the customer's concept and perception about the quality and quantity of requirements of the finished goods.

Information required to do process planning

- Details of product specification
- Quality of work to be completed
- Quantity of work to be done
- Availability of tools, equipments, and personnel at proper time and proper place
- Sequence in which operations will be performed on the input raw material
- Standard time for each operation
- When and in what sequence the operations will be performed

6.2.6.1   Process planning procedure

Selection of process: A process is necessary to shape, form, condition, and/or join materials and components with the help of machines and labour in order to convert raw materials into finished product. The objective is to select the most economical process and sequence that satisfies the product specifications. Selection of the process depends on:

- Current production commitments
- Delivery date
- Quantity to be produced
- Quality standards

Selection of material: Materials should be of right quality and right chemical composition to suit the specification. The shape and size of the material should restrict the scrap and save the conversion/machining time.

Selection of jigs, fixtures and other special attachments: These supporting devices not only reduce the cost of production per piece but also increase the productivity and the rate of the production.

Selection of cutting tools and inspection gauges: A proper selection of cutting tools and inspection gauges leads to reduction in production time and allows efficient inspection.

Make the **process layout** indicating each operation and the sequence in which each operation is required to be performed.

Find out and fix up the **set-up time** and **standard time** for each operation.

Manifest process planning by documents such as operation and route sheets which summarize the operations required, the preferred sequence of operations, auxiliary tools required, estimated operation time etc.

6.3   SCHEDULING

Scheduling is defined as the time phase of loading which decides the duration of time for a certain defined work, as well as the sequence in which the work will be done.

Scheduling decides when the work will start and the duration of completion of the work as well as the sequence of doing the work and activities. Scheduling may be called the time phase of loading. Loading means the work or the task allocation to a facility whereas scheduling specifies the time and sequence of taking up the work or the task for completion. The production planning, control and scheduling department prepares the production schedule which is a statement of target date for all the orders and operations to be performed with their starting and finishing dates.

6.3.1 Objectives of Scheduling

There are five distinct objectives of scheduling as detailed below:

Knowing the current job status: The total job contents as well as the status of the current job and its positioning should be known to the production planning, control and scheduling department. This helps in guiding the operations to be performed systematically. This also helps in arranging the resources, men, machines and material of the right quantity at the right time and the right place. The production planning, control and scheduling department should be aware of the production target, what are the jobs that are under process and they are at what state and located where.

Guiding future job operation: The production planning, control and scheduling department guides the future job operation in a synchronized manner looking at the final objective so that there is optimum use of resources and the end objective is achieved in time. The department ensures that there is no piling of inventory, no bottlenecks and ensures smooth flow of materials through the entire process of conversion to the final finished product. The department should determine what job should be the next and on which workstation across the entire plant.

Ensuring the adequacy of material and capacity: The production planning, control and scheduling department ensures that there is adequate material available at all the workstations and assembly lines as per schedule to ensure continuity (no stoppage) of production. On the other hand, the department also has to ensure that there is adequate capacity available on the machining canters as per the production plan. The department should also ensure that there is adequate capacity and tools available to work on them.

Maximizing operational efficiency: The department ensures maximum operational efficiency in terms of minimizing the input resources of raw material, men and manufacturing aids by reducing their wastages and optimum use. On the other hand, production planning, control and scheduling activities should ensure that the end objective of customer satisfaction and maximizing the return on investment are achieved in time as per schedule. The department should maximize the labour and machine utilization and minimize inventory, set-up cost and other overheads while meeting the market schedule and service objectives.

Maintaining operational control: Finally, the department should maintain operational control over the entire activities of production planning, control and scheduling right from sales forecasting or demand measurement to the process of deciding the best alternative for the achievement of the end objective in time as well as arrangement of the resources and ultimately ensure that all deviations are detected in time and corrected so that the end objective is achieved as per plan. In short, the production planning, control and scheduling department should monitor the job status and lead times, measure progress and signal corrective actions when necessary.

6.3.2 Types of Scheduling

There are **two types** of scheduling. The conventional method of scheduling is forward scheduling. The current trend in world-class manufacturing system is to schedule as per the customer's requirement or the market need. This is known as backward scheduling.

Forward scheduling: Forward Scheduling starts with a known start date and precedes from the first operation to the last operation to determine the completion date of the final product. This concept tries to make maximum use of the plant capacity by mass producing the products at the least cost of production. However, this concept of forward scheduling has lost its importance to the production planning, control and scheduling department due to frequent change in the product design and shorter product life cycle. This market trend creates a grave danger to mass produced products which may become obsolete.

Backward scheduling: Backward scheduling starts with a given due date and works backwards to determine the required start date and ensure the finished product is completed on the given due date. The norm of production planning, control and scheduling department in the current global customer-oriented business environment is manufacture only after demand measurement, i.e. manufacture only that much as the customer wants. This is precisely what backward scheduling is all about.

6.3.3 Factors Affecting Scheduling

There are multiple factors affecting the scheduling and they are broadly classified into external factors and internal factors.

External factors: The external factors of scheduling are basically concerned with the customers' demand, customers' committed delivery dates and the stock of goods with the dealers and depots/branch offices. The main external factor of scheduling is accuracy in measuring the customers' demand in terms of product-mix, product range and product features and making the products and services accordingly. For the standard product, the customer may not agree to wait. Hence, assured delivery dates and availability of previous stock of the products are important for the organization's market share and salability of the products to the customers.

Internal factors: The internal factors of scheduling are manyfold. The production planning, control and scheduling department must consider internal factors like the finished goods inventory, the processing time of converting the raw material and components into finished products. The department should also consider the availability of the right type material in adequate quantity as required, the trained and skilled manpower suitable for carrying out the machine operation and assignment to the desired level of accuracy and performance. The production planning, control and scheduling activity should ensure the availability of equipments, tools, manufacturing aids and machines with their total capacity and specifications. All these activities have to take place economically and with provision of additional facility as and when required.

6.3.4   Scheduling and Loading Guidelines

The scheduling department follows certain guidelines for loading and scheduling so that the customer orders are completed as per the schedule. The department normally does an FSN analysis. The FSN analysis consists of classifying the products into fast moving items, normal moving items and slow moving items. Normally 80% of the plant capacity is planned against customer orders. The balance 20% is filled with fast moving items so that if the men, machines and materials are available, there should not be any production loss and these items can be taken up for manufacturing. Since the items are fast-moving, they can be sold easily in the market. Apart from the above considerations, the scheduling department works with the following guidelines.

- Provide a realistic achievable schedule
- Conduct time and motion study and allow adequate time for operations, before, after and between operations
- Arrange availability of men, machine and material
- Do not release all available jobs to the shop at a time
- Do not schedule all available capacity on the shopfloor with customer orders
- Load only selected loading centres
- Allow for necessary changes
- Get the acceptance of the schedule by the shopfloor
- Decide on control points and ensure periodic monitoring

6.3.5   Scheduling Methodology

The scheduling methodology is specific to the type of industry, the type of organization, its plant capacity and machine availability, the product range, the type of manufacturing technology and the extent of automation desired. There are three types of scheduling methodology as given below:

1. Gantt charts
2. Priority decision rules
3. Mathematically programming methods

6.3.5.1   Gantt charts

The Gantt chart consists of time-scale on the X-axis and activities on the Y-axis. The X-axis shows the dates when the activities start and the dates on which they finish. The Y-axis lists the number of activities. The Gantt chart reveals the planning, loading and scheduling decisions graphically (see Figure 6.10). The chart quickly gives information on

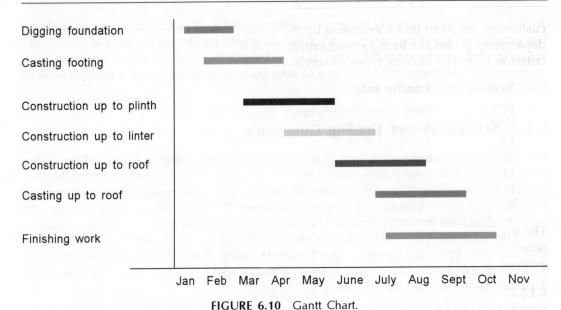

FIGURE 6.10 Gantt Chart.

the current planning and performance as well as the status of their completion. The three types of Gantt charts are as follows:

- *Scheduling or progress chart*: The scheduling or the progress chart depicts the sequential schedule.
- *Load charts:* The load charts assigns work to the group of machines and workers.
- *Record charts:* The record charts record the actual operating times and performance of the workers and machines.

The Gantt chart is a popular method of depicting the working of an organization for routine production for executing individual orders as per the customers' requirement. The Gantt chart is also a powerful tool for planning and scheduling for project execution in network analysis, including PERT and CPM. The chart with milestones shows the inter-relation between various activities as well as the sequence of operations and their interdependence for speedy execution of the laid out plan.

6.3.5.2 Priority decision rules

The priority decision rules are simplified guidelines for determining the sequence in which the job will be done. There could be more than one criterion for prioritizing the sequence of executing the customer orders. The priority decision rules include simulations and sensitivity analysis to analyze the effects of processing time, labour utilization, inventory and other costs.

6.3.5.2.1 Single criterion rule: The production planning, control and scheduling department uses the single criterion for giving priority to the execution of a particular order of a particular customer. The sequence in which the pending orders, placed by the customers, are taken up for execution by the production planning, control and scheduling department is decided by a focused criterion declared by the organization as the single criterion rule. The various types of single criterion are detailed below:

Symbol	Priority rule
FCFS	First Come First Served
EDD	Earliest Due Date
LS	Least Slack
SPT	Shortest Processing Time
LPT	Longest Processing Time
PCO	Preferred Customer Order
RS	Random Selection

The single criterion rule is extremely popular with the production planning, control and scheduling department as it is simple and easy to implement, easily understandable and achievable.

6.3.5.2.2 Johnson's rule: The Johnson's rule is a simple rule which yields minimum processing time for sequencing the jobs on machines or on the work centres. The Johnson's rule is a useful tool to the production planning, control and scheduling department to ensure minimum machine or workstation idle time, as well as the fastest method of job processing. The following example is a simple case where the Johnson's rule is applied by the scheduling department. The job is moulding various types of pots and baking the same in the oven. The table below gives five different types of pots, with different times for moulding and baking, to be scheduled to achieve the maximum plant utilization.

Johnson's Rule

Time Required

Work Centres	A	B	C	D	E
• Molding	4	4	6	9	5
• Baking	2	8	3	5	10

The sequence is B-E-D-A-C to ensure that there is minimum idle time for both the work centres and the starting of the work centres should be phased out so that they work to maximum efficiency. The B pot and E pot are taken first since they take minimum time

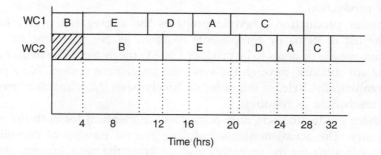

for the first operation and maximum time for the second so that the time utilization can be optimized with no idle time.

6.3.5.3 Mathematical programming methods

The production planning, control and scheduling department may adopt the mathematical programming method. The mathematical programming method mainly involves the linear programming—simple transportation methods or the linear programming—assignment model.

    This methodology of planning and scheduling is already explained in the North-west corner method under the section of production planning in this chapter. The graphical technique is also explained in detail in the same section.

6.3.6 Master Production Schedule (MPS)

A product is the final assembly of individual parts and components in the subsequent stages of value addition by conversion either by way of machining, fabrication as explained at the beginning of this chapter or by assembly. The final product can be used by the end-user for its intended use. This is the level zero. We break the product into sub-assemblies, sub-assemblies into individual parts and components till the parts or raw material is sourced from outside. This process is known as the **Explosion** of the product into individual components and raw materials at various levels of zero, one, two, etc. These levels show the entry point of the part or the components and after entry how many times it will undergo conversion to be part of the final assembly. After this process, the parts are grouped together depending upon the similarities in the process of manufacturing. This is known as formation of *groups by segregation*. The final process is adding up all the identical parts in the same group together known as *aggregation*. This process of grouping the parts and components into groups of similar process of manufacturing is known as the process of *explosion, segregation and aggregation*.

    This list of items that has to be either procured from outside or produced in-house is known as the master production schedule. The scheduling normally starts with a master production schedule. It translates the aggregate plans into the specific-end items. The master production schedule formalizes the production plan and converts it into specific material and capacity requirement. The master production schedule evaluates alternative schedules and selects the best one which maintains the customer's valid priorities, along with effectively utilizing the capacity in terms of men, machines and materials with the least cost of production.

    The master production schedule prepares the aggregated production plan and separates the list of items or components required as per the same into items to be procured from outside or items to be produced inside the factory. The items to be procured from outside are obtained through the vendor management system. Now plan and load the facility realistically. Release the order on timely basis. Now monitor inventory levels closely and reschedule as required.

    The master production schedule principles are identical for both the assembly and process industry. The actual master scheduling process consists of consolidating gross requirements adjusting for the inventory and lot sizing the net requirement into planned orders of either purchase order or the work order in a time-phased schedule.

The production planning, control and scheduling is the most important element of an organization which helps in controlling the inventory as well as making the products available at the right time in right quantity at the right time and at the right place. The input of the entire activity is accurate demand forecasting on whose accuracy depends the accuracy of the entire process of production planning, control and scheduling. One of the most effective ways of increasing the accuracy of the demand measurement and effectiveness of production planning, control and scheduling activity is to reduce the lead time between demand measurement and making the product available at the market place as per ATP or available to promise. The lesser the time for the demand fulfillment by the reduction of the manufacturing cycle, the more accurate is the production planning, control and scheduling in an organization. The other factors which are important consideration of an effective production planning, control and scheduling system are the method study, motion study and time study to ensure the optimized and best way of production planning, control and scheduling of the machines, along with the right choice of machineries and technology required for manufacturing.

EXERCISES

1. Explain the steps in detail to arrive at the accurate demand forecasting for an industry and what are the factors which will influence the demand in the market?

2. Explain the relationship between accurate demand, measurement and accurate production planning and control.

3. Define 'production planning and control' and explain the procedure for the same in detail.

4. How will you do the 'production planning and control' for (a) a CTV industry, (b) an automobile component industry (c) a textile industry, (d) a computer software development industry.

5. Elaborate the 'strategies and techniques' to absorb the fluctuations in demand.

6. Explain with an example both the 'graphic technique' and the 'linear programming method' for the same.

7. An organization's sales figure is given below for the entire year.

Month	Market demand
April	5000
May	5500
June	6500
July	5500
August	7000
September	6000
October	7000
November	8000

December	9000
January	8000
February	9000
March	10500

Indicate the average market demand per month for the entire year, for each quarter and each half of the year. How does this figure help you to arrive at the optimum level of planning per month?

Let us assume that the average production per worker is 50 units per month. The average inventory carrying cost per unit is Rs. 100.

Please compare the two plans. One with an average production capacity per month for the entire year and the other with two types of average production per month continuously for the first six months and another average production figure per month continuously for the next six months.

8. Explain the concept of the **Economic Batch Quantity**.

9. Find economic batch quantity using data given below:

    Set-up cost = Rs. 50 per set-up. Annual requirement of parts = 10,000, inventory carrying cost = 10% of value, i.e. 1 and cost per part = Rs. 5.

10. Explain in detail 'process planning'.

11. Define 'scheduling' its objectives, factors, guidelines, methodology and scheduling procedure.

12. Explain the process of 'master production scheduling' in detail.

7

Productivity Improvement Techniques

7.1 DEFINITION AND CONCEPT OF PRODUCTIVITY

World-class companies create "surplus" through productive operations, i.e. the output is always more than the input of resources.

Productivity is defined as "the ratio of output to input within a defined time period with due consideration for quality."

$$\text{Productivity} = \frac{\text{Output (within a defined time and good quality)}}{\text{Input}}$$

This formula can be elaborated as:

- Both the output and input should be quantified into measurable monetary terms for a correct assessment.
- Productivity can be improved by
  - Increasing output with the same input
  - Increasing output more than the increase in input
  - Decreasing input for the same output
  - Increasing output with decreasing input
- Productivity implies effectiveness and efficiency in individual and organizational performance. Here *effectiveness* means the achievement of the set individual and the organizational target or the objective whereas *efficiency* is the output—input ratio or the value addition to input resources minus the cost of value addition, i.e. surplus generated by a process or an organization as a whole.
- Managers should clearly know their goals and those of the organization to ascertain whether they are productive or not. It is therefore important for the organization to declare its mission, vision and annual objectives to chart out a clear unambiguous path without any confusion in the organization.

We are giving below a few more definition of productivity.

As per 'International Labour Organization', *productivity* is the ratio between *output* of *wealth* to the *input* of *resources* used in the process of manufacturing.

$$\text{Productivity} = \frac{\text{Output of wealth}}{\text{Input of resources}}$$

The input resouces are normally land, material, machine and men.

As per the Organization of European Economic Co-operation (OEEC) in 1950 currently known as the European Union or the EU, productivity is the quotient obtained by dividing output by one of the factors of production. It could be men, material, machines, etc. This is typically the definition of partial productivity.

As per Davis (1955), productivity is defined as the change in product obtained for the resources expanded.

Kendrick and Creamer (1965) gave a functional definition of partial, total factor and total productivity.

7.1.1 Productivity and Performance

$$\text{Performance} = \frac{\text{Actual achievement in terms of efffective work done}}{\text{Standard target of achievement}} \times 100$$

Performance is expressed as performance index which is the percentage of standard target. This is, in other words, the effectiveness of the productivity.

$$\text{Productivity Index} = \frac{\text{Output}}{\text{Input}} = \frac{\text{Performance achieved}}{\text{Resources consumed}}$$

$$= \frac{\text{f(effectiveness)}}{\text{F(efficiency)}}$$

whereas the production is the quantum of output with utility.

7.1.2 Partial Productivity

Partial productivity can be defined as the ratio of *output* to any one class of input, i.e. either material or capital or labour or energy, etc.

e.g. $$\text{Labour productivity} = \frac{\text{Output}}{\text{Labour hours}}$$

The partial productivity figure gives a measure of the impact of any one type of the input on the overall productivity of the organization. This can be measured of course by keeping the other factors of the inputs constant. This partial productivity figure also helps an organization to determine the relative importance of any type of input resources as compared to the others.

Advantages:
- Easy to understand the effect of individual factors of input on output
- Easy to obtain and analyse the data
- Easy to compute the indices
- It is a diagnostic tool to find areas of productivity improvement.

Disadvantages:
- It is overstresses one factor of production ignoring the others.
- If used alone, it may lead to costly mistakes.
- It cannot explain overall cost increase.
- In this methodology, profit control is not precise.
- In this system, there is a tendency to shift the blame to other areas.

7.1.3 Total Factor Productivity

Total factor productivity can be defined as the ratio of net output to the sum of associated labour and capital (factor) inputs.

Here the Net Output = Total Output – Intermediate Goods or Services purchased.

The intermediate goods and services outsourced include the raw material and components, money, energy, fuel for boiler/generator, expenses, fees for consultants, etc. Only the labour expense is considered to be the organization's own cost. This is an important index to compare the productivity between two similar organizations. An export trade house or a marketing organization with five employees may have Rs 10 million turnover. But for a manufacturing industry to have Rs 10 million turnover will need many employees probably in number more than 100 employees. The total factor productivity is the right index to compare the productivity of these two organizations on equal footing when the same is measured in terms of value addition.

Advantages:
- The data is easy to obtain.
- It gives bird's eye-view of the overall performance vis-à-vis labour and capital.
- It is a powerful tool for labour negotiation.
- It makes the productivity comparison between the two organizations from different sectors possible.
- It is an effective tool for measurement of the value addition to the input by the organization.

Disadvantages:
- It does not consider the impact of material, machine and energy inputs as material alone constitutes 50–60% of cost of production.

7.1.4 Total Productivity

Total productivity is defined as the ratio of total output to the sum of all input factors, i.e. it gives the combined impact of all the inputs in producing the output.

$$\text{Total productivity} = \frac{\text{Measured period output in base period price}}{\text{Measured period input in base period price}}$$

The total productivity index gives the absolute measurement between the output and the input. All the outputs and the inputs are converted into rupee value terms. The ratio therefore gives the overall productivity measurement. The total productivity between two different years or periods can only be measured when we take the common cost of inputs and selling price between the two periods.

The partial productivity figures can also be assessed from the total productivity figures by conducting sensitivity analysis. The relative importance of various input resources on the output can also be assessed by the same methodology.

Advantages:
- All quantifiable inputs are considered.
- Profit control is better and easier.
- It gives total productivity index.
- Sensitivity analysis can be done.
- It gives the overall picture to the top management.
- The data is easy to collect and the figure can be computed easily.

Disadvantages:
- It does not consider intangible factors of output and input.
- It is difficult to generalize all factors of input.

Productivity gain is net output minus the total factor input.

EXAMPLE 7.1

The output of the firm XYZ is Rs. 10,00,000. The labour cost for the above output is Rs. 2,00,000. The raw material purchased is worth Rs. 5,00,000, The capital cost is Rs. 1,20,000, The energy consumed is worth Rs. 50,000 and the other expenses are Rs. 30,000. Calculate the partial productivity for each of the factors, the total factor productivity, and the total productivity.

Solution:

(1) Partial productivity

$$\text{Human productivity} = \frac{\text{Output}}{\text{Labour cost}} = \frac{\text{Rs. } 10,00,000}{\text{Rs. } 2,00,000} = 5.00$$

$$\text{Material productivity} = \frac{\text{Output}}{\text{Material cost}} = \frac{\text{Rs. } 10,00,000}{\text{Rs. } 5,00,000} = 2.00$$

$$\text{Capital productivity} = \frac{\text{Output}}{\text{Capital cost}} = \frac{\text{Rs. } 10,00,000}{\text{Rs. } 1,20,000} = 8.33$$

$$\text{Energy productivity} = \frac{\text{Output}}{\text{Energy consumed}} = \frac{\text{Rs. } 10,00,000}{\text{Rs. } 50,000} = 20.00$$

$$\text{Other expenses productivity} = \frac{\text{Output}}{\text{Other expenses}} = \frac{\text{Rs. } 10,00,000}{\text{Rs. } 30,000} = 33.33$$

(2) $\text{Total factor productivity} = \dfrac{\text{Net output}}{(\text{Capital} + \text{Labour input})}$

$$= \frac{10,00,000 - (5,00,000 + 1,20,000 + 50,000 + 30,000)}{2,00,000 + 1,20,000} = 0.9375$$

(3) $\text{Total productivity} = \dfrac{\text{Total output}}{\text{Total input}} = \dfrac{\text{Rs. } 10,00,000}{\text{Rs. } 9,00,000} = 1.111$

Total Input = Labour + Material + Capital + Energy + Other Expenses

7.1.5 Applications of Productivity Technique

The productivity technique concepts can be applied to all the functional areas without exception. The concepts have universal application irrespective of the type of organization, i.e. for both the manufacturing and service sectors as well as to all functional areas in an organization. The concepts are vital to the success and survival of any organization in today's highly competitive global business environment. The measurement of productivity is not enough for an organization to survive. The continuous improvement in productivity in all the functional areas of an organization at a revolutionary rate, i.e. at a rate faster than its competitors, is a decisive business factor for the survival and success of an organization. We can now enumerate the various key parameters in each functional area for measurement of productivity and its continuous improvement.

- Management:
  - Management Information Service
  - Supply Chain Management
  - Enterprise Resource Planning
- Marketing:
  - Accuracy of Demand Forecasting
  - Competitor's Comparative Analysis in Terms of Value
  - Leadership and Cost Leadership
  - Effectiveness of Strategic Action Plan
  - Logistic Management
  - Servicing speed and Effectiveness
  - Most beneficial Product Mix
- Production:
  - Operation Research
  - Methods Study
  - Statistical Process Control
  - Plant Layout
  - Material Handling
  - Inventory Control
  - Just-In-Time-Production

- ■ Materials:
  - • Work Measurement
  - • Motion Study
  - • Production Planning and Control
  - • Just-In-Time Purchasing
  - • Materials Management and Control
  - • Material Requirement Planning
  - • Inventory Models
- ■ Personnel:
  - • Training
  - • Ergonomics
  - • Safety
  - • Management by objective
  - • Job Evaluation and Job Enrichment

7.1.6 The American Productivity Centre Model

This model derives an equation of profitability with productivity and price recovery factors (see Figure 7.1).

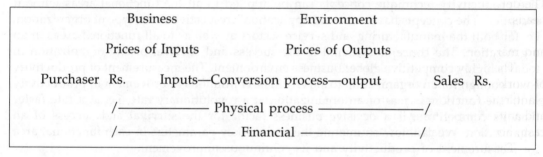

FIGURE 7.1 American Productivity center model.

$$\text{Profitability} = \frac{\text{Sales}}{\text{Cost}} = \frac{\text{Output Qty.} \times \text{Prices}}{\text{Input Qty.} \times \text{Unit cost}} = \frac{\text{Output Quantities}}{\text{Input Quantities}} \times \frac{\text{Prices}}{\text{Unit cost}}$$

$$= \text{Productivity} \times \text{Price Recovery Factor}$$

The price recovery factor indicates the inflationary effect and productivity gives the amount of resources consumed to produce the defined organizational output. In this American Productivity center model, the quantities of output and input are multiplied by the base year prices to have the comparison on equal footing. This gives an indication of the productivity performance index.

The prices and unit cost during each year are multiplied by the current year quantities to give the price recovery performance index.

Unit costs of labour, material and energy do not need any adjustments, but the capital input for any particular period is the sum of depreciation for that period and the product of return on investment in the base year period and current assets employed.

Capital input = Depreciation + (Return on assets in base period) × Current assets

7.2 TOTAL PRODUCTIVITY MODEL (TPM)

This Total productivity Model is developed by Sumanth. This is based on the total productivity measures. This total productivity model can be applied to any manufacturing company or any service organization with equal effectiveness.

$$\text{Total productivity} = \frac{\text{Total tangible output}}{\text{Total tangible input}}$$

Total tangible output = Value of finished units produced for sale as well as for internal use + Value of partial units produced for sale as well as for internal use + Dividends from securities + Interest from bonds + Other incomes

Total tangible input = Value of human input + Raw materials and bought out components + Cost of capital + Cost of energy + Other expenses

The details of the various inputs as given above are explained under the respective sub-heads.

The value of *human input* is the wages paid to the workers, salaries paid to the staff and managers and the consultancy fees paid to the professionals and bureaucrats.

The cost of *capital* is divided into two types. The cost of fixed capital and the cost of working capital. The *fixed component* of cost consists of the cost of investment on land, plant, machinery, tools, equipments, jigs and fixtures, amortized research and development and any other expenses. The *working capital* investment consists of investments in inventory, cash, accounts receivables and money receivables.

The *material cost* consists of the cost of raw material, purchased parts and consumables.

The *energy cost* comprises the cost of oil, gas, coal, water and the electricity.

The *other expenses* include the cost of travelling, taxes, fees, sale and distribution cost, information processing, research and development, administrative and general expenses.

Let us apply the theoretical principles of the total productive model into developing the mathematical models which can be conveniently used for getting more precise and quantitative evaluation of a particular firm's productivity performance. Total productivity model helps an organization to mathematically compute the productivity figure at the individual product level, operational unit level as well as at the overall organizational level.

$$\text{TPF} = \text{Total Productivity of a Firm}$$

$$= \frac{\text{Total output of the firm}}{\text{Total input of the firm}} = \frac{OF_t}{IF_t} = \frac{O_{it}}{I_{it}}$$

$$= \frac{\text{Total sum of output of individual products}}{\text{Total sum of input of individual products}}$$

$$\text{TPP} = \text{Total productivity of a product} = \frac{\text{Total output of product i}}{\text{Total input of product i}}$$

$$\text{Ppij} = \frac{\text{Oi}}{\text{Iij}} = \frac{\text{Oi}}{\text{IiH} + \text{IiM} + \text{IiC} + \text{IiE} + \text{IiX}}$$

Ppij = Partial productivity of Product i with respect to the input factor 'j'.

j = H, M, C, E, X
F = The figures at the firm level
O = Total output
I = Total input
T = Considered time period
I = Individual products
J = Individual inputs for each product (H, M, CEX)
H = Human input and cost of all employees
M = Raw materials and bought out components
C = Cost of the capital
E = Energy input including electricity, furnace oil, gas, etc.
X = Other expenses include taxes, travelling, administration, etc.
I = Number of products 1, 2, 3, ..., N.
N = Total number of products manufactured in the considered time period.

Total productivity index for a firm in period t is TPIF(t) where '0' is the base period or the reference year or month and t is the current period or year or the month's productivity measure,

$$\text{TPIF}(t) = \frac{\text{TPFt}}{\text{TPFo}}$$

Similarly the total productivity index for a period 't' for the product 'I'

$$\text{TPIit} = \frac{\text{TPit}}{\text{TPio}}$$

7.2.1 Salient Features of TPM

In Sumanth's total productivity model, the term operational unit is used to refer in general to the product or the service. The product unit can be a service unit like a student's education in an educational institution, patient care in a hospital, the transactions in a bank, etc. The salient features of the total productivity model are as follows:

- TPM gives both the productivity index at the aggregated organizational level as well as at the detailed operational unit level.
- TPM also gives the individual productivity indices for individual products.

- TPM indicates the profitability of individual operational unit as well as the overall organization, thereby giving an indication as to which unit's operation to continue and all its future investment decisions. At the same time, it clearly indicates which units are a liability and when to get out of these units.
- TPM determines the profitability of individual products and the correct product mix to optimize the profit as well as the optimum utilization of resources.
- TPM provides important and vital information for strategic planning.
- TPM shows which particular input resources are utilized inefficiently in a particular area or for a particular product so that its efficient and effective use can be ensured.
- TPM integrates the entire work of planning, execution, evaluation and improvement phases in the productivity cycle of an organization.
- TPM has developed individual and collective mathematical models for the productivity indices calculation. This makes the model validation and sensitivity analysis relatively easier and precise.

7.2.2 Causes of Poor Productivity

The major causes of poor productivity as well as productivity decline in an organization are to be found out on a regular basis and corrective and preventive steps should be taken for the eradication of the same. The reasons can be enumerated as follows:

Lack of productivity measures: The absence of a system to measure the productivity of all the employees in an organization, particularly the white-collared managers and supervisors, will create a group of non-productive and more often negative employees who are detrimental to organizational progress.

Faulty appraisal system: The appraisal system in an organization should be linked to the productivity measures. Rewards and benefits should be linked to performance. The best way to do it is by introducing employee-wise and function-wise implementation of 'Management by Objective (MBO)' and the identification of the Key Result Areas (KRAs) with quantified measurement of performance.

Complex organization: The Japanese management system has propagated the 'Lean Organization' for productivity improvement in an organization. A complex organization will always have some employees who will not have adequate work allocated to them, leading to idle hours and lower productivity.

Low employee involvement: If the employees are not involved in their own work as well as that of the organizational goals and their achievements, the organizational productivity will be extremely low. The productivity can be increased by involving workers in decision-making and continuous improvement activities like 'Kaizen Gemba', 'Quality Circle', etc.

Organizational expansion: As the organization keeps on growing, the new employees, new machines and new technology keep on entering the organization continuously. All these have to be learned, absorbed and implemented by the existing as well as new workers. This is an extremely difficult proposition and warrants the highest level of management skills to handle the situation or else it leads to big mess and confusion, bringing down the organization steadily to its end. Hence organizational expansions have to be planned and managed properly to ensure the consistency in performance.

Improper production planning: An efficient production planning and control system results in a highly productive manufacturing or service organization. The well-designed route cards, proper tools, jigs and fixtures, and other manufacturing aids, all contribute to the increase of productivity of the organization by an efficient manufacturing system with no idle men or machine time or piling up of inventories.

Human conflicts: The unresolved human conflicts and the inter-departmental politics play a negative role in the productive operation of the organization. The constructive positive effort of one department is negated by the other opposing group or individual resulting in net zero output. A productive organization will have no conflict among its work force and each one complementing and supplementing each other producing an extremely productive system of 1 and 1 forming 11 (synergic effect).

Lack of training and education: The current dynamic business environment with global competition, information technology revolution, frequent upgradation of products and processes puts a constant pressure on the existing work force to get themselves elevated to a higher level of performance. This challenge of the new industrial environment can only be met by education and training to the existing work force to enable them to learn and master the new technology, new processes and their operations resulting in improvement of productivity.

Legislative instructions: An organization should not have such a rigid working system that makes the operators to be more concerned about the maintenance of the system than the end result. The legislative instructions should be bare minimum and the operator should be given more autonomy to deliver the end result of higher productivity in terms of both quality, quantity and adherence to time schedule.

Technological changes: The buyers market and intense international competition have shortened the product life cycle, bringing in frequent product innovations, product modifications and emergence of the substitute products. The order of the day for world-class organizations is the practice of the world-class manufacturing system comprising the practice of the demand technology cycle. The frequently changing product designs require realignment and adjustment of the entire manufacturing set-up, including the changes in process, machines, training to workers, etc. All these factors reduce productivity substantially till the new system settles down.

Specialized processes: Specialized processes always slow down production and are detrimental to higher productivity. Specialized processes should be reduced to as minimum as possible. The more the standardization of the product, process and manpower, the more will be the increase in the productivity and efficiency.

Lack of latest information: The lack of latest information pertaining to the process, product and technology and the method of conversion of raw material into finished product leads to a slower and non-productive working system. The manufacturing system should undergo continuous improvement to remain competitive in the market place.

Idle time: All the idle time relating to men, machines, workstations and material have to be minimized to improve productivity. Idle time in any form is contradictory to the productivity improvement efforts.

The above factors are detrimental to productive operation. The enhancement of productivity is mandatory to survive and succeed in today's contemporary competitive business environment.

7.2.3 Sumanth's Five-Pronged Approach to Productivity Improvement

Sumanth has proposed a five-pronged approach to productivity improvement for an organization, irrespective of the fact whether it is in the manufacturing sector or in the service sector. The five productivity improvement techniques are detailed below. The points have been further modified keeping in mind the latest trends and contemporary knowledge on the subject.

7.2.3.1 Technology-based productivity improvement techniques

Technology-based productivity improvement technique brings about improvement in productivity by application of new scientific techniques for handling specific technical problems. The focus of the technological productivity improvement techniques are bringing in innovation in the technology of production and processing. The various techniques in this area are elaborated below:

CAD: The Computer Aided Design of products, processes or systems with speedy evaluation of best alternatives, resources optimization, error reduction, etc.

CAM: The Computer Aided Manufacturing involving CNC machine and Program Logical Controller (PLC), etc.

CIM: The Computer Integrated design and Manufacturing system with CAD and CAM integrated together. CIM reduces the set-up time as well as increases the accuracy and productivity of the machined components substantially.

Robotics: Robotics is that branch of technology which involves the design of reprogrammable multifunctional manipulators for material handling, welding, assembly, etc.

Laser technology: Laser technology is used for welding, cutting, for highly accurate measurement, etc. The use of laser technology is fast, accurate but costly.

Group technology: Group technology involves the organization, planning and production of parts and components in groups having similarity in size, shape, nature of operation, tolerance, etc. for better efficiency and optimization of resources. It is a form of modern-day plant layout.

Energy Conservation Technology (ECT): The energy conservation technology is a process of energy management through analysis and optimization of resources and preservation of energy as well as keeping the cost bare minimum.

Flexible Manufacturing System (FMS): The manufacturing system is designed in such a manner that it can take care of design change, optimum efficiency of manufacturing, customers' urgent orders, etc. This is basically a manufacturing system capable of taking up small lot sizes for production and frequent deliveries.

Water jet machining technology: This technology for machining components or parts using high speed water jet which machines the components as well as acts as a coolant during the machining.

7.2.3.2 Material-based productivity techniques

The material-based productivity improvement technique focuses on reduction in material wastages as well as inventory. At the same time, the material-based productivity improvement technique has to ensure that there is no material shortage or material pile up at all stages of material conversion from raw material to work-in-process to the finished goods store. The following are the material-based productivity improvement techniques.

7.2.3.2.1 Inventory control: The control of raw material, work-in-process, finished goods as per various inventory control models like ABC, HML, FSN, GOLF VED, etc.

7.2.3.2.2 Supply chain management

MRP–I: It involves the **Material Requirement Planning** and material management including procurement of raw material and bought out components from vendors and suppliers' end to the raw material stores so that they are of the right quality and right quantity and are available at the right place and right time, at the right cost. The activity includes vendor selection, purchasing decisions, demand assessment and arranging of the raw material and bought out components as stated above.

MRP-II: MRP-II involves the Manufacturing Resource Planning focusing on the conversion of raw materials and bought out components to finished products with the highest level of productivity, minimum time and optimum consumption of resources. The process includes capacity requirement planning, loading of workstations, assembly into final product, testing the same and dispatching to the finished goods store.

DRP: Distribution Requirement Planning or DRP is the inventory and distribution management system from the finished goods store to the end-consumer through distribution channel so that the products of right quality and right quantity are available at the right place, the right time and at the least cost leading to customer satisfaction and market leadership.

Logistics management: Logistics management is a support activity for the efficiency and effectiveness of the supply chain management. Logistics management ensures the timely and efficient flow of raw material, finished products and information through the entire supply chain. The logistics management activity involves information management, transportation management, warehousing management and material handling management during the entire supply chain management.

Quality assurance and control: The quality of the material is to be assured in terms of right quality and no field rejections. Quality control helps to reduce or eliminate material wastage, rejection or rework.

Material handling: Material handling is a non-value added activity. Hence it should be minimized by continuous improvement and, as far as possible, material handling should be automated and optimized. The material handling cost should be the least. Material handling should be automated, fast and minimum to increase the material handling productivity to the maximum level.

Material recycling: Material recycling productivity can be improved by fast and economical scrap and waste disposal after affluent treatment of the harmful ingredients of the wastages. Material rejection should be minimized by rectification, regarding and above all future minimization of the rejection by taking corrective and preventive actions. The reverse logistics of reusing the packing material of the products again can be looked into to reduce cost and increase material productivity.

Just-In-Time manufacturing and purchasing: The Just-In-Time manufacturing and the Just-in-Time purchasing system are part of the Toyota manufacturing system or the 'TPS' founded by Taiichi Ohno where idle inventory in the system is practically zero. The Just-in-Time manufacturing and the Just-in-Time purchasing system have minimum inventory, a customer pull-based system of manufacturing and purchasing, small lot sizes, and frequent deliveries to the market as per customer's demand make material productivity of the highest order and forms a world-class manufacturing system.

7.2.3.3 People/Employee-based productivity improvement technique

Total Quality Management or the world-class management system is basically a process driven by the people. The basic difference between an ordinary organization and an extra ordinary world-class organization is the difference in the quality of the people and their involvement in the organization. Some of the popular methods of improving the employee's involvement and productivity improvement are detailed below.

Financial incentives (Individual): Individual financial incentives help to reward the performing workers as compared to the non-performers or the average performers. This is purely a performance-based rewarding system which has a direct impact on productivity improvement. The popular incentive schemes in this regard are Piecework, Hasley plan, Bendeux plan, Rowan plan or a combination of the various plans.

Financial incentives (Group): Group financial incentive helps to reward the performing workers' group as compared to the non-performing department or the average performing teams. This is purely a performance-based rewarding system for groups of people working together with a high level of team-spirit or team-orientation in their work which has a direct impact on productivity improvement. The popular incentive schemes in this regard are the Kaiser plan, profit sharing, the Scanlon Plan, etc.

Fringe benefits: Fringe benefits like House Rent Allowances, medical treatment facility, Accident and illness insurance, leave traveling allowance, subsidized canteen etc. act as an incentive for increasing productivity.

Motivation, leadership, training and education: Motivation, leadership, training and education act as impetus to increase productivity by better job involvement and better skill development.

Job enrichment, job enlargement and job rotation, employee's participation: Activities like job enrichment, job enlargement, job rotation and employee's participation increase the workers' involvement in their job and increases their performance and productivity. Quality improvement activities like Kaizen Gemba, quality circle, employees' participation group enhance the employees' problem solving capability. These are also the scientific methods of increasing productivity in their work area.

Management by Objectives (MBO) and Key Result Areas (KRA): Management by Objective and breaking it into the key result areas is a scientific and systematic technique of measuring the employee's productivity and their contribution to the achievement of the organizational objective. This is a quantitative measurement technique of employees productivity on individual basis and is an objective measurement. This is a highly focused approach to increase employee productivity.

Learning curve: The learning curve technique is a measurement of productivity when you do a job for the first time and keep on repeating it. Productivity increases at a certain rate of learning by the reduction of time to do the job or the project till a number beyond which there is no further improvement.

Ergonomics: Ergonomics is a productivity improvement technique by way of improving the working condition including ventilation, lighting, working space, elimination of pollution and noise level and, above all providing a healthy working environment.

Time management: Time management is a productivity improvement technique at the level of employees, including the top management, that eliminates the time wasters and making optimum utilization of the time for productive use.

7.2.3.4 Product-based productivity technique

The product-based productivity improvement technique enhances the productivity level in a positive manner by cost reduction in designing, manufacturing, distribution and selling. In the current highly competitive customer-oriented business environment, continuous product innovation and improvement is key to success in the market place.

Value engineering: Value engineering or value analysis is a scientific way of increasing value of a product from the customers' point of view for which he is ready to pay higher than otherwise. On the other hand, this technique leads to reduction in the cost of manufacturing by elimination of parts or components which do not add value to the end product.

Product diversification: Product diversification is a process of introducing new products as per the market demand to retain and improve the organization's market share.

Product simplification and product standardization: Product simplification and product standardization is a method of product rationalization to reduce the cost element of product management. These steps will make the product cheaper and more competitive to the market as well as increase its usage.

Research and development: After conducting a SWOT analysis and identifying the weaknesses of the product and process of manufacturing research and development brings about product innovation, product alterations and modifications to convert these weaknesses into strengths, increasing product salability in the market as well reducing the cost of manufacturing.

Benchmarking and Emulation: Benchmarking and emulation is a universally accepted way of learning from others who are the best in their field and increasing an organization's performance to the level on each area and attributes that is the best in its class.

Advertising and sales promotion: Advertising and sales promotion is a methodology of sensitizing the customer about the organization, its product range, and the product features. Advertising and sales promotion increase the sales of the organization and hence contribute to its productivity improvement.

7.2.3.5 Task-based productivity technique

The task-based productivity improvement technique enhances the productivity level in a positive manner by cost reduction in designing, in work content, doing the work in a better cost-effective manner as well as by proper planning, control and scheduling of the job activities. The task-based productivity improvement techniques are detailed hereafter.

Work measurement: Work measurement techniques, including **Method Study, Time Study and Motion Study,** are the most effective time-tested productivity improvement techniques. This is the best way to improve labour productivity. These techniques also provide the basic data without which other productivity improvement and control activities like production planning and scheduling will not be possible.

Job design, job evaluation and job safety: Job design, job evaluation and job safety are important analytical tools for perfect job design, job improvement and job simplification leading to ease of manufacturing as well as reduction in the cost of production thereby increasing job productivity.

Production planning, control and scheduling: The Production planning, control and scheduling activity is a vital new activity for effective and smooth running of an organization. The scheduling activity maximizes plant productivity by ensuring the maximum productivity of the workstation, proper distribution of work load, smooth flow of production, proper line balancing, minimum inventory stocks and most effective and economical manufacturing system. The scheduling activity is equally important for both manufacturing and service sectors.

The five-pronged approach to productivity improvement technique adopts a holistic system approach covering all the aspects. This methodology invariably becomes the most effective approach for customer satisfaction by providing customer-oriented products and services, highest employee morale due to a number of employee-related activities, along with material and labour productivities. Hence, it can be concluded that this is the most powerful productivity improvement and management technique.

7.2.4 Implementation of Total Productivity Model

The step-by-step implementation of TPM is detailed below:

Sales, profit and cost analysis: The first step in TPM is to assess the current situation and its measurement to compare it with the future and past performance in an objective manner. The most important performance criterion are the sales, profit and cost analyses along with the computation of the return on investment.

Familiarization with products, process and personnel: The next step in TPM is the familiarization process with products, process and personnel. Once the familiarization process is over, the scope of improving productivity in all these three key areas is looked into.

Allocation of total output and input to a particular operational unit: The third step in TPM is the allocation of total output and input to a particular operational unit. Then add all such input and output figures to arrive at the overall organizational level figure and assess the current situation.

Data collection and design: The most cumbersome step in TPM is the data collection and designing the productivity improvement strategies and their effective control. The data collected should be factual, quantitative and specific and collected with a defined objective.

Obtaining deflator information: The next step in TPM is to obtain the deflator information and select the base period with which to compare the productivity improvement figures.

Data collection and recording areas for improvements: The important step of TPM is the data collection from the point of view of recording critical and weak areas suitable for improvements.

Data synthesis: The TPM now integrates all the data collected with a unified organizational objective. This data synthesis is important from the point of view of undertaking a unified holistic approach for a world-class organization. A sporadic dispersed productivity improvement will not be effective in an organization-wide performance improvement.

Productivity computation: TPM now does the productivity computation and its analysis with respect to the base year as well as that of the competition and the customer's expectations.

Charting productivity indices and productivity trend analysis: TPM charts the productivity indices for individual products, individual operational units and the overall productivity indices and undertakes the productivity trend analysis. This analysis is done with reference to the competition, market situation, emerging technology and products as well as the individual contribution and the future of the products and operational units in line with the organization's business plan and vision.

Evaluation and implementation of productivity programme: TPM will now finally undertake the evaluation and implementation of the productivity improvement programme. The periodic measurement of the performance and the control points have to be defined. The back-up actions in case of deviation have to be kept ready for correction of likely deviations. The objective is not only to achieve the business plan but also give a performance which is world-class and the best in its category.

7.2.5 Limitations of the Total Productivity Model

- Complexity of data computation.
- Deficiency of bringing all the inputs and outputs under the same value of cost.
- Difference in fixing a base period for having a common subscript of cost value to Input factors.
- Difference in selection of inflator and deflator for base period.

EXERCISES

1. Define and explain the concept of productivity. Explain the importance of productivity in the successful operation of a business organization.

2. Define and explain the concept of partial productivity, total factor and total productivity with the advantages and disadvantages of each type of productivity measure.

3. Write short notes on:
   a. Productivity and performance.
   b. American productivity centre model.
   c. Application of productivity technique.
   d. Causes of poor productivity.

4. The output of a firm XYZ is Rs. 10,00,000. The labour cost for the above output is Rs. 2,00,000. The raw material purchased is Rs. 5,00,000, the capital cost is Rs. 1,20,000, the energy consumed is worth Rs. 50,000 and the other expenses are Rs. 30,000. Calculate the partial productivity for each factors, the total factor productivity, and the total productivity.

5. Explain in detail the tangible inputs and outputs. Elaborate in detail the Sumanth's Total Productivity Model.

6. Describe in detail Sumanth's five-pronged approach to productivity improvement.

7. Explain the salient features of TPM. How can it be implemented and what are its limitations?

8

Work Study

8.1 WORK STUDY

The foundation of operations management lies in this section. To begin with we convert both the manufacturing and the service sector processes of value addition by conversion to the input into final output by way of a flow process chart which breaks up the organizational main process into sub-processes to individual activities. Each activity where the value addition takes place has also input and output with resources (or the entity relationship) required for the value addition at each stage. The output of one process becomes the input for next process. The processes are arranged and aligned in a synchronized manner in sequence of their manufacturing technology. This is known as the flow process chart. In the 'method study procedure', the flow process chart is systematically studied for the improvement and elimination of wastages. Fundamentally, five symbols are used for drawing the flow process chart, namely, the operation, transportation, delay, storage and inspection. If one examines critically, it becomes apparent that except the operation, all other activities are non-value added activities or wastages of time and resources. In the method study, we try to modify and improve the flow process chart by eliminating the non-value added activities and maximizing the operation or combination of two or more activities together. This is the main objective of the method study.

After the flow process chart is improvised to the most efficient and effective process of value addition, the four sets of rules of motion study are applied to further improve productivity and reduce the fatigue of the operators. The motion study principles include in their paradigm the optimization and effectiveness of the human body motions, time management, design of the work place layout in the most efficient manner and the ergonomics.

Now the final process of manufacturing or the value addition process is complete. The next step is to measure the time taken for each individual activity and add the various allowances so that the time schedule for the completion of the job, deciding on the delivery dates to the customers and sequencing of the machines and the operations can be done. This in short is the operations management where the efficiency and effectiveness of each and every process are enhanced and optimized as per the goal or the end objective.

The work study fundamentally consists of three types of labour productivity improvement techniques, namely, the method study, motion study and time study. These are the three basic productivity improvement techniques which are synchronized together for the optimum use of the men, machines and material for carrying out a specified activity in the most efficient and effective manner.

Frank B. Gilbreth and Lillan M. Gilbreth were the pioneers in generating the concept of the work study and work measurement, including motion analysis and time study for completing a specified element of the job.

Work Study is defined by the British Standard Institution as a generic term for those techniques particularly *Method Study* and *Work Measurement* which are used in the examination of human work in all its contexts and which lead systematically to the investigation of all the factors which effect the efficiency of the situation being reviewed in order to seek improvements.

Work study investigates, i.e. records and critically examines the work done in an organization and finds the best and the most efficient way of using the available resources to achieve the best quality production in the least possible time at the least cost. The crux of the work study is to achieve maximum productivity at the least cost by optimum utilization of input resources by giving each worker in each workstation a definite task to be performed in a well-defined manner with defined manufacturing aids in a defined time.

Time study can be defined as the application of scientific techniques to measure the work content of a particular activity in a normal defined situation and establish the time required to execute the job by a qualified worker at a defined level of performance.

8.2 APPLICATION OF WORK STUDY

The principles of work study are universally applicable to all the activities in an organization pertaining to all the functional areas. The main focus of work study is of course the manufacturing area or the productive operations. The other areas like research & development, marketing, sales, distribution, office, stores and warehouses all fall under the paradigm of work study with the objective of productivity improvement and reduction in wastages. Work study is uniformly applicable all the industrial activities like machine loading, job execution, and machine scheduling, material handling, designing, logistics and supply chain management, etc.

Similarly, the principles of work study are universally applicable to all the industries like the building and other construction, manufacturing, service sector like information technology, automobile manufacturing, transportation industry, hospitals, defence and agricultural industry.

8.2.1 Advantages/Objectives of Work Study

The advantages of work study are many fold. This is the basic requirement for an organization to work productively and efficiently. Work study helps in deciding the resource requirements at the right time and the right place. There are many advantages of work study. A few can be enumerated hereunder for ready reference.

- Uniform production flow.
- Production smoothing due to line balancing.
- Minimum inventory in the system due to removal of bottlenecks.
- Higher productive efficiency.
- Reduced manufacturing cost.
- Fast and accurate delivery dates to customer as per commitment.
- Better employee–employer relation.
- Better service to customer.
- Leads to attainment of market leadership due to timely delivery, competitive rates due to reduction in wastages and better all round productivity.
- Job security and job satisfaction to workers.
- Better working and other conditions.
- Reduces fatigue to workers by proper design and ergonomics of the work place and its design.
- Higher wages to workers due to productivity-linked incentive schemes.

8.3   METHOD STUDY

"**Method Study**" can be defined as the systematic and scientific analysis of the proposed method of doing a job in order to develop and install a simple, fast, efficient, effective and less fatiguing procedure of doing the same job at the least cost by optimum utilization of the input resources".

Method study uses five different basic activities, namely, operation, delay, storage, inspection and transportation, while drawing the flow process chart. On critical examination of the above-stated activities, the operation is the only value addition activity whereas the other four are non-value addition activities. The main objective of method study is to improve the process of value addition or conversion into finished component or simply the method of performing the task. This is accomplished by the maximization of the value adding activity of operation and minimizing or eliminating the other four activities of delay, storage, transportation and inspection. The flow process chart is modified as stated above by minimizing the four non-value addition activities and maximizing the value added activity of operation.

8.3.1   Objectives/Advantages of Method Study

Method study is the most scientific way of increasing labour productivity. The study hits at the root cause of productivity and improves the process, thereby permanently improving productivity without affecting or depending on any other factor. The basic advantages are listed below:

- Improved work process leading to higher productivity.
- Standardized procedure leading to consistency in performance.
- Better work place layout and positioning and arranging the facilities and machines.
- Neat and clean working environment and working conditions.
- Improved working process leads to decreased fatigue to workers.

- Method study improves product quality
- Method study ensures better safety at work place.
- Method study ensures effective utilization of men, machine and materials.

8.3.2 Method Study Procedure

- Select the work to be studied and define the objectives to be achieved.
- Record all the relevant information about the existing method in detail. The method of recording is in the form of a chart or diagram.

  Methods of recording are:
  (a) Process charts:
    (i) Outline process chart
    (ii) Flow process chart—Men, Materials and Equipment type
    (iii) Two-handed process chart
    (iv) Multiple activity chart
  (b) Diagrams:
    (i) Flow diagram
    (ii) String siagram
  (c) Motion and film analyses:
    (i) SIMO chart
    (ii) Models, etc.
- Examine the recorded events critically and sequentially. An activity can be eliminated, simplified or combined. Purpose, place, person, means and sequence have to be analyzed in the backdrop of: why they are necessary, what are the alternatives and the best methods of doing.
- Develop the best method which should be practical, feasible, safe, effective and economical.
- Install the improved method through the phases of planning.
- Arrange and implement with a proper time schedule and arrange for proper resources.
- Maintain the new method and ensure proper functioning.

8.3.3 Flow Process Chart

A chart recording graphically or with a diagram in sequence, the operation connected with a process is called a process chart.

Process charts are of three types:

- Outline process chart: It surveys and records an overall picture of the process and states only the main events sequence-wise.
- Two-handed process chart: It records the activities of the left hand and right hand of an operator as related to each other on a time-scale duly synchronized.
- Flow process chart: It is a detailed version of the outline process chart recording all the events.

  (a) It sets out the sequence of flow of a procedure or product.
  (b) It records all the events in sequence using process chart symbols.

(c) It marks distances travelled and time taken for completing an activity.

(d) It mentions the other important or key points if any.

(e) There are three types of flow process chart—men, material and equipment.

The flow process chart is drawn after arranging the activities in a sequential manner and allocating the resources. The flow process chart is analyzed critically to find out the scope of improvement. Accordingly, a modified flow process chart evolves, increasing the efficiency of the entire process by optimizing the value adding activities and eliminating or substituting the non-value adding activities.

The various symbols used for drawing the flow process chart are depicted below. They are basically five symbols of operation, storage, delay, transport and inspection. Out of the five symbols, only the operation adds value to the process. The rest of the activities are non-value adding.

8.3.4 Symbols for Drawing the Flow Process Chart

Event	Symbol	Description
1. Operation	◯	Operation is a change in the location or condition of a product.
2. Storage	▽	Represents a stage when a finished good or raw material awaits an action.
3. Delay	D	Occurs when something stops the process and the product waits for the next event.
4. Tranport	⇦	Transport indicates the movement of an item.
5. Inspection	☐	Inspection is an act of correctness of the quantity and quality of the items.
6. Operation	⬖	Articles are being painted as transported by the chain conveyor
7. Inspection	⊡	A powder milk tin is being weighed

8.3.5 Flow Diagram

A flow diagram is a drawing which shows the relative position of the production machinery, jigs, fixtures, gangways, etc. drawn to scale and marks the path followed by men and/ or materials. In short, flow diagram is drawn on the plant layout where the movement of men and material are drawn in different colour lines and the relative position of the machines are shown on the diagram. The flow diagram and the string diagram are similar. The flow diagram makes use of pencils or pens to draw the path of the men or material whereas the string diagram makes use of threads to draw the same.

The steps in drawing the flow diagram are detailed below:

(a) Draw the layout plan of the shopfloor area to scale.
(b) Mark the relative positions of machine tools, aisles, storage area, inspection benches, etc.
(c) Depending on the technological requirement of processing, the materials, parts and components decide the 'route chart' of each particular set of products being manufactured.
(d) From the different requirements, draw the actual movements of the material or the worker on the diagram in sequence as per the process requirement and indicate the direction of movement.
(e) Different movements can be marked in different colours and the process symbols are used.
(f) Take an overview of the entire process and check that everything is in order and in sequence.
(g) Now look for repetition of the tasks or the operations as well as excessive movement of the men or the materials. Identify such activities and list them.
(h) Improve on the existing flow diagram by eliminating, substituting or combining such operations or activities with the value added activities and optimize the flow diagram and make it as efficient as possible.

The flow process chart or the flow diagram are the most powerful and established techniques to improve the productivity and performance of a manufacturing or the service unit.

8.3.6 Operation Analysis

- Operation analysis is a detailed study of different operations involved in doing a work with the objective to find out defects in the existing method and to develop an improved procedure.
- It aims at optimum utilization of men, machines and material with minimum fatigue to workers.
- It considers the optimum utilization of both hands and legs.
- The procedural steps of a task are analyzed and the motions are studied, synchronized and/or eliminated and an operation chart is constructed.

- The different motions involved are subjected to specific and detailed questioning in order to eliminate unnecessary motions and to arrange the remaining motion in logical and better sequence.

  (a) Worker—fitness, fatigue, training needs and motivation.
  (b) Set-up—availability of tools, jigs, fixtures, moulds, etc.
  (c) Material—right quality, form, composition, size, quantity, etc. Cheaper and better substitutes.
  (d) Material handling—material handling equipments, distance, backtracking, etc.
  (e) Operations—can some operations be eliminated, combined, substituted or automated to save cost and time.
  (f) Working conditions—adequate light, ventilation, safety factors, housekeeping, etc.

After carrying out the detailed operation analysis, the final method or process of manufacturing is determined, optimizing all the resources for the attainment of the end objective. The operation analysis is a scientific method of improvising on the performance of an organization by focusing on all the activities and their interrelation.

For ready reference, a method study diagram depicting the details of operations with relevant symbols and activities of both the hands are given below for ready reference.

Job: Putting thread in needle

Left hand	Symbols LH	RH	Right Hand
Pick up needle	◯	◗	Idle
Hold	▽	◯	Pick up thread
Hold	▽	⇨	To left hand
Hold	▽	◯	Put thread in needle

There are three types of flow process charts namely the **material type** flow process charts, the **man type** flow process charts and the **machine or work place type** flow process charts. Each of these flow process charts are explained in detail, with example.

8.3.7 Material Type Flow Process Chart

Activity	Operations	Distance Moved (Metres)	Time (Minutes)
PVC granules lying in store		—	—
R.M. moved to plastic molding machine by trolley		10	3
Moulding machine being set		—	5
Material injected in die		—	2
Opening the die		—	3
Deflashing operation		—	3
Wait for trolley		—	10
Moved to assembly shop by trolley		20	6
Inspected before assembly		—	5

8.3.8 Man Type Flow Process Chart

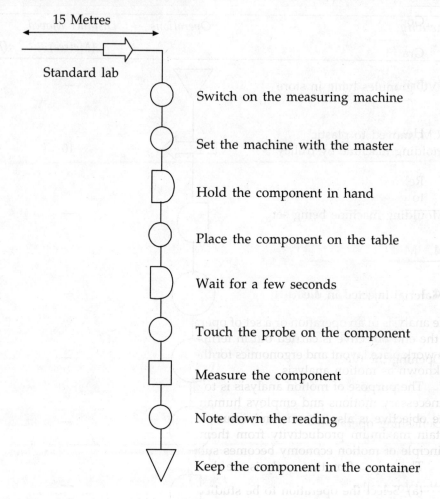

15 Metres

Standard lab

Switch on the measuring machine

Set the machine with the master

Hold the component in hand

Place the component on the table

Wait for a few seconds

Touch the probe on the component

Measure the component

Note down the reading

Keep the component in the container

8.3.9 Machine Type Flow Process Chart

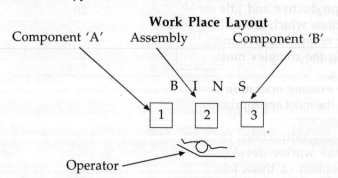

Work Place Layout

Component 'A'   Assembly   Component 'B'

B I N S

1   2   3

Operator

Left hand description	Symbols	Right hand description
Goes to Bin 1		Goes to Bin 3
Grasps 'A'		Grasps 'B'
Brings over Bin 2		Brings over Bin 2
Holds and grasps 'A'		Assembles 'B' with 'A'
Releases the assembly to drop on Bin '2'		Releases the assembly to drop on Bin '2'

8.4 MOTION STUDY

8.4.1 Analysis of Motion

The analysis of an operation or a set of operations arranged sequentially for the attainment of the end objective is carried out in terms of individual motions of a worker as well as his work place layout and ergonomics for the attainment of the highest level of productivity is known as motion analysis.

The purpose of motion analysis is to design an improved method which eliminates unnecessary motions and employs human efforts more productively.

The objective is also to cause minimum fatigue to the operators and at the same time obtain maximum productivity from them. For accomplishing the above objective, the principle of motion economy becomes substantially helpful.

The steps of motion analysis are detailed below:

(a) Select the operation to be studied.

(b) List and chart various motions performed by the operator. The process can also be videographed for better analysis.

(c) Identify the productive and idle motions. Separate them out. Also identify the complex motions which are difficult to perform.

(d) Eliminate the non-productive and unnecessary motions. Look into the possibility of simplifying the complex motions. Try to standardize the activities as far as possible.

(e) Redesign the existing operating procedure by employing the minimum number of motions in the most appropriate sequence and in accordance with the principles of motion economy.

(f) Impart necessary instructions to the worker so that he develops a proper habit cycle. Once the worker develops the habit cycle in performing the repetitive jobs, the execution of these jobs happens automatically with lesser stress or fatigue and with better accuracy and speed.

(g) Check once again the procedure in the light of the step (e) above.

(h) The procedure should now be standardized.

The principles of motion economy act as a guide to develop better and improved methods of doing the operation more effectively efficiently and with lesser fatigue to the operators.

8.4.2 Principles of Motion Economy

A set of rules were designed by Gilberth in order to develop better method. These are the rules of motion economy and have been developed keeping in mind better productivity with minimum stress or fatigue to the workers. The rules focus on developing better method of performing the tasks which consumes minimum amount of efforts and energy in performing limb motions in order to complete the task.

The rules of human motions were modified by Barnes, Lowry, Maynard, and others. The rules are of four types, namely, rules considering the human body, rules concerning work place layout and material handling, rules concerning time conservation and rules pertaining to the design of tools and equipments. The rules are described below in brief.

8.4.2.1 Rules concerning human body

The following are the rules related to human body motion.

- Both the hands should be used for doing productive work.
- Both the hands should start and finish their motions at the same time.
- Except for the rest period, the two hands should not be idle at one time.
- Motions of both the hands or arms should be symmetrical, simultaneous and opposite to each other.
- Motions should be simple and involve minimum number of motions of the limbs to perform work in the shortest duration and with minimum fatigue.
- A worker should employ momentum to assist himself.
- Motions should be smooth and continuous; they should not involve frequent stops and sharp directional changes.
- Ballastic movements, wherever feasible, like driving a nail into the wall should be preferred over controlled movements, because the ballastic movements are easy, fast and more accurate.
- A worker may use mechanical aids to assist him to overcome muscular effort.
- If possible, work movements should be rhythmical and automatic.

All these rules pertaining to the human body motion are principally aimed at reducing the mental and physical strain on the operators, ensuring that they are at the peak of their physical and mental ability. This kind of state of mind leads to high level of motivation, thereby achieving the maximum amount of productivity and efficiency in operations management.

8.4.2.2 Rules concerning work place layout and material handling

The rules regarding the work place layout and material handling are explained in detail and how to improve the efficiency of material handling with minimum wastages of motions.

- There should be a definite, fixed and easily accessible location for materials and tools near the place of work.
- Materials, tools and other mechanical devices should be kept close to the work place with proper arrangement.
- Gravity should be employed wherever feasible with a conveyor for transportation and delivering materials at the work place between various workstations and departments.
- An assembled or final product should be dropped on a conveyor by a chute below the work table.
- Hands should not be employed for non-productive work as far as possible.
- Tools and materials should be located in the order or sequence in which they will be required for use at the place of their need. It reduces mental strain and eliminates the wastage of time.
- Adequate light should be at the place of work for proper visibility, fast operation and better safety.
- In order to impart rest to some of the limbs, an operator may work in sitting or standing position while working. This necessitates certain design considerations and relationship between the chair height and the height of the table or workplace.
- In order to reduce fatigue, the seating arrangement of the worker should be adjustable and ergonomically designed.
- The heavy parts should be handled by the material handling automatic devices.
- The switches which need to be operated frequently should be foot-operated as far as possible.

The rules regarding the work place layout and material handling make the work execution scientifically designed to increase the speed of work execution with minimum effort and effective utilization of the limbs and other resources available in an organization.

8.4.2.3 Rules concerning time conservation

The rules pertaining to time conservation are elaborated below:

- Stoppage of work by a man or machine should not be encouraged.
- Machine should not run idle as it leads to loss of production and power.
- Two or more jobs should be done at the same time, or two or more operations should be carried out on a job simultaneously.
- Number of motions involved in completing a job should be simplified and minimized.
- The loading and unloading of the job and the cycle time should be synchronized in such a manner that one operator can be multifunctional or can simultaneously operate a number of machines.

The time conservation tactics are employed to speed up the cycle time and productivity of the process.

8.4.2.4 Rules concerning tools and equipment design

The tools and equipment design is a critical component of both productivity enhancement as well as the ease of completion of the job competently with least fatigue. The jigs and fixtures can increase the productivity in geometric proportion, reducing the job to complete in minutes or seconds which otherwise requires hours. The tools like dies and moulds are mandatory for production and forging processes like in the production of rubber and plastic components, non-ferrous metal parts/components. Certain rules for the effective design of tools and equipments are detailed hereunder:

- Jigs and fixtures should be employed to reduce the work loads and increase the ease of handling of the job and productivity.
- Foot-operated switches and controls should be designed as far as possible to reduce the workload on the hands.
- Tools should be multipurpose and easy to handle.
- Tools and materials should be properly arranged and located near the workplace.
- There should be maximum surface contact between the handle of the tool and the hand. It helps proper application of hand force and minimizes fatigue.
- Where the work is carried out by fingers (as while operating the computer keyboard) the load distribution on to each finger should be as per the normal capacity of the finger.
- Tools and materials should be located in the order of their use.
- Gravity should be used for delivery of material and finished products.
- The operator should have comfortable posture. The height of his seat should be such that the worker table is about 50 mm below the elbow level of the operator.
- A worker should have the flexibility to stand or sit freely while working.
- A worker should be able to operate levers and handles without changing the body position, i.e. ideally they should be located in front of the operator.
- The work place should have proper ergonomics in terms of illumination, proper conditions of heat, cold and humidity, reduced dust and noise, etc.

The most convenient work area can be worked out in the form of a diagram as detailed in Figure 8.1.

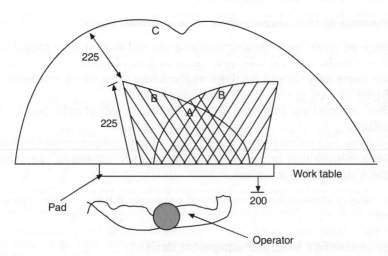

FIGURE 8.1 Workplace layout showing different areas and typical dimensions in mm.

'A' is the actual working area. It is the most convenient area for working. This is the area between the overlapping of both the hands with an area above elbow till the hand. Though it varies from operator to operator, the average length is normally taken as 225 mm or 9". This is normally the assembly area of the components or the parts of the work table.

'B' is the normal working area. It is within the easy reach of the operator but non-overlapping area stretched from hand to the elbow of 225 mm on either side of the overlapping area as shown in the figure number. Normally, the parts and components to be assembled are kept here, depending on which hand to pick up which parts for the assembly.

'C' is the maximum working area. It is the area accessible with full arm stretch that is another 225 mm or totally 50 mm. This is the maximum reach of the hands fully stretched out. Here occasionally required tools are kept while assembling so that they are needed once in a while.

The distance of work table from the body of the operator is normally kept at 200 mm or 8". A soft pad is kept between the table and the body to facilitate ease of working. There can be a cut in the table through which the assembled components can be dropped on a conveyor which will take it to the next workstation for assembly or further processing.

The height of the work table should be such that it is 50 mm or 2" below the elbow so that it is convenient to work both in the standing and sitting positions. The chair should be ergonomically designed to make long hours of working comfortable.

This work place arrangement satisfies most of the principles of motion economy in designing a work place layout.

8.4.3   Therbligs

Therbligs are the micro-motion study elements and were originally suggested by Gilbreth. Therbligs were used to describe the basic elements of movements or the fundamental hand motion of the work cycle. Every therblig is represented by a symbol, a definite colour and with a word or two to record the same.

A SIMO chart employs therbligs which are of microscopic nature, whereas a process chart uses symbols like operation, inspection, transportation, etc., which are macroscopic. A single operation may consist of many therbligs. The following elaboration can be a good example.

Macroscopic motion	*Microscopic motion*
Operation of picking up a component (therbligs)	1. Reach the hand for the component (transport empty)
	2. Grasp the same (grasp)
	3. Pick up the component (move)
	4. Place the component (transport loaded)

Though it is cumbersome to deal and chart the microscopic motions, they possess decisive advantages over the macroscopic motions for better understanding, analysis and improvements. As explained above, one macroscopic motion may contain a number of microscopic motions.

Since microsystem is more detailed, it is simpler to understand what precisely the worker is doing. Therbligs colours make the chart more meaningful.

SIMO or the Simultaneous Motion Cycle Chart is used to draw these microscopic motions. SIMO is an extremely detailed left- and right-hand operation chart. It shows on a common time-scale, the simultaneous minute movements or therbligs performed by the two hands of an operator. Besides the hand movements, other limbs of the operator may also be recorded. The time-scale is represented in wings (1/2000 of a minute). SIMO is generally used for micro-motion analysis of short cycle repetitive jobs, skilled jobs of high order, and finds application in jobs like component assembly, packaging, repetitive use of jigs and fixtures, inspection, etc. A SIMO chart shows the relationship between the different limbs of an operator. The SIMO chart balances the relative movements of the limbs with respect to each other, along with balancing the durations of the micro-motions.

The construction of a SIMO chart is carried out by using a 16 mm movie camera/video camera. A number of short and repetitive work cycles are filmed as the worker performs the job. For recording time, a timing device (wink counter) is placed in the field of view.

The film thus obtained is viewed and the one hand-cycle most efficiently performed is selected for analysis. A cycle involves complete series of motions from the beginning to the end for completing a unit of work. A specialist is employed to study the work cycle recorded on the film. The work study engineer analyzes the film—frame by frame, studying one frame at a time and concentrating first on the left-hand and then on the right-hand movements.

The data noted is recorded in the form of a Therblig chart. The duration of actual movements are also read from the wink counter. The SIMO chart is then drawn for further study and analysis. After the detailed analysis and effecting the scope of the improvements, a new SIMO chart is then drawn incorporating the new method. The new method is then checked to ascertain its benefits. Once the benefits are established and accepted, the new method is implemented and the gains are made part of the regular working system.

8.5   TIME STUDY (WORK MEASUREMENT)

Objectives/advantages of work measurement

- It determines the time required to do the job
- Compares the alternative methods and establishes the fastest method
- Decides manpower required for the job
- Decides equipments required
- Provides information for effective production planning and maintenance procedure
- Aids at calculating exact delivery dates
- Decides realistic labour budgeting
- Provides basis for standard costing system
- Provides a basis for a fair and sound incentive scheme
- Results in effective labour control.

8.5.1 Stop Watch Procedure for Collecting Time Study Data

- Establish the quality to be achieved for the product. Strike a balance between low quality and very high quality. Low quality means more rejection and scrap and high quality leads to increase in the cost of production.
- Identify the operations to be timed.
- Obtain the improvement procedure from the method study department.
- Collect the necessary equipments like stopwatch, calculators, steel rules, time study board, time study forms, etc.
- Select the worker to be observed.
- Take the worker as well as supervisor into confidence and explain to them the objectives of the project.
- Explain to the worker the improved working procedure and the tools, jigs, fixtures and other attachments.
- Break the operation into small elements and write to them on the paper form.

An element may be defined as a distinct part of an operation or working procedure. The element, being a small entity, makes it convenient to observe, measure and analyse it. The different objectives of element breakdown are as follows:

- To separate productive and unproductive activities or effective and idle times
- To get complete and accurate information
- To accurately define the operator's performance
- To produce detailed work specification
- To select the best method by comparing the work element to two or more given methods.

To collect information to compile standard data.

- Separate constant (time) elements from variable (time) elements. (Machine elements and manual elements are the examples of constant time and variable time elements).
- Determine the number of observations to be timed for each element.
- Conduct the observations (of timing the element) and record them on the time study form (Section 8.5.5)
- In continuous timing method, a non-fly back type of stopwatch is employed. It is started as soon as the first element begins and the reading is taken as the first element ends and the second element begins.

Element No.	Total time read at any instant (minutes)	Actual time for an element (minutes)
1	20	20
2	40	40 − 20 = 20
3	70	70 − 40 = 30
4	100	100 − 70 = 30
		and so on.

- Rate also the performance of the worker during the previous step.

- Repeat previous two steps for taking more than one observation.
- Compute observed time from the measures of central tendency.
- Calculate normal from observed time by using performance rating factor.
- Add process allowance, rest and personal allowances, and special allowances to the normal time in order to obtain standard time or allowed time. Policy allowance are in addition to standard time.
- Stopwatch study is employed.
- For checking standard time obtained by other methods.

For timing repetitive operations employed in manufacturing different jobs.

Where it becomes necessary to breakdown an activity involving motions of limb, leg, foot, etc. in detail and study.

8.5.2   Standard Time

The standard time may be defined as the amount of the time required to complete a unit of work:

- Under the existing working conditions
- Using specified method and machinery
- By an operator, able to work in a proper manner, and
- At a standard pace

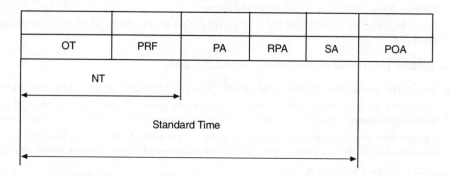

OT   : Observed Time
PRF : Performance Rating Factor
NT   : Normal Time
PA   : Process Allowances
RPA : Rest and Personal Allowances
SA   : Special Allowances
POA : Policy Allowances

FIGURE 8.2   Standard time is the amount of time required to complete a unit of work, including allowances.

8.5.3 Allowances

Allowances are added to the normal time to arrive at the standard time.

- Types of allowances
- Process allowances: They are the allowances allocated to compensate workers for enforced idleness due to the character or nature of a process or an operation.
- Personal/rest/relaxation allowance: These allowances are given to the workers to compensate for physical and mental fatigue, provision to attend nature's call, difficult working conditions, etc. It varies from 12% to 20% of normal time, depending on a particular situation.

Special allowances: These allowances are given for activities which are not generally part of the work cycle but are considered essential for performing the work satisfactorily. It could be the periodic activity allowance like machine set-up time, tool grinding time, or interference allowance when the worker is operating more than one machine, etc.

8.5.4 Standard Data

Standard data is a catalogue of normal time values for different elements of jobs.

- This catalogue is prepared by compiling the timings of a number of standard elements.
- Similar elements or motions are involved in many different jobs. Hence the standard data helps in work measurement of new and existing jobs accurately without actually doing the time study and motion study every time.
- Once the standard data is ready, the minute motions of an operation of the job elements, read their time from the standard catalogue and add them up.
- The total time thus obtained is an estimate of the normal time of a job which can be converted into standard time by adding suitable allowances.
- Standard data eliminates the need for a large number of time studies.
- Standard data being collected from a large number of observations are more accurate and reliable, thereby giving a better estimation of production time.

The standard data can also be used:

- To estimate standard time for new jobs.
- For estimating production times for pricing enquiries.
- For cost computation of the profit centre concepts.
- In job designing, process planning and scheduling.
- To measure productive labour for cost checks.
- As a realistic base for incentive plans.
- For machine and operator loading and balancing.
- To find standards for small batch quantity of production where production runs are too small to employ time study.
- For estimation of repair and maintenance jobs.
- For project work.

8.5.5 Time Study Form

Product .... Time study engineer ....

Operation no............................. Data ....

Operation description...................

Number of cycles.............................

Standard time found..

Element description	Observed time (Stop watch reading)	Averaged observed	Rating normal factor time	Allowances	Standard time
1	2	3	4	5	

Performance Rating: Means gauging and comparing the pace rate or the performance of a worker against a standard performance level set by the time study engineer. The standard performance level is different for different jobs. The (performance) rating factor is used to convert observed time into normal time.

Normal time = Observed time
Performance level of the worker
Standard performance level expected

EXERCISES

1. Define work study and explain the concepts, applications, importance and features of work study.

2. Define method study and explain its concepts.

3. Describe the flow process chart and symbols and the types of flow process charts, and flow diagram.

4. Explain the procedure of method study and method improvement procedure.

5. Define motion study and explain its concepts, features and applications. State the motion study rules and their applicability.

6. Define and explain time study and its importance in productivity improvement and machine scheduling. Define and explain normal time, standard time, performance rating, and various allowances.

7. Write short notes on:
   a. Therbligs.
   b. Time study procedure.

9

World-Class Manufacturing Technique

9.1 VALUE ANALYSIS (VA) AND VALUE ENGINEERING

9.1.1 Definition

Value Analysis (VA) and value engineering can be defined as the organized and systematic approaches to provide a required function at the lowest cost consistent with specific performance, quality and reliability.

9.1.2 Features of Value Analysis

Value analysis is a functionally-oriented scientific method to improve the product value from the customer's point of view with reference to elements of the product cost in order to accomplish the desired functions at the least cost of the resources deployed to produce the product.

Value analysis pertains to the existing products and services whereas value engineering is concerned with the design of new products.

The main objective of value analysis is to increase the profit by critical examination of the areas of high cost in the manufacturing of a product or a service and finding out the ways and means of reducing or eliminating unnecessary costs. Value analysis aims at achieving lowest cost by improving the essential functions reliably.

The focus of value analysis is on the reduction of the material cost while method study and time study are mainly concerned with the reduction in labour cost.

Value can be increased in three ways:

(a) Retain the value but reduce the cost.
(b) Retain the cost but increase the value.
(c) Increase the cost if necessary, but increase the value much more than the cost.

Value analysis is a group activity. The value analysis team is a cross-functional team. The leader of the value analysis team is normally the most affected person. If the objective of the value analysis is the enhancement of market value, then the value analysis team leader will be the head of the marketing department. If the objective of the value analysis is to reduce the cost or the product innovation then the value analysis team leader will be the head of the manufacturing.

9.1.3 Concept of Value

The value is of two types, namely the use value and the esteem value. They can be elaborated as follows:

Use value: The Product quality is fundamentally defined as *'fitness for use'*. Having a product and not having a product makes a tremendous difference to the user. Value analysis is primarily concerned with the *'use value'*. This is also known as the primary or the basic value of the product. This is basically the usefulness of the product or the service in fulfillment of a stated, implied or the latent need at the least cost for the required expectation of the performance standard or the quality level.

Esteem value: This is the enhanced value associated with a brand or a product created by the smart marketers. This is a notional or snob value for which the customer is ready to pay higher. This is also known as the secondary value associated with the product. Esteem value is the value associated with a brand, product or service created by the virtue of its positioning in the society or in the market place. It can be the product or the service factor positioning or an additional feature for which a certain segment of market with higher paying capacity is ready to pay as it adds to the consumer's social positioning in the society at a relatively higher echelon.

9.1.4 Steps in Value Analysis

The following steps are to be followed for the value analysis.

- Collect data about cost function, customer needs, history and likely future developments related to the product and its use. Determine the function of the product.
- Develop alternative designs. The selected alternatives should be able to fulfill the functional requirement of the product as detailed above.
- Ascertain the cost of the alternatives.
- Evaluate the alternatives in all respects. The alternative which fulfills all the 'basic' or primary value considerations and the maximum number of secondary value considerations is the ideal alternative subject to the cost consideration which should be minimum.
- Recommend and implement the best solution. Identify the control point and devise a plan for periodic measurement of the performance and correct the deviations if any.

9.1.5 Factors Influencing Product Design or Redesign

The factors influencing product design or redesign are either from the customer's perspectives or from the organizational perspectives. Let us discuss it first from the customer's perspective, then we shall discuss it from the organizational perspective.

9.1.5.1 Customer's perspectives

The product redesign should be as per the customers' requirements. The product alteration should be customer-oriented. The aim of the product redesign or alteration or modification is to fulfill the customers' stated, implied and the latent needs. The customers' perspectives are normally in four different sectors as detailed hereafter.

Functions: The product or the service should be fit for use by the customer. The functions of the product or the service can be divided into two types of needs—the 'musts' and 'wants'. The 'musts' are the basic requirements the product or the service has to fulfill and the 'wants' are the desirable features of the product or the service. The product or the service which fulfills all the musts and the maximum number of wants is functionally the best product or the service.

Aesthetics: The aesthetics or the external look of the product or the service constitutes of the basic requirements of any product or the service to decide its market acceptability and the value or the price it can command in the market. The aesthetics is a marketing requirement across the products or the services to be marketed.

User-friendliness: The user-friendliness of the products or the services decides its market share or the market leadership. Many of the good products or the services have failed to take off in the market place because the products or the services were either introduced before time, i.e. before the customer was ready to accept the product. The user-friendliness or the ease-of-use, service and maintenance adds substantial value to the end products or the services.

Esteem associated with possession: All the products or the services in the market have two types of values, i.e. the 'use' value and the 'esteem' value. The products or the services must fulfill the basic needs of a customer to survive in the market. The products or the services in the upper end of the market have 'esteem value' over and above the use value for gaining their market share. In this market segment the customer wants the products or the services with special or additional distinguishing features for which he is ready to pay substantially higher price. The products or the services possessed by him should increase his social esteem or prestige because others in the society cannot afford such costly products. The products or the services and the associated brand name should be a status symbol in the society where he lives. The example could be possession of cars like Rolls Royce or the Limozine.

9.1.5.2 Organizational perspective

The products or the services manufactured and marketed by an organization have certain internal factors to be taken into consideration while undertaking a value analysis of the products or the services. This is pertaining to the optimum utilization of the internal resources used for the production of products or services by the organization. This will enable the organization to keep low its cost of production so that it can defend its profitability and offer the products or the services at competitive rates than the competition thereby gaining a higher market share.

Intrinsic cost of material: The main objective of value analysis is to reduce the material cost by way of elimination of wastages, reduction in material consumption and elimination or substitution of the non-value adding components in the products or the services. The reduction in the cost of material can also come from cheaper and better substitute parts and components in the products or the services. As the material cost is normally 50% of the selling price of the products or the services, a small reduction in material cost is going to reduce the cost of production substantially.

Intrinsic cost of labour: A more important aspect than the cost of labour is the quality and the productivity of the labour, how much value the labour is adding to the products or the services and in what amount time. The intrinsic cost of labour is an important aspect of the value analysis of the products or the services. This aspect of labour cost and productivity is handled more effectively by management techniques like work measurement, time study, motion study and method study. These techniques bring down the intrinsic cost of labour, add better quality to the products or the services, and increase labour productivity.

Replacement, exchange and disposal: The cost of replacement, exchange, disposal or removal of men, machine or material due to the product design or redesign is an important aspect of value analysis which has to be looked into not only from the point of view of direct impact but also from the point of view of the effect on the product, market, employees and the management. This is a major area which has to be looked into critically or otherwise it may spell disaster to the organization or it may also be a boon to it.

9.1.6 Methods of Value Analysis

The method of value analysis pertaining to products or services is by asking certain fundamental questions in relation to the elimination, simplification, substitution, relaxation or standardization of operations, materials, tolerances or components. Let us examine critically all these possibilities:

Eliminate redundant parts: Critically examine all the parts and components which are part of the final assembled product and see if each one of them is adding any value to the products or the services. If the answer is no, then eliminate that component from the product or the service. For example, the earlier car radio and aerials were eliminated from the cars due to poor reception of the medium wave and short wave radio signals in a moving car, because it was not adding any value. Now with the clarity of FM Radio channels in moving cars and continuous music channels on them with contemporary music, the car stereo system is back because now it is adding value to the customers.

Simplify parts: After critical examination of parts and components, if it is found that a part or a component cannot be eliminated, then look into the possibility whether it can be simplified or combined with the other parts and components performing the same function effectively. The best examples could be the multi-functional switches in four-wheelers and two-wheelers.

Substitute alternative materials: After a critical examination of parts and components, if it is found that a part or a component can neither be eliminated nor simplified or combined with other parts or components, then look into the possibility whether it can be substituted by cheaper and better alternative materials. An excellent example of value analysis in this regard is the substitution of the heavy rigid steel car bumpers with light weight collapsible fibre glass reinforced ABS plastic bumpers. In case of an accident, the steel bumper will have marginal dent, the car will be relatively safe and the entire impact load of accident will be transmitted undiminished through the chassis of the car to the steering rod. The body of the driver will surge forward due to the sudden impact on the vehicle. The driver of the vehicle will be hit by the steering rod on his chest with such magnitude of the impact load of the accident that he will die on the spot. The light weight collapsible fibre glass reinforced ABS plastic bumpers, in case of an accident, absorb 75% of the impact load in rupturing of the car bumper and only 25% of the impact load will be transmitted further. There is a weak point deliberately incorporated in the steering wheel which collapses when the safe impact load goes beyond the limit. In this design based on value analysis, the driver of the car is safe as well the car.

Use standard parts in materials: Today, the emphasis in the manufacturing and service sectors is on the modular manufacturing, where the sub-assemblies and parts are standardized. This gives flexibility to the product range and also leads to reduction in the cost of manufacturing—both are attained at the shortest possible lead time between the receipt of the order and its execution. The concept of modular manufacturing which has already become popular in the construction and furniture industry is now being tried out in the automobile industry by various leading car manufacturers in the world.

Relax manufacturing tolerances: The more the number of manufacturing tolerances specified, the more is the cost of production and controlling. Also tighter the tolerance specified than required, the more is the cost of production in maintaining the same. Hence in value analysis, the parts and the components are critically examined to reduce the number of specified tolerances as well as the relaxation of the closeness of the tolerances. For example, now-a-days nobody specifies the radius of the sharp corners. Only one sentence is written at the bottom of the drawing that all sharp corners to be rounded off.

Use standard manufactured parts: The use of standard manufactured parts makes things cheaper and quality-consistent. There will be no need to keep excess inventory since such type of items are readily available.

Eliminate unnecessary design features: Unnecessary design features that do not add value to the final product or service should be eliminated to bring down the cost of production. Specify only that many dimensions that are required bare minimum.

Change design to suit manufacturing: Every organization has a well-defined manufacturing facility. The design of the parts and components should be so changed or modified that they can be processed in-house and at the least possible cost. This also helps in closer monitoring of the parts and components.

Buy if cheap than make: The emphasis of the most of the organizations currently is to outsource an item if feasible. In case the parts or components are outside the technical competence of the firm or the cost of manufacturing the components in-house is higher, the decision is to outsource manufacturing of the parts and components.

Use pre-finished materials: To speed up the manufacturing and assembly operations as well as execution of the projects, pre-finished materials are used. The pre-finished parts and components also reduce the inventory and reduce the cycle time of production process.

Use pre-fabricated parts: To speed up the manufacturing and assembly operations as well as execution of the projects, the pre-fabricated parts are used. The pre-fabricated parts and components also reduce the inventory and reduce the cycle time of the production process.

Rationalize product range: The profitability of the individual products, the positioning of the product at the product life cycle graph and the contribution to an organization has to be considered together to arrive at the product range that gives the best results in terms of the customer satisfaction, return on investment and future expansion. The rationalization of the product range is an important decision in the redesigning of the product.

Substitute labour cost manufacturing process: The product redesign should have a focus on eliminating or substituting labour cost in manufacturing processes. This will minimize the human error in the manufacturing process resulting in lower cost of production and better quality of the end-product.

Rationalize and standardize low cost purchased parts: The redesign of the parts and components should be able to rationalize and standardize the low cost purchased parts so that there is no shortage for these items during production. The cost of holding inventory will also be minimum in view of their low cost.

Eliminate material waste: The redesign of the product should ensure the optimum utilization of material and avoid excessive use of material. All causes of material wastages should be eliminated.

9.1.7   Value Analysis—Areas of Improvement

In value analysis, improvements are basically identified in four areas. These areas are the functional aspects of the products and services, the intrinsic cost of the materials, manufacturing and specification. While the functional aspect is related to the adding of value to the products and services, the other three factors of material, manufacturing and reworking the specifications, are aimed at reducing the cost of production. Certain questions are asked from the check list in all the four areas. The answer to these questions gives the scope and means of improvements in these areas.

Functions:
- Details of the basic functions.
- Details of secondary functions.
- Are all the functions necessary?
- Substitute the factors.
- Combination of factors.

Materials:
- What materials are used?
- Look for alternative materials.
- Reduction in waste materials.
- Standardization of materials.
- Use of cheaper and better substitute materials.
- Price of materials.
- Make or buy decision.

Manufacturing:
- Define operations.
- Can it be eliminated?
- Can it be substituted?
- Can it be simplified?
- Can it be standardized?
- Can standard tools be used?
- Can pre-fabricated parts be used?
- Make or buy the parts.

Specifications:
- Define specifications.
- Can the dimensions be reduced?
- Are the parts oversized?
- Are the tolerances very close?
- Are the tolerances very critical?
- Can the tolerances be increased?
- What type of finish is required?
- Are the finish standards too specific?

9.1.8 Phases of Value Engineering

Value analysis or value engineering is normally carried out in eight successive phases as enumerated below in chronological order:

- Orientation
- Information
- Function
- Speculation/Creation
- Evaluation/Analysis
- Recommendation
- Implementation
- Audit/Follow-up

Now let us take the phases one-by-one and understand the activities and objectives at each stage of the activity.

9.1.8.1 Orientation phase

The orientation phase of value engineering consists of imparting training to the members of a department or the organization proposing to undertake the value engineering activity. The next value engineering activity will involve selecting the 'subject of study'. Once the subject of the study is selected, the 'selection of the project' is normally done by priority depending on the urgency and criticality of the situation. The project prioritization can be done by either ABC analysis, Pareto analysis, contribution analysis, new product development or the new system/process development.

The value engineering team consists of members from different functional areas and should be as heterogeneous and creative as possible. The team leader is normally the most affected person by the exercise. In case the objective of value engineering is value addition to the products and services, the leader could be the head of marketing. If the main objective of the value engineering team is cost reduction, the leader will be the head of manufacturing.

9.1.8.2 Information phase

The information phase of value engineering starts only after deciding the *objective* or the *mission* of the value engineering activity. The information to be collected should hover around the *key question of cost* and collection of data about *special waste* and *work procedures* and install the facts about the correctness and validity of the data collected, as well as the source of the information. The sources of information can be government publications, government reports, information from suppliers, commercial information provided by the competitors about their products and services, project data, historical data and experimental data, etc.

9.1.8.3 Functional phase

The next phase of value engineering is the functional aspect of the products and services. The value engineering activity starts with determination of the *objective* and the *key question of function*. The functional phase of value engineering has to answer the following important questions:

> What does it do?
> What must it do?
> How much does it cost?
> What is its function/work?

Once these questions are answered, the value engineering team analyzes the answers and determines the functional requirement of products and services.

9.1.8.4 Speculation/creation phase

The next phase of the value engineering activity looks for *alternatives*. This phase of activity consists of *brain storming* session by the value engineering team where the number of alternatives are blasted and created. Then all these alternatives are analyzed to find out which alternative will satisfy the needed function. Most of the alternatives are eliminated, leaving behind a few most likely and feasible alternative substitutes.

9.1.8.5 Evaluation/analysis phase

The next phase of the value engineering activity is the evaluation of the ideas created during the brainstorming session. What is the cost of implementation of each idea? Will they perform the basic function or the 'musts'? Will they perform the secondary functions or 'wants' and to what extent? Will it work satisfactorily? What will be the savings? The idea which satisfies all the musts and the maximum number of wants is the best solution. However, this idea should be better than the existing way of doing things and should either add value to the products and services or reduce the cost of production.

9.1.8.6 Recommendation phase

Now develop a prototype of the idea into the controlled condition and conduct trials. Get the feedback from the market and the customers and assess the customer satisfaction; assess the management's needs in terms of profitability and return on investment; pre-empt any objections for the acceptability of the idea and make presentation to the customers; organizational people and the dealers for the acceptance of the idea. If everything goes favourably and the chances of the idea becoming successful are high, recommend the same for implementation as a validated idea.

9.1.8.7 Implementation phase

After finding out the best solution, the value engineering team will work out an action plan for systematic implementation of the idea with the required resources and in a time-bound manner. The value engineering team will now translate the ideas into actions and remove the bottlenecks as and when they arise. The progress of the implementation of the ideas will have to be monitored by the value engineering team and they have to ensure their smooth implementation for obtaining the desired result.

9.1.8.8 Audit follow-up

The value engineering team keeps constant watch on the actual process even after the same has been successfully implemented. The team prepares periodic reports after evaluating that the desired results are obtained also under normal working conditions by the regular people handling the matter as usual. After being certain about the success of the idea and its implementation, the value engineering team looks for spin-off projects in other similar areas and initiates new projects and the process repeats again.

9.1.9 Darsiri Method

Darsh in Sanskrit means to reconsider. The Darsiri method of value engineering is a systematic approach to improve the value of the products and components by reconsideration of cost and quality. The quality of the product is reconsidered and reviewed, based on its functions, esteem value and cost.

9.1.9.1 Steps of Darsiri method

Data collection: The data is collected based on the functional aspects of the products and services. The cost associated with each function is also ascertained during the data collection process.

Data analysis: The data analysis is focused on saving in cost with improvements in the product features without compromising on the performance and reliability of the product and the related services.

Recording of ideas: After the data collection, the team goes through the process of the generation and recording of ideas through a brainstorming exercise.

Speculation and selection: The ideas are selected based on whether they have been previously tried and failed, technological viability, availability of material, etc. and a few best ideas are approved.

Investigation: After a detailed analysis and investigation, suitable prototypes are developed on the approved ideas. These prototypes are tested to ascertain their performance against the required level. A comparative study is done to select the best alternative which satisfies all the basic functions and the maximum number of secondary functions.

Recommendation: The value engineering team now recommends the implementation of the best alternative as discussed above and arranges for the required resources.

Implementation: The value engineering team now shifts the responsibility of implementing the best alternative by the most affected department. If the exercise is for a better market share, the department will be the marketing department. On the other hand, if the objective of value engineering is cost-reduction, the implementing department will be the manufacturing department.

A periodic review is always required after implementation to find out the scope for further improvement as well as for implementing in the other relevant areas.

9.2 SMED (SINGLE MINUTE EXCHANGE OF DIES)

An increased variety or small lot sizes lead to increase in the number of change-overs. Each change-over leads to a new set-up and the loss of valuable production time due to enhancement of idle time. Sheigo Shingo worked for many years to solve this problem and came out with a methodology to ensure that change in all the dies over time is restricted to less than 10 minutes, thereby saving a lot of useful production time otherwise lost in machine set-up time. Normally, dies are needed to manufacture a lot of components. All the plastic and rubber components need dies for their manufacturing. The castings of steel and non-ferrous metal need dies. The forging process need dies for manufacturing. SMED is a structured procedure of reducing the set-up time to between 1 and 9 minutes.

As set-up cost reduces, the total cost of production reduces substantially as also the pressure on the lot size enhancement also reduces. (refer Figure 9.1)

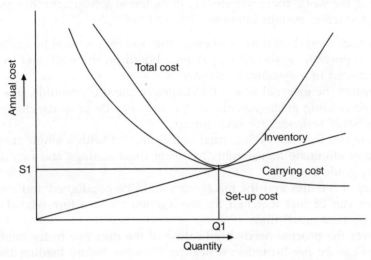

FIGURE 9.1   Relationship between set-up cost, inventory carrying cost and total cost.

9.2.1   Steps of SMED

In 1950, Shigeo Shingo first introduced this study in Toyo Kogyo's Mazda Plant. He introduced the following four-step procedure for SMED:

Step 1:   Observe and analyze how the set-up is being currently performed—observe the set-ups carefully draw the activity charts, worker machine charts and if possible, videotape the process and look for improvements. Break up the process into sub-processes and look for the time wasting factors. Eliminate the time wasters and combine the operations for reducing the set-up time as well as to carry it out effectively and efficiently.

Step 2:   Separate internal and external operations of set-up activity—internal operations are those for which the production has to be stopped, e.g. actual changing of the die.

External operations are those which can be carried out concurrently without stopping the production activity, e.g. arranging for the tools, bolts, materials beforehand.

The objective is to reduce both the operations as far as possible and, if the operations cannot be eliminated, they should be at least converted into external operations so that the machine stoppage time is reduced to the bare minimum.

Step 3:   Convert internal operation set-up activities to external operation set-up activity. Activities like pre-arrangement of tools for changeover, cleaning of machine and closeby area of old material, etc. bringing and arranging new material for production, preheating of dies and moulds, providing duplicate alignment facility, etc. should be completed before the machine is actually shut down for the changeover. The internal operation set-up time should be as low as possible.

Step 4: Simplify and streamline the activities—after assigning as many activities as possible to external set-up, internal set-up time can be further reduced by simplifying and streamlining the work, thereby reducing the internal set-up activities and ultimately reducing the production system idleness. For example,

(a) Each workstation should have its own tools and they should be easily retrievable. As far as possible, it should be put on a board on the wall next to the machine and arranged in a systematic manner.

(b) Standardize the external sizes and shapes of the dies, moulds, jigs and fixtures and their holding arrangements so that they can be of quick change type.

(c) Use the same fasteners for each set-up.

(d) Use fasteners that can be loosened and tightened with a single turn.

(e) Reduce or eliminate adjustments by using fixed settings and markings on dies, moulds, guide bars, etc.

(f) The axes of the dies and the machines should be prealigned and marked so that the lines can be just matched for the alignments in a few seconds which may otherwise take much time.

(g) Whenever the process needs pre-heating of the dies like in the rubber industry, the dies can be pre-heated in a heating chamber before loading the die on the machine.

9.2.2   Success Stories of SMED

- Shingo reduced the set-up time of a bolt making machine at Toyota from eight hours to one minute.
- Shingo reduced the set-up time for boring machine at Mitsubishi Heavy Industries from 24 hours to less than three minutes.
- Ford Motor Company reduced the time for a die change on one of its presses from five hours to five minutes.

9.2.3   Examples of SMED

- Cap of jam bottle opens in half turn.
- Metal clip on wrist watches takes less time than leather strap and buckle.
- Twin razor is quicker than shaving stick.
- Press buttons on zippers are faster than loop buttons.
- Changing of dies on presses is like changing cassettes and in tape-recorders due to standardization of sizes and shapes.

9.2.4   Four Principles by Shingo for Achieving SMED

- No matter what the current set-up time may be (hours, days, weeks, etc.), it is possible to reduce the set-up time to a single digit value in minutes, i.e. less than ten minutes.

- The reduction in set-up time should be done in stages and not in one go.
- Only a small amount of money should be spent for reducing set-up time at each stage.
- Only through participation of all, can SMED be attainable.

SMED along with the Computer Integrated Manufacturing (CIM) has reduced the loss of production and idle manpower due to set-up time to practically single digit minute or almost negligible. This has reduced the pressure on manufacturing for taking up economic batch quantity to compensate for the setting time. Hence, the modern manufacturing concepts like Just-In-Time could be implemented. Smaller lot sizes with frequent deliveries to the market or the customer have become the norm of the world-class manufacturing system. All these modern manufacturing techniques have been made possible to a great extent by SMED. The underlying principle of SMED has been applied to the concept of *Modular manufacturing* which is quite popular in the construction and furniture industries and is under the process of implementation in the automobile industry.

9.3 TOTAL PRODUCTIVE MAINTENANCE

Due to sudden breakdown of machine tools, there is substantial loss of production due to stoppage of the production line as well as rejection of the products. Before the machine actually breaks down, it produces lots of products which are substandard in terms of quality due to deteriorating condition of the machine tools. The cost of breakdown maintenance is higher than the preventive maintenance for a machine. The effects of poor maintenance are detailed below:

9.3.1 Effects of Poor Maintenance

- It is expensive and harmful.
- Fixing major machine failures is costlier than the cost of preventive maintenance.
- When machines are being repaired, the workers are idle.
- Production reliability is lost due to machine breakdowns, leading to product shortages and late deliveries.
- Breakdown wastes capacity.
- Production is lost due to unplanned shut-downs as a result of machine failures.
- Inadequately maintained machines may produce defective parts.

9.3.2 Causes of Machine Failures

The causes of machine failures are enumerated below:

- Inadequate and irregular preventive maintenance leads to deterioration of the machines and ultimately their failure.
- Overusing and operating machine at excessive speeds exceeding their specified limit results in reducing the life of the machine as well its accuracy and consistency of performance.

- Improper cleaning of the machines leads to accumulation of dirt, oil, etc., on the machine parts resulting in chemical changes causing erosion and corrosion of the machine parts. This makes the machine to work in a defective manner, producing non-conforming product.
- Inadequate maintenance of the machines results in loosening of the parts including nuts and bolts. The parts may fall off leading to the collisions and accidents.
- Incorrect machine set-up for operation by loading with parts beyond the machine's capacity and taking cuts or performing an operation beyond the machine's capability will result in the machine breakdown, the cutting tool breakage and the slippage of the job under operation.
- Materials fed into the machine may be processed inadequately due to the inconsistency in the quality of the material or its specifications leading to the quality problem or rejection of the parts produced on the machine.

9.3.3 Focus of Total Productive Maintenance

- Total productive maintenance aims to eliminate the six causes of machine failures.
- Total productive maintenance aims at maximizing the effectiveness of equipment throughout its entire life.
- Total productive maintenance involves everyone in all the departments and at all levels.
- Total productive maintenance motivates people for plant maintenance through small group and voluntary activities.
- Total productive maintenance develops a maintenance system.
- Total productive maintenance provides training in basic house-keeping, problem solving skills and activities to achieve zero breakdowns and prevents six big loses, namely
  (1) Breakdown due to equipment failure.
  (2) Set-up and adjustment time lost.
  (3) Idling and minor stoppages.
  (4) Reduced speed.
  (5) Defects in process and reworks.
  (6) Start-up loss of yield.

9.3.4 Features of Total Productive Maintenance

Total productive maintenance can be achieved by installing a sense of ownership in the mind of the operator for the machine being run by him for years together. Total productive maintenance work can include both routine maintenance and preventive maintenance work to be done regularly by the machine operator himself. The preventive maintenance work should be delegated from specialized maintenance staff to the routine machine operators. Preventive maintenance should be done as normal part of the operator's job so that it is more reliable and regular. It is also inexpensive since it can be done while the machine is running or when it is idle for other reasons.

To make the total productive maintenance work effective, an elaborate training on the fault finding, noticing early warning signals of machine malfunctioning and preventive maintenance should be imparted to the regular machine operators. Machine failures are maximum when it is run for a long time regularly without break and also if it is run more than 80% of its rated speed (refer Figure 9.2).

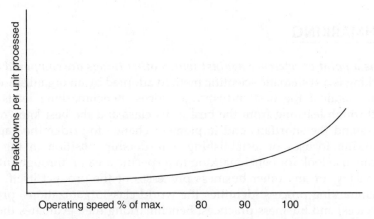

FIGURE 9.2 Relation between the machine speed and the machine failure rate.

Cleanliness and good housekeeping not only prevent machine failures, but also reduce accidents, rejections, rework, etc. A major cause of machine failure or poor product quality is the buildup of dirt, chemicals or oil on the machine or the material. The dirt, chemicals and oils corrode the machine parts leading to faulty working resulting in poor quality of the components produced and weakening of the machine parts.

Structured set-ups driven by SMED technique ensure quick changeovers, better quality of product and no rejections. Incorrect set-ups lead to material jamming in the machines and other processing problems, leading to malfunction of the machines and accidents. Proper set-ups on the machines can only be ensured by the machine operators and not by the maintenance personnel.

Proper job design and work aids ensure that no time is wasted in looking for materials or other work aids. They also ensure the optimum utilization of the input resources of men, machines and materials safely and securely. This also can be ensured by the machine operator only.

Machines should be as simple as possible and standardized while still accomplishing the required functions effectively. The machine operator should be properly trained to handle the machine and work on the same efficiently. The workers being trained on the use of the machine, maintenance of the machine, and various problem-solving techniques should also be trained how to effectively implement total productive maintenance.

Machine history cards should be properly filled in and maintained to prepare adequate data for preventive maintenance work. This will enable the operator to plan the routine spare parts requirements like V-belts, bearings, etc. for the machine in advance and as per schedule. Procurement should be carefully planned so that all the parts are available when needed as well as that they are not excess in inventory.

When one part of the machine wears out, it affects other parts also. It is better to change all such related parts in one go rather than opening the machine frequently. Hence, under the total productive maintenance philosophy, the machine operator not only takes responsibility for the quality and quantity of production, but also the routine preventive maintenance of the machine.

9.4 BENCHMARKING

A benchmark is a point of reference against which other things are compared or measured. The benchmarking is a systematic scientific method adopted by an organization to measure its performance against the best industry practices. Benchmarking leads to superior performance through learning from the best in its class and the best known practices. It helps to understand the shortfalls and implement change to bridge the gap.

Benchmarking focuses on establishing a leadership position in the market. An organization can also look for benchmarking in a specific area of 'throughput', 'a product attribute', 'servicing' or any other business processes or the product itself.

The benchmarking process identifies the world-class organizations, products (both goods and services) and business practices. Benchmarking then evaluates the reasons for those being the world-class. Benchmarking, systematically and continuously integrates that knowledge into an organization's products and services as well as their processes. Benchmarking is for world-class leadership.

The objective of benchmarking is to understand the competitor's strength and how they operate and wherever it is beneficial to adapt and build upon their excellent practices for a company's use. The benchmarking process can extend beyond the competition also for a particular product and/or service attribute.

Identify companies renowned as functional leaders. These organizations can be picked up for the process of the benchmarking. The benchmarking process focuses on activities towards customer satisfaction and market leadership. The benchmarking process is a continuous process and leads to openness to new ideas. Benchmarking can be applied to both manufacturing and service industries.

9.4.1 Types of Benchmarking

Internal benchmarking: The internal benchmarking process is benchmarking against a particular department and function which is excelling compared to other departments or functions. The internal benchmarking could be against a process or individual performance under a certain category which can be implemented in other areas also.

Benchmarking against the competition: This is the most common benchmarking exercise mandatory to be carried out for organizational survival and performance excellence. As per Michael Porter's theory of Competitive Advantage, it is mandatory for an organization for benchmarking against the competition in terms of value advantage, product differentiation or cost advantage for market leadership and salability of the product or service. This is the normal practice of benchmarking in most of the industries.

Benchmarking outside the industry: On a particular attribute applicable to a product, organization may go outside the boundary of competition and benchmark itself against the best in that particular sector. For example, internationally a world leader in the field of entertainment electronics, particularly the 'colour television' sector, benchmarked against 'Bose' for the sound system. One of the benchmarked criteria of Xerox Corporation was against a courier company.

Functional Benchmarking: This is the most common benchmarking process which is concerned with product performance vis-à-vis the competition. Quality is defined by Dr. Joseph Juran as *The fitness for use* and by Philip B. Crosby as *'the conformance to requirement'*. Dr. Edward Deming stated that 'quality performance by a product is the key factor for the market leadership'. If we combine the theories of all these management gurus, we shall come to the conclusion that functional benchmarking is not only essential but also mandatory for an organization to survive and excel in its performance.

Business process Benchmarking: The benchmarking process pertaining to various business processes like customer satisfaction, market leadership, order fulfillment, maintenance of machines and services, billing and collection, financial management, asset management, information technology, human resource development, etc. The best practices from the same group of industries as well as the best in each class is taken up as the benchmarking partner for attaining perfection in the respective business operations.

9.4.2 Three Reasons for Benchmarking Competition

Stay in business: The benchmarking process enables an organization to assess its position in a particular market segment vis-à-vis the competition. The organization has to offer the products and the services at least in line with what is being offered by its competitors to enable it to survive in its business in that particular market segment. The organization has to do a gap analysis of products and services feature by feature with reference to its competition and bridge the gap. This is the bare minimum effort the organization has to take in surviving in its business.

Delight the customer: When the organization can bridge the gap and go beyond in providing the products and services better than the competition at the same price to the customers, the customer will be delighted and switch over to the organization's products and services, thereby ensuring it a market leadership in that particular market segment.

Become the world-class leader: After having attained the position of market leader in a particular market segment, an organization can extend its network to other potential areas of its product and service usage. By steadily following the practice of benchmarking in various market segments and learning from the best in each respective area, combine the knowledge gained from each area of the products and services to reach world-class level. This process, if monitored and practised continuously, will make the organization invariably a world leader.

9.4.3 Elements of Benchmarking

The elements to be chosen for benchmarking could be anything which are superior to the organization elements in any particular area. The benchmarking process could have benchmarking partner as one of the following organizations.

Direct competitor: The most common benchmarking partner is from direct competition and it is a bare minimum requirement of an organization to survive in today's global business environment. The basic benchmarking process with the competition is the product related features and after sales service or the distribution service. This practice of benchmarking is followed when the organization is a follower or laggard in the industry.

Admired company in the same industry: When an organization attains a powerful position in the industry it shifts its focus of benchmarking to the best in the same industry as it is rearing to go beyond the competition. It is of course assumed that the admired company in the same industry has similar customers and it has attained the position of admiration by better understanding of the market and obviously the consumers and customers.

Admired company in any industry: The benchmarking process pertaining to business processes looks for a benchmarking partner who has attained the position of an admired company in any industry and excels in its performance in one or more business processes. It is much easier to benchmark processes of an admired company outside the competition as the flow of data and relevant information can be collected easily with the help and co-operation of the benchmarking partner as his business interest does not clash with that of the organization. This will also help the organization to go beyond the competition in best business practices as the choice of selecting the benchmarking partner is wide and from a much better breed of organization to choose from.

Best of breed on different aspects: When an organization has attained a very high level of performance in terms of its products and processes, it needs to progress further and now has to increase the level of its benchmarking partner to the best of breed on a particular aspect. The fine-tuning of the benchmarking process will lead the organization to an all-round excellent performance level.

Chasing multiple competitors: When the benchmarking process reaches a high level of standard and maturity over the years, an organization may have different benchmarking partners for different attributes of a product or for each of the different business processes. The objective of the organization is clear. It wants to attain world-class performance level in each individual segment of the product or the process collectively, the organisation attains superior features as compared to any of its benchmarking partners individually.

The organization starts with the process of benchmarking against an organization which is better at the moment. Some time later, the organization bridges the gap and reaches the same level and then goes beyond through continual improvement. Now the organization has reached a performance level beyond the originally benchmarked organization. The organization then looks for a new benchmarking partner whose performance is much above the earlier benchmarking partner (refer to Figure 9.3).

9.4.4 Benchmarking Measurements

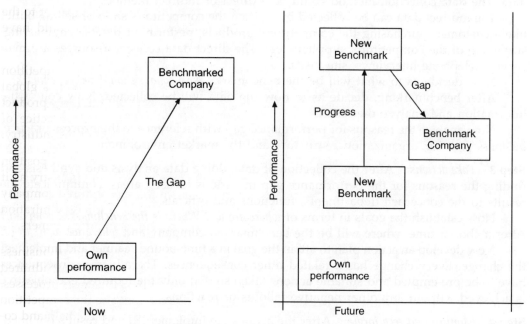

FIGURE 9.3 Process of benchmarking.

9.4.5 Process of Benchmarking

The benchmarking process consists of four distinctive steps. It follows the steps successively in a systematic and scientific manner, highly structured and oriented towards the specified and well-defined objectives.

Step 1 *Prepare to benchmark:* The benchmarking process starts with the top echelon of an organization accepting the fact that its performance in various sectors of products and processes needs to be improved at the earliest. Once the above objective is accomplished, involve the Chief Executive Officer and the heads of the functions and build the quality council support. Decide 'what to benchmark' and the 'scope' of the benchmarking—broad, shallow, narrow, and in-depth. The benchmarking topic could be either the products and processes that are critical success factors for the organization either by way of market leadership, the financial parameter or both.

Now assign the change agent for the benchmarking process and assemble a team. The benchmarking team now prepares to collect data and understands its own operation. Now the benchmarking team documents the data collection procedure and communicates to all concerned. The team now meets periodically on a fixed day and time and devotes enough time. It is extremely important for the benchmarking team to thoroughly understand and document the current product and the current process.

Step 2 *Discover facts:* The benchmarking team now starts collecting data. The data collection process starts with the identification of sources of data, determination of the method of data collection, sharing of information and finding the right contact for the data. The data collection method could be a direct or indirect method.

The indirect data can be collected by visiting the competitor's shop or selling outlet like a customer, purchasing the competitor's products, performing reverse engineering, surveying of the competitor's suppliers, etc. The direct data collection sources are mail survey, telephone interviews, site visits.

Now decide as to what will be the benchmark? And *whom should we benchmark*?

After benchmarking, decide as to how the data will be collected. Now collect the information and analyze the result.

Now analyze the reasons for performance gap with reference to the process practice, business practice, organizational structure and the market environment.

Step 3 *Take actions:* After the collection of data, doing data analysis and synthesis and finding the reasons for the performance gap in various focused areas, communicate the results to the concerned departments, functions and officials.

Now establish the goals in terms of *where are we? Where is the benchmarked company?* After a chosen time, where will be the benchmarked company and *where we want to be*.

Now develop an action plan to attain the goal in a time-bound manner and implement the change. Every change has a related other consequences. The adverse consequences have to be pre-empted and suitable actions taken so that only the required end objective is achieved without any other negative fallouts or reactions.

Step 4 *Monitor and recalibrate:* After the actions are implemented and results obtained, monitor the progress. The benchmarking process continues with the measurements identified, results communicated to the concerned departments, including the senior management. Monitor the progress of the satisfactory implementation of the action plan. Now update the benchmarks against a better competitor, a better process, a better technology, etc.

The stages of benchmarking are detailed in Figure 9.4. The process starts with the selection of the weak areas or the benchmark areas which are critical for the business success as well as the areas where there is substantial scope for improvement in performance, then the benchmark organizations and the areas of benchmark are decided. The performance of the organization vis-à-vis the benchmark organization is compared in the next stage.

Benchmarking is an adaptive learning process. An organization learns from the best, i.e. the benchmarked organizations and implements the learning into action to bridge the gap in performance and knowledge. Once the benchmark parameters are achieved, then revise the benchmark to the next higher order and set new benchmarks.

Now again bridge the gap and go beyond. Now go for multiple benchmarking on multiple product and business process attributes and reach an overall higher performance level. Derive competitive advantage and become the market leader. Upgrade the organization on a continual basis and attain the level of a world-class organization as depicted in Figure 9.5.

Benchmarking is an effective management tool to improve the performance of organization in the shortest possible time. It is a process of adaptive learning from the best and a case of reverse engineering. Benchmarking improves the organizational performance in all the three areas of product, process and system.

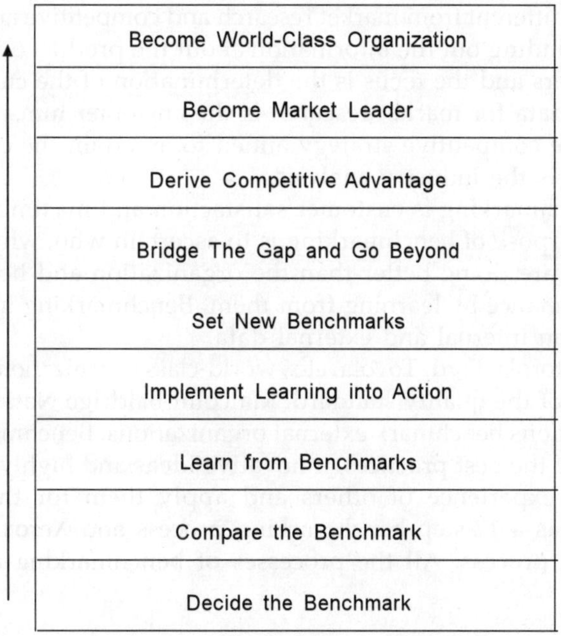

```
┌─────────────────────────────────────────┐
│         Become World-Class Organization  │
├─────────────────────────────────────────┤
│         Become Market Leader             │
├─────────────────────────────────────────┤
│         Derive Competitive Advantage     │
├─────────────────────────────────────────┤
│         Bridge The Gap and Go Beyond     │
├─────────────────────────────────────────┤
│         Set New Benchmarks               │
├─────────────────────────────────────────┤
│         Implement Learning into Action   │
├─────────────────────────────────────────┤
│         Learn from Benchmarks            │
├─────────────────────────────────────────┤
│         Compare the Benchmark            │
├─────────────────────────────────────────┤
│         Decide the Benchmark             │
└─────────────────────────────────────────┘
```

FIGURE 9.4   Stages of benchmarking.

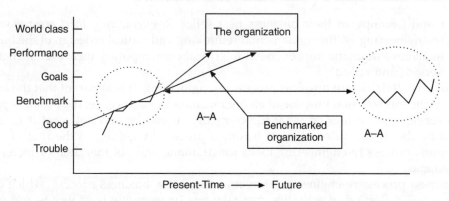

FIGURE 9.5   The process of upgrading an organization on a continual basis to attain the level of world-class organization.

Benchmarking is not a performance evaluation tool, a quick fix programme, a panacea, a fad or a public relation tool. It is not something you do half heartedly or in a perfunctory manner. Benchmarking is not a mechanism for determining resource reduction and is a highly structured scientific management process to improve on a continual basis and attain perfection in the shortest possible time.

The common benchmarking metrics are customer satisfaction, market share, cost as a per cent of revenue, cycle time, quality, return on assets, logistics, etc.

Benchmarking is different from market research and competitive analysis. The purpose of market research is finding out the information about the product/service requirements and about the customers and the focus is the determination of the customers' needs and wants. The source of data for market research is the customer himself. The competitive analysis focuses on the competitive strategy aimed to ascertain the competition and the source of information is the industry analysis.

The focus of benchmarking is customer satisfaction and maximization of the return on investment. The purpose of benchmarking is to ascertain who, why, how and in what areas the benchmarks are doing better than the organization and how to reach quickly to their level of performance by learning from them. Benchmarking involves the original research work based on internal and external data.

Xerox, AT&T, Motorola, Ford, Toyota, etc., world-class organizations use benchmarking as a common element of the quality standard. Malcolm Baldrige National quality awards the applicant organizations benchmark external organizations. Benchmarking is systematic search and adoption of the best practices, innovative ideas and highly effective operating procedures from the experience of others and apply them for the improvement of organization. AT&T has a 12-step benchmarking process and Xerox Corporation has a 10-step benchmarking process. All the processes of benchmarking are similar to each other.

9.5 BUSINESS PROCESS RE-ENGINEERING (BPR)

Hammer and Champy in their business best seller *Re-engineering the Corporation* have defined re-engineering as 'the fundamental rethinking and radical redesign of the business process to achieve dramatic improvement in critical contemporary measures such as cost quality, service and speed'.

From the definition of business process re-engineering, it is apparent that the activity focuses on the fundamental purpose of an organization's existence, i.e. the business process re-engineering concentrates on what the company should be and not what it is. This is achieved by the 'Radical Redesign' of business process by getting to the root of things. The business process re-engineering looks for dramatic and not marginal or incremental improvements.

Business process re-engineering hovers around the 'business process' which can be described as a collection of activities that take one or more kinds of inputs and creates an output that is of value to the customers. The entire activities are process-oriented and not task- or job- or structure-oriented.

BPR is oriented towards the customer and it views business as a system with sub-systems organized around processes with common goals for the entire organization.

The companies that undertake BPR are either companies that find themselves in deep trouble or those that are not in trouble at present but foresee trouble in future. The business process re-engineering is also equally important for those companies that are leaders in their fields whose positions are threatened by the competition which can dislodge them from the leadership position.

9.5.1 The Concept of Business Process Re-engineering

Among the many methodologies adopted for business solutions, BPR has emerged as one of the vital management tools. The concept of radically changing business practices promising significant performance improvement makes BPR an effective management tool which solved management problems. This concept has received both acclaim and criticism as corporations world-wide have geared their processes to meet the challenges of intensive global competition.

In BPR, several jobs and operations are combined into one whereever feasible. The workers are empowered to make decisions. The work is performed at the point where it makes the most sense. Rejection, reconciliation and rework are minimized. Checks and controls are reduced as the focus is more on controlling the process rather than the product.

After examining their BPR results, most companies were disappointed as their expectations were much higher. A survey of *Fortune 500* companies and the top 100 U.K. companies was carried out by Price Waterhouse. According to the survey, 67% of the companies reported that increased speed with which new products and services were developed and brought to the market was the strongest motivation for BPR. Apart from the above, the following five objectives were met. The objectives accomplished by BPR were the streamlining of business processes, increase in productivity, reduction in cost of manufacturing, reduction in manpower and increasing efficiency of the workforce as well as eliminating low value work.

A few myths pertaining to BPR need to be cleared before we move further. BPR is not a panacea for all the problems prevalent in a company which may be caused by poor management or unhealthy business practices. Business process re-engineering is not an organization-wide computerization even though I.T. has played a major role in many success stories of BPR implementation.

BPR involves changes that may impact the existing functions and egos. The involvement of the CEO is likely to be intensive throughout the process.

Re-engineering has worked well in many Indian companies like Mahindra & Mahindra Ltd. For the effective implementation of the BPR, there must be eagerness to tackle the critical issues that lead to the quick and effective fulfillment of the customers' needs. BPR challenges the old mindsets and creates an interest in using the technology available.

Information Technology plays a critical role in the implementation of BPR. BPR is the industrial engineering principles and practices enabled by the information technology. BPR makes use of IT to transform the work procedures in an effective manner rather than merely hastening the office work.

Time has now come for business processes and technology to be integrated in order to function effectively in realtime world, e.g. the airline and railway reservation system. The system is updated and the status is made available to all the terminals on a transaction to transaction basis. The implementation of supply chain management is the ultimate manifestation of the integration of the business processes and information technology for the effective and efficient operation of business enterprises. The information technology should enable simplification of the business process and the use of technology should perfect the business process.

9.5.2 Implementation of Business Process Re-engineering

The business process re-engineering implementation is done in four phases.

9.5.2.1 Focus phase

In this phase, the quality council decides to implement the BPR in the organization and defines the objectives for implementing the same. The quality council then sets up a cross-functional core processing reengineering group. The team conducts a Pareto Analysis and identifies the key processes that are of high priority for the re-engineering. The focus phase considers the following factors.

The business vision and goals are normally customer-driven and contain in them the survival values and critical success factors of the enterprise. They also include actions for the maximization of the return on investment. Achievement of the business vision may involve re-engineering of one or more processes. The BPR process decides the vital process attributes like cost, quality, time, wastages and the process measures. BPR examines these processes critically for their improvements in terms of quality, reduction of cost and time. The probable benefit realization opportunity of these processes decides the focus area and works out a rough cut implementation plan, along with the details of activities and resources requirements. The process looks for a radical examination of re-engineering with the resultant likely benefit to justify such changes and related efforts to be taken.

9.5.2.2 Design phase

In this phase the organization makes a serious effort to measure the performance of the existing processes on identifiable and well-defined attributes. First the chosen existing process and its enabling technology are analyzed and assessed. Now the viable alternative processes are designed and prototypes of the alternative processes are built up. A comparison is made of the alternative processes with the existing one and its benefits and drawbacks. The one alternative which satisfies all the musts and the maximum number of wants related to the products and the services at the least cost is the chosen solution to the BPR process.

9.5.2.3 Implementation phase

Here, the new solutions and processes as outcomes of the BPR process need proper change management. First of all, the top management and quality council members have to give their approval to the findings and go ahead for the implementation. This acceptance will be followed through training the work force, staff and managers both from the concept point of view as well as the individual training angle to operate the new process by respective individuals. The control points and the units of measurements of the new process have to be established. Once all these are done, the BPR process can be implemented as a fresh plan along with focus on the key areas. The periodic measurement of the performance as per the plan and correction of deviations if any will complete the implementation phase.

9.5.2.4 Benefit realisation phase

The new process is now actually implemented in a pilot situation and eventually into full stream implementation. The BPR process implementation takes about a couple of years but the benefits of the BPR process starts coming in from the end of the third month onwards.

The final stage needs a lot of business acumen and skill for all the companies as it involves issues that are multidimensional in nature relating to technology, attitudes of the people, creating new organizational structure, etc.

Such issues are highly enterprise-specific, and the methods to be adopted depend largely on the organizational climate prevailing at that time. The BPR implementers have to be cautious of not imposing too many change programmes with too many goals competing with each other. Involvement of key individuals, coordinated and integrated effort, careful and optimum resource planning and allocation are the important aspects of the benefit realization of the BPR process. Effective communication within and outside the organization is going to be the critical element of approach.

The approach should now shift from defensive to an offensive approach which not only encompasses the cost cutting approach but also gives a strong thrust to customer satisfaction.

Hence a six-layer approach as suggested by Price Waterhouse should be adopted:

1. Markets and customers
2. Products and services
3. People and culture
4. Technology
5. Business processes
6. Structure and facilities

The first two are at the strategic level while the other two are at the operational level. Such a methodology will not only re-design the business but most importantly it will evaluate the shareholders, products, markets, services, etc.

Despite all the publicity and enthusiasm surrounding reengineering, many organizations remain in a state of confusion and misunderstanding. BPR in India is yet to take off.

Many companies have realized the importance of the BPR process and the organizations which have implemented are ITC, L&T, M&M, Siemens, Crompton Greaves, etc.

The main hurdle in implementing the BPR is that the benefit is realized after many months of painstaking efforts for which normally the management may not agree to wait. The consultants and information system managers may be tempted to unnecessarily load the organization with costly IT hardware and software much more than what is required. In order to bring everything under the BPR, the organizations lose focus on the key issues of marketing and human resource management which are low cost areas to generate revenue and reduce the cost of manufacturing.

Hence to make BPR successful, the scope and objective of the re-engineering should be clearly defined at the beginning of the activities and all the wrong notions must be removed.

BPR as implemented as a sporadic activity without well-defined focus and long-term planning may not yield the desired result in many organizations. However, India is a developing country growing fast. Transfer of technology is taking place globally at a tremendous speed and low cost. The scope of implementing the BPR in India is fantastic and the returns from the same are also likely to come much faster than the global standards since there is a lot of re-engineering of business processes has to be done in such a short time for the survival and performance excellence of Indian organizations.

9.5.3 Case Study

The organization is one of the top 20 manufacturing companies in India. This company is engaged in the business of manufacturing the Sports Utility Vehicles (SUV) and tractors. Around the mid-eighties, the organization had been facing intense competition from the new entrants and multi-nationals, leading to a reduction in its market share. Hence it decided to go for BPR. The organization hired an expert consultant from the United Kingdom. However, the first 3–4 years went only in the process planning exercise. The company faced the problem of reduction in market share, higher inventory, large amount of non-value adding activity, low productivity level, frequent change in production planning and idle machine capacity. The company had the further problem of multi-tier organization, poor communication, strong departmental orientation, centralized control system and the lack of process ownership.

After identifying all these problems, the CEO of the organization kept a 10-year target to achieve the following parameters (this is an example of areas of concentration of BPR).

- Customer complaints should reduce by 90%
- Sales per employee should increase by 175%
- Price of vehicles should reduce by 15%
- Cost of material as percentage of sales should reduce by 10%
- Stock turnover ratio should improve to four times a year
- Lead time should reduce by 70%
- Schedule adherence should be 100%

However, the target could not be achieved as per stipulation and it was extended further by a year and a half.

Some of the good results achieved due to this effort of BPR were inventory reduction in the axle division by almost 50% in these 11 years. Unloading time came down from 48 hours to 2 hours. The modvat credit was available on the same day. Lead time was reduced from 45 to 30 days. Rejection was lower by 25%. However, the organization could not show any significant improvement in its bottom line. Even if there was some improvement in selected areas, is the long duration of over 11 years it took and the heavy investment in BPR justified?

QUESTIONS

1. Explain the high points of the case.

2. Is the BPR successful or failure in India?

3. What are the areas where you can get easy success through the BPR?

EXERCISES

1. Define and explain the concepts *value analysis* and *value engineering*. Describe in detail the phases of *value analysis*.

2. What are the benefits of *value analysis*? What are the areas of *value analysis*? Explain the method of value analysis?

3. Explain the concept of the Single Minute Exchange of Dies (SMED) and its significance in the manufacturing industry. Explain the SMED process.

4. Elaborate the concept and process of Total Productive Maintenance.

5. Define benchmarking. Explain the concept and process of benchmarking in detail.

6. Define Business Process Reengineering. Explain the concept and process of BPR in detail.

7. Of all the Total Quality Management practices discussed in this chapter, explain which of them can be applied to an automobile manufacturing industry and how.

10

Supply Chain Management

10.1 SUPPLY CHAIN MANAGEMENT

Supply Chain Management (SCM) is probably the most talked about subject in the management of an organization but also the least understood one. The topic is usually discussed in part with many misnomers like inventory management system and the inclusion of suppliers in an organization structure. Supply chain management is in a way an extension of the Porter's theory of Value Chain Management, but goes much beyond.

Let us give the description of the supply chain as given in ISO 9000:2000 edition-Clause No. 3. "The following terms are used in the edition of ISO 9001 to describe supply chain, have been changed to reflect the vocabulary currently used".

$$\text{Supplier} \longrightarrow \text{Organization} \longrightarrow \text{Customer}$$

However, this definition, as given in ISO 9001 has been updated into a more advanced definition of the supply chain as elaborated below in a simple manner. Please refer to Figure 10.1.

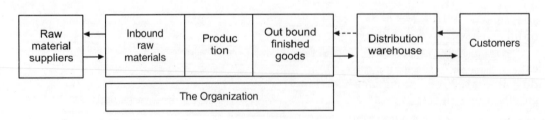

→ Flow of material, products and services

◄--- Flow of information

FIGURE 10.1 The desciption of supply chain management according to ISO 9000:2000.

10.2 LOGISTICS AND SUPPLY CHAIN MANAGEMENT

In a conventional organization and in a situation where, through licence raj, the demand was more than the supply, manufacturing is always based on the maximization of plant capacity. After manufacturing the product, the organization looks for a customer and tries to 'push' the product in the market. However, in the current scenario after doing away with the licence raj through liberalization, signing of WTO and globalization leading to intense global competition, shortened product life cycle, this 'push strategy' does not work due to fast product obsolescence, non-competitive product features and ultimately no buyers for the product.

Hence the only way to survive in the current business environment is to switch over to pull strategy wherein the customer pulls the entire supply chain. Only products and services, that are capable of providing customer satisfaction by fulfillment of customers' stated and implied needs, are going to survive. This, in short, is the need and objective of supply chain management. The main objective of SCM is the maximization of customer satisfaction by providing the right quality products and services, in the right quantity, at the right time, at the right place and at the right price. The internal objective is to maximize the return on investment (ROI) by compressing the cycle time. Both the objectives are attained by the compression of cycle time and producing only the goods that are needed to fulfill the customer's requirement.

10.2.1 The Concept of Right Quality

The definition of quality was already discussed in detail. However, two definitions are more pertinent. The first is given by Dr. Joseph Juran and also accepted by W. Edward Deming. These two persons are known as the fathers of TQM.

Quality of products and services is defined as "Fitness for use and free from product non-conformities".

ISO 9000:2000 defines quality as: "The degree to which a set of inherent characteristics fulfil requirement". This product feature fulfilling customer requirement is changing today at a fast rate due to intense global competition, more focus by manufacturers on R&D, technological innovations, development of additional product features, shorter product life cycles and fast changing consumer's preferential life styles. If an organization cannot adapt fast to all these changes, its products and services become obsolete and it goes out of business.

Let us look at the current practices of the Indian industries. First of all they are extremely poor in deploying resources in finding out customer requirements. They normally do a monthly production planning. They arrange for inputs to products like raw material, etc. Planning precedes production by a month. The production cycle is about a month. The average finished goods inventory is for a couple of months. The average finished goods stock held at branch offices/distribution warehouses and dealer's end combined together is another two months stock. Combining all this cycle time together, the consumer always gets the products and services more than seven months later and often outdated compared to what the consumer wants today. The products are hence more likely to be obsolete and not as per customer's requirements. This is definitely not the right quality we are talking about. International organizations today like Zaras, a Spanish firm dealing in readymade garments for teenagers, has compressed this cycle time, from market research to market delivery to 15 days.

There are many more examples in this context like the United Colors of Benetton, an Italian garment manufacturer having thousands of retail outlets spread over a 100 countries. The company's cycle time, from the moment the orders are placed by the retail outlet to the goods replenished from the central warehouse at Italy, is less than a week.

10.2.2 The Concept of Right Quantity

Consumer has a buying habit in terms of quality of the products. If you feel thirsty, you will buy a bottle of cold drink and not consume three bottles just because there is a quantity discount unless otherwise you have somebody else to share with.

Normally, you purchase soaps, toothpastes, shaving creams, etc. in a unitary mode. The retailer purchases the same from wholesalers in boxes with each box having 100 pieces so packed together that the wholesaler purchases in container which the distributor may purchase in full truckload. The packaging, as well as storing, have to be done accordingly for compressing the cycle time, ease of handling and economics of transportation cost, storage space, etc. Hence the primary packing should be done in an attractive packet in which it is sold to consumers, as the distributor receives a full truck-load goods stacked in a container.

When the container is opened by the distributor, the goods are in crates to be delivered to the next stage of wholesalers. The distributor needs material handling equipment and storage space for storing the containers and crates. The wholesaler has material handling arrangement and storage space for crates and boxes. When the crates are opened, the material is duly packed in boxes to be delivered to retailers, where the storage space is designed to store boxes and when the retailer opens the boxes, the goods are available in packets to be sold to consumers.

Various powerful products have failed to take off in the market, because companies tried to sell more quantity than the buying behaviour of the consumers permits. Various schemes to sell soaps giving one soap free with six soaps failed. But when the same scheme was given as one free with two soaps succeeded as consumers buy at the most one month's requirement and not more than that. Jyoti Laboratory's sales promotional schemes of giving one 'Ujala' free with six bottles failed to take off for the same reason. The shirt sellers scheme of one shirt free with the purchase of two shirts failed as a promotional scheme because consumers don't have the habit of buying three shirts at a time.

10.2.3 The Concept of Right Place

Customers do not like to travel 10 km to buy sugar, soap or toothpaste, i.e. products of day-to-day need even if it is available there at a cheaper rate. We all know that these products are available at a cheaper rate at wholesale market a few km away, but still we prefer to buy from the shop next door.

This is place utility and mainly created by dealers and retailers. Coca-Cola Ltd. was smart enough to foresee the importance of place utility and took over Parle Soft Drinks, the makers of popular Thumps Up brand of cool drink with a wide distribution network and gained market share. Its competitor Pepsi Foods Ltd., in spite of having heavy television, newspaper and other advertisements popularizing the brand, could not gain market share even in a premium market like Mumbai. This is due to lack of place utility as for this kind of products as customers will not even visit the next shop for Pepsi if both brands are available. Hence it was forced ultimately to enter into a strategic alliance with Dukes Ltd. to gain market share. Similar is the case with P&G and Godrej alliance. The place utility is created by proper supply chain management only.

10.2.4   The Concept of Time Utility

The demand for every product peaks at a certain time. The sale of every product is seasonal to some extent. Hence the supply chain management must keep the seasonal cycle time in mind and should immaculately plan and ensure that the products and services are available at the right time to the customer. This doesn't happen automatically but needs to be managed and controlled.

For example, sales of fans, refrigerators, air-conditioners, water-coolers and air coolers surge in the months of April and May. Assume that a certain organization manufacturing these products has scheduled its peak sales in mid-May. Due to delay in receipt of raw material by 10 days and delay in transit time due to a transporter's strike by seven days the consignment arrives in the market by mid-June. The entire goods will remain unsold at the company's distribution godown for the next 6 to 10 months. By this time, the consumer's preference may change and the products may become obsolete. Also the cash flow will be disturbed and the minimum loss will be 10% to 15% due to loss of interest alone. Then there is a chance of defects getting developed due to the environmental effect of moisture, etc.

Apart from the above example, many times it has been observed that companies advertise for a new product that is about to be launched or start sales promotion scheme immediately after the product leaves the factory without considering the transit time and other elements of cycle time. The entire effort, including the lakhs of rupees on advertisement are wasted. When the consumer visits the dealers' shop, the products are not available. The effect of the advertisements is lost as human beings have short memory. This is due to the fact that time utility has not been created. Recent examples are launching of TVS Vector by TVS Suzuki Ltd. Margo Glycerin Soap by Calcutta Chemicals Ltd., 50% discount on All Out mosquito mats.

10.2.5   The Concept of Price Utility

All the other four utilities, quality, quantity, time and place, being equal, price plays a dominant role in customer satisfaction and leads to better salability of the product. In short, the product available with the same features and utility but at a lower price means better value for money for the customer. Products with the same quality but demanding a higher price due to esteem value associated with their brands have totally disappeared in the case of industrial products and the same trend is becoming visible in consumer durables and non-durables.

10.3 BENEFITS OF SUPPLY CHAIN MANAGEMENT

- Getting a higher return on investment due to effective supply chain management and multiplying the same is the main benefit for management. Please refer to the example given in the chapter under the concept of right quality. Over the cycle time of seven months, add another three months as outstanding debtors. Then the working capital cycle time becomes 10 months. The average profit is 20% and we earn one profit per completion of one working capital cycle, i.e. from the time we pay and procure raw material and convert the same to finished products, sell it to the customer and receive the money. From this, we earn only (12/10) × 20% profit, i.e. 24% over the completion of one working capital cycle of 10 months in the current case. To the quantity of one month's sale of Rs. 1,00,00,000 (one crore), our working capital involvement is roughly around Rs. 9,00,00,000 assuring the cost of raw material and WIP is 50% value of sales and equating money blocked in excise and sales tax as equal to 20% bridge of profit. Our net earning is only Rs. 24,00,000. Hence the ROI is 2.6% on our working capital investment, which is marginal.

  Now if we can compress the cycle time by proper supply chain management to 7 days production cycle instead of monthly production cycle, the resultant raw material inventory will be one week, production cycle time one week, finished goods inventory two weeks. Compress the goods in transit time from one month (four weeks) to two weeks and stock at distribution houses of two weeks and debtors as one month, i.e. four weeks, and retain profit at the same level of 20%. The cycle time now becomes 12 weeks, i.e. 3 months. Hence now the organization earns 20% on a month's sale every three month. Hence in a year it will earn (12/3) × 20 = 80% of a monthly sale, i.e. Rs. 80,00,000 per annum. The blocked money is Rs. 2,75,00,000. Hence the return on investment is 29% which is more than 10 times of the earlier case.

- Benefits that are derived out of proper supply chain management are substantial and manifold.
- In today's competitive world, increase in earnings by increase in price is rarely possible. Cutting down the COPQ and reducing the cost of production thereby increasing the profit also takes substantial effort and time. On the contrary, SCM is the fastest method of increasing the earnings within the shortest possible time.
- Return on investment (ROI) = Profit × number of working capital cycles turnover.

  While Supply Chain Management cannot directly contribute to increase in profits, profit can be either be increased by 'price increase' and/or 'reducing the cost of production'. Both have marginal effect. But, proper SCM increases the working capital cycle turnover multiple times. One complete working capital cycle means one profit. A normal organization to remain healthy should have four working capital cycle turnover, thereby earning profit four times. Hence ROI can be increased many times by proper SCM only.

- It maximizes customer satisfaction by providing goods and services of the right quality, in the right quantity, at the right time, at the right place and at the right price. Achieving all these above five parameters by supply chain management is a tremendous achievement for customer satisfaction.
- SCM gives 'competitive advantage in the market place'.
- It avoids product obsolescence. Decreasing the cycle time to market, it always provides contemporary products in the market place thereby preventing product obsolescence.
- It helps an organization to enhance its market share and attain leadership position.
- It leads to the practise of CRM—Customer Relationship Management and ECR—Excellent Customer Response.
- Proper SCM leads to reduction in blocked capital and hence improves the cash flow and fund flow situation.
- SCM adds more value to organization and system at least cost.
- SCM principles can be applied universally and are bound to give benefits.
- Proper SCM is mandatory in a world-class organization and is a basic infrastructure requirement.
- SCM can cater to a customer's delivery requirements.
- SCM integrates the entire system from suppliers to customers online with a single unified objective of maximization of customer satisfaction externally internally maximization of return on investment internally.

10.4   PRE-REQUISITES FOR EFFECTIVE SUPPLY CHAIN MANAGEMENT

- Regular updating of the entire network by all the concerned parties is mandatory.
- Correct feeding of data in the system is important for the SCM to function properly.
- Uniform software package interacting each other's system through the Internet should be there to make the system operative. Normally Visual Basic at front-end and Oracle at back-end make a good support system for this Data Base Management System (DBMS) of computerization for SCM.
- Proper education and training on operations and day-to-day servicing of the equipment and system must be imparted to all the concerned in the supply chain for making the system effective and properly working.

10.5   FLOW IN THE SUPPLY CHAIN AND LOGISTICS MANAGEMENT

What flows backward in the supply chain is the 'information'. Customer is the driver of the entire supply chain. The flow of information means the customer's requirements and demands. His purchase orders origin, order acknowledgment, technical clarifications and subsequent realization of purchase order is the flow of information.

In response to this backward flow of information, what flow forward are the raw materials, finished goods and numerous products and services. This flow is from the supplier to the organization. This makes the raw materials to flow within an organization.

Value is added to this raw material by converting it into finished product. The finished product flows from the finished goods store to the customer.

This backward flow of information from the customer to the manufacturer and then to the supplier is online and is integrated. In response to this information pertaining to customer's requirement of goods and services, the SCM ensures flow of raw material from the supplier's end to the manufacturer's end and conversion of the raw material to finished goods inside the manufacturer's organization and ultimately to the customer.

10.6 LOGISTICS MANAGEMENT

SCM and logistics management go hand in hand. Logistics is the support for the supply chain. All the concerned members of the supply chain, including the suppliers, the organization, its branch offices/distribution houses and the dealers should have the Internet facility with e-mail, i.e. they must have telephone line, computers with modem, Internet connection and a uniform software package as detailed earlier. This is the logistic support needed for the flow of information through the supply chain in backward direction. The logistic support needed for the flow of raw materials, products and services are as follows:

Transportation management: The cycle time for the goods-in-transit has to be minimized at the least cost. In the transportation management, the latest trend is the 'multi-modal transportation' to economize the cost, increase the speed and have effective transportation. Another trend, which is emerging in this arena, is keeping 'specialized logistic managers' with tremendous amounts of infrastructure back-up. Examples are Airfreight Ltd., DHL Ltd., Sembium SemCop., American President Lines, Dynamic Logistics Ltd., Gati (TCI Ltd.), etc.

Warehouse management: Storing materials in a safe and secure manner at various storing points of stocking and distribution is another important aspect of logistics management. Safe and secure storage, minimization of storage cost and time, keeping proper records, required retrieval, prevention of deterioration during handling and proper **material handling** are all part of the warehouse management in the logistic area.

Proper packaging: Primary, secondary and tertiary packaging are also subjects of logistics management. Simultaneously, the statutory requirement pertaining to packaging and levelling has to be taken into consideration for packaging. A detailed study to keep goods in safe and secure condition without deterioration at the least cost during storage and transportation has to be done.

Flow of information: Proper status of the processing of raw materials into finished goods, stock availability status of goods-in-transit, etc. is an important information for the customer. He will be interested to know at what time, at what place and in what quantity the products and services will be made available. This again is possible through proper computerized network of system with common interactive software. A good logistics manager may not provide mobile phone with roaming facility to his executives but will provide to the truck driver who is carrying lakhs of rupees worth of goods.

Logistics management cost is very important for products which have a lower price/ kg of the raw material, i.e. weight of materials like cement, salt, steel, etc. Here the transportation and handling cost forms a good percentage of the selling price and economizing on the same through proper multi-modal transportation and the least warehousing is the key to the success of the organization in the market place.

The main cost involved in supply chain management is holding of more inventories than required and holding the inventory longer than the required time. Here the required time and quantity are decided by the customer and the organization so that there is no shortage and the concepts of the right time, the right quantity, and the right place are fulfilled.

10.7 INVENTORY MANAGEMENT

Inventory can be defined as all the movable items held in temporary storage. Inventory can include raw materials, component parts, partly processed materials which are inputs to the next state and finished goods.

Inventory does not add any value to the product, i.e. inventory is a non-value adding activity. Therefore, inventory has to be minimized. At the same time, we have to maximize the customer service by making the products and services available at the right time, the right place, in the right quantity and at the right price. This objective is accomplished only by proper supply chain management or control of raw material, finished goods (products) and the related services.

Inventory classification: Inventory is a broad-based term and covers a wide spectrum of entities, which are summarized below:

(a) *Raw material:* They constitute basic raw materials like steel, aluminum, rubber, plastic granules, etc. which are processed further and converted into components which are useful in the final assembly of products. Its location could be at the ancillary's place or at the manufacturing unit itself.

(b) *Work-In-Progress (WIP):* They are the in-process inventory at various stages of conversion process of raw material into finished products. They could be semi-finished and awaiting assembly into the final product.

(c) *Bought out items*: They are the items which are sourced from outside. They are those parts which are either
   • Technically not feasible to manufacture in-house.
   • Economically not viable for in-house manufacturing, or
   • Difficult to meet customers delivery priorities.
   They are sourced from outside even if it can be made in-house but not at the time when required. These products could be raw materials, semi-finished products or finished products.

(d) *Finished goods inventory:* They are the final assembled products lying at the finished goods store, at central warehouse, at regional warehouse and at dealers' showrooms. It is the finished goods, i.e. final product and services, which should be made available to the customer when he needs, where he needs and in required shape, form and quantity to satisfaction of the customer.

(e) *Goods-in-transit:* It can be shown separately or it can be shown by adding to the raw material in transit, which is paid by an organization. Similarly, it is paid in bought out items. The bulk value of the goods-in-transit is the finished goods on its way from the manufacturing unit to the dealer's sales outlet via various warehouses. Logistic support plays a vital role in minimizing goods-in-transit. The quantity of goods-in-transit is always to trade off between cost and time.

(f) *Indirect and/or other inventories:* They can be broadly classified into four categories:

 1. *Manufacturing aids*—they constitute the stock of tools, jigs, fixtures, inspection gauges, dies and moulds, cutting oil, etc.
 2. *Maintenance spares*—V-belts, bearing, electrical items, lubricants, etc.
 3. *Servicing spare parts*—the stock of spares to supplement the after-sales service at dealer's outlet or service centre.
 4. Fuel for boilers, generators, etc.

10.8 DEPENDENT DEMAND AND INDEPENDENT DEMAND

A component's sub-assembly or assembly is classified under 'dependent demand' when the demand for that particular part, component's sub-assembly or assembly is directly proportional to the number of finished products sold. It is normally all the components that are used as standard features of a finished product. For example, each motor cycle needs two wheels. If a firm produces 10000 motor cycle units, it will need 20,000 tyres, 20,000 tubes. The requirement of tyres and tubes is dependent demand. On the other hand, the motor cycle offers an optional feature of push button start for which it needs a battery. Since every motor cycle is not offering push button start, the requirement of the number of batteries is not dependent on the number of motor cycles sold. It is classified under independent demand.

Every pen needs a refill, hence the demand for refill is a dependent demand. Hence the standard feature of the products and related components, all fall under the category of dependent demand. Inspite of such a large category of items falling under independent demand items, it constitutes only 3–5% of the inventory items, whereas dependent demand items constitute more than 95% to 97% of the inventory.

Since the dependent demand items follow logic, they can be easily computerized which give tremendous amount of flexibility and speed in data handling. The dependent demand items are handled under various computer-based modern techniques of inventory handling like Material Requirement Planning (MRP-I), Manufacturing Resource Planning (MRP-II) and Distribution Requirement Planning (DRP). Independent demand items are handled by the conventional inventory management systems like: the concept of Order–Reorder model and Economic Order Quantity (EOQ).

10.9 INVENTORY COST

The inventory and related cost could be broadly divided into two categories:

 A. The cost of material and
 B. The cost on material

Let us assume that 100 is the value of sales. Then as per industry norm, the component of this 100 will be 20 profit, and 80 costs of production (including direct and indirect). This 80 can be sub-divided as:

(1) 50 material related cost (2/3rd of 50, i.e. 33% as cost of material and 17% as cost on material).
(2) 7–8%—labour cost (wages)
(3) 7–8%—cost of power, fuel and consumables.
(4) 8–12%—marketing, selling, and administrative overheads.

It is interesting to mention that the average cost of labour for the Indian industry is 7–10% of sales value whereas the international norm for the same is 5–7%, contrary to the belief that Indian labour cost is cheap. The actual fact is that per unit head Indian labour is cheap, but they also happen to be least productive. An average Indian worker works for 3 to 3.5 hrs per shift of 8 hrs whereas an average worker as per international norm in Europe, America, Japan, and Korea works for atleast 6.5 hrs per 8-hr shift. These workers also handle more than one machine whereas in India workers are reluctant to handle more than one machine. The reason is over-protective labour laws and socialist type of government's working.

Whether this kind of working will sustain today's globally competitive environment is a big question to be answered. This topic may be out of place to discuss under the topic of inventory cost at first look but we should not forget that the major portion of cost on material is related to human productivity.

Nevertheless, we cannot do much in reducing 'cost of material', we can definitely reduce substantially and even can make it near to zero the 'cost on material', which is as high as 17% of sales value and is nearly as much as the total profit (20%) of the organization. This is one of the major reasons attributed to the current focus on SCM with a view to reducing bulk of this 'cost on material'. Let us now understand what are the elements of 'cost of material' and that of 'cost on material'.

10.9.1 Cost Associated with Materials

Cost associated with materials is of two types:

(a) *Cost of materials:* It is about 33–35% of sales price and consists of
  • *Basic Price:* This is the consideration payable to the supplier. This is approximately 60% of the cost of material and 20–21% of the sale price.
  • *Government Duties:* They constitute excise duty, custom duty, sales tax, local tax (octroi), etc. This is approximately 35% of the cost of material and about 11–12% of sales price.
  • *Packing:* Primary as well as secondary packing cost for safety, preservation and presentation of the product.
  • *Transportation:* This is the cost of transporting materials and products in the least time and at the minimum cost.
  • *Clearing and forwarding:* The custom clearing and forwarding agents, the octroi clearing agents all charge their fees for clearing and forwarding of the goods.

- *Insurance:* To protect the goods-in-transit against loss, theft, spoilage, accidents etc. the goods are insured at cost.
- *Material Handling:* At every transit point, the material needs to be handled, i.e. loading and unloading charges.

(b) **Cost on material Inventory Carrying Cost—ICC:** This is approximately 33% of the material related cost and about 16–17% of the sale price.

- *Cost of Capital (interest cost):* The investment in inventory is hidden cost. Lot of capital gets blocked in inventory. Money as a resource costs (interest) about 15% p.a. as per current trend. The ROI depends on the speed with which the working capital turns round. Inventory constitutes a major component of working capital.
- *Storage Space (warehousing) Cost:* Additional inventory requires additional space for storage thereby incurring investment on land, building, storage racks, watchman, clerk for record keeping and incidental expenses.
- *Insurance Cost:* Raw materials and products when kept in stock need to be insured against various calamities like fire, earthquake, flood, riots, etc.
- *Inventory Risk Costs:* The inventory risk cost constitutes product obsolescence, pilferage, loss, damage, and deterioration.

10.9.2 Eight Areas of Inventory Control System

- Accurate demand forecasts
- Selection of inventory models
- Dependent demand items model—MRP-I, MRP-II, CRP and DRP (97% of inventory).
- Independent demand items model—ABC, HML, FSN, SOS, GOLF, etc. (absolutely 3% of inventory)
- Measurement of inventory cost
- Inventory Carrying Cost
- Ordering cost (EOQ)
- Method to record and account for items.
- Method for receiving, handling storage and issuing of items.
- Information procedure to report exception.
- Safe and secure primary and secondary packaging of the product.
- Safe and speedy transit of raw materials and products at the respective demand points.

10.10 MATERIAL REQUIREMENT PLANNING (MRP-I)

MRP is a computer-based planning and control system used to plan and control effectively internal production and material flow (see Figure 10.2).

Objective: To minimize inventory; to maintain delivery schedules.

Modalities: This is achieved by forecast of needs derived from a master plan (MSP) and Bill of material required which can be used to project, release and control orders.

The MRP-I system has the following four elements. Refer to Figure 10.2.

- Bill of material file containing product structure record.
- Inventory status file.
- The master production schedule.
- The MRP package.

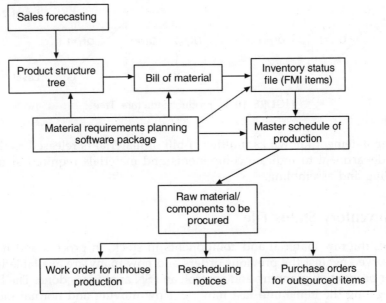

FIGURE 10.2 Material requirement planning (MRP-I)

MRP logic—demand for materials, parts and components depends on demand for end product.

10.10.1 Bill of Material (BOM)

MRP-I is the first stage of the supply chain management. It can only be applied to the dependent demand items, which form the basic raw material working process and finished goods inventory. The first stage of the MRP-I is a compilation of the bill of materials. Each product is exploded using the **Product Tree concept**. Refer to Figure 10.3. We keep on exploding the product into major assemblies and sub-assemblies till we arrive at the basic raw material or the bought out part to be sourced from outside.

Each stage of explosion has a separate stage number sequentially from zero onwards. Product at zero level is the final assembled product which can be used by the customer. At the end of the process of explosion, similar parts are segregated and aggregated to form the final list of materials and components to be procured for manufacturing the final product. This consolidated list is known as **the Bill of Material** which is given to the material department for sourcing.

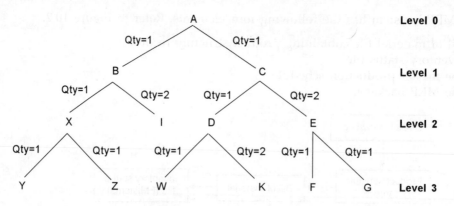

FIGURE 10.3   Product Structure Tree.

Another statement known as multilevel bill of material is released to the shopfloor production department to indicate components and materials required at each level of sub-assembling and assembling.

10.10.2   Inventory Status File

This indicates the raw material and components in stock, in process and how many of them are reserved against the previous orders and how many are available in free stock. Normally for production planning and control, an FSN analysis is done. The FSN analysis means segregating the items into fast moving, slow moving and normal moving items. The production capacity is filled up to 80% of the components and parts against the actual customer orders. The balance 20% of the plant capacity is filled in by the fast-moving items. These FMI items are normally available in stock. These are the items which are shown in the inventory status file.

10.10.3   Master Production Schedule

The master production schedule is derived from the customer demand and gives the quantity required under each product category. The basic data fed into the bills of material file is the quantity of raw material and components required to produce one number of final assembled product which can be used by the customer. The final list of bills of material is worked out based on "master production schedule" and the quantity required under each product category. This consolidated requirement is noted in the bills of material for the month. From this statement, the MRP package deducts the free inventory available and produces the final list of planned order release.

This planned order release is divided into two categories:

(i) Items to be produced in-house and
(ii) Items to be bought from outside.

At the stage of MRP-I, we release purchase order for those items for which the organization does not have the technological ability to produce in-house.

10.10.4 MRP-I Package

The material requirement planning package is the centre of processing the entire inventory and parts and components with the procurement right from the suppliers to the point of receipt in the raw material store and issue to the shopfloor for the manufacturing of the particular product. The product tree structure is already fed into this software package. The most successful software package for the SCM consists of 'Visual Basic' at the front end and Oracle or the SQL at the back end. The moment the product-wise sales forecast for the month is fed into the system, the MRP software package works out the bill of material and the requirement of the parts and components to meet the market demand. The MRP-I software package checks automatically the inventory status and deducts the parts/components available in the inventory and produces the final list of parts/components either to be produced in-house or to be sourced from outside. The MRP-I package also balances the requirement by issuing the rescheduling notices in case of shortages or the excess inventory available.

10.11 MANUFACTURING RESOURCE PLANNING (MRP-II)

MRP-II or the Manufacturing Resource Planning takes care of the balance items which are verified against the organization's manufacturing capability. The MRP package has all the information regarding various workstations, machines and their capacity and capability. This list of items is verified against their capacity known as capacity requirement planning and further two final lists are prepared:

- One for the items which can be economically and technically viable to be manufactured in-house up to full plant capacity utilization.
- The balance items are to be procured from outside. These items are either not economical to produce in-house or even if economical, the organization cannot produce the item in so much quantity within the stipulated delivery period.

This is known as MRP-II, and the output from MRP-II is either a work order for in-house production or a purchase order for bought out items (refer to Figure 10.4).

While booking the capacity for in-house manufacturing, the normal industrial practice is to fill up to 80% of the capacity, with planned order releases and the remaining 20% with the open order file which consists of fast moving items. Now the capacity is filled in, keeping in mind the load profile for each machining centre and the production routing file. MRP-I links the supplier to the organization and extends from supplier to the receipt of goods and parts at the incoming raw material stores. MRP-II extends from the incoming raw material to the finished goods store.

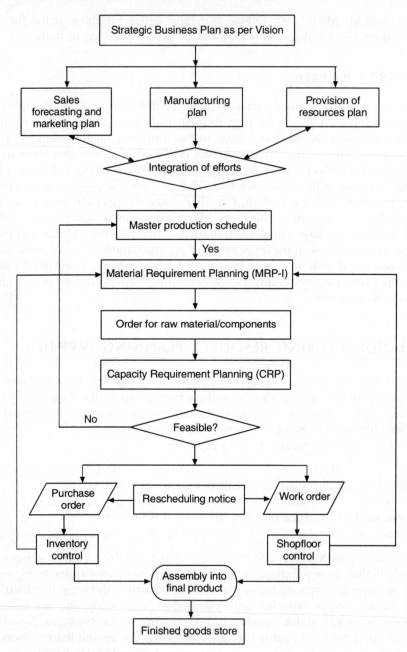

FIGURE 10.4 Manufacturing Resource Planning (MRP-II).

10.12 MATERIAL REQUIREMENT PLANNING AND MANUFACTURING RESOURCE PLANNING (MRP-I & MRP-II) COMBINED

- It contains the necessary logic to operate the system.
- The system tied together becomes a tool for planning and controlling a great number of inter-related parts and products.
- MRP considers the current and planned quantities of parts and products in inventories in addition to the time element in order to incorporate long and short run changes for inter-related parts and products.
- MRP needs all records and files to be updated on a continuous basis and containing accurate information.
- It is also vital to have all necessary records in a good database form for computer application.
- MRP can be applied for inventory control of items that have a discontinuous, non-uniform and dependent demand.
- It is suitable for assembly, production, manufacturing or fabrication operations and not suitable for wholesalers and traders.
- The software language used for development of MRP package is Visual Basic at the front-end and Oracle at back-end.
- Supply chain management integrates the working of the entire organization under one paradigm. The MRP input requirement integrates the requirement of business plan, marketing plan, resource management or financial plan and manufacturing plan.

10.13 DISTRIBUTION REQUIREMENT PLANNING (DRP)

The DRP is software supported, time-based planning of distributing resources in order to satisfy the demand at all stages of the distribution channel.

DRP provides a general method of inventory model for both dependent and independent demands. DRP extends the supply chain management to the customer's end. DRP begins with identification of the time and place at which product SKU (Stock Keeping Units) will be required. DRP analyses demand for individual SKUs at each customer service location and produces the aggregated time-phased requirement schedule for each level in the distribution system. These schedules are then fed into the master production schedule.

DRP ensures perfect co-ordination between production, marketing and distribution management. DRP improves performance and motivates the managers to think about and implement demand management by modifying the customer's behaviour while closely forecasting the demand for a product, product range or an individual item.

DRP implements the scheduled distribution closely specifying the conditions, specially the timing within which deliveries must be made. DRP is mainly responsible for creating the time and place utility for a particular product and service.

The most important feature of DRP, however, is the co-ordination of the manufacturing and distribution functions of the company to maximize customer satisfaction.

DRP ensures lower finished product inventories and better customer service. It provides opportunities for timely re-planning the distribution as market conditions change. DRP produces the 'production schedule' with valid priorities and common basis of information to enhance communication and hence build the company-wide plan.

DRP changes the paradigm from control to coordination in SCM. By moving away from the separate control of departments towards overall co-ordination of effort, all the major movement activities, both of information and materials/products are brought together into a single system.

10.14   OBJECTIVES OF SUPPLY CHAIN MANAGEMENT

The objective of Supply Chain Management (SCM) is to reduce pre- and post-production inventory levels, tending towards the minimum level. SCM leads to implementation of a 'flexible system'.

Small lot sizes in SCM prevent losses from unsold stock and allow flexibility through accommodating small changes. SCM prevents product obsolescence in today's shorter product life cycle. SCM ensures maximum efficiency in using labour, capital and plant throughout the company.

SCM provides scope for 'flexible planning and control' procedures. It also ensures the controlled customer service performance.

SCM leads to a system of performance with minimum variances due to reduced uncertainty.

SCM creates an organization which incurs minimum total cost. It also ensures product quality by preservation of added value by faster delivery to the point of consumption from the point of manufacturing. This is particularly true for food and pharmaceutical products.

10.15   PRE-REQUISITES FOR THE SUCCESS OF MRP, DRP, AND SCM

The following points need to be kept in purview for the success of SCM:

- For all these systems to be effective, accurate information and control to the extent of at least 98% is mandatory.
- The fool-proofing of the system is necessary.
- Adoption of methods like bar coding, Kanban or JIT, computer communication and linkage for ordering and billing, cycled stock taking, statistical expertise and education and training are must.
- All the parties including the supplier, materials, stores, production, marketing, logistics, distributors, branches and dealers are all to play well-coordinated, and well-versed role for making the above activities successful.
- The security of the system implementing SCM is extremely important since the system will provide limited access to the network to so many of its vendors and dealers apart from the organizational offices.

10.16 JUST-IN-TIME (JIT)

JIT is defined as a highly integrated system of production, sales and distribution, leading to continuous flow through the entire supply chain.

Concept: The finished goods inventory of one department becomes the raw material inventory for the next downstream department requiring that particular part.

10.16.1 Core Japanese Practices of JIT

The ultimate manifestation of SCM as well as the implementation of Total Quality Management is reflected in the Toyota Production System or TPS. The JIT is an integral part of the Toyota Production System which is designed and practised by Taichii Ohno.

The core practices followed by JIT are the use of the 'Kanban' system or the card system in the production which ensures that the items are manufactured only against an actual customer's order and not otherwise. To achieve this, the production system is adapted to accommodate the demand change. The set-up time is reduced employing techniques like SMED and computer-integrated manufacturing to reduce the production time and the operations are standardized to attain line balancing.

For the implementation of JIT, the machine layout is the 'Group Technology' or the 'cellular manufacturing technique'. The machine operators are multifunctional for the flexible work concept. There is implementation of activities by the small group and a suggestion scheme to reduce the work force and increase the worker's morale. The visual control systems are installed to achieve the autonomation concept that is integrating quality control and the production together. The organization should be practising total quality management and a functional quality management system to promote companywide quality control.

All the employees of the organization should be oriented towards JIT. It should promote practices that promote "continuous flow manufacture". The organization should eliminate wastage or the *Muda*, i.e. any activity that does not add value but adds costs like rejection, rework and wastage, etc. These practices are described in detail in Chapter 2. The organization should make efforts to improve activities that add value.

The organization should reduce activities such as inventory, reserve stock, lead time, over-production, reduce machine set-up times etc., that add cost. The organization should also ensure negligible order processing or changeover costs.

JIT activities belong to four categories, namely people, process, planning and quality.

The JIT system should opt for mixed model scheduling as per the production rate and demand by flexibility of production lines to allow concurrent assembly of different models on the same lines. This enables the JIT system to achieve synchronized scheduling and regularity in end product scheduling and delivery as per market demand.

The JIT system should incorporate frequent deliveries, small lot size production and buffer stock removal and manufacturing the products only as per the market and the customers demand.

The JIT system eliminates the need for inspection of incoming goods and outgoing goods by opting for the Six-Sigma system of production process control and standardized container so that there is no need to count the products or the parts produced.

10.16.2   JIT Enablers

We can now try to summarize the main factors which enable the implementation of the JIT system. They are detailed below:

- *Housekeeping:* Using 4S for good housekeeping can be suggested here, viz.
  - *Seiri:* orderliness.
  - *Seiton:* tidiness.
  - *Seiso:* clarity.
  - *Seiketsu:* cleanliness.
- *Problem Solving Techniques*: They include implementation of Pareto analysis, Ishikawa diagram and brainstorming backed up by techniques like quality circles, Kaizen Gemba and Juran's quality improvement.
- *Waste reduction*—Using of 3Ms practice
  - *Muri:* unreasonableness.
  - *Mura:* unevenness.
  - *Muda:* waste.
- *Visibility:* Visibility and transparency in production as well as in the entire organizational operation is mandatory for success of JIT.
- *Standardization:* It includes standardization of parts, processes, dies and mould sizes.
- *Total Productive Maintenance:* It refers to shifting of routine maintenance to operators and focus on preventive maintenance.
- *SMED:* Reduction of set-up times to single digit minutes enables small lot size production feasible.
- *Statistical process control:* SPC is an important aspect of quality control and quality management. It leads to process orientation and zero defect.
- *Autonomation:* This helps in automatic defect control and prevention of poor quality in production.
- *Total Employee Involvement (TEI):* This is a JIT prerequisite. This is achieved through teamwork, education, training, job enrichment, quality improvement project, etc.
- *Design:* Design of modular manufacturing technique and simplicity is an integral part of JIT.
- Flexible process and equipment
- Management control
- Other contributing factors include a high level of technical support and production engineering.

10.16.3   Just In Case Stock (JIC)

The JIT system can be implemented step-by-step over a number of years by successive reduction in inventory. Every time the inventory is reduced a new problem surfaces needing immediate action to prevent any stock-out of raw material and production stoppage or stock-out of finished products leading to shortage in the market.

The four factors which are responsible for such occurrence of stock-outs and failure of the JIT system are late deliveries, rejections, sudden increase in market demand and machine breakdown (refer to Figure 10.5).

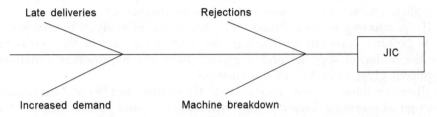

FIGURE 10.5 Ishikawa diagram that explains the four factors that can lead to stock-outs and the failure of JIT system.

The problem can be eliminated progressively by finding out the root cause through 'Ishikawa' or the 'Cause and Effect' diagram, followed by a brainstorming session. Once the root cause is determined, suitable corrective and preventive actions are taken for the elimination of these four factors responsible for JIT stock which is a measurement of the inefficiency of the entire system. The objective of the JIT system is to reduce the Just-In-Case stock to zero over a period of time.

10.16.4 Just-In-Time System

The JIT system consists of two major parts: JIT purchase and JIT production or the Kanban system. We shall discuss first the JIT purchasing which is primarily responsible for the vendor management system and raw material and components inventory.

10.16.5 JIT Purchasing

In the JIT purchasing system, quality has superseded price to become the primary consideration in the selection of a supplier. The word quality implies both quality of components and parts supplied by the vendor as well as the reliability of timely supply.

The goals of JIT purchasing is to filter out the wastes in the production processes and to improve upon the quality of the products and the services. JIT purchasing should be able to satisfy consumer demand in an efficient and reliable manner. JIT purchasing should ensure that value is added to the products.

JIT purchasing system should look into the following aspects of the organization to do an efficient and effective work.

Inventory: The objective of JIT purchasing is to have only the correct part in the correct place at the correct time. To achieve this objective, the JIT purchasing approach is to remove bottlenecks and have only as small inventories as possible. JIT purchasing is possible only if the suppliers have fast set-ups, small lots size for production and frequent delivery. The JIT purchasing system should have flexible labour and equipment. At the management level, there should be consensus management and integrated technical support. JIT purchasing always challenges as usual attitude and looks for improving everything.

Suppliers: The JIT purchasing system has a few suppliers preferably, according to Edward Deming, one or two suppliers per component. JIT purchasing should give preference to nearby suppliers and repeat business with the same suppliers.

The JIT purchasing system should make active use of analysis to enable desirable suppliers to be price competitive. The supplier who is the best of the two is rated as A-class or the preferred supplier and is given 70% of the requirement orders and the other supplier is given only 30% of the business.

If at all certain items are not available with the nearby supplier and the organization is forced to go to a remote supplier, the organization should form a cluster of remote suppliers at a place where the company is already sourcing some of its requirements.

Competitive bidding is mostly limited to new items and commercial terms are discussed only once a year and an annual rate contract is signed between an organization and its suppliers.

The suppliers are encouraged to extend JIT buying to their suppliers. An organization has to ensure that all its suppliers are implementing statistical process control.

Quality: The JIT purchasing system imposes minimum product specifications on the suppliers. The parent organization helps suppliers to meet quality requirement. There is a close relationship between buyers and suppliers quality assurance procedures. The suppliers are encouraged to use control charts and implement statistical process control so that the parts are of zero defect and do not need any inspection at the organization level. The suppliers are also required to supply the components in standardized containers so that no time is wasted in counting the parts supplied.

Quantities: The JIT purchasing system expects a steady output rate and frequent delivery in small lot quantities from its suppliers. The JIT purchasing system has long-term contract agreements with the suppliers and there is minimum or zero paper work.

The JIT purchasing system fixes the delivery quantities variable from release-to-release but fixed for whole contract term between the buyer and the seller organizations.

The JIT purchasing system does not allow any 'overage' or 'underage' of receipts in terms of quantity and suppliers are encouraged to package in exact quantities in standardized containers. The suppliers are encouraged to reduce their production lot sizes.

Deliveries: The JIT purchasing system schedules the in-bound deliveries. The organization gains control of the delivery time by the use of company-owned or contracted transportation system. The   delivery and storage   of the components and parts are kept under the control of the organization wherever possible.

10.16.6   Just-In-Time Production

After the execution of the JIT system of purchasing, the JIT system of production is deployed, also known as the Kanban system.

There are two types of Kanban system: production ordering Kanban known as POK and withdrawal Kanban known as WK.

These two together execute the pull type of JIT production. JIT produces only that much as is needed for customers. The output from the previous process becomes the input to the succeeding process without any delay or being held in stock. Similarly, when a product reaches the final stage, it is immediately dispatched to the customers as the products are produced only against active customer orders.

10.16.6.1 *Kanban*

- It is an integral part of the JIT production system.
- Kanban system is designed to produce only the number of units needed by a pull or demand feeding process.
- It leads to smaller set-up times, smaller production lots and reduced in-process inventories.
- Kanban is a card of two types (refer to Figure 10.6).

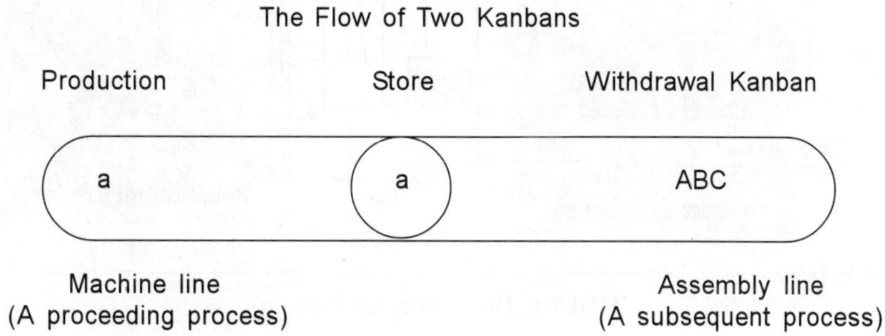

The Flow of Two Kanbans

Production	Store	Withdrawal Kanban
a	a	ABC
Machine line (A proceeding process)		Assembly line (A subsequent process)

FIGURE 10.6 The flow of two Kanbans.

- A Withdrawal Kanban shows the quantity of items that the subsequent process should withdraw from the preceding or one.
- Production ordering Kanban shows the quantity that the preceding process should produce.
- The Kanban system provides an additional close link between operations, reinforces previous linkages that lead to improved quality and productivity.
- The Kanban system of inventory control works well in a situation with standardized parts and products cycled in the manufacturing system.
- The Kanban system goes well with MRP and inventory control.
- The Withdrawal Kanban (WK) details the quantity that the subsequent process should withdraw (refer to Figures 10.7 and 10.8).
- Production Ordering Kanban (POK) shows the quantity, which the preceding process should produce.
- Carrier of the subsequent process goes to the store of the preceding process with the necessary number of WKs and empty containers.
- When this process carrier withdraws the parts from the store, he detaches the POK attached to physical units in pallets and deposits this in the Kanban receiving post. He also leaves behind the empty pallets.

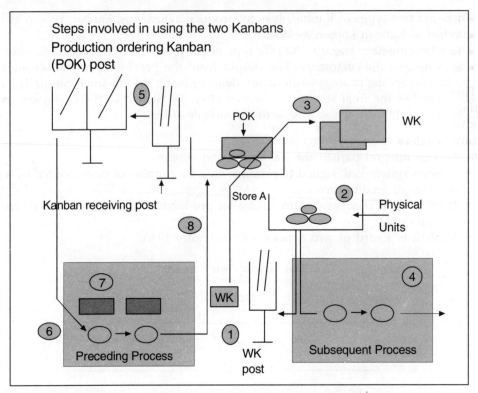

FIGURE 10.7 The Kanban process.

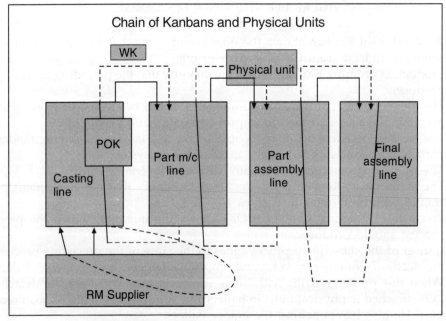

FIGURE 10.8 Chain of Kanbans and physical units.

- Each POK he replaces with his WK after checking the quantity.
- When work begins in subsequent process, WKs are put in WK post.
- In the preceding process, POKs are withdrawn with empty pallets.
- Reproduce the POKs as per original sequence.

The JIT production system and the Kanban system are an integral part of JIT manufacturing. This is a demand pull system of manufacturing where only the amount of products required by the customers are manufactured. This process ensures zero wastages and minimum lead time for processing from raw material to finished product. The JIT system ensures zero inventory and maximum efficiency in manufacturing.

11

Service Quality

This chapter covers the following: (i) quality management in service industries, (ii) the definition of service sector and its importance, (iii) the definition of service quality, (iv) the benefits from service quality based on research work done abroad, (v) the importance of customers in service quality, (vi) the difference between goods and services, (vii) the techniques for determining customer needs, (viii) the importance of service leadership, and (ix) the dimensions of service quality (customers view of service quality).

11.1 PREFACE ON QUALITY MANAGEMENT PRACTICES IN SERVICE INDUSTRIES

Macroeconomic data suggest that the service sector is becoming the primary source of wealth, trade, and economic growth throughout the developed and also in the developing world. The proportion of purchasing effort focused on goods is declining rapidly due to the impact of a number of forces; (i) the commodisation of branded goods; (ii) the shattering of the mass market into a mosaic of millions of pieces and (iii) the resultant growing power of the trade. By comparison, the purchasing of services is becoming increasingly widespread. The global communication networks will soon provide home shopping on demand.

Recent tendencies in globalisation and privatisation are confronting service organizations with new challenges and causing an urgent need for the design and development of management concepts and techniques specifically geared for the service sector. Achieving competitive advantages in service requires the integration of service quality with service delivery to meet or exceed customer requirements at present and in the future.

Services permeate every aspect of our lives. We use transportation services when we travel, often to and from work; when we travel away from home, we use restaurant services to feed us and hotels to provide us accommodation. At home, we rely on services such as electricity and telephone. At work, we need postal, courier, and maintenance services to keep our work places running. We use the services of hairdressers to maintain our personal self-image, and our employers use the services of public relations and advertising firms to maintain our corporate image. Lawyers, doctors, dentists, stockbrokers and insurance agents look after our personal and financial health. In our leisure time, we use a battery of services ranging from cinemas to swimming pools to theme parks for amusement and relaxation. And when we do buy goods, such as a new car or a washing machine, we often rely on services to keep them running and repair them when they break down.

Services allow us to budget our time as well as our money. We use some services to generate increased disposable time so as to buy other services. A family might, for example, eat in a restaurant in order to save time that would have been spent cooking a meal at home and that 'extra' time might be 'spent' at a cinema or at a theme park, using another service to provide recreation. A company might buy a service, such as advertising or research or catering, rather than spending its own valuable time in the field and then be free to concentrate on its core business. Many of these services have always been present to some degree, but the complexity and diversity of services has increased dramatically over the past century.

Contrary to popular belief, services, not manufactured goods, have fuelled modern economic growth. The Industrial Revolution of the 18th century involved changes not only in production, but also in financial structures and in transportation and communication networks. It is no coincidence that two of the biggest service sectors, banks and transportation, boomed at the same time as the Industrial Revolution. Without the emergence of these and other services, the economic benefits of the large production units could never have been realized. Economic growth has in its turn fuelled the growth of the service sector, as increasing prosperity means that companies, institutions and individuals are increasingly willing to trade money for time. Recently, services have seen a dramatic growth. Services now generate more than 50% of the world gross domestic product. Also, service firms are emerging bigger than manufacturing firms. This is reflected in the *Fortune* 500 listings. Now, Wal-Mart tops the list of *Fortune* 500, pushing GM down. Service firm AT&T comes fifth, Sears ninth, insurance companies like State Farm and Prudential 12th and 13th respectively, and Citicorp 17th. Even within the manufacturing companies, the share of service component in total revenue is rising fast. General Electric, for example, derives over 40 per cent of its revenue from services. Services were responsible for most of the new jobs in the year 2005. New technology has led to considerable changes in the nature of many services and in the development of new ones.

Many views of scope of services do not agree with the facts:

(1) Contrary to popular opinion, services are not responses to marginal demands that people satisfy only after they meet their product needs. People value services at least as highly as they value manufactured products and purchase them in much less cyclical patterns than manufacturers.

(2) Companies generate value-added services at comparable or higher rates than the product companies.

(3) Service sector is at least as capital-intensive as the manufacturing sector, and many industries within it are highly technological.

(4) Service industries tend to be as concentrated as manufacturing industries and to have companies of sufficient scale to be sophisticated buyers and even producers of technology.

(5) Service industries lend themselves to productivity increases great enough to fuel continuing real growth in per capita income.

Excellent service will be a genuine key to a better future—for those who give service, as well as, for those who receive it; for companies that make things, as well as for companies traditionally labelled service businesses; for our country's national pride as well as its economic competitiveness. This is the new age of the service economy in India. What kind of future is in store for our citizens, our communities, our industries, our economy, and our national self-respect if our service is slovenly, uncaring, and incompetent?

11.2 INTRODUCTION TO QUALITY MANAGEMENT PRACTICES IN SERVICE INDUSTRIES

In 1878, Margaret Wolfe Hungerford wrote, "Beauty is in the eye of the beholder. The *Quality Control Supervisor's Bulletin* has paraphrased this and says, "Quality is in the eye of the customer." Quests for quality and beauty are eternal and evasive. Once you think you have found them, your perceptions will change. Perceptions of quality are also flexible. Edwards Deming emphasized this when he said: "We shall learn that impressions of quality are not static. They change." These thoughts are as much applicable to the service sector as they are to the manufacturing sector.

When we started this chapter on service quality, we expected to find a varied and rich literature that would guide us. We found nothing of that kind. Instead we found a literature almost exclusively devoted to the quality of tangible goods, defined in terms of conformance to manufacturers' specifications. As a result, quality control principles and practices we discuss so far, while pertinent to evaluating and ensuring goods quality, were inadequate for understanding service quality. This inadequacy stems from the three fundamental ways services differ from goods in terms of how they are produced, consumed, and evaluated.

First, services are basically intangible (although opinions on services vary from customer-to-customer, time-to-time and one provider to another, i.e. customer-centric, time-centric, and server-centric). Because they are performances and experiences rather than objects, precise manufacturing specifications concerning uniform quality can rarely be set. Unlike automobiles and audiocassettes, service quality of airline transportation and aerobic exercises cannot be measured, tested, and verified in advance of sale to assure quality. Moreover, when what is being sold is purely a performance, the criteria customers use to evaluate it may be complex and difficult to capture precisely.

Second, services—especially those with a high labour content are heterogeneous: their performance often varies from producer to producer, from customer to customer, from place to place and from day to day. The quality of the interactions that bank tellers, flight attendants, and insurance agents have with customers can rarely be standardized to ensure uniformity the way quality of goods produced in a manufacturing plant can.

Third, production and consumption of many services are inseparable. Quality in services is often understood during service delivery, usually in an interaction between the customer and the provider, rather than being engineered at the manufacturing plant and delivered intact to the customer. Unlike producers of goods, service providers do not have the benefit of a factory serving as a buffer between the production and consumption. Service customers are often in the service factory, observing and evaluating the production process as they experience the service.

Many service industries have hired consultants from manufacturing as 'foster parents', in order to gain an insight into raising baby quality assurance departments. To date, however, few have been willing to sign lifelong contracts for the infant departments' nursery care. Why is that a problem? Because services sector quality control has been an infant for over 20 years and promises to remain one for another 20.

Too many businesses still think of quality in terms of manufactured goods instead of products delivered by the vast and growing service sector. Management in the service industry views quality as a concept rather than a product, subject to the same rigorous analysis and control taking place on the shopfloor. In the book *Out of the Crisis*, author, W. Edwards Deming makes an observation that there is no distinction between quality practices in manufacturing and service industries. The service industries include government services, among which are education and posts and telegraphs. All industries, manufacturing and service, are subject to the same principles of management. It is estimated that only 10% of the American service companies have some form of a quality improvement process in place. But quality is critical to the products and processes of the service industry, which account for approximately three-fourths of America's gross national product and nine of the 10 new jobs.

The subject of quality management in manufacturing industry has been a matter of great interest and concern for business and academia alike. Several works have thoroughly investigated the various dimensions, techniques and organizational requirements for effective implementation of TQM. These dimensions include top management commitment and leadership, quality policy, training, product/service design, supplier quality management, process management, quality data and reporting, employee relations, workforce management, customer focus, customer involvement, benchmarking, SPC, employee empowerment, employee involvement, corporate quality culture and strategic quality management. These dimensions in essence, are tools of the intellect that were forged in the administrative theory, tempered in manufacturing quality management and therefore are naturally expected to be honed to aid quality management in the service sector. Most of these dimensions, techniques and strategies proposed by various theorists and practitioners, starting from the birth of the quality revolution, seem to provide universal remedies to the problems of the manufacturing business. But they are not a complete yardstick for service quality improvement. The reasoning here is that although from a logical point of view, most of the dimensions of manufacturing quality management should naturally apply to services, the transferability of manufacturing quality management dimensions to services calls for some serious soul-searching as services differ from the manufacture of goods in a number of different ways: service intangibility, simultaneity of production, delivery and consumption, perishability, variability of expectations of the customers and the participatory role of customers in the service delivery. Interestingly, the literature on TQM with respect to services, i.e. total quality service (TQS), seems to be bereft of an integrative framework that will include all the critical dimensions of TQS by addressing the issue of possible transferability of manufacturing quality management dimensions to services, and by focusing on those dimensions that are unique to a service organization.

Who needs improvements? An efficient system of quality improvement is helpful to anyone that turns out a product or service, or in research, and wishes to improve the quality of his work, and at the same time to increase his output, all with less labour and at reduced cost. Service needs improvement in the same way as manufacturing. Anyone that ever registered at a hotel will endorse this statement. Inefficiency in a service organization, just as in manufacturing, raises prices to the consumer and lowers his standard of living. The principles and methods for improvement are the same for service as for manufacturing. The actual application differs, of course, from one product to another, and from one type of service to another, just as all the manufacturing concerns differ from one to another.

Real quality service, however, is not sales slogans, buzzwords, or lip service. It is a deep, organization-wide commitment to achieving the best. It starts with a personal and professional commitment by the CEO and is ingrained in the organization's culture to the point where every employee feels a strong sense of commitment. This is particularly important for companies, such as large retailers, airlines, or banks, with front-line workers subjected to tremendous daily pressures from customers and managers.

11.3 QUALITY MANAGEMENT PRACTICES IN SERVICE INDUSTRIES IN USA

In the USA, governmental agencies were leaders in the field of service sector quality; Dr. A.C. Rosander has been working in this field since World War II. Some of his exploits are documented in his recent book *Washington Story and Applications of Quality Control in the Service Industries*. One reason, service quality has become such an important issue is that America's economy has become a service economy. Virtually all organizations compete to some degree on the basis of service. It is difficult to name even one industry for which service matters are unimportant. If one studies the strategies of manufacturing companies such as Ford Motor Company or Corning Glass Works and what one finds is a paramount role for service.

Indeed, starting with the 1990s, more and more executives have shown a keen interest in service quality in banking, healthcare, and transportation businesses. As manufacturing executives find it increasingly difficult to establish sustainable, technology-based competitive advantages, they are focusing their attention and resources on value-added services. And as manufacturers compete more on service, there will be less distinction between manufacturing and service businesses.

The central role of services in the American economy is a key factor behind service quality becoming an institutional and societal issue. Services are so much a part of what the Americans produce, consume, and export that it would be surprising if they were not concerned about quality. A second factor behind service quality's rising prominence is that superior quality is proving to be a winning competitive strategy.

The banking industry in USA also made major contributions towards recognizing the need for service sector quality. Eugene Kirby and Bill Latzko were pioneers in this area. Although much of Kirby's work was not published, he did document some of his ideas in *Quality Control in Banking*, which appeared in the 1975 Yearbook of the Administrative Applications Division of the American Society for Quality Control. Bill Latzko, the Chairman of the Administrative Applications Divisions (1985–87), is another poineer of 'quality in banking'. He is also a prolific writer; many of his publications are identified in the bibliography of his recent book *Quality and Productivity for Bankers and Financial Managers*.

The demand for customer service comes at a time in the United States when manufacturing has declined in importance relative to the service sector: 85% of the 12.6 million new jobs created in the United States between 1982 and 1987 were in the service sector. As America's economy becomes more dependent on the service sector, the real danger is that service organizations will make the same strategic mistakes over quality that manufacturing did. Due to their high quality of services, Japanese banks are already a threat to American banks.

Time magazine said: 'The potential of service business losing touch is chilling because it was the U.S. that practically invented the concept of good service on a mass-market scale.' ... 'The country's huge appetite for reliable services gave rise to such pioneers as AT&T, IBM, American Express.' Service organizations making the headway in USA include: government, banking, insurance, hospitals, and service sectors of manufacturing companies.

11.3.1 Surveys for Service Industries in USA

The ASQC/Gallup Survey of 1985 checked public opinion to determine why consumers thought services were poor. Service industries in the survey included auto repair, banking, insurance, government, hospital and airlines. Those experiencing problems with services reported the following:

Reason given	Per cent	Problem category
Work not done right	39	product
Too slow	30	timeliness
Too expensive	20	pricing
Indifferent personnel	20	attitude
Unqualified personnel	12	product
Lack of courtesy	10	attitude
Unspecified poor service	10	unknown
Lack of personnel	5	timeliness
Poor scheduling	4	timeliness
Reservation problems	2	product
Poor food	2	product
Miscellaneous	11	unknown

The interpretation of these findings is that defects of products, timeliness and attitude were the most prominent categories of problems identified by the survey. In this case, defects are identified as failure of service or products to meet the customer expectations.

Writing about the quality side of Disneyland, Lee Branst came up with similar data. Favourable guest comments received by the company included the following:

Comment	Comment Category
Cleanliness	facilities
Friendliness	attitude
Courtesy	attitude
Good show	product

Although not mentioned in the article, the worst shortcoming at Disneyland might be the long lines (timeliness). A different definition of defects might be used. The preferred wording is 'A defect is a characteristic that does not conform to requirements, such as drawings, standards or specifications.' A frown is an attitude defect if there is a requirement for a smile. A misspelt word is a product defect if there is a spelling requirement. A late delivery is a timeliness defect if there is a timeliness requirement. Products or services with one or more defects are called defectives.

11.4   QUALITY MANAGEMENT PRACTICES IN SERVICE INDUSTRIES IN JAPAN

Some service industries in Japan have been active in improvement of productivity from the start of 1950—for example, the Japanese National Railways, Nippon Telegraph and Telephone Public Corporation, the Tobacco Monopoly of Japan, the Japan Post Office, etc.

Service organizations have won the Deming Prize in Japan; for example, Takenaka Komuten, an architectural and construction firm, won the Deming Prize in 1979. They studied the needs of users (in offices, hospitals, factories, hotels, trains, subways, etc.). They reduced the amount and cost of rework in drawings using computer software. Research on soils, rocks, movement of earth, machinery, accomplished continual improvement in methods of construction. Kajima Corporation, another architectural and construction firm, won similar recognition in 1982; likewise the Shimizu Construction Company won in 1983. The Kansai Electric Power Company, serving Osaka, Nagoya, and other parts of central Japan, the biggest power company in the world, won the Deming Prize in 1984.

11.5   QUALITY MANAGEMENT PRACTICES IN SERVICE INDUSTRIES IN ASIAN COUNTRIES

In the mid-1980s, the Asian countries implemented service quality management (SQM) for the civil service work environment. The popularity of SQM was due to three groups of QM practitioners:

(1) Norman, who called it "service management" (Norman 1984);
(2) Albrecht and Zemke (1985) whose book, *Service America*, generated worldwide interests in service quality; and
(3) Parasuraman and his co-workers, who developed a conceptual model of service quality, which was refined into a measuring instrument called SERQUAL in 1988 (Parasuraman, Zeithaml, and Berry 1985; 1988).

Thereafter, the hotel industry, financial and banking services, and other service industries in Asia adopted SQM to improve their customer service. Today, service quality is accepted as a norm in the service industries. The reasons for this acceptance are summarized as follows:

(i) Singapore: The republic's civil services developed a world-class strategy to develop Singapore into a world centre for trade, finance, port, hotel, and service industry

(Singapore Competitiveness Report 1998). Supporting this was the Service Quality Centre, a joint venture between the Productivity and Standards Board of Singapore and Singapore Airlines. Later, the civil service conceptualized the "PS21" vision of public service in the twenty-first century (Singapore Competitiveness Report 1998).

 (ii) Malaysia: In 1989, the first Civil Service Excellence Work Culture initiative was launched to improve the service quality in the country. These initiatives were supported by many civil service recognition awards (Chan 1999b).

(iii) Brunei, Indonesia, and the Philippines: The civil services continued with its quality control circles, which were modified to include service quality techniques.

11.6   QUALITY MANAGEMENT PRACTICES IN SERVICE INDUSTRIES IN INDIA

In India, the service sector has been emerging as a dominant component of the economy. Agriculture and industry are growing at a slower pace, while services are growing more rapidly. Share of services in the country's GDP has increased from 36% in 1980–81 to 44% in 1997–98. In the latter year, the share of agriculture and industry in GDP was just 24% and 32%, respectively. The share of services was, in fact, just 25% in 1955–56. It increased to 40% in 1987–88 and 46% 1999–2000. Service industries today dominate our economy. (According to CMIE source GDPfc {Gross Domestic Product at factor cost at current price} service accounts for (Rs. crore) '1135508' out of '2242463' approximately 51%). According to an article in the *Times of India*. "Service without a smile: Govt to raise new taxes" dated 03/06/04, service accounts for 54% of Indian economy. The service sector accounts for more than 70% of jobs and it is on the rise and expected to reach 85% in the near future. Quality management and quality improvement are mandatory for the success of the service sector of our economy.

It seems the notion that the majority of people need only *roti, kapda* and *makaan* has to be given up. Even the poor seem to need and be availing of several services, especially the ones like education, entertainment, information and healthcare. The middle class and the affluent are, of course, availing of a much larger variety of services, including dining out, and travel.

Certain types of services have been growing particularly rapidly. Higher education service is one example. Healthcare is another. Financial services is yet another. Healthcare has, in fact, become the fastest growing sector of the economy, growing at a compound rate of 26% annually between 1993–2000. Entertainment too is now among the fastest growing sectors. Spending on hotels and restaurants has grown at a compound rate of 18%. Services backed by technology and equipment, like vending machines, coffee and sandwich dispensing machines, computerized patient history records, etc., have also registered good growth.

The next decade in India will belong to service providers. One of the key service-quality challenges in the future will be service design. Service design is a form of architecture that involves processes rather than brick and mortar. The aim will be to design high quality into the service system from the outset. In other words, to consider and respond to customers, expectations in designing each element of the service along the QFD (quality function deployment) path. Technology will be the foundation for enhancing the quality of service. The dimensions of service-quality will be tangibles, reliability, responsiveness, assurance and empathy.

The service sector in India has been growing not only in volume but also in variety and sophistication. However, a word of caution may be exercised here on the realities of service quality as is observed in our day-to-day life. The general attitude and low levels of morale of the service providers in the Indian service industry makes the quality of service far from desirable. The following table summarizes the service sector in India.

Traditional services
(i) Utilities such as electricity and water supply
(ii) Transport services—rail, road, air, etc.
(iii) Communication services—posts, telephone, broadcasting, telecasting, etc.
(iv) Educational services
(v) Legal services
(vi) Accountancy services
(vii) Medical services/hospitals
(viii) Insurance, banking, etc.
(ix) Financial services—stock brokerage, leasing
(x) Food, leisure and recreation services—restaurants, hotels
(xi) Catering, fast-food joints, etc.
(xii) Entertainment services—cinema and theatre clubs and casinos, video game parlours and amusement parks, etc.
(xiii) Miscellaneous services such as repair and maintenance
(xiv) Beauty parlours
(xv) Distributive trade/retailing

Modern services
(i) Travel agency
(ii) Real estate
(iii) Advertising
(iv) Public relations
(v) Market research
(vi) Physical fitness/health clubs
(vii) Car rental service
(viii) Courier service
(ix) Credit cards

New generation services
(i) Business services
(ii) Recruitment services
(iii) Computer software/solutions
(iv) Computer maintenance
(v) Management consultancy
(vi) Technical consultancy
(vii) Management training
(viii) Technical training
(ix) Computer training

   (x)   Value-added telecom services
  (xi)   Radio paging
 (xii)   Cellular phone
(xiii)   Fax
 (xiv)   E-mail
  (xv)   Internet
 (xvi)   V-sat
(xvii)   Video conferencing
(xviii) E-commerce

Several factors have contributed to this big growth in services. Economic, socio-cultural, automation of service delivery systems, increasing number of women in jobs, and lifestyle changes taking place over the years, have been the major factors. Increased affluence as well as leisure with select segments of the population is another important aspect here. The advent of many new and technical products, and the new complexities of life are two other relevant aspects. The economic reforms and liberalization have led to the advent of many new services. The explosion in the information technology has been another great contributor to the growth of service businesses. In itself IT has emerged as a mega service business. In addition, it has supported the growth of other service businesses.

More specifically, increased affluence has led to greater demand for services like laundry, interior decoration, care of household products, etc. Increased affluence and leisure in combination, have led to the growth of recreation and entertainment services, travel services, etc. The phenomenon of more and more women going to work has led to a greater demand for services like fast foods, crèches, baby sitting, domestic help, etc. The advent and spread of complex products such as air-conditioners, cars, home computers, etc., has led to a greater demand for maintenance services. Increasing complexity of life has led to greater demand for advisory services in income tax, accounting and legal matters. The growing pressure on time and competition has resulted in greater demand for services like 'home delivery'; people do not want to waste their time visiting shops, standing in queues and waiting for billing and packaging of products bought by them. They place the order over the phone and the storekeeper arranges home delivery. In more recent times, tele-shopping has caught up, especially in urban centres. As for higher education, rising consciousness of its benefits coupled with the growing ability to pay for it has led to an upsurge in the student population seeking higher education, especially technical, management and computer education. Demand for medical service has grown rapidly on account of population growth and increased health consciousness.

There are indications that in India, services will grow even more rapidly in the coming years. Economic, social and lifestyle factors all signal such an expansion. Investments as well as job-generation too will be far greater in services compared to manufacturing. It is estimated that the service industry of telecom alone can absorb an investment of Rs. 1,50,000 crores in a relatively short span of time. The fact that India is rich in human resources and the service sector is full of export potential are the driving factors behind growth of services.

Opening up of markets for services is an important part of the agenda of the World Trade Organization (WTO). India can press for the needed changes in the dispensation and try to maximize the export of its services. It need not confine itself to just computer software but can try its hands in many other areas with potential. India's comparative advantage in global terms lies not so much in manufacturing as in services. In the export context, often people refer to harnessing India's cheap skilled manpower in making products for export. But, the real scope in this regard actually lies in services export. It is quite limited as far as manufactured products are concerned. The labour content in most manufacturing activities are dropping steadily with developments in technology. In contrast, the labour content in services is quite high.

In the Indian context, service problems are of different dimensions. Why is Hinduja Hospital cleaner than other hospitals? Why is Bombay Gymkhana's grass greener and Azad Maidan's brown? Why is Jet Airways more responsive than other Airlines? Why is Orange phone service better than the services provided by the other providers? Why is Hotel Taj service superior to other hotels? ... And the questions can go on. Fact is numbers. Sheer numbers. It is huge, massive and unimaginable. There are a large number of customers to be serviced. There are a large number of employees to be managed. There is a large size of infrastructure to be maintained. These service providers are bending over, cracking up and crumbling down, with the weight of large volumes, severely affecting the quality of service. To overcome this we have to generate the thought of providing quality service with a sense of belongingness and make them efficient, friendly organizations. Then we no longer should contented with the poor services in Hospital, Airlines or Railways.

In India, customers are not quality-conscious. Customers are not willing to pay higher price. We have to assess quality of service vis-à-vis cost of providing service. The major question emerging whether the customers are willing to pay the price of quality service. In the Indian situation, for instance, in railway services, postal services, hospital services etc., people are willing to stand in long queues, rather than pay more for quicker services. It may be that serving the customer in our country (India) gets confused with service attitude and class barriers come up quickly. It may be that pay and other rewards are so poor in the retail trade that people are not motivated to look after customers. Perhaps they are just not trained or managed skillfully to do so. It could be that by allocating 'low status' to service jobs, those employees are 'programmed' for delivering poor service. Part of it must be due to the customers themselves, who are not assertive about what they want. On the other extreme, we have the elite customers. People who splash out 1000s of Rupees for an evening meal for two, expect the restaurant to be fully satisfying. The setting and service must be correct. The food has to be excellent and properly prepared. Any aspect of the dinner that goes wrong—cold soup, or an over-cooked roast beef, or the wrong wine, or a surly waiter, or a noisy room, or loud or inappropriate music—can diminish the satisfaction and even spoil the evening.

In the Indian context, quality in the service sector is hard to define and measure. Missiles that blow up on the launching pad get everyone's attention. But when insurance adjusters underpay claims, "quality" is harder to pin down; the average Indian customer (particularly in the rural areas) does not know the difference between good quality and poor quality services. In some cases, the adjusters save the company's money; in others, they lose customers. Disgruntled people seldom suffer in silence; they tell a 'chain' of friends. Phone customers who are put on hold may not complain; they do, however, evaluate the service. In time, they may look for a company that treats them better.

A survey showed that it costs five times as much to get a new customer as to retain those we already have. Companies continue to spend crores of rupees, seeking new customers through advertising and promotion while remaining oblivious to the fact that current customers are dropping out due to poor attention paid by the company towards their needs and desires. The old customers leave mainly because of service quality problems. Most Indian businesses continue budgeting internal issues. Customer-oriented action should take a large part of our energy. Unfortunately, 90% of our time is spent in solving internal issues, while customer seldom gets even 10% attention. Strategy issues for servicing the customer, who pays us, need to be built in our business. According to a CII study, 68% of customers turn away due to attitudes of an organization, reflected through their employees.

Today, more than 50% of the Indian workforce is employed in the service sector and well over 50% of those employed in manufacturing are actually doing service work, such as finance, IT and marketing. Despite the high number of service employees, there are yet a few companies who believe that improving service processes is less important than improving manufacturing processes. The cost of poor quality in the service sector is found to be of a higher magnitude. Probably, the service sector nurses costs of poor quality of the order of 30% of total costs. Imagine the implications at the national level.

Some Indian examples practising quality management compiled from magazines/journals:

(1) Hotel Windsor Manor, Bangalore, for example, has committed half-an-hour as the execution time for room service orders and has created the wherewithal to stick to the committed standard. It has, in fact, projected this service commitment prominently by informing the customers that they will not be required to pay the bills at all if their room service order is not executed within the stipulated interval.

(2) From the case study of Grid Corporation of Orissa Ltd., it becomes evident that the quality circle of the Core Skill Training Centre of Grid Corporation of Orissa Ltd. Bhubaneswar, provided remarkable improvement in productivity due to remarkable reduction in labour cost, reduction in accidental compensations and reduction in power interruption periods, i.e. downtime. Orissa has the unique distinction of being the first state in India to take an initiative for power sector reform and restructuring. The main objective of the power sector reform is to provide quality power supply to consumers at a low cost. Emphasis is made on quality improvement of employees by HRD techniques, viz; setting up Quality Circles (QCs). The recommendation of a quality circle was implemented in some electric supply companies. The study indicates that there is a remarkable productivity improvement due to reduction in manpower as well as reduction in accidents and deaths. The recommended method is gaining popularity and is being implemented in other electric utilities of the state.

(3) The Taj West End, Bangalore, differentiates its service offering, using time dimension. Their claim is stated below. two-minute check-in, four-minute baggage delivery, five-minute room service (for beverages). Additionally, to help customers to work efficiently, 24-hour business centre offers computers and workstations, while all their rooms have fax, data ports and modem connectivity. The hotel realizes that a businessman's most

precious asset is his time. So, they have set standards that allow the customer to make the most of it.

(4) Jet Airways: The Service Quality Experience: Case Study

Since inception in 1993, Jet Airways has always endeavoured to deliver a world-class service, on the ground and in the air, by borrowing from the best practices of airlines and other service-related fields in the world, and by adapting the same to the Indian environment. Forte believes service is emotional labour and this has to be sustained and managed. Further, the airline travel is not merely transportation, it is also an experience.

The liberalization process of the airline industry in India started on December 11, 1990 with the issuance of a new Air Taxi Guidelines. Private airlines were designated as Air Taxi Operators (ATOs). The major ATOs to start operations with jet aircraft in 1992–93 were: East West Airlines, Damania Airways, ModiLuft, Jet Airways, Sahara India Airlines, and NEPC. Jet Airways took to the skies on May 5, 1993. By the year 1995, all the major private operators were granted the scheduled airlines status. Jet Airways achieved a market share of 6.6% in its first year of operations (1993–94) and has, by 2000–2001, achieved a market share of 40% a growth that is nearly seven times as much. Today, the airline has, in its eight years of operations, carried over 25 million passengers. Years of ongoing and consistent efforts have won the Jet Airways recognition from various industry forums in the form of awards, such as India's Best Domestic Airline.

In the service industry, especially the competitive airline industry, knowing what to do is not difficult. But how to do and convincing the team why it should be done are more often the problems. To complicate matters further, the high financial risks and relatively low profit margins in the industry do not allow for experimentation. Doing all the right things—right in the service profit chain is required. The simple, effective plan includes actively managing every customers feedback. Every meeting of a customer with an employee is treated as a rare opportunity for the airline to distinguish itself favourably from the competition. Jet Airways believes that world-class service entails being warm and caring. The efficiency of the West, combined with the renowned warmth and hospitality of the East, is reflected in their blue and yellow corporate colours. The colour blue stands for professionalism and efficiency, while yellow symbolizes warmth and caring.

Recent research has indicated that excellence in the following areas is of vital importance for an airline to be considered an ideal airline: punctuality, safety, seating comfort, large network, friendly and caring, professional and efficient staff/crew service, quality of food served, cleanliness of aircraft, quick baggage clearance, ease in booking tickets, and easy check-in. It is therefore critical for an airline to continually achieve an excellent rating in all the above service criteria.

Without customer service standards to guide their activities, they are unlikely to be able to meet the expectations of their customers. **Hard standards** can be measured in the following areas: appearance, customer-contact areas, lounges, reservations, sales, check-in, system reliability, baggage handling, punctuality, delay handling, aircraft cleaning, maintenance.

Soft standards apply to all customer-contact areas. Research has shown that the following soft standards are considered by their customers as important aspects of personal service: staff who are attentive and ready to help, polite staff, competence in dealing with any eventuality, level of tact displayed by staff in difficult situations, staff that appear to enjoy dealing with people, availability of airline staff, responsiveness to individual needs, being treated as an individual, approachable staff, staff who are warm and friendly, and being greeted with a smile and pleasant service. Although soft standards in these areas are subjective and more difficult to monitor, they are the standards by which many customers are likely to judge their services. Soft standards present them with an opportunity to turn ordinary experiences into exceptional services. Hence they cannot be left to chance.

Hard standards have the potential to dissatisfy customers if we fail to meet them. However, they would more or less go unnoticed, and fail to impress or excite a passenger even if they are world-class standards—which are to be expected. Soft standards, on the other hand, are the powerful tools to impress the passengers, to make them feel special, to recognize and treat them as individuals.

The airlines are presently reviewing their standards and are working very closely with their contact staff to ensure their participation for the competitive standards they believe need to be in place in the next phase of their service improvement programme. Technical (hard) standards get them into the game while soft standards give them the opportunity to win. Airlines, in their opinion, will not be able to compete at a world-class level if they do not implement world-class standards.

Standards not only impact customer satisfaction, but also establish a common language. They also provide a sense of purpose and improve teamwork. These are some of the elements required to develop a strong service-oriented culture. They have, therefore, to close the gaps using the tested model developed by Prof. A. Parasuraman.

Gap 1: Management perceptions and customer expectations
Gap 2: Management perceptions and service quality specifications
Gap 3: Service specifications and service delivery
Gap 4: Service delivery and external communications to customers
Gap 5: Perceived and expected service.

Service quality team activities: The service quality department reports directly to the CEO. They were previously reporting to the head of customer services and were seen as a semi-operational extension of the airport and in-flight services. The service quality department has, worked with the CEO in setting targets and in supporting the operational teams. The following are the quality initiatives: Quality awareness programmes, outstation audits (in-flight and airport), set targets and follow-up action plans, quarterly customer feedback workshops, standards (minimum/competitive/world-class), on time performance —precision time schedule, quality monitor, service index, benchmarking, external measurement of quality, ISO 9000 for in-flight and engineering

Jet Airlines introduced a feedback mechanism on the ground through the customer comment form (CCF) and that more than doubled the then 8,000 service monitor questionnaire (SMQ) responses to 19,000 responses per month. Their sample size is therefore not only more representative but they are obtaining statistically valid responses for even the smaller stations. This information is collated in reports and linked with other feedback sources to determine their strengths and weaknesses. They group these weaknesses under a collective term *service detractors* and they are rated from *critical* to *concern*. A monthly overview, the *Quality Monitor*, is published to keep them on track. The management teams were previously given feedback on service issues in the form of ratings obtained from the SMQ distributed onboard, and, of course, customer complaints. They now use the quality monitor to analyze their service levels. The message to the organization was that quality of service was going to be the driving force in their quest for world-class recognition. Their service quality department has recently been actively involved in process mapping their core customer service processes, with an end to enabling them to review their functioning very objectively and pointing out means by which they can channelize their efforts more efficiently.

Jet Airlines are using the Parasuraman Berry and Zeithaml model as a checklist to ensure that they ask themselves the right questions in each customer service process. Through this checklist, they measure whether their processes or service are in order as viewed from a customer's perspective.

R-A-T-E-R Checklist

R-A-T-E-R   Y/N

Responsiveness

     Is our staff able to assist customers?

     Is their service delivery prompt every time?

Assurance

     Are we and our staff knowledgeable?

     About the company

     About the products and services

     About systems and procedures

     Do we create a sense of trust and confidence in the company?

     Are we courteous?

Tangible

     Are the company's physical facilities customer-friendly?

Empathy

     Do customers receive individual attention?

     Is our staff taught and do they practice individual customer care?

Reliability

     Can the customer depend on us?

     Do we deliver on promises made?

(5) Mumbai *dabawalas* case study: 5000 men deliver 1,75,000 lunches every day, making only one mistake in every two months, which is equivalent to one mistake in 8 million deliveries; a service failure of less than a Six-Sigma company. They earned a mention in *Forbes* Global. The drive for such a quality service is the desire to serve each customer without fail, so that he does not go hungry. In business, we need to realize that we need to serve every single hungry customer. As they say, if we don't take care of the hungry customer, someone else will.

11.7   HOW DO WE DEFINE SERVICE SECTOR?

It is extremely difficult to define pure goods or a pure service. A pure good implies that the consumer obtains benefit from the goods alone, without any added value from service; concurrently, a pure service assumes that there is no 'goods' element to the service, which the customer receives. In reality, most services contain some goods element. At

McDonald's the customer receives a hamburger; the bank provides a bank statement; the garage that repairs cars adds new parts to those cars, and so on. And most goods offer some service—even if it is only delivery.

A product or offering can consist of as many as three components: physical good(s), service(s), and idea(s). For example, a fast-food restaurant is supplying goods (hamburgers, fries, soft drinks), services (purchasing, cooking, seating), and an idea ('saves my time'). A computer manufacturer is supplying goods (computer, monitor, printer), services (delivery, installation, training, maintenance, repair), and an idea ('computation power'). A church offers less in the way of physical goods (wine, wafer) and more in the way of services (sermon, singing, education, counselling) and ideas (community, salvation)

The importance of physical products lies not so much in owning them as in obtaining the services they render. We buy a car because it supplies transportation service. We buy a microwave oven because it supplies a cooking service. Thus physical products are really vehicles that deliver services to us. In fact, other vehicles, such as people, places, activities, organizations and ideas, also supply services. If we are bored, we can attend a comedy club and watch a comedian (person); travel to a cool vacation land like Matheran (place); go to the health club (activity); join a hiking club (organization); or adopt a different philosophy about life (idea). Manufacturers often make the mistake of paying more attention to their physical products than to the services produced by those products. They see themselves as selling a product rather than providing a solution to a need.

Increasingly, firms in the goods sectors are using service offerings as a way of differentiating their products from those of their competitors. The goods/services dichotomy is a subtly changing spectrum, with forms moving their position within that spectrum overtime. In fact, an exact definition of services is not really necessary in order to understand services and the quality problems associated with them. That there are different problems associated with the two is readily apparent; Mills and Moberg describe two factors which set service operations apart from goods operations, namely differences in process and differences in output. It is probably of greater practical value to focus on these kinds of differences rather than on ultimate definitions.

Service has been defined as "a social act, which takes place in direct contact between the customer and representatives of the service company". A service might be as simple as handling a complaint or as complex as a home mortgage. Many organizations are pure service businesses, their products are intangible. Examples would include education, banking, insurance, defence, municipal services, welfare services, legal services, health services and so on. Other examples of services are marketing, travelling and tours, restaurants, and public utilities (including electricity, gas, water and telephone service). Some service industries provide a tangible product and an intangible component that affects customer satisfaction. Certain service functions are found in both the manufacturing and service sectors. For instance, customer services (after-sales service, warranty replacement, repairs under guarantee clauses, etc.) purchasing, accounting, payroll and personnel are service functions that support the manufacturing function in manufacturing organizations. Even research and development (R&D), providers of healthcare, including hospitals and nursing homes, day care centres for children and for old people, wholesale and retail establishments, transportation of goods and of passengers (by any mode), insurance companies, accounting services, painters (houses, buildings, furniture), printing, news service, software, communication (telephone, telegraph, transmission of voice and of data), real estate, maintenance of buildings, plumbers, electrical repair and alteration, security, sale and delivery of electric power, construction, laundry and dry cleaning are considered as service functions.

11.8 WHY IS SERVICE SECTOR QUALITY CONTROL SO IMPORTANT?

Some say it is because the need is so great. Since World War II, product quality has received a lot of attention—as if it were industry's favourite child. Service quality, on the other hand, is treated like an illegitimate relative with tattered tennis shoes and patched-up clothes. Poor-looking relatives with questionable heritage can control crores of rupees; similarly service sector quality can control a sizeable sum in the overall economy. Consider the budgets allotted to secretarial support, filling, data entry, customer service, consumer relations, computer operations, database management, sales, quality control, manufacturing engineering, purchasing and design. These parts of industry represent the service sector; they require many of the same skills as service industries like banking and insurance.

Companies that do not provide quality service not only fail to compete, they will not even exist. Just as true wisdom is knowing how much you do not know, true quality is knowing you can always do better. For quality service to exist and flourish, everyone in the organization must internalize the concept that quality is a journey, not a destination. One of the most frequently stressed differences between goods and services is the lack of ability to control service quality before it reaches the consumer. Service encounters occur in real time, and consumers already are involved in the factory; if something goes wrong during the service process, it is too late to institute quality control measures before the service reaches the customer, indeed, the customer or another customer may be part of the quality problem. If, in a restaurant, something goes wrong during a meal, that service experience for a customer is bound to be affected; the manager cannot logically ask the customer to leave the restaurant, reenter, and start the meal over again. It is impossible for a service to achieve 100% right quality on an ongoing basis. Manufacturing operations also may have problems achieving this sort of target, but they can isolate mistakes and correct them over time, as mistakes tend to be recurring parts of the process. Many errors in service operations are one-offs; in the restaurant example mentioned above, the waiter who drops a plate creates a technical problem that neither can be foreseen nor corrected ahead of time. Interestingly enough, such mistakes often can be used to create customer satisfaction by recovering the situation in an excellent fashion. Since mistakes cannot be corrected as they occur, the only answer is to attempt to eradicate them at the source. Again, as the consumer is both part of the process and the person who ultimately determines service quality, understanding consumer behaviour must be a basic part of the quality process. Service quality is an integrated function, which needs inputs from all parts of the service organization.

11.8.1 Why hasn't Quality Service Taken Hold?

The root causes of low quality service are economics and low quality consciousness both among providers and utilisers. The great inflation of the 1970s, set off by the oil crisis, caused businesses to cut service to keep prices from rocketing. This was followed by deregulation, which increased competition and caused more cutbacks. Computers and self-service replaced service personnel as further cost cutting took place.

The question "Why hasn't quality service taken hold?" in the Indian context, is not an easy one to explain. It brings to mind the familiar situation of the chicken and the egg: Without chickens, there are no eggs; without eggs, there are no chickens. Similarly, with few quality "missionaries" in the service sector, there are few success stories; with few success stories, quality assurance in the service sector is hard to sell. Many executives are like cannibals; they would rather eat the quality control missionaries than listen to them. Many companies are struggling to improve service, wasting money on ill-conceived service programmes and undermining credibility with management rhetoric not backed up by action. Keeping and developing relationships with current customers is a key business strategy.

11.8.2 What is Service Quality?

The importance of quality assurance in service industry can never be overemphasized. A service must be performed right the first time and every time. The damage done on any one occasion leaves a permanent scar and the effect of a badly rendered service cannot be mitigated by any sops. Ironically, while quality assurance is of utmost importance in service, it is difficult to assure quality here. Even measuring quality is difficult in services. In the first place, quality characteristics in respect of a service are more difficult to define, leave alone measure. Second, quality here includes many subjective elements. We can state that service quality is ensured when the service does what the customer expects of it. This means that quality assurance in services calls for: (i) a device for understanding customer expectations of quality in the service, (ii) a mechanism for ensuring that the service is performed matching customer expectations, and (iii) a device for measuring the service quality perceived by the customer as the service goes along and on completion of the service. Since quality assurance in services becomes difficult mainly because of the difficulty in measuring service quality, the latter becomes the crux in managing service quality.

The first step in the study is to understand the nature of quality service. Without this background, you will be like a missionary trying to talk cannibals out of having you for dinner when you cannot even speak their language. Quality service involves attitudes, timeliness, proper tools, quality products and customer satisfaction. If you take care of the first four elements, customer satisfaction is assured—as long as you have a product the customer wants, readily available at a reasonable price.

Morse, Roth, and Poston (1987) define quality as a set of attributes that enable a service to conform to customer expectations. The assumption, of course, is that some design specifications have been developed and must be followed for the service in question. As long as all the specifications are being met, the customer remains satisfied. When the specifications are not met, not only are the customers dissatisfied, but also that dissatisfaction can be measured.

"Service quality" includes both quality in service industries and quality in the service sector of manufacturing companies. Service industries like hotels, fast-food outlets, insurance companies, governmental agencies, hospitals and banks are not noted for their high-volume manufacturing operations. There are, however, some jobs common to both the service and manufacturing sectors; the control of raw materials is one. In addition, most manufacturing organizations have clerical operations and use computers. These activities involve either service quality or administrative quality control and fall under the service sector umbrella. Formal attempts to bring quality to these areas, however, are limited.

Service quality includes both the quality of core services and facilitating services, which enhances the value of core services to the customer. Facilitating services are also provided by businesses that produce tangible goods. For example, in banking services, checking an account is a core service product whereas additional services provided by banks, such as automated teller services, and 24-hour telephone access to account information are facilitating services. Sometimes facilitating services may be more valuable to the customers than the core services. For instance, a fast food restaurant may produce tangible goods in the form of pizzas and French fries, which are the restaurant's core products. However, the restaurant's distinctive features may be its quick service and friendliness of its service (which are the facilitating services).

In defining quality service, there are additional characteristics to be accounted for. Garvin (1988), for example, identified eight dimensions of quality, with each contributing to a set of requirements. In quality service, it is paramount that those dimensions be accounted for and planned in the service process. However, regardless of how the organization defines and/or derives its definition of quality in service, it must be understood by everyone that quality service must incorporate as many dimensions as possible. These dimensions are:

Function: The primary required performance of the service
Features: The expected performance (bells and whistles of the service)
Conformance: The satisfaction based on requirements that have been set
Reliability: The confidence of the service in relationship to time
Serviceability: The ability to service if something goes wrong
Aesthetics: The experience itself as it relates to the senses
Perception: The reputation of quality

11.8.2.1 The Concept of 'Service Value'

The concept of 'service value' is another useful contribution of researchers in this area. The concept reckons the benefits as well as the sacrifices inherent in the purchase and consumption of a service. The benefits include service quality and satisfaction enjoyed by the customer. The sacrifices include 'objective price' and the 'perceived risk' in the service. Studies have shown that the 'service value' concept is useful in predicting further the behavioural intentions of the customer, such as intention to repurchase, intention to increase the usage, intention to use other offerings of the firm and intention to recommend the service to others.

11.8.3 What is Total Quality Service?

If total quality management (TQM) in India was the ticket to success in the 1990s, then total quality service (TQS) is rapidly becoming the challenge of the 2000s for our country. Indian companies that want to achieve a certain goal will be successful through a cultural transformation that produces a TQS organization.

What is TQS? In its simplest form, it is a true commitment to operationalizing the concept of customer focus, establishing service performance standards, measuring performance against benchmarks, recognizing and rewarding exemplary behaviour, and maintaining enthusiasm for the customer at all times. In its most complicated form, it increases sales and market share. All within an organization should get involved in small group improvement activities with a different mindset. 'For example, even the activities of a driver receiving a guest at the airport may make or mar the image of an organization. He should be punctual, should spot the guest, should have good manners, should be well-dressed, should be safe in driving, should ensure that the car used by him is well-maintained both functionally and aesthetically'.

Various studies have shown that excellently managed service companies share the following common practices: a strategic concept, a history of top-management commitment to quality, high standards, systems for monitoring service performance, systems for satisfying customers' complaints, and an emphasis on employee and customer satisfaction.

The manufacturing landscape of the corporate world has undergone a quality revolution, resulting in a plethora of research works on the tools, techniques, critical dimensions and other organizational requirements for the effective implementation of TQM. But the same cannot be said with certainty of service quality management. Research works on total quality service TQS is not exhaustive in the sense that there appears to be a vacuum in literature as far as a holistic model (from the perspective of the management) is concerned.

The TQM concept can be of use in quality assurance in services. It is a mistaken notion to assume that TQM is applicable only to product marketing situations. We know that the principal elements of TQM are: people, appropriate technology, quality control through problem solving tools/procedures and a resolve for continuous improvement. All these elements are equally applicable to quality assurance in service marketing situations.

11.8.4 Does Quality Service Pay?

The importance of quality in services cannot be underestimated. Nowadays many firms offering service lose their customers because of poor service. Studies in the USA have shown that firms can boost their profits by almost 100% by retaining just 5% more of their customers than their competitors. This is because the cost of acquiring new customers is much higher than the costs of retaining them. Firms with loyal, long-time customers can financially outperform competitors with higher customer turnover even when their unit costs are higher and their market share is smaller.

Delivering excellent service is a winning strategy. Quality service sustains customers' confidence and is essential for a competitive advantage. It results in: more new customers; more business with existing customers; fewer lost customers; fewer mistakes requiring reperformance of services; challenged service providers performing to their potential.

11.8.5 Research Observations in USA in the Context 'Does Quality Service Pay?'

'In today's competitive market, no business can survive without satisfied customers. Findings from recent studies conducted by the Technical Assistance Research Program (TARP), a federal government-sponsored program in the USA, support this statement:

(i) 96% of the consumers who experience a problem with a small-ticket product (for example, small packaged goods) do not complain to the manufacturer. (Of these, 63% will not buy again.)

(ii) 46% of the consumers who experience a problem with a small-ticket service (for example, cable television or local telephone service) do not complain. (Of these, 45% will not buy again). {These figures may not apply to monopoly markets}

(iii) Not surprisingly, only 27% of unhappy consumers of large-ticket durable products (for example, automobiles, computers) do not complain. (Of these, 41% will not buy again.)

(iv) 37% of unhappy consumers of large-ticket services (for example, insurance, loans, HMOs) do not complain. (of these, 50% will not buy again.)

These numbers alone are significant and can make a major dent in future sales. But TARP has confirmed that negative word of mouth can create an even more formidable problem. Unhappy customers share their experiences with others. A dissatisfied customer with a small problem typically tells 10 other people; those with large problems tell 16 others, 13% of dissatisfied customers tell their experiences to more than 20 people. As bad as this sounds, the news is not all bad. Each customer whose small problem is satisfactorily resolved can be expected to tell five other people. Each customer whose large problem is satisfactorily resolved can be expected to tell eight other people. Of these people, some will then become new customers. The significance of these numbers is that most customers whose complaints are satisfactorily resolved go on to buy again. These figures range from 92% of purchasers of small-ticket products to 70% of customers of large-ticket services.

If quality is so evasive, is it an attainable goal or a budget-busting dream with no conceivable payback? Many executives in both manufacturing and service sectors agree that quality does pay. Variables they use to measure the payback include lower costs, good savings and improved productivity. The following quotes illustrate these points:

(i) *Lower Costs:* James E. Olson, president of American Telephone and Telegraph (AT&T), said, "Quality will cost us less money and better meet the needs of óur customers." The president of AT&T should know; his job depends on containing costs and maintaining profits.

(ii) *Savings:* Robin L. Lawton, president of Innovative Management Technologies, Inc., supports the savings theme. Lawton wrote about initiating a quality improvement programme for an accounting organization. They "identified systematic invoice errors causing over $750,000 per year in unnecessary costs." In another case, he writes about a customer service organization that "identified a declining trend in quality of service which threatened business survival."

(iii) *Productivity:* Another service company executive, Subhash C. Puri, Director at Agriculture Canada, stresses the interrelationship between quality and productivity: "Productivity and quality are completely intertwined—a neglect of one jeopardizes the other."

Quotes from these service-sector executives support the contention that quality in the service area contributes to corporate profits.

11.8.6 Importance of Customers in Service Quality

Total quality management is focused on the requirements of the customer. On the personal front people only go back to restaurants that fully satisfy them and they shop regularly at stores that meet their needs. They fly on airlines that provide friendly, efficient service. Industrial customers, likewise, have a set of expectations and requirements that must be met for the supplier to win repeat business. An industrial customer has the same range of emotions as a personal customer to being disappointed, cheated or short-changed. The industrial customer's response to poor service is similar—withdrawal of business and buying elsewhere.

Ken Cusack (Managing Director of Sorbus UK), whose firm has had a phenomenal growth in the computer maintenance business, refuses to let anyone in his firm talk about 'satisfying' the customer: 'we aim to positively delight the customer not just satisfy him.' In doing so he is in line with Deming's latest thinking: "It will not suffice to have customers that are merely satisfied", Deming wrote: "An unhappy customer will switch. Unfortunately, a satisfied customer might also switch, on the theory that he could not lose much, and might gain. Profit in business comes from repeat customers, customers that boast about your products and service, and bring friends with them."

Often experts, including Deming, talk about satisfying customers' needs now and in the future. The idea is to stay ahead of the customer, to anticipate his or her needs in the next few years so that when he or she articulates the need, you have already planned for it and are ready (ahead of the competition) to meet it. The emphasis for customer requirements must be on what he requires, not on what the company wants to impose on the customer. Customer requirements include specification, conformance, reliability, value-for-money and on-time-delivery. The insurance industry is awakening (lately) to the concept of meeting genuine customer requirement—as opposed to inventing new products almost in isolation from the customer and pushing them on to the market.

While the literature on quality has been predominantly goods-oriented, a few contributions have focused on service quality. From these writings emerge the following themes:

(i) Service quality is more 'difficult for customers to evaluate than goods quality. Therefore, the criteria customers use to evaluate service quality may be more difficult for the researcher to comprehend. How customers evaluate investment services offered by a stockbroker is more complicated and varied than how they evaluate insulation materials. Customers' assessment of the quality of healthcare services is more complex and difficult than their assessment of the quality of automobiles.

(ii) Customers do not evaluate service quality solely on the outcome of a service (e.g., how a customer's hair looks after a hair-cut).

(iii) Customers define the only criteria that count in evaluating service quality. Only the customers will judge quality; all other judgments are essentially irrelevant. Specifically, service-quality perceptions stem from how well a provider performs vis-à-vis customers' expectations about how the provider should perform.

The following statements underline the importance of customers in the service industry:

  (i) In the service industry, the people's skills in dealing with customers are as important as immediate behaviour.
 (ii) The information has to be translated over and over again for different customers.
(iii) All the employees have the responsibility and opportunity to deal effectively with the customers.
 (iv) All the employees must make the customer feel comfortable in the face of the customers irate behaviour.
  (v) The employees must answer the same questions over and over again with a smile, always showing concern and courtesy.
 (vi) The employee must appease the irate customer so that the customer will feel satisfied.

Indeed, it is a proven fact: when treated well, shown respect, and kept informed, customers respond more favourably, complain less, are more cooperative, become loyal customers, and their perception of quality improves.

Most Indian organizations now profess that, for them, customer is the king. The competition is at least forcing them to look at the customer with respect. India should have a passion for the customer-driven quality. Without this, little else matters. Customers are the final judges of how well the organizations perform, and what they say counts. It is their perception of the product or service that will determine whether they remain loyal or seek better providers. Employees must systematically listen to customers and act quickly on what they say. Dissatisfied customers must be heard closely, for they often deliver the most valuable information. If only satisfied and loyal customers (those who continue to do business with a company, no matter what) are given attention, the organization will be led astray. Most successful organizations keep tabs on customers who are not satisfied and work to meeting their demands and expectations.

11.8.7 Importance of Physical Environment in Service Quality

Physical evidence is the environment in which a service is delivered and where the firm and the customer interact; and any tangible commodities that facilitate performance or communication of the service. Physical evidence is particularly important for communicating about credibility service (such as auto repair) but it is also important for services, such as hotels, hospitals, and theme parks that are dominated by experience attributes. Physical evidence that is inconsistent with service delivery or that over-promises what the firm can do will lead to disappointment.

Because services are intangible, customers often rely on tangible cues, or physical evidence, to evaluate the service before its purchase and to assess their satisfaction with the service during and after consumption. General elements of physical evidence include all aspects of an organization's physical facilities as well as other forms of tangible communication. Elements of the physical environment that affect customers include both exterior attributes (such as signage, parking, landscape) and interior attributes (such as design, layout, equipment, décor). It is apparent that some services communicate heavily through physical evidence (e.g. hospitals, resorts, childcare) while others provide limited physical evidence (e.g. insurance and express mail). All of the elements of evidence listed for each service communicates something about the service to consumer and/or facilitate performance of the service.

Consumer researchers know that the design of the physical environment can influence customer choices, expectations, satisfaction, and other behaviours. For example, retailers know that customers are influenced by smell, décor, music, and store layout. Further, because services are generally purchased and consumed simultaneously, employees and customers will interact with each other in the physical environment. Thus, the same physical setting that communicates with and influences customers will also affect the employees of the firm.

On the basis of a totally separate area of research, we know that the design of work environments can affect the employees' productivity, motivation, and satisfaction. The challenge in many service settings is to design the physical space and evidence so that it can support the needs and preferences of both customers and employees simultaneously. For example, in a study of employee and customers preferences in a bank environment, customers tended to agree that "A bank should not look like it spent too much money on décor," while employees tended not to agree. Customers may perceive that they are paying for expensive décor. Employees, on the other hand, may perceive an investment in the environment as an indication of the management's concern for their feeling of job satisfaction.

At one extreme is the self-service environment where the customer performs most of the activities and few (if any) employees are involved. Examples of self-service environment include ATMs, movie theatres, express-mail drop-off facilities, and self-service entertainment, such as theme parks. In these primarily self-service environments, organizations can plan the facility focusing exclusively on marketing goals, such as attracting the right market segment and making the facility pleasing and easy-to-use. Creative use of physical design supports positioning and segmentation strategies as well. At the other extreme of use, dimension is the remote service where there is no customer involvement with the physical environment. Telecommunication, utilities financial consultants, editorial, and mail-order services are examples of services that can be provided without the customer ever seeing the service facility. In fact, the facility may be in a different state or a different country. In these remote services, decisions about how the facility should be designed can focus almost exclusively on the employees' needs and preferences. The place can be set up to keep employees motivated and to facilitate productivity, teamwork, operational efficiency, or whatever organizational behaviour goal is desired without any consideration of customers, since they will never need to see the physical environment.

Interpersonal services are placed between the two extremes and represent situations where both the customer and the employee must be present in the physical environment. Examples abound such as hotels, restaurants, hospitals, educational setting and banks. In these cases the physical environment must be planned to attract, satisfy, and facilitate the activities of both customers and employees simultaneously. Special attention must also be given to how the physical environment affects the nature and quality of the social interactions between and among customers and employees. A cruise ship provides a good example of a service setting where the physical environment must support customers and the employees who work there and also facilitate interactions between the two groups.

11.9 CATEGORIES OF SERVICE QUALITY CHARACTERISTICS

The following are the categories: attitude, timeliness, tools and facilities, product defects and customer satisfaction.

Attitude: The ASQC/Gallup Survey shows that dissatisfaction with indifferent workers is common for the service industries—especially with hospitals and government offices. Discourtesy also causes many complaints; hospital employees were the worst offenders. Disneyland overcomes most attitude problems by selective hiring and by thoroughly educating their employees. The United Services Automobile Association (USAA) is also attitude-conscious. The company has a need for prompt, polite and accurate customer service. Common attitude problems in the service sector include the following:

(i) Poor attention from the sellers makes most buyers unhappy. Few shoppers want a clerk to hover; most shoppers, however, expect some attention. As an example, a customer recently went shopping for a suit. The first shop had a Rs. 1500 outfit that looked like it fit his needs. The customer did not buy because the clerk kept wandering off; he also failed to answer questions promptly. Later, however, the customer bought a Rs. 3000 suit from another store. The clerk who made the sale had a better attitude; he also sounded more knowledgeable about his product. The suit the customer bought may or may not have been worth the extra price—but the quality of the service kept him satisfied.

(ii) A "know-it-all" attitude also turns off customers. As an example, many people pay more for computers than they should, because some stores with the best values have clerks with the worst attitudes. No one wants to be browbeaten by sales personnel, just because they do not know the difference between hardware and software. Clerks with good attitudes accept customer shortcomings and help them select what is the best for them.

(iii) A 'we're the good guys' attitude can cause difficulties, too. This problem often shows up when working with vendors. In the old days, it was customary to assume that the vendor should resolve vendor problems, with no assistance from the buyer; suppliers were the bad guys. The current trend is to acknowledge that vendor problems hurt buyers as well as sellers. Many vendor problems are the result of poor communication between the two. The more vendors know about the product, how it will be used and what it interfaces with, the more responsive they can be to the buyer. The example highlights the fact that quality service is not limited to service industries; it also applies to the service sector of manufacturing companies, including their purchasing departments.

(iv) An "I'm the expert" attitude hampers communications. For example, computer programmers and analysts with this attitude seldom ask the right questions. When they think they know everything, they make assumptions about what the user wants. As a consequence, the finished computer program may fit the programmer's idea of what is needed without coming close to the user's actual requirements. Similar problems occur when purchasing departments do not ask manufacturing departments the right questions; or design departments do not talk to marketing departments; or sales departments talk to production departments.

(v) The "you're the expert" attitude is the opposite of the "I'm the expert" attitude; both create problems. It is not unusual for managers to give too much freedom to computer analysts and programmers. After all, "they are the experts." This approach results in the development of computer programmes that appear perfect to the computer people but useless to the user. Then, each blames the other.

(v) "Grumpy" attitudes extend beyond the service sector. One shop supervisor in an aerospace company was so unpleasant that the manufacturing engineers refused to work with him. Eventually, a new engineer decided to put up with the verbal abuse long enough to find out what the problem was. Persistence paid off. The engineer helped the supervisor solve a technical problem that had been bugging him for months. Once the supervisor found an engineer who was willing and able to help him, his attitude toward engineers improved. Quality service paid.

Timeliness: Problems with timeliness ranked second among customer complaints listed in the 1985 ASQC/Gallup Survey; it was most obvious when government employees were involved, although insurance companies and banks had timeliness problems too. Rosander divides timeliness into the following categories: time to order a service, waiting time before service can be performed, service time, post-service time, repeat-service time.

Time to order a service can involve reaching the right person by phone. We all get tired of waiting in line. Have you ever walked out of a bank or store because the lines were too long? When people walk out, they are unhappy and many unhappy customers do not return. (In the Indian situation, this may not always be true) A typical service-time problem can occur when you get your car fixed. Post-service time can involve waiting in line to pay your bill: some cashiers take forever. Repeat-service time often occurs when the service was not performed properly. Improperly repaired automobiles, faulty calculations and typographical errors are typical.

Tools and Facilities: These have a major impact on customers' perceptions. With fast-food operations, for instance, appearance and cleanliness are critical. In some other service areas, customers look for state-of-the-art equipment. Examples for showing the effect of tools and facilities on customer satisfaction includes the following:

(i) Greasy-spoon restaurants have a bad reputation. Flies buzz around the food, empty tables are full of dirty dishes and the cooks' aprons look like the dresses of car mechanics.

(ii) Accounting offices are expected to have state-of the-art computer equipment. Those using hand-written ledgers and low-paid clerks have refused to enter the age of automation.

(iii) Computer organizations that still use keypunch machines are not state-of–the-art. Keypunch machines are data processing equipment used to punch holes in computer cards—those sacred forms that are not supposed to be 'spindled, folded, punched or mutilated.' Some payroll checks and bills still come from these sources.

Product defects: Quality in the service sector has much in common with quality in manufacturing. Both services and products should be free of defects. It is difficult, however, to monitor or improve a service until you have determined what "defects" you should be looking for'.

If we take care of the four dimensions, viz. (i) attitude, (ii) timeliness, (iii) tools and facilities and (iv) product defects, then customer satisfaction is automatically ensured.

11.10 KNOWING THE CUSTOMERS

It is only the salesman and the serviceman of manufactured products—apparatus, machinery, utensils, automobiles, trucks, railway cars, locomotives, and the like—that see the customer. These men do not make the items that they sell, repair, and maintain. They are in a service organization, independent or owned by the manufacturer. Many people work in a bank. The officers and tellers see customers; the rest do not. People at the front end in a department store, restaurant, hotel, railway, trucking company, or bus company see customers; the inside officials do not. Everyone, whether he sees the customer or not, has a chance to build quality into the product or into the service offered.

The people who see customers have a role that is not usually appreciated by supervisors and other management. Many customers form their opinions about product or a service solely by their contacts with the people that they see. It is the customers who keep a company in business, both in manufacturing and in service industries. Ability to please the customers should be, for good management, top priority for hiring and training of employees.

Many people who serve customers in restaurants, hotels, elevators, banks, and hospitals would enjoy the job much more were it not that customers come in and interrupt their conversations. A bus driver of a private travels is obviously an expert at driving the bus, and knows his route. Customers board and descend. His job would have been so much more enjoyable to him were it not for those passengers that boarded and descended or needed directions and help. Actually, the job might be enjoyable to him were he to understand that a sizable proportion of the people who ask questions for directions and guidance are a potential source of future revenue for the company, and that he can help to build up business to ensure his job in the future. Likewise in hotels, stores, restaurants, banks, trains, and a multitude of other types of shops and services, the people that see the customers are the marketing department. Do they know it? Does the management teach drivers that they are not only drivers, but also a potential influence to increase patronage? How about screening applicants for their adaptability to this role? The man who runs the elevator in a department store plays an important role in the customer's opinion of the quality of everything for sale in the store. The Japanese know this. The man who runs the elevator in a department store in Japan receives training over a period of two months on how to direct people, how to answer questions, and how to handle them in a crowded elevator—this in spite of the gracious manners in a Japanese home.

Starting a service company with little knowledge of the potential customers is like swimming in the Gulf of Mexico with a broken leg, a bleeding cut and no shark repellent. The risk-taker cannot keep head above water very long. Julie MacLean, quality manager, marketing and international sector for Hewlett-Packard, supports this contention when she says: "Quality products and services are those that meet or exceed customer expectations. A company's definition of quality must be customer-driven." W. Edwards Deming adds support by saying, "Quality should be aimed at the needs of the consumer, present and future."

Warren L. Nickell, in his article on quality in marketing, defines a customer as "the recipient of any of your work ... (both inside and outside the organization)." In other words, your customer is anyone benefitting from your services—directly or indirectly. Philip B. Crosby has a similar approach. He asks the question, "Who is our customer inside the company?" Then he answers himself with, "It could be another department, the president, or whoever receives the result of our work."·

In an article published in the March 1999 edition of the *Quality Times*, the Australian management consultants Andrew Gorecki and Susanne Siggins gave five major guidelines for delivering consistently good customer service. They are:

(1) The entire service delivery process needs to be analyzed and improved: All the process elements must be mapped down and reviewed. Those vulnerable to variation due to reliance on people need to be changed, to minimize this dependence.
(2) The service delivery system needs to be formalized: There must be clear rules, quantitative process design, and unambiguous allocation of responsibilities and accountabilities. Consistency requires that the service delivery process is stable.
(3) Staff should be trained to enhance their skills and abilities: The service system needs to be based on a set of intuitive, self-guiding checklists and procedures, supplemented by graphical operating manuals and even specialized tools like the scoop they use at McDonalds for filling boxes with French fries.
(4) Staff who works directly with the customers must have the right personality: Employ the right people in the first place
(5) Continuing improvement: The process of continuous improvement consists of delivering service that is not only consistently good, but getting better all the time.

To meet the customers' requirements means to listen to the customer and to respond to what he or she wants and to what is agreed. But as stated earlier, customers are not only external to the company—the people outside who are the end-users of a firm's products and services. There is also the internal customer, the person within the company who receives the work of another and then adds his or her contribution to the product or service before passing it on to someone else. In manufacturing, the internal customer is the next person down the line who builds the product.

For example (i) At shoes manufacturing in Bata, a pair of shoes will pass through a hundred hands from the start to the finished product—the chain of internal customers stretches round the factory. (ii) Suppose the service you provide is entering data into a computer database. The head of the department responsible for the database is one of your customers. If you enter the wrong data, the department head's reputation will suffer. Members of your chain of command are also your customers; they pay you for your services. If you make an error, they feel bad. In addition, individuals using the database are your customers. They make decisions based on the assumption that the data they get from the database is correct. If it is faulty, their work is prone to errors. Poor quality often has a ripple effect; one instance of poor service may hurt many people. (iii) In software engineering as the 'man-years' grow, the computer programme passes from one internal customer to another until a 'bug free' programme is offered to the external customer. (iv) In a restaurant, the chef has the waiters and waitresses as internal customers and the chef must meet their requirements if they are all to please the guests.

If the internal customers' requirements are agreed and met, a chain of quality is made that reaches out to the external customer. Making people to identify the internal customers for the main outputs of the work group is the beginning of the total quality process. To touch off a dialogue between the internal 'supplier' and the internal customer that leads them to agree with the end customer requirements is the beginning of creating a total quality culture.

11.11 DIFFERENCE BETWEEN GOODS AND SERVICES

According to Theodore Levitt, "There are no such things as service industries. There are only industries whose service components are greater or less than those of other industries. Everybody is in service". A service is any act or performance that one party can offer to another that is essentially intangible and does not result in the ownership of anything. Its production may or may not be tied to a physical product. A company's offer to the marketplace often includes some services. The service component can be a minor or a major part of the total offer. Five categories of offer can be distinguished:

(i) *Pure tangible good:* The offer consists primarily of tangible goods such as soap, toothpaste, or salt. No services accompany the product.

(ii) *Tangible good with accompanying services:* The offer consists of tangible goods accompanied by one or more services to enhance its consumer appeal. For example, an automobile manufacturer must sell more than an automobile. Levitt observes that "The more technologically sophisticated the generic product (e.g., cars and computers), the more dependent are its sales on the quality and availability of its accompanying customers services (e.g., display rooms, delivery, repairs and maintenance, application aids, operator training, installation advice, warranty fulfillment). In this sense, General Motors is probably more service-intensive than manufacturing-intensive. Without its services, its sales would shrivel." In fact, many manufacturers are now discovering opportunities to sell their services as a separate profit centre.

(iii) *Hybrid:* The offer consists of equal parts of goods and services. For example, people patronize restaurants for both their food and their service.

(iv) *Major service with accompanying minor goods and services:* The offer consists of a major service along with additional services and/or supporting goods. For example, airline passengers are buying transportation service. They arrive at their destinations without anything tangible to show for their expenditure. However, the trip includes some tangibles, such as food and drinks, a ticket stub, and an airline magazine. The service requires a capital intensive good—an airplane—for its realization, but the primary item is a service.

(v) *Pure service:* The offer consists primarily of a service. Examples include baby-sitting psychotherapy and massages.

As a consequence of this varying goods-to-service mix, it is difficult to generalize about services unless further distinctions are made.

Schwartz (1992) presents a very thought-provoking argument as to why the difference between a product and a service is important and why it is not a mere semantic issue.

He claims, and rightfully so, that failure to distinguish between a products and a services contributes to lack of quality in both. Economists break down the overall category of products into two classes: The tangible products are called goods and the intangible are called services. The word 'product' is sometimes used in quality literature to refer to both goods and services, consistent with the economists' definition. For example, Juran and Gryna (1980) state that 'we will frequently use the word 'products' as a short generic term to designate both goods (milk, clothes, houses, vehicles) and services (electrical energy, bus rides, health care, education).'

An important difference is that a production worker in the manufacturing sector not only has a job, he is aware that he is doing his part to make something that somebody will use in some way. In spite of the problems illustrated, he has some idea about what his job is, and some idea about the quality of the final product. He visualizes the final customer, satisfied or unhappy with the product of his organization. In contrast, in many service organizations, the people who work there only have a job. They are not aware that they have a product, and that this product is service; that good service and happy customers keep his company in business and provide jobs; that an unhappy customer may bring loss of business and of his job as well. (Contributed by Carolyn A. Emigh).

Another difference between a service and a manufacturing establishment is that most service establishments have a captive market. Service organizations rarely have to compete head to head with a foreign firm. Our choice of restaurants, laundries, transportation, and mail is narrow. Yet another difference between service and manufacturing is that a service organization does not generate new material for the world market. A freight carrier, for example, can only haul what someone else produces. He cannot generate material to haul. To him, the only way to get ahead, when industry is in decline, is to take business away from a competitor, with the hazard of starting a cutthroat war. A better plan for freight carriers would be to improve service and thus to decrease costs. These cost savings, passed on to manufacturers and to other service industries, would help industry to improve the market for products, and would in time bring new business to carriers of freight.

Service industries have to be particularly careful when evaluating customer needs; their problems are different from those of the manufacturing sector. Differences cited by Carol A. King, and others are the following:

   (i) Services involve complex delivery systems.
  (ii) Services are often time-sensitive.
 (iii) Customer involvement is unpredictable.
 (iv) Services are usually intangible as opposed to goods, which are tangible.
  (v) Services are perishable. They are often produced and consumed simultaneously. For example, a surgeon executes (or produces) an operation, which is "consumed" by the patient as it is produced or executed.
 (vi) Services are often unique. For example, the mix of financial coverage, such as investments and insurance policies may vary for each customer as per his/her unique requirements. Goods may be standardized to meet most of the requirements of a large number of customers.

(vii) Services have high customer interaction. Services are often difficult to standardize, automate and made as efficient as we wish because customer interaction demands uniqueness.
(viii) Services have inconsistent product definition. Product definition may be rigorous, as in the case of an auto-insurance policy, but inconsistent because policyholders change their cars.
(ix) Services are often-knowledge-based, as in the case of educational, medical and legal services.
(x) Service delivery cannot be standardized.

In most service industries, one finds:

1. Direct transactions with masses of people: customer, householder, depositor, insured, taxpayer, borrower, consumer, shipper, consignee, passenger, claimant, and another bank.
2. Large volume of transactions; as in the main business in sales, loans, premiums, deposits, taxes, charges, interest.
3. Large volumes of paper involved in the main business: sales slips, bills, cheques, credit cards, charge accounts, claims, tax returns, mail.
4. Large amount of processing—for example, transcription, coding, calculation of freight charges, calculation of division of revenue, calculation of interest to pay, punching, tabulation, construction of tables.
5. Many transactions with small amounts of money. However, some transactions involve huge amounts (as a transfer from one bank to another, or a huge deposit).
6. An extremely large number of ways to make errors.
7. Handling and rehandling of huge numbers of small items—for example, in communications, mail, federal, state, and city governments, your own payroll department, your own purchasing department.

A denominator common to manufacturing or any service organization is that mistakes and defects are costly. The further a mistake goes without correction, the greater the cost to correct it. The cost of a defect that reaches the consumer or recipient may be the costliest of all, but no one knows what this cost is (an invisible figure). One finds in service organizations, as in manufacturing, the absence of definite procedures. There is an unstated assumption in most service organizations that the procedures are fully defined and followed. This appears to be so obvious that authors avoid it. Yet in practice this condition is often not met. Few organizations have up-to-date procedures. Consider a manufacturer who has full specifications for making a product, but whose sales department does not have guidelines of how to enter an order. A control on errors on placing orders would require procedures for the sales department. There are numerous service-oriented operations functioning without them.

The definitions of quality that apply to manufactured products apply equally to service products. The very nature of service implies that it must respond to the needs of the customer. The service must meet or exceed customer expectations. The production of services differ from manufacturing in many ways and these differences have important implications for quality management in services.

11.12 SOME GENERALIZATIONS REGARDING SERVICE SECTOR

(i) services vary as to whether they are equipment-based (automated car washes, vending machines, etc.) or people-based (window washing, accounting services, etc.). People-based services vary by whether they are provided by unskilled, or professional workers.

(ii) some services require the client's presence. Thus brain surgery involves the client's presence, but a car repair does not. If the client must be present, the service provider has to be considerate of his or her needs. Thus beauty shop operators will invest in their shop's décor, background music, and engage in light conversation with the client.

(iii) services differ as to whether they meet a personal need (personal services) or a business need (business services). Physicians will price physical examinations differently for private patients versus employees on a prepaid company health plan. Service providers typically develop different marketing programmes for personal and business markets.

(iv) service providers differ in their objectives (profit or nonprofit) and ownership (private or public). These two characteristics, when crossed, produce four quite different types of service organizations. Clearly, the quality programmes of a private investor hospital will differ from those of a private charity hospital or a Veteran's Administration hospital.

The following table summarizes some of the important differences mentioned above:

Differences in manufacturing and services sector

Manufacturing Sector	Service Sector
Product is tangible	Service consists of tangible and intangible components
Back orders are possible	Services cannot be stored
Producer or the company is the only party involved in the making of the product	Producer and consumer are both involved in the delivery of service
Product can be resold	Services cannot be resold
Customer usually provides formal specifications for the product	The consumer need not provide formal specifications. In fact, in monopolies involving public utilities, such as electricity, gas, telephone etc. federal and state laws dictate the requirements.
Customer acceptance of the product is easily quantifiable	Customer satisfaction is difficult to quantify because a behavioural component associated with the delivery of the service is involved.
Ownership of a product changes hands at a specific point of time.	Rendering of a service takes place over an interval of time.

11.12.1 Techniques for Determining Customer Needs

11.12.1.1 Face-to-face programme

The Walt Disney Company's face-to-face programme is called 'cross utilization.' It involves making their executives put on theme costumes and take over customer-contact jobs for a full week. These jobs range from selling hot dogs to parking cars. That way, they get to feel the pulse of the organization. They also get direct feedback from the customers without the screening that usually occurs when information passes through multiple layers of management.

11.12.1.2 Correspondence

Joe Girard, an outstanding car salesman mentioned in *'In Search of Excellence'*, used just about every gimmick he could think of to keep in contact with his customers. As an example, he sent out over 13,000 cards per month as thank-you notes, Happy-New-Year's cards, Happy-George-Washington's Birthday cards and many other innovative excuses for keeping in touch. Frequent contacts like these kept the buyers coming back. This exposure also encourages customers to bring their problems and ideas to him. In the end, both paid off. According to *'In Search of Excellence'*, Joe Girard sold more new cars and trucks per year than any other salesperson for 11 successive years.

11.12.1.3 Toll-free hotlines

Procter & Gamble improved its customer contacts by putting a toll-free number on its packaging. During one year time, the company received 200,000 calls on this line. Many of the calls were complaints. Others, however, were suggestions. The company executives valued these calls so much that they had them summarized for monthly board meeting. With hotline; you have an excellent chance to solicit information from the callers. Will they give more details? Can they identify individuals and products involved? What made them happy or unhappy with the service? Phone calls, however, should be handled with care and diplomacy. Unhappy customers can escalate the problem and haul you to court if not satisfied with the treatment they receive. Are all complaints justified? No! but even the unjustified calls should be taken seriously.

11.12.1.4 Surveys

Surveys are popular for measuring customer satisfaction, and customer satisfaction is a key to success. Jeffry W. Marr, at Walker Research, the 14th largest marketing research firm in the USA, supports this claim when he says, "The firms that are known to measure customer satisfaction are usually market leaders." Sources of surveys include departments within a company, market research companies, newspapers, magazines, trade organizations, chambers of commerce, governments and universities. Subjects surveyed range from "Was there service with a smile?" to "Rate our performance on a scale of one to ten." The possibilities are limitless. Public information of this type, found in newspapers or other publications, can help almost any service organization. The percentages may be different from company to company and from one area of the country to another. The basic information, however, can be used. Poor service is costly; quality service pays.

11.12.2 Tools for Tracking and Measuring Customer Satisfaction

Customers do not buy services as such; they buy satisfaction; hence service quality researchers must be clear about the satisfaction the customer is seeking and check out whether he is actually getting it. There are several methods, used to monitor customer satisfaction.

11.12.2.1 Complaint and suggestion systems

A customer-centred organization makes it easy for its customers to deliver suggestions and complaints. Many restaurants and hotels provide forms for guests to report their likes and dislikes. A hospital could place suggestion boxes in the corridors, supply comment cards to the existing patients, and hire a patient advocate to handle patient grievances. Some customer-centered companies—Procter & Gamble, General Electric, and Whirlpool —establish customer hotlines with toll-free 800 telephone numbers to maximize the ease with which customers can inquire, make suggestions, or complain. These information flows provide these companies with many good ideas and enable them to act more rapidly to resolve problems.

11.12.2.2 Customer satisfaction surveys

Studies show that while customers are dissatisfied with one out of every four purchases, less than 5% of dissatisfied customers will complain. Most customers will buy less or switch suppliers rather than complain. Therefore, companies cannot use complaint levels as a measure of customer satisfaction. Responsive companies obtain a direct measure of customer satisfaction by conducting periodic surveys. They send questionnaires or make telephone calls to a random sample of their recent customers and ask if they were very satisfied, satisfied, indifferent, somewhat dissatisfied, or very dissatisfied with various aspects of a company's performance. They also solicit buyers' views on their competitors' performances.

11.12.2.3 Ghost shopping

Companies can hire persons to pose as potential buyers to report their findings on strong and weak points they experienced while buying the company's and competitors' products. These *ghost shoppers* can even pose certain problems to test whether the company's sales personnel handle the situation well. Thus, a ghost shopper can complain about a restaurant's food to test how the restaurant handles this complaint.

11.12.2.4 Lost customer analysis

Companies should contact customers who have stopped buying or who have switched to another supplier to learn why this happened.

11.13 EFFECTIVE SERVICE RECOVERY

Despite the efforts of the service organizations, problems and complaints are bound to occur over the lifetime of customer relationships. Handling these effectively is vital to maintaining customer satisfaction and loyalty. The impact of recovery strategies on a company's revenue and profitability is dramatic. The ability to deal effectively with customer problems is also closely related to employee satisfaction and loyalty, which are critical concerns in industries where customer relationships are more closely associated with individual service provider than with the organization.

Most complaints are lodged when customers experience what they perceive to be a serious problem. Thus, once customers have voiced complaints, they expect action. More specifically, they want justice or fairness. Customers form perceptions of fairness by assessing three aspects of service recovery: outcomes, procedural features and interactional treatment. Outcome fairness concerns the results customers receive from complaints. Procedural fairness refers to policies, rules and timeliness of the complaint process. For each of the three aspects of service recovery, most customers believe that they had been treated unfairly and overall were dissatisfied with the way their complaint was handled. Research results indicate that there is a critical need for firms to devote far more attention to recovery. Poor recovery following a bad service experience can create 'terrorists', customers so dissatisfied that they actively pursue opportunities to criticize the company. Research has found that customers previously loyal to the company expressed the most negative reactions to poor recovery. Loyal customers expect problems to be dealt with effectively and are disappointed when they are not, making service recovery the key to maintaining the loyalty of those customers. While resolving a problem helps achieve the loyalty of one customer, using complaint data as an input into process improvement contributes to current and prospective customers' satisfaction. Sustaining satisfaction over many encounters builds equity with customers, strengthening loyalty and further driving profitability.

In addition, customer complaints provide valuable insights into the root causes of operations failures. Suggestion forms found in hotel room and company "hot lines", such as those run by Procter & Gamble and General Electric, serve this purpose. These companies hope that customers will call them with suggestions, inquiries, and even complaints. 3M claims that over two thirds of its product-improvement ideas come from listening to its customer complaints. The company must respond constructively to the complaints. Many quality-award winners, including Federal Express, Xerox and Ritz Carlton, use failure data when making decisions on process improvements, coupling service recovery with initiatives to increase customer satisfaction in the future. Research indicates that resolving problems effectively has a strong impact on customer satisfaction and loyalty. Studies show that some customers are actually more satisfied with a firm that follows a service failure with a remarkable recovery than they would have been had the failure not occurred in the first place. Further, data from Xerox and American Express have demonstrated that only customers scoring the highest level on satisfaction measures tend to be both loyal purchasers and "apostles", customers who encourage others to buy from the company. Since recovery is closely tied to satisfaction, the revenue and profitability impacts of service recovery can be dramatic. Studies on the return on investment in complaint-handling units in several industries, including retailing, banking and automotive service, indicate that service recovery investments provide substantial returns, ranging from 30% to 150%. J. Willard Marriott, Jr. offers the following advice on service recovery: "Do whatever is necessary to take care of guests. Also track, measure, and follow up on how to handle it better next time, the first time". Marriott's approach reflects the Malcolm

Baldrige National Quality Award scoring system, which provides service-recovery points for 'complaint resolution that leads to quality improvement". The system also requires organizational learning, defined as "the capacity or processes within an organization to maintain or improve performance based on experience'.

Another important profitability question for companies to consider is how service recovery affects the employees involved. In examining the customer descriptions of service recovery, two interesting themes relate to employees. First, customers who found the service recovery handled fairly commented that the employee was concerned about the problem, eager to help and happy that the complaint was resolved to customer' satisfaction. Second, when the customers indicated that the complaint was handled unfairly, employees were frequently observed to be rude and defensive, indifferent to providing assistance, and increasingly angry as the dispute progressed. These findings suggest that individual service recovery incidents affect the satisfaction of not only the customer but also the employees involved. Research further suggests that employees faced with a large number of complaints to handle and no effective ways to deal with them are likely to be very dissatisfied. Therefore, developing effective recovery programmes and improving the service system should enhance service quality and increase employee satisfaction and loyalty, contributing to customer value and ultimately to improved profitability.

A market-driven approach to service research consists of many tools in addition to identifying and responding to complaints. Berry and Parasuraman have developed a 'Service Quality Information System', a comprehensive approach to service-improvement planning and resource allocation. The system includes, but is not limited to: customer, employee, and competitor surveys; mystery shopping, focus groups, customer and employee advisory panels, and service operating performance data. In identifying opportunities to improve services, many firms integrate complaint data with data gathered through one or more of these research methods. The multiple methods and sources of data provide a comprehensive view of service quality.

Despite the benefits offered by effective service recovery strategies, research shows that the majority of customers are dissatisfied with the way companies resolve their complaints. This result is consistent with other findings, indicating that most customers have more negative feelings about an organization after they go through the service-recovery process. Further, the vast majority of companies do not take advantage of the learning opportunities afforded by service failures.

The greatest barrier to effective service recovery and organizational learning is the fact that only 5% to 10% of dissatisfied customers choose to complain, following a service failure. Instead most dissatisfied customers silently switch providers or attempt to get even with the firm by making negative comments to others. Why are customers reluctant to complain? Research has uncovered four key reasons: customers believe that the organization will not be responsive; they do not wish to confront the individual responsible for the failure; they are concerned about the high cost in time and effort of complaining. In addition, some customers anticipate negative ramifications. The firms can remove these barriers and encourage dissatisfied customers to complain by identifying service failures. Examining the recovery practices of leading firms highlights several approaches that have been effective in identifying service failures.

11.13.1 Identifying Service Failures

Since customers complain about problems that they find important, complaints represent a valuable form of market information. However, because customers rarely complain when a service fails, companies seeking to improve service quality need to locate additional sources of information. The goal of data management is to ensure that the organization gathers relevant, credible, timely information and disseminates it to everyone involved in decisions on investments in service quality.

Information from call centres and customer databases are also valuable. Maintaining databases of customer purchases is particularly helpful in cases where the only indication that a service has failed is that the customer has stopped purchasing from the firm. Information systems can generate a list of monthly cancellations, which could be used to trigger calls to customers to determine the cause of the defection, assess the situation and try to win the customer back (data mining).

Different approaches to identify service failures are explained below:

(i) Setting performance standards; (ii) Communicating the importance of service recovery; (iii) Training customers on how to complain and (iv) Using technological support through customer call centres and the Internet.

(i) *Setting performance standards:* Comparing services with tangible foods, Levitt observed that with services "You don't know what you aren't going to get until you don't get it". His comment reflects customers' unclear expectations about many services and helps explain why they do not complain when they are dissatisfied. A way to overcome the problem of unclear expectations is to implement service standards, which are often communicated through service guarantees.

'Developing guidelines for service recovery that focus on achieving fairness and customer satisfaction represents a direct approach to improving the performance. For example, the AAA action plan principles guide specific policies for the recovery programme: The As stand for: anticipate and correct problems before they occur; Acknowledge mistakes when they occur without placing blame or making excuses; sincerely Apologize for the mistake, even if you are not at fault; and make amends for the mistake by taking corrective action and following up to ensure the problem has been resolved. Developing standards for service-recovery responsiveness and accessibility like a five-day turn-around on correspondence; a 20-day closure on complaints and 95% accessibility to incoming callers and a maximum hold on calls of 30 seconds is also effective.'

(ii) *Communicating the importance of service recovery:* Companies that are committed to developing lifetime customers recognize the significance of service recovery in achieving customer satisfaction and enhancing customer relationships. Through their values, these companies signal to employees the importance of taking responsibility for service failures and resolving problems. Employees become important listening posts, discovering customer concerns and facilitating recovery. Companies also use physical symbols to communicate the importance of service recovery, e.g. by providing every employee with a wallet-size card that lists the organization's core values, along with statements referring to service recovery. Communicating the value of service recovery creates an atmosphere conducive to identifying failures and achieving effective recovery.

(iii) *Training customers in how to complain:* Some companies explicitly tell customers how to lodge a complaint and what to expect from the process. This is done by prominently placing pamphlets, explaining the process designed to help customers to get their complaint heard and resolved. The pamphlet should stress the importance the organization places, on maintaining to whom, the customers should initially lodge complaints and describe how to make appeals and provide phone numbers of the organization's ombudsperson or vice president for customers who are dissatisfied with the initial resolution. The strategy is designed to both encourage the use of the complaint option and enhance the responsiveness of the process. Further, the pamphlet reinforces to employees the value placed on service recovery.

(iv) *Using technological support:* The use of toll-free telephone call centres to handle customer contacts, including complaints, is a growing trend. Since the introduction of the 1–800 service in the United States 30 years ago, the number of calls has grown from 7 million a year to more than 10 billion a year. Call centres offer several advantages over written correspondence in providing customer with convenient, low cost access to service recovery. For example, research has found that oral communication is better suited to conveying compassion and empathy to irate customers than written communication. In addition, customer may feel more comfortable complaining over the phone than face-to-face or via mail.

11.13.2 The Following are the Strategies for Recovering Successfully

(i) When services fail, customers expect to be compensated. The typical forms of compensation are refunds, credits, correction of charges, repairs, and replacements, either singly or in combination. It was found that apologies also contribute to customers' compensation for being inconvenienced or treated rudely. Most customers judge the outcomes they received to be unfair. The driving force behind unfair assessments was the failure of companies to compensate adequately for the harm done or to recognize the costs incurred by customers in getting their complaints resolved. The most negative reactions are in response to complaints that were never resolved. Clearly, firms need to better understand the outcomes that customers expect from a service failure and to construct compensation packages that better acknowledge the costs of the failure to the customer. The small number of customers who are favourably impressed typically pointed to compensation that includes reimbursement for the inconvenience associated with the failure as well as basic exchanges or repairs. Customers also reacted more positively when the firm gave them options, than when it unilaterally prescribed the outcome.

(ii) Study findings indicate that providing fair procedures is important and begins with the firm assuming responsibility for the failure. The complaint must be handled quickly, preferably by the first person that is contacted. Other aspects of procedural fairness include having a flexible system that takes individual circumstances into account and obtaining input from the customer on what the final outcome should be. Less than half the customers surveyed found the recovery procedures they experienced to be fair. When the procedures were rated as fair, it was mostly because they were clear to the customer and the problem was dealt with quickly and without hassles. In the more frequent cases where customers judged procedures to be unfair, those surveyed were frustrated by a prolonged inconvenient process that required them to repeat their complaint to several firm representatives who seemed unconcerned about the situation. These employee responses prompted one respondent to comment that the firm operated on the principle that "the customer is always wrong". According to respondents, the employees' indifferent behaviour is typically driven by an attitude that the firm is not responsible for the problem and that they are not going to resolve it.

(iii) Research indicates that successful service recovery is highly influenced by the effectiveness of the front-line employee who receives the complaint. This is not surprising since 65% of the complaints are initiated with front-line workers. What it means is that the design of a recovery system must focus on the initial contact and on developing policies that enable employees to resolve the complaint efficiently. Service recovery performance must therefore be incorporated into human resources management practices. Developing hiring criteria and training programmes that take into account the employee's service recovery role directly affects the customers' fairness evaluations. Training before job assignment and regular training during employment and putting candidates through an assessment centre to evaluate skills that are particularly relevant to service recovery, like written and oral communication, listening skills, problem analysis, organizing and following through, resilience and stress management are effective tools.

The real test of service quality/customer satisfaction is that the customer will keep coming back to the service provider every time he needs a service and that he will strongly recommend it to others. In other words, the extent of customer retention is the prime indicator of service quality/customer satisfaction.

11.14 SERVICE LEADERSHIP SPELLS PROFITS

'The company exists only to satisfy customers, earn revenue, create wealth and grow'. The most important parameter that can enable the company to accomplish these goals is 'Quality'. "CEO has no other job but to manage quality and so he has to find time for Quality". This was stated by Sri Venu Srinivasan, CEO of TVS Suzuki. He has not only defined the role of CEO, he has also practised it to prove his point. TVS Suzuki is one of the Indian companies that has already crossed many milestones in the world-class journey.

The CEO, expressing good intentions and delivering a lecture once a year, and going back to his original style of management does not help. He has to spend bulk of his time focusing on quality and quality management-related issues. The CEO has to demonstrate his commitment to quality by appointing one of the most talented managers to lead quality initiatives. He has to project 'quality improvement' as a strategic imperative. He has to ensure deployment of improvement objectives up to actionable elements. He has to review progress and stay focused. He has to demonstrate his commitment through uncompromising stand and firmness when 'deviations' and compromises come up. Employees learn more from the behaviour of leaders than from their talks and lectures.

He has to ensure that the senior managers under his direct command have identical role towards quality and that they too demonstrate similar behaviour. They have to demonstrate to the whole organization that 'quality is first' by not accepting compromises when quality vs. quantity or quality vs. cost situations come up. This demonstration will go a long way in developing a culture that will take the organization from quality vs. quantity and cost to quality and quantity with cost. This has been the practical approach adopted by the Japanese CEOs when they took up 'quality improvement'. They had the spirit to sit through days of learning sessions where Deming taught them the SQC tools and Juran, the quality management principles.

There is enough research evidence documenting the central role that leadership plays in delivering excellent service. It has been observed that strong management commitment to service quality energizes and stimulates an organization to improved service performance. On the other hand, role ambiguity, poor teamwork, and other negatives, and leaderless environment, can hamper an organization's service quality. True service leadership builds a climate for excellence that prevails over operational complexities, external market pressures, or any other impediments to quality service that might exist.

Mediocre service in India is common. However, in every single industry we have examples of companies delivering superb service. Excellent service is not a pipe dream; it is possible to overcome the conditions that foster service mediocrity. The key is genuine service leadership at all levels of an organization—leadership that offers the direction and inspiration to sustain committed servers. Managing is not enough. To manage, one must lead. To lead, one must understand the work that he and his people are responsible for. Who is the customer (the next stage), and how can we serve the customer better?

An incoming manager, who wants to lead and manage at the source of improvement, must learn. He must learn from his people what they are doing and must learn a lot of new subject matter. It is easier for an incoming manager to short-cut his learning and responsibilities, and focus on managing the outcome—get reports on quality, on failures, proportion defective, inventory, sales, people. Focusing on the outcome is not an effective way to improve a process or an activity.

Service work can be difficult and demoralizing: Customers can be rude and company policies can be suffocating. Sheer numbers of customers to serve can be overwhelming. End-of-the-day fatigue can be desensitizing. Over time, many service employees get 'beat up' by the service role and become less effective with customers even though they gain technical experience. People in service work need a vision in which they can believe, an achievement culture that challenges them to be the best they can be, a sense of team that nurtures and supports them, and the role models that show them the way. This is the stuff of leadership. In their book, "Leaders: The Strategies for Taking Charge", Bennis and Nanus point out that the principal distinction between the leaders and the managers is that leaders emphasize the emotional and spiritual resources of an organization, its values and aspirations, whereas managers emphasize the physical resources of the organization, such as raw materials, technology, and capital.

The root cause of quality dissatisfaction today—the reason service is not better than it is despite the fruits of excellent service—is the insufficiency of service leadership. Too many service workers are over-managed and under led. Thick policy manuals rule management's belief in good judgment of frontline servers. Memoranda from above supersede face-to-face, give-and-take dialogue with employees. The goal of profit takes precedence over the goal of providing a service good enough that people will pay a profit to have it.

Service leaders fundamentally believe that high quality pays off on the bottom line. Many executives, however, are not so sure. Many executives are not yet convinced that hard-rupee investments to improve service will come back as profit gains. And these executives may be right. Investments to improve service may not come back as profit gains. Indeed, a lot of money is wasted in organizations every year in the name of quality improvement. From adding costly service features that are unimportant to customers to spending money unwisely on training, it is quite common for organizations to throw money away pursuing better service quality.

11.14.1 Characteristics of Service Leaders

The following are some of the most important characteristics:

1. *Service vision:* Service leaders see service quality as a success key. They see service as integral to an organization's future, not as a peripheral issue. They believe fundamentally that superior service is a winning strategy and a profit strategy. Regardless of the markets targeted, the menu of services offered, or the pricing policies followed, service leaders see quality of service as the foundation for competing. Whatever the specifics of the vision, the idea of service excellence is a central part. Service leaders never waver in their commitment to service quality. They see service excellence as a never-ending journey in which the only effective option is to plug away towards better quality every day of every week of every month of every year. They understand that service quality is not a programme; that there are no quick fixes, no magic formulas, and no quality pills to swallow.

2. *High standards:* True service leaders aspire to legendary service; they realize that good service may not be good enough to differentiate their organization from other organizations. Service leaders are interested in the details and nuances of service, seeing opportunities in small actions that competitors might consider trivial. They believe that how an organization handles the little things sets the tone for how it handles the big things. They also believe that little things add up for the customer and make a difference. Service leaders are zealous about doing the service right, the first time. They value the goal of zero defects, striving continually to improve the reliability of the service.

3. *In-the-field leadership style:* Service leaders lead in the field, where action is, rather than from their desks. They are visible to their people, endlessly coaching, praising, correcting, cajoling, sermonizing, observing, questioning, and listening. They emphasize two-way, personal communications because they know this is the best way to give shape, substance, and credibility to the service vision and the best way to learn what is really going on in the field. Service leaders also employ their hands-on approach to build a climate of teamwork within the organization. They challenge the organizational unit to be excellent in service, not just the individual

employee, using the influence of their offices to bring the team together frequently for meetings, rallies, and celebrations.

4. *Integrity:* One of the essential characteristics of service leaders is personal integrity. The best leaders value doing the right thing—even when inconvenient or costly. They place a premium on being fair, consistent, and truthful—and, as a result, earn the trust of associates. As Peter Drucker writes: "The final requirement of effective leadership is to earn trust. Otherwise there will not be any followers— the only definition of a leader is someone who has followers" Service leaders recognize the impossibility of building a service-minded attitude in an organization whose management lacks integrity. They recognize the interconnection between service excellence and employees' pride and understand that employees' pride is shaped in part by their perceptions of management fairness.

11.15 FACTORS INFLUENCING CUSTOMER'S EXPECTATIONS

Actually, improving service in the eyes of customers is what pays off. When service improvement investments lead to perceived service improvement, quality becomes a profit strategy. The essence of services marketing is service. Whereas the marketing textbooks stress the four Ps of marketing—product, place, promotion, and price—in a service business the most important competitive weapon is the fifth P of performance. (Although, theoretically, this may get included in the product). It is the performance of service that separates one service firm from others; it is the performance of service that creates true customers who buy more, are more loyal, and who spread favourable word of mouth. The following are some of the factors influencing customer expectations:

   (i) What customers hear from other customers—word-of–mouth communications— is a potential determinant of expectations.
  (ii) Expectations appeared to vary somewhat depending on their individual charac- teristics and circumstances, suggesting thereby that personal needs of customers might moderate their expectations to a certain degree. For example, in credit-card focus groups, while some customers expected credit-card companies to provide them with the maximum possible credit limits, other customers wished that their credit-card companies should charge less interest and less penalities on occassional defaults.
 (iii) The extent of past experience with using a service could also influence the customers' expectation levels. More experienced participants in the securities—brokerage focus groups, for instance, seemed to have somewhat lower expectations regarding brokers' behavioural attributes, such as friendliness and politeness; however, they appeared to be more demanding with respect to brokers' technical competence and effectiveness.
 (iv) External communications from service providers play a key role in shaping customers' expectations. Under external communications we include a variety of direct and indirect messages conveyed by service firms to customers.

11.16 SERVICE QUALITY (CUSTOMER'S PERSPECTIVE)

In the book *Delivering Quality Service* by Valarie A. Zeithaml, A Parasuraman and Leonard Berry, the authors used focus groups of four service sectors: retail banking, credit cards, securities brokerage and product repair and maintenance, to determine the criteria used by customers in judging service quality. Ten general criteria or dimensions are listed below:

Tangibles: Appearance of physical facilities, equipment, personnel, and communication materials.

Reliability: Ability to perform the promised service dependably and accurately.

Responsiveness: Willingness to help customers and provide prompt service.

Competence: Possession of the required skills and knowledge to perform the service.

Courtesy: Politeness, respect, consideration, and friendliness of contact personnel.

Credibility: Trustworthiness, believability, and honesty of the service provider.

Security: Freedom from danger, risk, or doubt.

Access: Approachability and ease of contact.

Communication: Keeping customers informed in a language they can understand and listening to them.

Understanding: Making effort to know customers and their needs.

From their exploratory study the authors were able to (1) define service quality as the discrepancy between customers' expectations and perceptions; (2) suggest key factors like word-of-mouth communications, personal needs, past experience, and external communications that influence customers' expectations; and (3) identify 10 general dimensions that represent the evaluative criteria customers use to assess service quality.

Figure 11.1 below provides a pictorial summary of these findings.

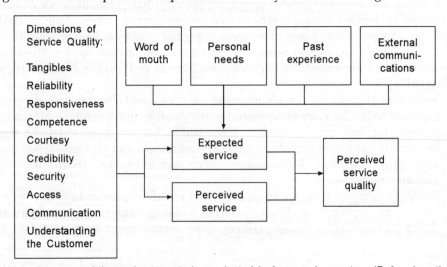

FIGURE 11.1 Summary of the exploratory study conducted in four service sectors (Ref. subsection 11.16)

One of the important ways to differentiate a service firm is to deliver consistently higher-quality service than competitors. The key is to meet or exceed the target customers' service-quality expectations. Customers' expectations are formed by their past experiences, word of mouth, and service-firm advertising. The customers choose providers on these bases and, after receiving the service, compare the perceived service with the expected service. If the perceived service falls below the expected service, customers lose interest in the provider. If the perceived service meets or exceeds their expectations, they are apt to use the provider again.

Building on the conceptual definition of service quality and the 10 evaluative dimensions, the authors embarked on a quantitative research resulting in a parsimonious instrument (SERVQUAL). The various statistical analysis conducted in constructing SERVQUAL revealed correlation among the last seven dimensions listed above. The following exhibit shows correspondence between SERVQUAL dimensions and original 10 dimensions for evaluating service quality.

Original 10 dimensions for evaluating Service quality	*SERVQUAL dimensions*
Tangibles	Tangibles
Reliability	Reliability
Responsiveness	Responsiveness
Competence	Assurance
Courtesy	Assurance
Credibility	Assurance
Security	Assurance
Access	Empathy
Communication	Empathy
Understanding the customer	Empathy

The definitions of dimensions defined in SERVQUAL are as follows:

Tangibles: Appearance of physical facilities, equipment, personnel, and communication materials.

Reliability: Ability to perform the promised service dependably and accurately.

Responsiveness: Willingness to help customers and provide prompt service.

Assurance: Knowledge and courtesy of employees and their ability to convey trust and confidence.

Empathy: Caring, individualized attention the firm provides to its customers.

The SERVQUAL instrument had widespread applications in a variety of organizations ranging from tyre retailing, dental service, hotels, travel and tourism, car servicing, business schools, hospitality, higher education, business-to-business channel partners, accounting firms, architectural services, recreational services, hospitals, airline catering, banking, apparel retailing and local government. On the other hand, the efficacy of SERVQUAL in measuring service quality has also been severely criticized for various reasons by many researchers (see Buttle, 1996, for a detailed discussion).

11.17 ISO 9001:2000 QUALITY MANAGEMENT SYSTEMS

The adoption of a quality management system should be a strategic decision of an organization. Varying needs, particular objectives, the products and services provided, the processes employed and the size and structure of the organization influence the design and implementation of an organization's quality management system. It is not the intent of this International Standard to imply uniformity in the structure of quality management systems or uniformity of documentation. The quality management system requirements specified in this International Standard are complementary to requirements for products. Internal and external parties, including certification bodies, can use this International Standard to assess the organization's ability to meet customer, regulatory, and the organization's own requirements.

ISO 9001 is not TQM, but is a subcomponent of TQM and a good start of the TQM path. ISO 9001 is only the minimum required quality standard that a service provider must demonstrate to receive the ISO 9001 accreditation. TQM by contrast is much more comprehensive in linking quality to customer satisfaction.

The quality management principles stated in ISO 9000 and ISO 9004 has been taken into consideration during the development of this International Standard. The eight quality management principles defined in ISO 9000:2000 and in ISO 9004:2000 are as follows: (i) Customer focus, (ii) Leadership, (iii) Involvement of people, (iv) process approach, (v) System approach to management, (vi) Continual improvement, (vii) Factual approach to decision-making, and (viii) mutually beneficial supplier relationships.

11.18 BENCHMARKING

Benchmarking is the art of finding out how and why some companies can perform tasks much better than other companies. There can be as much as a 10 fold difference in the quality, speed, and cost performance of an average company versus a world-class company. Comparing one company's performance with that of another is a reflex of TQM. Competitive benchmarking is a continuous management process that helps firms to assess their competition and themselves and to use that knowledge in designing a practical plan to achieve superiority in the market place. To strive to be better than the best competitor is the target. The measurement takes place along the three components of a total quality programme—products and services, business processes and procedures, and people. The idea is to benchmark performance, not only with one's direct competitors, but also with other firms as well to discover the best practice and bring that in to one's own company.

Benchmarking involves the following seven steps: (1) Determine which functions to benchmark; (2) identify the key performance variables to measure; (3) identify the best-in-class companies; (4) measure performance of best-in-class companies; (5) measure the company's performance; (6) specify programmes and actions to close the gap; and (7) implement and monitor results.

The Japanese used benchmarking tirelessly in the post-World War II period, copying many U.S. products and practices. Xerox in 1979 undertook one of the first U.S. major benchmarking projects. Xerox wanted to learn how Japanese competitors were able to produce more reliable copiers and charge a price below Xerox's production costs. By buying Japanese copiers and analyzing them through 'reverse engineering,' Xerox learned how to greatly improve reliability and costs in its own copiers. Another early benchmarking pioneer was Ford. Ford was losing sales to Japanese and European automakers. Don Peterson, the then chairman of Ford, instructed his engineers and designers to build a new car that combined the 400 features that Ford customers said were the most important. If Saab made the best seats, then Ford should copy Saab's seats, and so on. Peterson went further: he asked his engineers to 'better the best' where possible. When the new car (the highly successful Taurus) was finished, Peterson claimed that his engineers had improved upon, not just copied, most of the best features found in competitive automobiles.

Today many companies (including AT&T, IBM, Kodak, Du Pont, and Motorola) use benchmarking. Some companies benchmark only the best companies in their industry. Others choose to benchmark the "best practices" in the world. In this sense, benchmarking goes beyond standard competitive analysis. Motorola, for example, starts each benchmarking project with a search for 'the best of breed' in the world. According to one Motorola executive, "The further away we reach for comparisons from our industry, the happier we are. We are seeking competitive superiority, after all, not just competitive parity." As an example of seeking best of the breed, Robert C. Camp, Xerox's benchmarking expert, flew to Freeport, Maine, to visit L.L. Bean to find out how Bean's warehouse workers managed to "pick and pack" items three times as fast as Xerox workers. On later occasions, Xerox benchmarked American Express for its billing expertise and Cummins Engine for its production scheduling expertise.

EXERCISES

1. What are the three fundamental ways services differ from goods in terms of how they are produced, consumed, and evaluated?
2. What are the quality management practices in service industries in the USA?
3. What are the quality management practices in service industries in Japan?
4. What are the quality management practices in service industries in Asian countries?
5. What are the quality management practices in service industries in India?
6. How do we define service sector?
7. Why is the service sector quality control so important?
8. What is service quality?
9. Explain the concept of 'service value'.
10. What is 'total quality service'?
11. Explain how quality service pays.
12. Explain the importance of customers in service quality.
13. Explain the importance of physical environment in service quality.
14. What are the categories of service quality characteristics?

15. Explain the difference between goods and services.
16. What are the techniques for determining the needs of customer?
17. What are the methods of identifying service failures?
18. What are the strategies for recovering customers successfully?
19. Explain the importance of service leadership.
20. What are the characteristics of service leaders?
21. What are the factors influencing the customers expectations?
22. Explain the customer's perspective of service quality.
23. Explain the ISO 9001:2000 quality management systems for service quality.
24. Explain the importance of benchmarking in service quality.

12

Service Quality Research and Subject Development

This chapter covers the following: (i) Research using secondary data, (ii) Research using initial primary data, and (iii) the models for TQM and Service Quality.

12.1 RESEARCH ON SERVICE QUALITY

A lot of research in service quality has been done in the areas of Total Quality Management in service industries (from management perspective) and service quality (from customers perspective). The following are the excerpts compiled from research papers:

(i) Hasan studied quality management practices in service organization in Australian companies and has identified that the role of top management, customer satisfaction and employee involvement are the most important factors influencing organizational performance.

(ii) Hansson & Jonas analysis of small organizations in Sweden indicates that some of the core values of TQM, which are often described as the basis of the concept, are more adequate than others when initiating the quality development work. These core values were leadership, everybody's commitment and customer focus. In addition, the studies also visualize the importance of committed management and co-workers in order to accomplish the substantial organizational change that is necessary in order to implement TQM.

(iii) Another case study "Quality Practices And Customer/Supplier Management in Australian Service Organizations" reports on a cross-sectional study conducted in the Australian service sector in which the extent of implementation of quality management practices with customers and suppliers, and the links between specific practices and performance outcomes are considered. The sample for the study (N = 141) is drawn from small to medium-sized service organizations. Overall, the findings indicate that quality management practices are not widely implemented with customers and suppliers in services. Significant factors include the use of customer satisfaction surveys, and the existence of strategic alliances. The implication of these findings for managers in service organizations, who are seeking more value from their customer/supplier interface, is that organizations should involve suppliers in their system changes and improvement projects.

(iv) Another research study on "Comparative Analysis of Cultural, Conceptual and Practical Constraints on Quality Management Implementations—findings from Australian and Korean Banking Industries" found significant relationships and path links between the perceived service quality, customer satisfaction and customer loyalty as well as between TQM practices and employee satisfaction. These findings suggest that organizations, which are interested in long-term business success, should focus on the satisfaction of customers. A total of 11 banks, five in Seoul, Korea and six in Sydney, Australia, were chosen, which responded positively to questionnaires distributed to both bank customers and employees.

(v) Another research study on "The Role of Quality Practices in Service Organizations" by Anders Gustafsson land Lars Nilsson Service Research Center, Sweden, and Michael D. Johnson University of Michigan Business School, USA, reports that many organizations use quality management to improve their performance, but the results do not always come quickly. Using data from 281 firms to investigate the role of quality practices in service organizations, the authors support that the relationship between quality practices and business performance is dependent on an organization's size. In addition, they provide insight into how the business results are influenced by individual quality practices, such as employee management, process orientation and customer orientation, depending on the organization's size.

(vi) Case Study: Revolutionizing the Service Industry, The Ritz-Carlton Hotel Company wins the Coveted Malcolm Baldrige National Quality Award for the second time:

At Ritz-Carlton Hotel, every employee has over 100 hours of customer service training annually. Customers always check-in efficiently and quickly. Guest room is never more than 90 days old because of a revolutionary maintenance programme. Every employee in the customer service department will break away from his or her duties to help a guest. Consistent, reliable services such as these are just a few of the reasons why The Ritz-Carlton Hotel Company, has been named a winner of the 1999 Malcolm Baldrige National Quality Award by the United States Department of Commerce.

The Atlanta-based company, a previous Baldrige recipient in 1992, joins only one other American company that has earned the distinction more than once. The Ritz-Carlton is the only company in the hotel industry to have ever achieved the award, which recognizes exceptional achievement in the practice of total quality management principles. Winning this award confirms that quality is not a short-term approach to doing business. Instead it is a roadmap that allows the hotel to achieve the highest customer and employee satisfaction in the industry.

Seven categories make up the award criteria: Leadership, Strategic Planning, Customer and Market Focus, Information and Analysis, Human Resources Focus, Process Management and Business Results. At Ritz-Carlton, the focus on these criteria has resulted in higher employee and customer satisfaction, increased productivity and market share. Perhaps most significant is increased profitability.

Research shows that the stock price of companies with effective TQM implementation outperformed the S&P 500 Index by approximately 30% over a five-year period.

What quality means to the guest at Ritz-Carlton: The daily SQI (Service Quality Indicator) is displayed throughout the hotel, enabling all departments to monitor the key production and guest service processes up to the minute to address the challenges and areas of need immediately. The SQI of all hotels is displayed on flat screen monitors in the corporate office, ensuring immediate communication of hotel issues and strategies.

All Ritz-Carlton employees are empowered to make a difference. Using tools ranging from nine-step quality improvement teams to guest surveys, Ritz-Carlton employees examine every process in the hotel to ensure that the most efficient, customer-service driven practice is in place. Examples include: A front desk project team at The Ritz-Carlton, Osaka reduced check-in time by 50%. A cross-functional team from the two Atlanta hotels and the corporate office developed a guestroom child safety programme, POLO (Protect Our Little Ones), in response to an increase in family travel. The team spent two years benchmarking children's programmes, interviewing customers, testing products and piloting the programme to ensure successful implementation. A cross-functional corporate and hotel team created the functional model for CLASS (Customer Loyalty Anticipation Satisfaction System). This guest recognition database is the company-wide tool used to meet and anticipate repeat customers' preferences and requirements. Hotel engineers from resorts and city hotels developed a system called CARE (Clean And Repair Everything) to create the most defect-free guestrooms in the industry. Merging the deep cleaning housekeeping processes with the engineering preventative maintenance schedule ensured that all guestrooms are guaranteed to be defect-free every 90 days. At Hotel Arts Barcelona, a cross-functional team of hourly employees and managers tackled the problem of guestroom readiness when a guest checks in. Staggering the lunch hours of the housekeeping supervisors streamlined the guestroom inspection process and eliminated the problem, ensuring a guestroom is always ready when one wants to check-in. Based on the results of a nine-step customer problem solving team, business and leisure travellers on The Club level of The Ritz-Carlton, Buckhead are checked in according to their specific needs. Business travellers are checked in quickly and efficiently whereas leisure guests are given the option of a more pampered check-in with champagne and a more lengthy presentation of the hotel services and amenities. A team of catering managers from Ritz-Carlton Hotels worldwide created the first comprehensive wedding programme in the hospitality industry. After two years of surveying guests, benchmarking the competition, meeting with wedding experts and media, a five-tier programme, designed to meet the bride's needs from initial telephone call to the first anniversary, was successfully launched.

(vii) In the case study, "Learning from TQM (TQM—How can we make the implementation effective?), Abhay Ojha, takes an overview of TQM principles. The author has looked at the TQM implementation issues and their resolution. The case of TQM implementation at Canada healthcare is studied in detail and a scientific approach is taken to co-relate various factors like vision, leadership, momentum of change, teamwork, availability of resources, focus and training playing major role in the TQM implementation process.

(viii) Continuous quality improvement process at West Florida Regional Medical Center identifies that there are eight dimensions of health quality improvement process: leadership constancy, employee-mindedness, customer-mindedness, process focused, statistical thinking, PDCA-driven, innovativeness, and regulatory proactiveness.

(ix) Total Quality Management at Robert W. Baird & Co.

Associates at Baird Co. (investment products and services company) are expected to conduct themselves according to Principles revolving round the following topics: Integrity, Client Satisfaction, People, Consultative Sales (Leadership), Communication, Teamwork, Growth, Balance, Community Involvement, and Stability. These principles are expanded and defined below:

Integrity is irreplaceable. We will strive to uphold the highest standards of business conduct in all dealings with our clients and associates.

Client Satisfaction is our primary goal. We believe that in all our endeavours, the clients' interests come first.

People are the most important asset. We are committed to hiring the best people and to encourage individual growth through training, recognition and respect for each other.

Consultative Sales are the by-product of leadership. It is not sufficient to simply take our clients' order. Our goal is to fully understand their needs and to deliver complete financial solutions, building long-term relationships in the process.

Communication is critical to our success. Clear, direct and frequent communication creates an atmosphere of understanding, confidence, and trust with our clients and associates.

Teamwork is essential. Optimal client satisfaction can only be obtained when all the Baird associates coordinate their efforts.

Growth is the direct result of providing quality, value-added client services. Growth comes naturally from doing things right and always being in a position to take advantage of opportunities—be they new people, new skills, new geography, or new business.

Balance is a key to success. By providing a broad range of products and services, our clients and we are able to diversify and insulate against the cyclical nature of securities markets. Equally important is the balance in our personal lives, giving appropriate consideration to business and family needs.

Community Involvement is strongly encouraged. It is our opportunity to give something back to the communities in which we live and work.

Stability is the result of our efforts. Stability of people, culture, and capital has served our clients, associates and shareholders very well over the long-term.

Another research study by Sureshchandar et al. has reported the following literature:

(x) Quality management has been considered a major driver in enhancing business performance. Many studies have provided ample evidence that quality and all aspects of quality have always scored highly as an important competitive capability (Corbett, 1994; Kim, 1995). The decision as to which management practices should be given importance for effective TQM implementation has been a major concern of practitioners in the field (Flynn et al. 1995). Madhu et al. (1996) reasoned that although many conceptual models have emphasized the usefulness of certain quality dimensions (such as customer satisfaction, employee satisfaction and employee service quality) in improving organizational performance, no empirical study up to that time verified such claims.

(xi) The US Government Accounting Office Study (GAO, 1991) examined the influence of formal TQM strategies on the performance of 20 US companies that had scored well on the 1988/89 Malcolm Baldrige National Quality Award. The results revealed a strong relationship between the company's practice of TQM (such as strong customer focus, senior management leadership, a commitment to employee training, empowerment, involvement and the application of systematic fact-finding and decision-making processes) and organizational performance (measured by employee relations, quality, productivity, customer satisfaction and profitability).

(xii) Samson and Terziovski (1999) attempted to find the relationships between the various TQM practices, individually and collectively, and a firm' performance. The results showed that the intensity of TQM practice does contribute significantly to the performance. In another research work Terziovski and Samson (1999) tested the relationship between TQM practice and organizational performance with and without the covariates, company size, industry type and ISO9000 certification statute. The authors concluded that there were significant differences in the relationship between TQM and organizational performance across industry type and size, especially on the effect of defect rates, warranty costs and innovation of new products. In a recent work Agus et al. (2000) investigated the simultaneous linkages between TQM, customer satisfaction and financial performance. The results have indicated that proper implementation of TQM can positively influence customer satisfaction, ultimately leading to enhanced financial performance.

(xiii) In a significant research work, Powell (1995) provided valuable insights into the 'soft issues' of TQM. The work explored TQM as a potential source of sustainable competitive advantage and found that the most generally acceptable features associated with TQM, such as quality training, process improvement, benchmarking, etc. may not be that useful for effective TQM implementation, but that certain tacit, behavioural, imperfectly imitable features, like open culture, employee empowerment and executive commitment, are vital for an environment conducive to TQM. It was concluded that these tacit resources, not mere TQM tools and techniques, are instrumental for success and organizations that acquire them can win over their competitors with or without the TQM label.

(xiv) TQM is an approach for continuously improving the quality of every aspect of business life, i.e. it is a never-ending process of improvement for individuals, groups of people and the whole organization (Kanji & Asher 1993, 1996). It is an integrated approach and set of practices that emphasizes, inter alias, management commitment, continuous improvement, customer focus, long-range thinking, increased employee involvement and teamwork, employee empowerment, process management, competitive benchmarking, etc. (Ross, 1993).

(xv) Saraph et al. (1989) identified eight critical factors of quality management: the role of management leadership and quality policy; the role of the quality department; training; product/service design; supplier quality management; process management; quality data and reporting; and employee relations. Operational measures of these factors were developed and were found to be reliable and valid. By using such measures, decision-makers can assess the level of quality management in their organizations in order to devise strategies for further improvements.

(xvi) Flynn et al. (1994) identified and accentuated seven key dimensions of quality management that included top management support, quality information, process management, product design, workforce management and supplier and customer involvement. These dimensions were then tested for reliability and validity and, by doing so, described a clear framework for subsequent research and established a standard by which practitioners could evaluate the effectiveness of their quality management programmes.

(xvii) Ahire et al. (1996a) identified 12 constructs of integrated quality management strategies, namely, top management commitment, customer focus, supplier quality management, design quality management, benchmarking, SPC, internal quality information usage, employee empowerment, employee involvement, employee training, product quality and supplier performance.

(xviii) Black and Porter (1996) presented a research methodology that could be used to improve self-assessment frameworks and make organizations more effective in the development of total quality systems. Their research focused on the important elements of the Baldrige Award model and other established literature, and identified 10 critical components of TQM, viz. corporate quality culture, strategic quality management, quality improvement measurement systems, people and customer management, operational quality planning, external interface management, supplier partnerships, teamwork structures, customer satisfaction orientation and communication of improvement information. These factors were found to be reliable and valid, and provided key contributions for a better understanding of TQM. Black and Porter (1995) also developed a model for TQM, which provided visual information on the various factors of TQM, relationships between those factors, strength of those relationships and the relative importance (or criticality) of those factors.

(xix) Joseph et al. (1999) identified 10 factors of TQM. These include organizational commitment, human resource management, supplier integration, quality policy, product design, role of quality department, quality information systems, technology utilization, operating procedures and training. A measurement instrument was also developed which can be used to evaluate the extent of TQM practice in an organization.

(xx) The subject of service quality as perceived by the customers has been researched extensively. Gronroos (1978, 1982, 1983) was one of the first few researchers who recognized the need to develop valid and distinct measures of service quality. In an effort to explain how customers perceive service quality, Gronroos (1984) developed a model of service quality based on three dimensions, viz. (a) functional quality—how the service is performed and delivered, (b) technical quality—what the consumer receives and (c) the image of the service firm. These efforts and the author's later works on service quality (Gronroos, 1990, 1993) triggered a lot of interest in service quality research.

(xxi) The importance of service culture has been widely discussed and emphasized in a TQM literature (Bowen & Schneider, 1988; Harber et al., 1993a, b; Schneider & Bowen 1992, 1993; Schneider et al., 1994, 1996a, b). As certain unique features such as intangibility characterize service businesses, inseparability of production and consumption, heterogeneity, perishability, etc., management finds it very difficult to supervise directly employees when they interact with customers as this would affect the seamlessness of service (Schneider & Bowen, 1995). It is therefore highly prudent to establish a service climate and culture that will guide employee behaviour indirectly—through the values, mores and beliefs captured by the procedures, policies and routines and behaviour in the various functional systems of the organization, such as marketing, operations and human resource management (HRM).

(xxii) In another work, Schneider and Bowen (1992) explored four classic personnel/ HRM procedures (entry, socialization/ training, compensation/rewards and effectiveness criteria) as organizational processes for creating a service climate. Zeithaml et al. (1996) proposed a conceptual model of the impact of service quality on particular customer behaviours and demonstrated that improving service quality could increase the likelihood of positive behaviour and decrease negative attitudes towards the organization.

(xxiii) In an empirical research, Bitner (1992) explained how the 'built environment' in service organizations (i.e. the man-made physical surroundings) influenced both customers and employees. Many other researchers have also emphasized the influence of these 'servicescapes' on customers (e.g. Baker, 1987; Berry & Clark, 1986; Bitner, 1986; Booms & Bitner, 1982; Kotler, 1973; Rapoport, 1982; Shostack, 1977; Upah & Fulton, 1985; Zeithaml et al., 1985) and employees (e.g. Baker et al., 1988; Becker, 1981; Davis, 1984; Steele, 1986; Sundstrom and Altman, 1989; Wineman, 1986) in physiological, psychological, emotional, sociological and cognitive ways.

(xxiv) Petro et al. reported the service quality in hotels. The hotel is a system where the vital aim is to satisfy (and hopefully delight) the customer. Each identifiable subsystem (viz. reception, room, bathroom, restaurant, support services) concurs to realize this aim by means of a peculiar process. The customer actively participates in several service processes and affects the result in terms of quality and added value. The customer is both the recipient and the judge of the service. Therefore, to design the hotel service, customers' needs and expectations should be identified and translated into hotel quality elements. Vice-versa, to assess the hotel service quality, the specific impact of each quality element on customer's satisfaction should be taken into account. With regard to this impact, the service quality elements may be classified (Kano et al., 1984; Center for Quality Management, 1993; Rust et al., 1994; Mazur, 1995) into: (i) Must-be quality elements: Service attributes which are so basic that the customer may fail to mention them, until the service provider fails to provide them. They fulfill basic expectations therefore their absence is extremely dissatisfying. On the other hand, they often go unnoticed by most customers. (ii) One-dimensional quality elements: Service attributes which customers generally mention as desirable or determinants in their choice of a service. These service quality elements satisfy in proportion to their level of presence. (iii) Attractive quality elements: Service attributes, which are far beyond the customer's expectations. They fulfill the customer's latent needs therefore their presence would surprise and delight the customer. On the other hand, the absence of such service quality elements would not cause customer dissatisfaction.

Each customer can effectively evaluate a whole range of standards, from 'hard' standards to 'soft'. A 'hard' standard is easy to spot, since it is anything, which is 'expected' by a normal customer, e.g. 'Do the lamps work?' 'Is the bedroom clean?' 'Soft' standards are less easy to spot, but they may be more memorable. By achieving soft standards, the hotel succeeds in making the customer feel a special guest. Examples of soft standards may be 'Did the staff use your name?' 'Were you thanked and bid farewell?' A warm welcome, cleanliness, attractiveness, punctual service and choice food are the main customer requirements from a restaurant service.

(xxv) Brady et al. reported some new thoughts on perceived Service Quality. Although it is apparent that perceptions of service quality are based on multiple dimensions, there is no general agreement as to the nature or content of the dimensions. Gronroos (Gronroos 1982; Lehtinen and Lehtinen 1982; Mels, Boshoff, and Nel 1997) identifies two service quality dimensions. Functional quality represents how the service is delivered; that is, it defines customers' perceptions of the interactions that take place during service delivery. Technical quality reflects the outcome of the service act, or what the customer receives in the service encounter. Rust and Oliver (1994) offer a three-component model: the service product (i.e., technical quality), the service delivery (i.e. functional quality), and the service environment. Rust and Oliver do not test their conceptualization, but support has been found for similar models in retail banking (McDougall and Levesque 1994) and healthcare samples (McAlexander, Kaldenberg, and Koenig 1994). Parasuraman, Zeithaml, and Berry (1988) propose five: reliability, responsiveness, assurances, empathy and tangibility characteristics of the service experience. Parasuraman, Zeithaml, and Berry 1985) had earlier proposed 10 dimensions. Several studies advance modified versions of the SERVQUAL model (e.g., Boulding et al. 1993; Cronin and Taylor 1992; De Sarbo et al. 1994; Parasuraman, Zeithaml, and Berry, 1991, 1994; Zeithaml, Berry, and Parasuraman 1996). These modifications drop expectations altogether (e.g., Cronin and Taylor 1992), add dimensions to the expectations portion of the model (such as "will" and "should" expectations; see Boulding et al, 1993), or employ alternative methods (such as conjoint analysis) to assess service quality perceptions (Carman 2000; DeSarbo et al. 1994). Because of the reports of SERVQUAL's inconsistent factor structure, Dabholar, Thorpe, and Rentz (1996) identify and test a hierarchical conceptualization of retail service quality that proposes three levels: customers' overall perceptions of service quality, primary dimensions, and subdimensions. This multilevel model recognizes the many facets and dimensions of service quality perceptions.

(xxvi) The quality of services offered in an academic library in India has been investigated by Banwet & Datta. Service quality and consumer satisfaction have been found to be indispensable for retaining and attracting consumers in service-providing institutions, such as libraries (Banwet & Datta, 1999). Tangible and intangible aspects of service performance affect the level of service quality and consumer satisfaction, which, in turn, determine whether consumers will re-visit the library and advise others to visit it in future (Banwet & Datta, 2000a). However, the level of service performance may change over time. Service quality and consumer satisfaction can also change because of a shift in the attribute weights determining service satisfaction (Mittal et al., 1999). The quality of library services can be classified into two dimensions: technical (outcome) dimension and functional (process) dimension (Gronroos, 1988). Technical quality or tangible quality can be expressed primarily as the quality and volume of literature available in the library. Functional quality or intangible quality refers to the manner in which the library services are delivered. The service achieves quality in perception when its performance meets or exceeds the level of consumer expectations.

Responses to service importance scale clearly indicated that students placed more importance on the outcome of library services than other service dimensions. This was consistent with past research where the outcome of a service was rated as the most important factor affecting service satisfaction and value (Banwet & Datta, 2000b; Patterson & Spreng, 1997). Reliability of service had been rated as the most important intangible service quality dimension.

The outcome dimensions, such as availability of books, journals and other literature and the ease with which they can be found, rated among the most important factors affecting service satisfaction. The availability of staff, their sincerity, trustworthiness, knowledge, problem-solving ability and record keeping accuracy were rated to be important factors, determining a high level of service quality in the library. The conditions of physical facilities, general ambience in the library and convenient operating hours were also important for satisfying the readers."

(xxvii) The study in Indian banks carried out by Sureshchandar et al. strives to examine the influence of Total Quality Service (TQS) dimensions on customer-perceived service quality. Multiple regression analysis has been used to investigate the relationship between different dimensions of TQS and the various factors of service quality. The results have indicated that TQS dimensions, as a whole, are indeed good predictors of service quality. Further, the soft issues of TQS (such as human resource management, customer focus, service culture, employee satisfaction, top management commitment and leadership and social responsibility) seem to be more vital than do hard issues in positively influencing customer-perceived service quality.

Decision-makers are continuously concerned and interested in ascertaining the exact nature of relationships between quality management practices and business performance. What are the key quality management practices that result in improved business performance? What practices contribute more to performance and what practices contribute less? Do the different quality management practices act synergically to improve performance or do they act independently? These are some of the questions that are constantly thought about by researchers and quality management practitioners. The solutions to such questions are vital for researchers for the process of theory building, and would help decision-makers to sustain a true competitive advantage.

In a recent research work Sureshchandar et al, (2001b) identified the critical dimensions of TQS (from the perspective of the management) by addressing the different facets of TQS, such as human and non-human aspects of service production and delivery, service design and operations, aesthetics of the physical environment, information technology, industrial relations, corporate citizenship behaviour, etc. A review of literature on quality management implied that the critical dimensions of TQS could be broadly categorized under three groups as follows:

Those dimensions of manufacturing quality management (i.e. TQM) that can be effectively used in service organizations as well (these include dimensions such as top management commitment and visionary leadership, human resource management, design and management of processes, information and analysis, benchmarking, continuous improvement, employee satisfaction and customer focus and satisfaction).

Those dimensions that are seldom addressed in literature, but are nevertheless key elements of TQM in both manufacturing and service organizations (e.g. union intervention and social responsibility).

Finally, those factors that are highly unique to service organizations (namely, servicescapes—the manmade physical environment and service culture).

Based on a thorough review of the prescriptive, conceptual, practitioner and empirical literature on TQM and TQS, the authors have identified the following 12 dimensions as critical for the institution of a TQM environment in service organizations: top management commitment and visionary leadership, human resource management, technical system, information and analysis system, benchmarking, continuous improvement, customer focus, employee satisfaction, union intervention, social responsibility, servicescapes, and service culture.

High correlations were observed among the TQS dimensions that were treated as independent variables here. This problem is bound to happen, as the very concept of TQS is built on the assumption that it is an integrated approach where there is a lot of interdependence among its dimensions. Many TQS gurus and practitioners have proposed this notion time and again, which has been reemphasized by several researchers as well as through their research findings.

The TQS dimensions that have turned out to be significant in service quality are: human resource management, service culture, social responsibility, customer focus and employee satisfaction (with respect to core service); service culture (with respect to human element of service delivery); service culture and social responsibility (with respect to systematization of service delivery); service culture and social responsibility (with respect to tangibles of service); and top management commitment and visionary leadership (with respect to social responsibility).

It can be observed that the dimensions that have turned out to be significant happen to be the people-oriented issues of TQS (such as top management commitment and visionary leadership, human resource management, service culture, social responsibility, customer focus and employee satisfaction). This finding underlines the importance of the 'people-oriented' issues over the technology-related issues in delivering high service quality. This finding also goes in line with the results of some earlier studies that have highlighted the importance of the soft issues in improving business performance.

An examination of the few dimensions that have turned out to be significant has offered some interesting conclusions. The dimensions that are significant have been found to be the soft issues of TQS (such as top management commitment and visionary leadership, human resource management, service culture, social responsibility, customer focus and employee satisfaction). This observation underscores the importance of the 'people'-oriented issues over the technology–related issues in dispensing 'quality service'.

The bottomline for this result may be that the advancement of technology in banks has, to a very great extent, resulted in the standardization of technological factors. Therefore, in such a scenario, the soft issues are more likely to determine the success of quality management programmes. Therefore, it becomes imperative for the management to lay greater emphasis on 'high touch' quality management rather than 'high tech' quality management.

(xxviii) According to G.S. Sureshchandar et al., "The research literature on service quality and satisfaction are copious, with various contributions from numerous researchers over the past few years (e.g. Cronin & Taylor, 1992, 1994; Parasuraman et al., 1985, 1988, 1991, 1993, 1994a, b; Teas, 1993, 1994; Zeithaml et al., 1985, 1990, 1993, 1996). However, the SERVQUAL instrument of Parasuraman et al. (1988), a 22-item scale that measures service quality along five dimensions, forms the keystone for all the other works. Though the effectiveness of SERVQUAL in evaluating service quality has been questioned by different authors for diverse reasons, there is a general agreement that the 22 items are reasonably good predictors of service quality in its entirety. But a meticulous investigation of the scale items reveals that most of the items relate to the component of human interaction/intervention in service delivery and the rest on the tangibles facets of service (such as the effect of atmospherics, design and door elements, appearance of equipment, employee dress, etc.). The point to be underscored here is that the SERVQUAL instrument seems to have left out certain other momentous aspects of service quality, such as the features associated with a service, namely, the service product or the core service, systematization/standardization of service delivery in order to establish the seamlessness in service, and the image/goodwill a service firm could establish for itself in terms of being responsible to the society in which it operates.

The credit for heralding service quality research goes to Parasuraman, Zeithaml and Berry (see Parasuraman et al., 1985, 1988; Zeithaml et al., 1985, 1990). The authors, based on qualitative research, formulated a measure of service quality derived from data on a number of services, instead of counting on earlier dimensions of goods quality in the manufacturing sector. The initial results, based on some focus group findings, yielded 10 dimensions of service quality that included tangibles, reliability, responsiveness, competence, courtesy, credibility, security, access, communication and understanding the customer. Further empirical scrutiny (Parasuraman et al., 1988) resulted in a 22-item scale, called SERVQUAL, which measures service quality based on five dimensions, viz. tangibles, reliability, responsiveness, assurance and empathy. The entire approach was formulated on the tenet that customers entertain expectations of performances on service dimensions, observe performance and later form performance perceptions. The authors defined service quality as the degree of discrepancy between customers' normative expectations for the service and their perceptions of service performance. Rust and Oliver (1994) noted that the SERVQUAL instrument captured the crux of what service quality might mean, i.e. a comparison to excellence in service by the customer.

In their empirical work, Cronin and Taylor (1992) controverted the framework of Parasuraman et al. (1988) with respect to conceptualization and measurement of service quality, and propounded a performance-based measure of service quality called SERVPERF by illustrating that service quality is a form of consumer attitude. They argued that the performance-based measure was an enhanced means of measuring the service quality construct.

In another empirical work, Teas (1993) investigated conceptual and operational issues associated with a 'perceptions-minus-expectations (P-E)' service quality model. The author developed alternative models of perceived service quality based on Evaluated Performance (EP) and Normated Quality (NQ). It was concluded that the EP model could overcome some of the problems associated with the P-E gap conceptualization of service quality.

Parasuraman et al. (1994a) responded to the concerns of Cronin and Taylor (1992) and Teas (1993) by demonstrating that the validity and alleged severity of many of those concerns were questionable. Parasuraman et al. (1994a) elaborated that though their approach in conceptualizing service quality could and should be revised, relinquishing it altogether in preference of the alternative approaches proclaimed by Cronin and Taylor and Teas did not seem warranted. This triggered an interesting controversy in service quality research.

In another empirical work, Parasuraman et al. (1994b) revamped SERVQUAL's structure to embody not only the discordance between perceived service and desired service (labeled as measure of service superiority, or MSS), but also the discrepancy between perceived service and adequate service (labeled as measure of service adequacy, or MSA).

Critics of SERVQUAL have also disputed the logic and requirement behind the measurement of expectations (Cronin & Taylor, 1992, 1994), the decipherment and operationalization of expectations (Teas, 1993, 1994), the reliability and validity of SERVQUAL's difference-score formulation (Babukus & Boller, 1992; Brown et al., 1993) and SERVQUAL's dimensionality across various service scenes (Carman, 1990; Finn & Lamb, 1991).

The point worth debating here is that the comprehensiveness of the 22-item scale proposed by Parasuraman et al. (1988) in addressing the critical dimensions of service quality is in question, for the simple reason that a careful examination of the scale items divulges that the items at large focus on the human aspects of service delivery and the remaining on the tangibles of service (like the effect of atmospherics, design and décor elements, appearance of equipment, employee dress, etc.).

The notability of the element of human interaction/intervention in service delivery has been, without an iota of skepticism, acclaimed and reiterated by various other researchers as well (e.g. Harber et al., 1993a, b; Mills & Morris, 1986; Norman, 1991; Schneider & Bowen, 1985, 1992, 1993, 1995; Schneider et al., 1994, 1996a, b; Stebbing, 1993). Of the five SERVQUAL dimensions, four, namely, reliability, responsiveness, assurance and empathy, relate to this aspect.

The fifth one, i.e. the tangibles, pertains to the effect of physical facility, equipment, personnel and communication materials on customers. The effect of this atmospherics, popularly known as 'servicescapes' (Bitner, 1992), does affect customers in many ways. Bitner (1992) elucidated how these servicescapes influence both employees and customers in physiological, psychological, sociological, cognitive and emotional ways. Various authors have also dealt with in detail the impact of these tangibles on the service perceptions by customers and their effects on employees (Baker et al., 1988; Berry & Clark, 1986; Sundstrom & Altman, 1989; Upah & Fulton, 1985; Zeithaml et al., 1985). But, while accentuating the significance and high relevance of these two momentous dimensions, one should also admit that the highly subjective concept of service quality not only confines to the realms of these elements, but also encompasses other critical factors, such as: the service product or the core service, systematization/standardization of service delivery (the non-human element), and the social responsibility of the service organization.

The core service portrays the 'Content' of a service. What is delivered is as substantial as how it is delivered. Schneider and Bowen (1995) clarified that many a time managers become so involved with all the procedures, processes and contexts for service, that they tend to overlook that there is also something called the 'core service'. Rust and Oliver (1994) defined that the service product is whatever service 'features' are offered. Schneider and Bowen (1995) also argued that fancy facilities, modern equipment, stylish uniforms and terrific signs can never countervail for bad/mediocre food, poor financial advice, an inappropriate will, or lousy music. Hauser and Clausing (1988) also demonstrated the influence of diverse product (or service) attributes on customers' perceptions. To put everything in a nutshell, the core service itself has discernible, tangible and multidimensional quality features that could discriminate services and could preponderate over other issues, such as delivery. The quality of this core service largely influences and sometimes may be ultimate determinant of the overall service quality from the viewpoint of the customers (Schneider & Bowen, 1995).

The service delivery represents the 'how' of a service. It has two distinct and disparate features: Human element of service delivery, which has been effectively addressed by SERVQUAL. The processes, procedures, systems and technology that would ensure seamless service. The second aspect is as crucial as the first one. Customers would always like and expect the service delivery processes to be perfectly standardized, streamlined and simplified so that they could receive the service without any hassles, hiccups or undesired/inordinate questioning by the service providers. Zemke and Schaaf (1990) quoted a study of 1500 consumers by Cambridge Reports, a Massachusetts-based research firm, which found that 44% of the respondents indicated that 'ease of doing business with' was the fundamental reason for choosing a financial firm.

Milakovich (1995) noted that process improvement has become the prime focus of the service quality revolution, as he observed that the key to total quality service (TQS) depends on understanding the process, as mechanism to transmute knowledge and respond to customers faster than the competitors. Ahire et al. (1995) explained that the overall quality of the products or services could be made better by improving the quality of the processes either directly or indirectly. Spenley (1994) claims that the basic business processes go a long way to substantiating the quality of an organization's products or services. Enhancement of technological capability (e.g. computerization, networking of operations, etc.) plays a crucial role in establishing the seamlessness in service delivery.

In addition to abetting as a potential market signal, social responsibility helps an organization to lead as a corporate citizen in encouraging ethical behaviour in everything it does. This critical factor has seldom found a place in the quality management literature, even though it does come into picture in the Malcolm Baldrige National Quality Award Criteria (Malcolm Baldrige National Quality Award Guidelines, 1998) under the heading 'Company responsibility and citizenship'. A study conducted by 'Consumer Reports' on consumers of non-banking financials (Zemke & Schaaf, 1990) found that one of the predominant consumer concern on service quality was: "Equal treatment tempered by pragmatism, stemming from the belief that everyone, big or small, should be treated the same". They were also concerned about getting good service at a reasonable price, but not at the expense of quality.

The point which merits articulating here is that an organization cannot count only on financial performance to survive in this ever-changing scenario of global competition, but also has a responsibility to the society in which it exists. Albeit this feature sounds highly abstract and intangible, it does contribute to the formation of quality perceptions by customers. For example, a hospital that gives free treatment to the economically downtrodden, an educational institution that grants scholarships for the poor, or a financial institution that provides loans to needy ones with less rigid loan conditions, would certainly be adored and appreciated by the customers. These subtle, but nevertheless forceful, elements send strong signals towards improving the organization's image and goodwill and consequently influencing the customers' overall evaluation of service quality and their loyalty to the organization.

In essence, it is postulated that service quality is based essentially on five dimensions namely: core service or service product, human element of service delivery, systematization of service delivery non-human element, tangibles of service (servicescapes), and social responsibility."

In summary, finding out what customers expect is essential to providing service quality, and service quality research is a key vehicle for understanding customer expectations and perceptions of services. In services, as with any offering, a firm that does no service quality research at all is unlikely to understand its customers. In many of the research abroad, national culture has been recognized as an independent variable influencing an organization culture and practices. Hence, even though researchers have developed new concepts in eastern and western countries, there is a huge potential of studying these concepts from the Indian perspective.

Service quality research methods used in services are similar in many ways to the research conducted for physical products; both aim to assess customer requirements, satisfaction, and demand. Service research, however, incorporates additional elements that require specific attention. Service research must continually monitor and track service performance because performance is subject to human variability and heterogeneity. Conducting performance research at a single point in time, as might be done for a physical product, such as an automobile, would be insufficient in services. A major focus of service research involves capturing human performance—at the level of the individual employee, the team, the branch, the organization as a whole and the competition. Another focus of service research is documenting the process by which a service is performed. Even when a service employee is performing well, a service provider must continue to track performance because the potential for variation in service delivery is always present.

Both qualitative and quantitative research are important and need to be included in service research programmes. Insights gained through qualitative methods, such as unstructured interviews, informal conversations with individual customers, critical incidence research and direct observation of service transactions show the researcher the right questions to ask of consumers. Qualitative research also gives managers the perspective and sensitivity that are critical in interpreting data and initiating improvement efforts. Because the results of qualitative research play a major role in designing quantitative research, it often is the first type of research conducted. Researchers often need qualitative inputs—inputs that cannot be meaningfully expressed in the form of numbers—to understand their consumers and the efficacy of their strategies. Qualitative research helps gather such inputs. It probes feelings, attitudes, predispositions and the perceptions of respondents. It is as important and valuable as quantitative research.

Qualitative research assumes that there is a common thread among the consumers belonging to a particular segment. It attempts to get a feel of this common thread. Since, in order to get such a feel, it is not necessary to interview a large sample of population, it does a sensitive probing of a small, purposive sample. The non-structured and small-sample features render it particularly suitable for gaining initial insights into the given problem. It is true that qualitative research is subjective. The theory, methodology, and findings of qualitative research are not as hard and tangible as those of its quantitative cousin. Qualitative research findings are neither valid nor reliable in the strict statistical sense, for there is no number crunching here. Interestingly, its subjectivity is its main strength.

Quantitative research gives managers data from which they can make broad inferences about customer groups and provide yardsticks to evaluate and track the firm's service performance. It deals with quantitative aspects. It is used more in conclusive research projects. It expresses and summarizes data numerically/quantitatively. It tackles a large number of respondents; often amounts to large-scale surveys. It involves limited probe with limited questions. It involves structured questioning/observations. It provides insights on quality problems. The final course of action can depend on its findings.

12.2 SUMMARY AND SYNTHESIS OF OBSERVATIONS

This chapter has been specific in coverage. It covers the service sector. It addresses the definition and concept of service quality and other aspects of its management. The literature sources are textbooks on total quality management both international and Indian editions, research papers both international and Indian journals. The following observations can be derived from the above literature:

1. *Definition of Service Quality:*
   (a) Service quality involves a set of dimensions like attitudes, timeliness, facilities etc. that enable a service now and in the future to meet or exceed customer expectations.
   (b) Service quality is defined by a customer's perception of the reliability, responsiveness, empathy, assurances, and tangibles associated with a service experience.

2. *Essentials for TQM Implementation in Service Sector:*
   The prerequisites of TQM in the service sector are: (i) Customer focus, (ii) Organizational culture, (iii) Employee satisfaction and (iv) Continuous improvement.

   The important factors in implementing TQM in the service sector are: (i) Top management leadership, vision, support and commitment, (ii) Measuring customer satisfaction (iii) Teamwork (quality teams), (iv) Training of personnel, (v) Involvement and empowerment of employees, (vi) Design quality systems (process management), (vii) Supplier involvement, (viii) Benchmarking, (ix) Servicescapes, (x) Good relations with unions.

3. *Dimensions of Service Quality:*
   The dimensions of service quality are strongly influenced by the nature of the services. The following dimensions have been observed over a number of services like hotels, airlines, banks, after-sales service, insurance, hospital, academic library, investment services, etc.
   (i) Reliability (dependable performance), (ii) Timeliness (responsiveness), (iii) Service price, (iv) Attitude (courtesy), (v) Facilities (tangibles), (vi) Knowledge (competence/skill), (vii) Credibility (trust/honesty), (viii) Security (risk/danger), (ix) Ease of contact (access), (x) Communication (language), (xi) Customer 'need' understanding, (xii) Service product (outcome of service/core service), and (xiii) Social responsibility.

As mentioned in the literature survey, Valarie A. Zeithaml, A Parasuraman and Leonard Berry embarked on a quantitative research resulting in a parsimonious instrument (SERVQUAL). The various statistical analysis conducted in constructing SERVQUAL revealed correlation among some of the dimensions listed above. Figure 12.1 shows the correspondence between SERVQUAL dimensions and original dimensions for evaluating service quality.

In light of the SERVQUAL dimensions, the above 13 dimensions for service quality may be modified to the following eight dimensions: (i) Tangibles, (ii) Reliability, (iii) Responsiveness, (iv) Assurance, (v) Empathy, (vi) Social responsibility, (vii) Service product, and (viii) Service price·

12.3 SERVICE QUALITY MANAGEMENT (FROM CUSTOMER'S POINT OF VIEW)

The following eight dimensions are important for service quality: (i) Tangibles, (ii) Reliability, (iii) Responsiveness, (iv) Assurance, (v) Empathy, (vi) Social responsibility, (vii) Service product, and (viii) Service delivery·

The service quality model is defined here as the representation of the system that is constructed to study some aspects of that system or the system as a whole. It represents the phenomenon through the use of analogy. It describes the behaviour of elements in a system where theory is inadequate.

The hypothesis is that each of the eight factors listed in the model are individually and jointly influencing service quality. The factors are interrelated, therefore interdependence of the factors is assumed. Refer model drawing given in Figure 12.1:

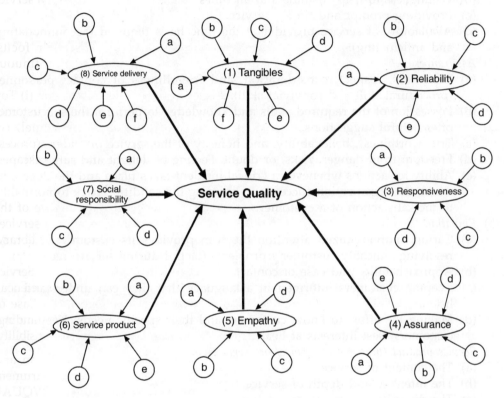

FIGURE 12.1   Dr. Kachwala's model for service quality from the customer's point of view.

The dimensions defined in the service quality model are as follows: (Operational definition of the terms)

(1) *Tangibles (Facilities):*
    (a) Appearance of physical facilities, equipment, etc.
    (b) Classy ambient conditions, such as temperature, ventilation, noise and odour.
    (c) Well-dressed personnel (neat, clean and professional appearance).
    (d) Visually appealing signs, advertisement boards, and other facilities.
    (e) Physical layout of equipment and other furnishings/facilities.
    (f) Proper housekeeping.
(2) *Reliability:*
    (a) Service provider's ability to display a positive moment of truth.
    (b) The interest the service provider shows in solving customer problems.

   (c) The right delivery of service first time and every time.

   (d) The ability to perform the promised service dependably and accurately.

   (e) The ability to provide error-free records, bills and other transaction documents.

(3) *Responsiveness (timeliness):*

   (a) Ability to communicate provision of services as per desired schedule.

   (b) Willingness to help customers at all times.

   (c) Providing prompt and timely service.

   (d) Availability of service provider at the time he is required (accommodating and anticipating).

(4) *Assurance:*

   (a) Politeness, respect, consideration, and friendliness of contact personnel (procedural skill and convivial skill).

   (b) Possession of the required skills and knowledge to perform the service, and offer helpful suggestions.

   (c) Trustworthiness, believability, and honesty of the service provider.

   (d) Freedom from danger, risks, or doubt. Feeling of delight and satisfaction.

   (e) Ability for actions whenever a critical incident takes place and the degree to which the organization succeeds in bringing the condition back to normality to the satisfaction of a customer.

(5) *Empathy:*

   (a) Caring, individualized attention the firm provides its customers. Attitude resolving amicably customer's problems (tactful during service recovery).

   (b) Approachability and ease of contact.

   (c) Keeping customers informed in a language that they can understand and listen.

   (d) Making the effort to know customers and their specific needs. Keeping the customers' best interests at heart.

(6) *Service product (outcome of service/core service):*

   (a) The content of service.

   (b) The intensity and depth of service.

   (c) The diversity and range of services.

   (d) Service Innovation.

   (e) Convenient and flexible operating/service availability hours.

(7) *Social responsibility:*

   (a) Equal treatment stemming from the belief that everyone should be treated alike.

   (b) Giving good service at a best value (reasonable cost), but not at the expense of quality.

   (c) A social responsibility characterized by 'deserving service' to people belonging to all strata of the society (e.g. concessions to economically and socially downtrodden people, needy ones, etc.).

   (d) Extent to which the organization leads as a corporate citizen, the level to which it promotes ethical conducts in everything it does and a sense of public responsibility among employees.

(8) *Service delivery:*

   (a) Standardized, simplified and structured delivery processes so that the service delivery times are minimum and without any bureaucratic hassles.

(b) Enhancement of technological capability (e.g. computerization, networking of operations, etc.) to serve customers more effectively.

(c) Degree to which the procedures and processes are perfectly foolproof.

(d) Extent to which the feedback from customers is used to improve service standards.

(e) Effectiveness of customer grievance procedures and processes.

(f) Adequate and necessary personnel and facilities for good customer service.

12.4 THE CRITICAL DIMENSIONS OF TQM (TQS) {FROM MANAGEMENT'S POINT OF VIEW OR SERVICE PROVIDER'S POINT OF VIEW} AS DEFINED IN THE DRAWING

Refer model drawing in Figure 12.2.

The following 14 dimensions are important for Total Quality Management: (i) Top management leadership and commitment, (ii) Customer focus, (iii) Organizational culture, (iv) Employee commitment, (v) Continuous improvement, (vi) Training of personnel, (vii) Employee satisfaction, (viii) Involvement and empowerment of employees, (ix) Benchmarking, (x) Servicescapes (physical environment and facilities), (xi) Good relations with union, (xii) Social responsibility, (xiii) Process management, (xiv) Supplier involvement.

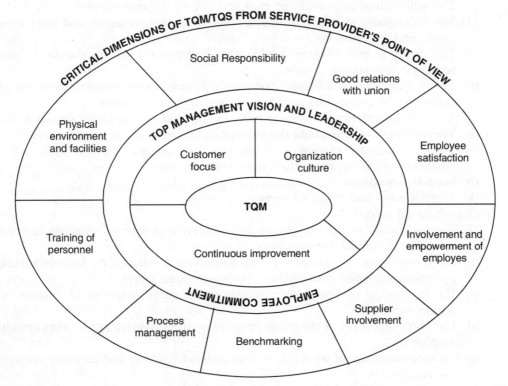

FIGURE 12.2 Dr. Kachwala's model for Total Quality in Service from the service provider's point of view.

The hypothesis is that each of the 14 factors listed in the model are individually and jointly influencing total quality. The above factors are interrelated, therefore interdependence of the factors is assumed.

(a) The following five factors are prerequisites for effective implementation of Total Quality Management (Total Quality Service) (Operational definition of the terms)

(1) *Top management leadership and commitment:*
   (a) The commitment to the philosophy of TQM and a clear quality vision.
   (b) The allocation of adequate resources and time for continuous improvement efforts.
   (c) The ability to recognize employees/teams as valuable and long-term resources.
   (d) The effort to remove the root causes of problems.
   (e) The active participation in creating customer focus throughout the organization.
   (f) The commitment to energize and simulate an organization to improve service performance.
   (g) The wholehearted involvement and commitment to a clearly defined road map for implementing and sustaining TQM activities.

(2) *Customer focus:*
   (a) The consideration of customer focus as the driving force behind day-to-day operations.
   (b) The pleasing and courteous behaviour of employee towards the customers.
   (c) The willingness to provide prompt services to the customers.
   (d) The willingness to help customers, respond to their requests and meet their needs and expectations.
   (e) The ability to use customer feedback to improve the service standards, and redress customer-grievances.
   (f) The willingness to address customer's future needs and involvement of customers in continuous quality improvement programmes.
   (g) The willingness to go the extra mile, i.e. beyond the customer expectations.
   (h) The willingness to provide the content, intensity and depth of a service.
   (i) The extra mile the employee will go to satisfy the unexpressed needs of the customer by giving more than what they expect.
   (j) Service innovation.
   (k) The diversity and range of services.

(3) *Organizational culture:*
   (a) The realization of the employees at all levels that the real purpose of their existence is 'service to customers'.
   (b) The overcoming of resistance of the employees to change by fostering trust, openness and good relationships among the employees.
   (c) The facilitation of fast decision-making and quick response to customers' requirements.
   (d) The encouragement of the philosophy of accurate service at all times among employees.
   (e) The encouragement of work culture that fosters friendship and harmony amongs the employees.

(f) The encouragement of open door policy where the subordinates can freely interact with their superiors.

(4) *Employee commitment:*
  (a) Provide services right the first time and every time.
  (b) Give individual and caring attention as much as possible to the customers by having the customers' best interests at heart.
  (c) Necessary skills and abilities for actions whenever a critical incident takes place (i.e. when a problem arises).
  (d) Actively gather, integrate and communicate information that is critical to the implementation and practice of TQM.
  (e) Foster a feeling of comradeship and brotherhood among all levels of employees.
  (f) Actively participate in the initiatives of quality improvements set by the top management.

(5) *Continuous improvement:*
  (a) The belief that 'continuous improvement' results in a competitive advantage.
  (b) The emphasis on continuous improvement in all operations and at all levels.
  (c) The ability to make continuous improvement a way of incremental process improvements.
  (d) The ability to use continuous improvement as a tool of self-development.

(b) The following nine factors are essential for effective implementation of Total Quality Management (Total Quality Service) (Operational definition of the terms)

(6) Training of personnel:
  (a) The ability to link education and training of employees to its long-term plans and strategies.
  (b) The conduct of TQM and other training programmes such as ISO9000 for employees working in all functional areas.
  (c) The training of employees as per identified needs of the employees.
  (d) The training of employees as per a defined schedule (training calendar).
  (e) The process of evaluating and improving the effectiveness of the training programme.

(7) *Employee satisfaction:*
  (a) The recognition and encouragement for achievements in quality.
  (b) The willingness to devise strategies to improve employee satisfaction.
  (c) The willingness to effectively redress grievance of employees.
  (d) Effective performance appraisal system.
  (e) The ability to foster environment devoid of fear or reprimand.
  (f) The ability of the management to demonstrate that they care for the welfare of the employees and their families.

(8) *Involvement and Empowerment of Employees:*
  (a) Authority and operational independence for the employees to achieve results.
  (b) Encouraging the employees to voice their opinions, criticisms and feedback on organizational functioning and performance.
  (c) Providing employees with enough support and encouragement to offer suggestions and using innovative methods to solve problems.
  (d) Fostering involvement of employees in TQM programmes.

  (e) Support to employees during setbacks and undesired outcomes.

  (f) Involvement of the employee in defining the road map and identifying the resources required for implementation of TQS.

(9) *Benchmarking:*

  (a) Benchmarking the services and processes with respect to other companies.

  (b) Benchmarking the service recovery process with respect to other companies.

  (c) Benchmarking the level of servicescapes (i.e. the aesthetics, appeal, comforts and facilities) with respect to other companies.

  (d) Benchmarking the level of commitment for the society as a whole with respect to other companies.

(10) *Servicescapes (Physical Environment and Facilities):*

  (a) The employees will have a pleasant and neat appearance.

  (b) The ambient conditions such as temperature, ventilation, noise, odour, etc. prevailing in the organizational premises will be comfortable to customers as well as employees.

  (c) The infrastructure facilities will be modern and visually appealing to the employees and to the customers.

  (d) The physical layout of premises, facilities and other furnishings will be comfortable for the employees and for the customers to interact with the employees.

  (e) Housekeeping is kept as a priority in the organization.

  (f) The signs, symbols, advertisement boards, pamphlets and other artifacts in the organization will be appealing to the customers.

(11) *Good relations with union:*

  (a) Clearly defined role played by the employees' union in establishing the policies and strategies of the organization.

  (b) Employees' union's co-operation and support for the drive for improved customer focus and service quality in the organization.

  (c) Establish congruence between the management, the union and the employees with the belief that their functions are complementary, not contradictory, towards improving organizational performance.

  (d) Involvement of the union for redressal of grievances of employees and customers.

(12) *Social responsibility:*

  (a) Lead as a corporate citizen, and promote ethical conduct in everything you do.

  (b) Equal treatment to all customers, stemming from the belief that everyone should be treated alike.

  (c) Sense of public responsibility among employees (in terms of being punctual, regular, sincere and without going on strikes).

  (d) Sense of social responsibility characterized by assisting the deserving, economically and socially downtrodden students with less rigid loan conditions without compromising on quality.

  (e) Evaluate possible impact of its services on society and effectively satisfy the needs and expectations of the society at large.

  (f) Promote truthful advertisements and publishing campaigns that reflect only facts in all communications.

(13) *Process management:*
   (a) Integrating customer feedback in the design of standardized, simplified and foolproof operational procedures and processes.
   (b) Coordinating activities among different departments/branches during the service development processes.
   (c) Enhancing technological capability (e.g. computerization, networking of operations, etc.) to serve customers more effectively.
   (d) Documenting procedures for the investigation of causes of errors and subsequent corrective actions.

(14) *Supplier involvement:*
   (a) Evaluate supplier performance with specified requirements/parameters through mutually agreed plans.
   (b) Involvement of the suppliers in establishing quality and punctuality requirements.
   (c) Constantly endeavour for development of capabilities of its suppliers.
   (d) Treating suppliers as an integral part of the organization.
   (e) Ensuring prompt and timely payment to the suppliers.

EXCERCISES

1. Explain some of the research findings on service quality? What are the common observations among research?

2. Briefly enumerate the case study: "Revolutionizing the service industry, the Ritz-Carlton Hotel Company wins the coveted Malcolm Baldrige National Quality Award for the second time".

3. Explain the research study an Indian banks carried out by Sureshchandar et al.

4. Explain the essentials for TQM implementation in the service sector.

5. Explain service quality management (from customer's point of view).

6. Explain the critical dimensions of TQM (TQS) {from the management's point of view or service provider's point of view}.

ANNEXURE

An Instrument (Questionnaire) for Measuring Service Quality

GENERAL DIRECTIONS

Based on your experiences as a student of management education institute offering MBA programme, please think about the kind of management education institute that would deliver excellent quality of service. Think about the kind of management education institute with which you would be pleased to do your studies. Please demonstrate the extent to which you think such a management education institute would possess the features described below:

Part A

The section below contains eight features pertaining to management education institute and the services they offer. I would like to know how important each of these features is to you when you evaluate a management education institute's quality of service. Please allocate a total of 100 points among the eight features according to how important each feature is to you—the more important a feature is to you, the more points you should allocate to it. Please ensure that the points you allocate to the eight features add up to 100.

1. The appearance of the management education institute's physical facilities, equipment, personnel, and communication materials.

    _____ points

2. The management education institute's ability to perform the promised service dependably and accurately.

    _____ points

3. The management education institute's willingness to help students and provide prompt service.

    _____ points

4. The knowledge and courtesy of the management education institute's employees and their ability to convey trust and confidence.

    _____ points

5. The caring, individualized attention the management education institute provides its students.

_____ points

6. The range of subjects, electives, competent faculty and placement facilities the management education institute provides its students.

_____ points

7. The equitable treatment, financial assistance to the needy students, reasonable fees, the promotion of ethical code by the management education institute.

_____ points

8. The effective simplified and fool-proof procedures and processes, enhanced technology, use of student's feedback and handling critical situations effectively by the management education institute.

_____ points

Total points allocated

100   points

Part B

The section contains 39 statements to ascertain the general expectations of the students concerning service in management education institutes. Please show the extent to which you think an excellent management education institute would possess the features described by each statement. If you feel a feature is not at all essential for excellent management education institute such as the one you have in mind, circle the number 1. If you feel a feature is absolutely essential for excellent management education institute, circle number 7. If your feelings are less strong, circle one of the numbers in the middle. There are no right or wrong answers—all I am interested in, is a number that truly reflects your feelings regarding a management education institute that would deliver excellent quality of service.

	Not Essential						Absolutely Essential
1. An excellent management education institute will have modern teaching facilities and equipments like computers, LCD projectors.	1	2	3	4	5	6	7
2. Infrastructure like library, computer centre classrooms and other facilities at an excellent management education institute will be visually appealing.	1	2	3	4	5	6	7
3. Employees (faculty) at an excellent management education institute will be neat and clean and well-dressed.	1	2	3	4	5	6	7
4. Written material associated with the services (such as handouts or grade sheets) will be visually appealing in an excellent management education institute.	1	2	3	4	5	6	7

	Not Essential						Absolutely Essential

5. An excellent management education institute will have housekeeping as a priority and of the highest order in the organization.   1 2 3 4 5 6 7

6. An excellent management education institute will have physical layout of equipment and other furnishing comfortable for the students to interact with the employees.   1 2 3 4 5 6 7

7. When an excellent management education institute promises to perform certain activities by a certain time, they will do so.   1 2 3 4 5 6 7

8. When a student has a problem, an excellent management education institute will show a sincere interest in solving it.   1 2 3 4 5 6 7

9. An excellent management education institute will deliver the service right the first time and every time.   1 2 3 4 5 6 7

10. An excellent management education institute will provide their services like examination at the time they promise to do so.   1 2 3 4 5 6 7

11. An excellent management education institute will insist on error-free records like student attendance or examination grade sheets.   1 2 3 4 5 6 7

12. Employees in an excellent management education institute will tell students exactly when services like regular teaching classes, exams will be performed.   1 2 3 4 5 6 7

13. Employees in excellent management education institute will give prompt service to students like the issue of library books.   1 2 3 4 5 6 7

14. Employees in excellent management education institute will always be willing to help students for example selection of elective subjects, administrative assistance, hostel accomodation.   1 2 3 4 5 6 7

15. Employees in excellent management education institute will never be too busy to respond to students' requests.   1 2 3 4 5 6 7

16. The behaviour of employees in the institute will instill confidence in students.   1 2 3 4 5 6 7

	Not Essential					Absolutely Essential	

17. Students of the institute will feel safe, secure, satisfied and delighted in their interactions with faculty.

    1 2 3 4 5 6 7

18. Employees in excellent management education institute will be consistently pleasing and courteous with students.

    1 2 3 4 5 6 7

19. Employees in excellent management education institute will have the knowledge and competence to answer students' specific request.

    1 2 3 4 5 6 7

20. Employees of the institute will try to relate to and resolve amicably student's problems.

    1 2 3 4 5 6 7

21. Excellent management education institute will have operating hours convenient to all their students, e.g. library and computer facilities for 24 hours X 7 days

    1 2 3 4 5 6 7

22. Excellent management education institute will have employees who give students personal attention, for example, counseling.

    1 2 3 4 5 6 7

23. Excellent management education institute will have the student's best interests at heart.

    1 2 3 4 5 6 7

24. The employees of the excellent management education institute will understand the specific needs of their students.

    1 2 3 4 5 6 7

25. Excellent management education institute will provide the latest, current, state-of-the-art subjects and electives in the curriculum.

    1 2 3 4 5 6 7

26. The institute will provide a range of teaching tools like lectures, case studies, field projects.

    1 2 3 4 5 6 7

27. The institute will provide proper campus placements for the students.

    1 2 3 4 5 6 7

28. The institute will provide faculty with sound subject knowledge and industry experience, maintain the necessary rigour both in class and by the way of industry based assignments/projects for overall develop-ment of the students.

    1 2 3 4 5 6 7

29. The institute will provide equal opportunities for all students.

    1 2 3 4 5 6 7

30. The institute will provide education at reasonably minimum cost.

    1 2 3 4 5 6 7

	Not Essential					Absolutely Essential

31. The institute will provide loans and other financial assistance for the economically backward and needy students.   1 2 3 4 5 6 7

32. The institute will promote ethical conduct in every thing it does.   1 2 3 4 5 6 7

33. The institute will have effective procedures and processes for student's grievances.   1 2 3 4 5 6 7

34. The institute will have standardized and simplified service processes so that the service delivery time are minimum.   1 2 3 4 5 6 7

35. The institute will ensure procedures and processes are perfectly foolproof.   1 2 3 4 5 6 7

36. The institute will enhance technological capability to serve students more effectively.   1 2 3 4 5 6 7

37. The institute will ensure that feedback from the students will be used to improve service standards.   1 2 3 4 5 6 7

38. The institute will have the willingness of the employee for actions whenever a critical incident takes place.   1 2 3 4 5 6 7

39. The institute will bring critical incidents back to normalcy to the satisfaction of the students.   1 2 3 4 5 6 7

Part C

Please document your views:

  (i) Identify three most important factors that characterize the institute?
  (ii) Identify three least important factors that characterize the institute?
  (iii) Any other observations?

Part D

Please fill up the following personal details:

Name: Contact email:

Institute name: Name of the course:

Class

An instrument (Questionnaire) for measuring Total Quality Service (TQS/TQM) from the perspective of the management (Service Provider) [Annexure 2 TQM-MEI]

GENERAL DIRECTIONS

Based on your experiences as a service provider (management / faculty / employee) of management education institute offering an MBA programme, please think about the kind of management education institute that would deliver excellent quality of service. Think of the kind of management education institute where you would be pleased to offer your services. Please demonstrate the extent to which you think such an institute would possess the features described below:

Part A

The section below contains 14 features pertaining to a management institute and the services it offers. We would like to know how important each of these features is to you when you evaluate TQS for management institute. Please read all the 14 features before you allocate the points. Please allocate a total of 100 points among the 14 features according to how important each feature is to you—the more important a feature is to you, the more points you should allocate it. Please ensure that the points you allocate to the 14 features add up to 100. In case your total exceeds 100 points, the allocated points will be proportionately reduced to 100 points.

(1) Leadership and commitment of the top management (Director HOD)	_____ points
(2) Customer (student) focus	_____ points
(3) Organizational culture (academic and administrative staff)	_____ points
(4) Employee (faculty and administrative staff) commitment	_____ points
(5) Continuous improvement	_____ points
(6) Training of personnel (faculty and staff)	_____ points
(7) Employee satisfaction	_____ points
(8) Involvement and empowerment of employees	_____ points
(9) Benchmarking (for improvements)	_____ points
(10) Servicescapes (physical environment and facilities)	_____ points
(11) Good relations with union	_____ points
(12) Social responsibility	_____ points
(13) Process management (operational procedures and processes)	_____ points
(14) Supplier (visiting faculty) involvement	_____ points

Total points allocated   100 points

(or proportionate 100 points)

Part B

This section contains 40 statements to ascertain the general expectations of management (service provider) concerning TQS (TQM) in management education institutes. Please show the extent to which you think an excellent management education institute would possess the features described by each statement.

If you feel a feature is not at all essential for an excellent management education institute such as the one you have in mind, circle the number 1. If you feel a feature is absolutely essential for an excellent management education institute, circle the number 7.

If your feelings are less strong, circle one of the numbers in the middle. There are no right or wrong answers since we are only interested in a number that truly reflects your feelings regarding the features that are important for TQS in the management education institute.

In the questions given below, we are using an acronym EMEI for Excellent Management Education Institute.

1. The top management of EMEI will have an inclination to allocate adequate resources and time for continuous improvement efforts.   1 2 3 4 5 6 7

2. EMEI will provide a range of teaching tools like lectures, case studies, and field projects for the students.   1 2 3 4 5 6 7

3. EMEI will overcome resistance of the employees to change by fostering trust, openness and good relationships among the employees.   1 2 3 4 5 6 7

4. Employees in EMEI will give individual and caring attention as much as possible to the students by having the students' best interests at heart.   1 2 3 4 5 6 7

5. EMEI will emphasize on continuous improvement in all operations and at all levels.   1 2 3 4 5 6 7

6. EMEI will have TQM and other training programmes, such as ISO 9000, conducted for employees working in all functional areas.   1 2 3 4 5 6 7

7. EMEI will actively devise strategies to improve employee satisfaction.   1 2 3 4 5 6 7

8. EMEI will have the employees encouraged to voice their opinions, criticism and feedback on organizational functioning and performance.   1 2 3 4 5 6 7

9. EMEI will benchmark the training programmes with those of other management institutes.   1 2 3 4 5 6 7

10. EMEI will ensure that ambient conditions such as temperature, ventilation, noise, odour, etc. prevailing in the organizational premises are comfortable to students.   1 2 3 4 5 6 7

	Not Essential					Absolutely Essential	

11. EMEI will foster employee union's co-operation and support in the drive for improved student focus and service quality in the organization. 　1　2　3　4　5　6　7

12. EMEI will give equal treatment to all the students, stemming from the belief that everyone should be treated alike. 　1　2　3　4　5　6　7

13. EMEI will co-ordinate activities among different departments/branches during the service development processes. 　1　2　3　4　5　6　7

14. EMEI will effectively evaluate if visiting faculty members are meeting its quality and punctuality requirements. 　1　2　3　4　5　6　7

15. The top management of EMEI will try to remove the root causes of problems and not just 'fire-fight' the symptoms. 　1　2　3　4　5　6　7

16. EMEI will willingly help students, respond to students' requests and strive to develop the necessary capabilities in terms of manpower and facilities to meet the needs and expectations of students. 　1　2　3　4　5　6　7

17. EMEI will encourage the philosophy of accurate service at all times among employees. 　1　2　3　4　5　6　7

18. Employees in EMEI will actively gather, integrate and communicate information that is critical to the implementation and practice of TQM. 　1　2　3　4　5　6　7

19. EMEI will have the ability to use continuous improvement as a tool of self-development. 　1　2　3　4　5　6　7

20. EMEI will have training of employees as per a defined schedule (training calendar). 　1　2　3　4　5　6　7

21. EMEI will have an effective appraisal system, giving each appraised person an idea of what is expected of him/her in the future. 　1　2　3　4　5　6　7

22. EMEI will foster involvement of employees in TQM programmes, like quality control circles (QCs), cross-functional and quality Improvement teams (QIT) for problem-solving. 　1　2　3　4　5　6　7

23. EMEI will benchmark the level of commitment for the society as a whole with those of other management institutes. 　1　2　3　4　5　6　7

	Not Essential					Absolutely Essential

24. EMEI will ensure that the physical layout of premises, facilities and other furnishings are comfortable for the employees and for the students to interact with the employees. 1   2   3   4   5   6   7

25. EMEI will involve the union for redressal of grievances of employees and students. 1   2   3   4   5   6   7

26. EMEI will have a sense of social responsibility characterized by giving loans to deserving economically and socially downtrodden students with less rigid loan conditions without compromising on quality. 1   2   3   4   5   6   7

27. EMEI will document procedures for investigation of causes of errors and subsequent corrective actions. 1   2   3   4   5   6   7

28. EMEI will consider visiting faculty as an integral part of its faculty team. 1   2   3   4   5   6   7

29. The top management in EMEI will have the commitment to energize and simulate the organization to improve service performance. 1   2   3   4   5   6   7

30. EMEI will address the students future needs taking in to account competitors and changing student expectations and will involve students in continuous quality improvement programmes. 1   2   3   4   5   6   7

31. EMEI will encourage an open door policy where the subordinates can freely interact with their superiors. 1   2   3   4   5   6   7

32. Employees in EMEI will actively participate in the initiatives of quality improvements set by the top management. 1   2   3   4   5   6   7

33. EMEI will have the ability of the management to demonstrate that they care for the welfare of the employees and their families. 1   2   3   4   5   6   7

34. EMEI will involve employees in defining the road map and identifying the resources required for the implementation of TQS. 1   2   3   4   5   6   7

35. EMEI will have signs, symbols, advertisement boards, pamphlets and other artifacts in the organization that will be appealing to the students. 1   2   3   4   5   6   7

	Not Essential						Absolutely Essential

36. EMEI will have truthful advertisements and publishing campaigns that reflect only facts in all their communications. 1 2 3 4 5 6 7

37. EMEI will provide the latest, current, state-of-the-art subjects and electives in the curriculum. 1 2 3 4 5 6 7

38. EMEI will have a process of evaluating and improving the effectiveness of the training programme. 1 2 3 4 5 6 7

39. EMEI will pay honorarium and other remunerations to the visiting faculty on time. 1 2 3 4 5 6 7

40. EMEI will encourage pleasing and courteous behaviour of the employees towards the students. 1 2 3 4 5 6 7

Part B

Second set of 40 statements

	Not Essential						Absolutely Essential

1. EMEI will have commitment of the top management to the philosophy of TQM and a clear quality vision (based on student focus and employee focus). 1 2 3 4 5 6 7

2. EMEI will provide faculty with sound subject knowledge and industry experience, maintaining the necessary rigour both in class and by way of industry-based assignments/projects for the overall development of the students. 1 2 3 4 5 6 7

3. EMEI will make the employees at all levels realize that the real purpose of their existence is 'service to students'. 1 2 3 4 5 6 7

4. Employees in EMEI will provide services right the first time and every time. 1 2 3 4 5 6 7

5. EMEI believes that 'continuous improvement' results in a competitive advantage. 1 2 3 4 5 6 7

6. EMEI will link education and training of employees to its long-term plans and strategies. 1 2 3 4 5 6 7

7. EMEI will provide ample recognition and encouragement for achievements in quality. 1 2 3 4 5 6 7

	Not Essential					Absolutely Essential	

8. EMEI will give employees the authority and operational independence to achieve results. — 1 2 3 4 5 6 7

9. EMEI will emphasize on benchmarking the services and processes with respect to those of other management institutes. — 1 2 3 4 5 6 7

10. EMEI will encourage the employees to have a pleasant and neat appearance. — 1 2 3 4 5 6 7

11. EMEI will clearly define the role played by the employees' union in establishing the policies and strategies of the organization. — 1 2 3 4 5 6 7

12. EMEI will lead as a corporate citizen, and the level to which it promotes ethical conduct in everything it does. — 1 2 3 4 5 6 7

13. EMEI will integrate student feedback in the design of standardized, simplified and foolproof operational procedures and processes. — 1 2 3 4 5 6 7

14. EMEI will evaluate visiting faculty's performance with specified requirements/parameters through mutually agreed plans. — 1 2 3 4 5 6 7

15. The top management of EMEI will recognize employees/team as a valuable, long-term resource. — 1 2 3 4 5 6 7

16. EMEI will provide prompt services to the students as promised and also as per the defined schedule. — 1 2 3 4 5 6 7

17. EMEI will facilitate fast decision-making and enable quick response to students' requirements. — 1 2 3 4 5 6 7

18. Employees in EMEI will have the necessary skills and ability for actions whenever a critical incident takes place (i.e. when a problem arises). — 1 2 3 4 5 6 7

19. EMEI will have the ability to make continuous improvement a way of incremental process improvements. — 1 2 3 4 5 6 7

20. EMEI will have training of employees as per identified needs of the employees. — 1 2 3 4 5 6 7

21. EMEI will effectively redress grievances of employees. — 1 2 3 4 5 6 7

	Not Essential					Absolutely Essential

22. EMEI will provide employees with enough support and encouragement to offer suggestions and use innovative methods to solve problems.　1　2　3　4　5　6　7

23. EMEI will benchmark the level of servicescapes (i.e. aesthetics, appeal, comforts and facilities) with those of other management institutes.　1　2　3　4　5　6　7

24. EMEI will have modern infrastructure facilities that are visually appealing to the employees and to the students.　1　2　3　4　5　6　7

25. EMEI will establish congruence between management, union and employees with the belief that their functions are complementary, not contradictory, towards improving organizational performance.　1　2　3　4　5　6　7

26. EMEI will have a sense of public responsibility among employees (in terms of being punctual, regular, sincere and without going on strikes).　1　2　3　4　5　6　7

27. EMEI will enhance technological capability (e.g. computerization, networking of operations, etc.) to serve students more effectively.　1　2　3　4　5　6　7

28. EMEI will constantly endeavour for development of capabilities of its visiting faculty.　1　2　3　4　5　6　7

29. The top management in EMEI will actively participate in creating and reinforcing student focus throughout the organization.　1　2　3　4　5　6　7

30. EMEI will use student feedback to improve the service standards, and redress student-grievances.　1　2　3　4　5　6　7

31. EMEI will encourage work culture that fosters friendship and harmony among the employees.　1　2　3　4　5　6　7

32. Employees in EMEI will foster a feeling of comradeship and brotherhood among all levels of employees.　1　2　3　4　5　6　7

33. EMEI will have the ability to foster environment devoid of fear or reprimand.　1　2　3　4　5　6　7

34. EMEI will support the employees during setbacks and during undesired outcomes.　1　2　3　4　5　6　7

35. EMEI will ensure that housekeeping is a priority and is of the highest order in the organization.　1　2　3　4　5　6　7

	Not Essential					Absolutely Essential	
36. EMEI will evaluate possible impact of its services on society and effectively satisfy the needs and expectations of the society at large.	1	2	3	4	5	6	7
37. EMEI will have the willingness to go the extra mile, i.e. beyond the student expectations.	1	2	3	4	5	6	7
38. The top management in EMEI will have the personal visible involvement and commitment to a clearly defined road map for implementing and sustaining TQM activities.	1	2	3	4	5	6	7
39. EMEI will provide proper campus placements for the students.	1	2	3	4	5	6	7
40. EMEI will ensure that the student focus is the driving force behind day-to-day operations.	1	2	3	4	5	6	7

Part C

Please document your views:

   (i) Identify three most important factors that characterize EMEI
   (ii) Identify three least important factors that characterize EMEI
   (iii) Any other observations

Part D

Please fill up the following personal details

Name: Contact email:

Name of the Institute: Designation:

13

Theory of Constraints (TOC)

13.1 INTRODUCTION

The production control approach of managing bottlenecks, or constraint management, was popularized by Dr. Eliyahu Goldratt. He refers to this approach or philosophy as the theory of constraints (TOC), and he has presented seminars on TOC around the world to all types of industry and academic groups. Some people refer to this philosophy of TOC as synchronous manufacturing, because all parts of the entire organization work together to achieve the organization's goals.

13.2 *THE GOAL* BY DR. ELIYAHU GOLDRATT JEFF COX

To illustrate the effects of TOC, Dr. Goldratt and Jeff Cox wrote *The Goal: A Process of Ongoing Improvement*, an intriguing and highly readable book that dramatically illustrates the implementation of TOC in a factory. Alex Rogo, a factory manager who is the main character in the goal, searches for a way to save his factory, which is about to be deep-sized by the uncaring and ignorant top management. By following the advice of Jonah, a consultant who continually asks easily understood questions which have very difficult answers, and the factory survives.

The process followed by the factory manager in *The Goal* is at the heart of TOC. First, the factory manager measures the production rates of the major operations in the factory. He discovers one operation that is much slower than all the others—a bottleneck.

Next, he asks a team of his best people to come up with ways to increase the production rate of the bottleneck operation. Then, after the production rate of the bottleneck operation is increased, the whole factory's production rate is observed to increase. The team then goes to the next slowest operation and repeats the process. The output of the factory increases as the production rate of each bottleneck operation is increased. This procedure results in the production rate of the factory being dramatically increased with little additional cost and with a consequent rise in profits.

A key aspect of the philosophy of TOC is the continuous improvement of production performance. Rather than using the traditional accounting measurements of unit cost and utilization of workers and equipment, the new measures of throughput (the rate that cash is generated by the sale of products), inventory (money invested in inventory), and operating expenses (money spent in converting inventory into throughput) are used to measure production performance. The idea is to increase throughput while reducing both inventory and operating expenses.

13.3 SOME PRINCIPLES OF SYNCHRONOUS PRODUCTION

Synchronous production, developed by Eliyahu Goldratt, is based on the theory of constraints. This theory was developed from three empirical observations: (1) In multistage production systems not all stages have the same production capacity; (2) Variations and randomness in production systems reduce effective capacity and output; and (3) The procedures in classical production systems generally amplify rather than solve the problems created by capacity imbalance and production variations.

13.3.1 Empirical Observation One

Goldratt's first observation: In a multistage production process, the maximum rate of production (the throughput) is dictated by the stage with the smallest production capacity. A bottleneck resource is any resource that limits the flow of production through the system. Alternatively, a bottleneck resource is one that has a capacity less than or equal to the demand put on it. A non-bottleneck resource is one that has a capacity greater than demand and therefore does not restrict the system throughput. For example, in Figure 13.1, workstation 3 would be a bottleneck resource and workstations 1, 2 and 4 would be non-bottleneck resources. A third category, a capacity-constrained resource, is not a bottleneck but is operating close to capacity and could become a bottleneck if not operated efficiently.

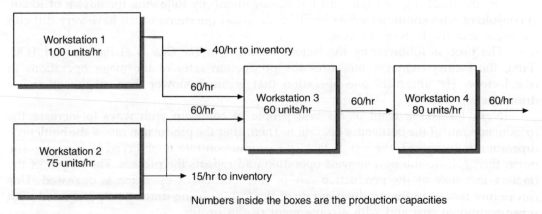

Numbers inside the boxes are the production capacities

FIGURE 13.1 Over-production by non-bottleneck resources.

An important consequence of having capacity imbalances among the stages is that an hour of production lost at a bottleneck resource will decrease the throughput of the entire system by the equivalent of one hour of production. In addition, an improvement that saves an hour of time at a non-bottleneck resource simply increases an amount of idleness at the resource by an hour without increasing the system throughput. These facts lead to the key principle of the theory of constraints: To manage production effectively, one must focus on the constraining resources—the bottlenecks.

13.3.2 Empirical Observation Two

Goldratt's second observation: variations in processing times due to machine breakdowns, defects, material shortages, or worker fatigue can reduce the effective capacity of a production system and increase inventories and throughput time. These variations can turn non-bottleneck resources into bottlenecks and vice-versa.

13.3.3 Empirical Observation Three

Finally, the production systems are often operated in ways that amplify problems. For example, consider the production system in Figure 13.1. Because of the measures of productivity normally used to evaluate operations, such as machine utilization, the managers of workstations 1 and 2 will try to keep their workstations operating all the time. As long as materials are available, such as for stock items, workstations 1 and 2 will keep processing items that may not be sold for months. But workstation 3 cannot handle all the production form workstations 1 and 2, so large inventories develop in the front of workstation 3. These large inventories begin to create material-handling problems and misplaced inventories. Workstation 4, on the other hand, is starved for material to process. Synchronous production is designed to prevent these problems.

13.4 THE DRUM–BUFFER–ROPE MECHANISM

The solutions recommended by Goldratt are wide-ranging and include many aspects of JIT: better maintenance, more efficient set-ups, and smaller lot sizes. However, his key recommendation is a mechanism for coordinating production so that the flow of production (rather than the capacities) among the stages is balanced, and inventories are kept to a minimum except where they are really needed. This scheduling method is called the **drum–buffer–rope** method, as illustrated in Figure 13.2.

Production is controlled at control points or bottlenecks, which are collectively referred to as the drum because it establishes the beat to be followed by all other operations. The drum provides the rhythm that is consistent with the bottlenecks of production. A time buffer in the form of inventory is kept before a bottleneck so that it always has material on which to work. These buffers provide the insurance that delivery promises to customers can be made with high reliability. A rope is some form of communication, such as a schedule, that is communicated back upstream to prevent inventory from building up and to coordinate the activities required to support the MPS. The rope ensures that every production stage is synchronized to the MPS.

13.4.1 The Drum

The drum is the mechanism that controls the pace of production; that is the drum 'beats' the rhythm of production. In a JIT pull system, the drum is the final product demand; production occurs only at the pace of actual demand. In a push production system such as MRP, the drum is the master production schedule, which tells all the production stages what to produce and when. In synchronous production, the drum is the bottleneck resource(s). The production schedule is developed around the bottleneck, which pulls production from earlier stages and pushes it to the subsequent stages. In this sense, synchronous production is a hybrid of the push and pull systems. The demand pattern driving the bottleneck could be either an assured demand system, as in JIT, or a speculative demand system.

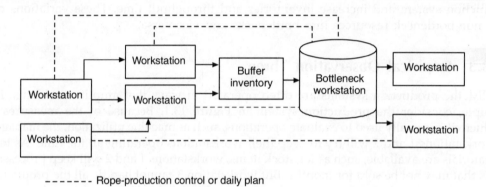

------- Rope-production control or daily plan

FIGURE 13.2 Drum–Buffer–Rope Methods.

13.4.2 The Buffer

Regardless of how carefully production is planned, there will be variations in the production system, and the units scheduled to be produced at some workcentre will not be available on time. If a non-bottleneck resource stops because of a material shortage production will not normally be lost because the non-bottleneck resource has idle time available and can quickly catch up. However, if a bottleneck operation must stop because of a shortage of material to process, then the entire system will lose production, which cannot be regained. Therefore, in synchronous production we normally keep inventories in front of non bottleneck operations very low, but in front of bottleneck operations, a supply of safety stock is maintained to buffer or protect the bottleneck operation from material shortages; the bottlenecks must be kept operating.

Synchronous manufacturing also encourages the use of inventories in front of assembly operations because of shortage of a single item can stop the entire process. Final product inventories, however, can be kept to a minimum if an assured demand approach is used to drive the bottleneck.

13.4.3   The Rope

Although the drum is supposed to set a production rythm that everyone follows, a communication link is needed to ensure that all stages are working at the same pace. The rate of production for operations that follow the bottleneck will be controlled directly by the amount of material made available to them by the bottleneck for processing. But non-bottleneck operations preceding the bottleneck are frequently evaluated using measures that encourage them to overproduce, so they must be controlled. We do not want non-bottleneck operations running simply to keep workers busy. The rope is the link between the bottleneck and the preceding workstations that keep them for running ahead of the bottleneck. In JIT scheduling the rope is the Kanban pull mechanism. In synchronous production, the rope can also be Kanbans pulling production, or flow can be controlled by using a daily production schedule based on the production of the bottleneck.

EXCERCISES

1. To illustrate the effects of TOC, Dr. Goldratt and Jeff Cox wrote *The Goal: A Process of Ongoing Improvement* that dramatically illustrates the implementation of TOC in a factory. What are the key learnings of the book *The Goal*?

2. What are the principles of synchronous production?

3. Explain the "drum–buffer–rope mechanism".

14

Basic Inventory Concepts

In this chapter, we will consider basic inventory concepts such as the reasons for holding inventory and the various types of inventory.

14.1 FIVE REASONS FOR HOLDING INVENTORY

Formulation of an inventory policy requires an understanding of the role of inventory in manufacturing and marketing. Inventory serves five purposes within a firm:

1. It enables the firm to achieve economies of scale.
2. It balances supply and demand.
3. It enables specialization in manufacturing.
4. It provides protection from uncertainties in demand and order cycle.
5. It acts as a buffer between critical interfaces within the supply chain.

14.1.1 Economies of Scale

Inventory is required if a firm is to realize economies of scale in purchasing, transportation, and manufacturing. For example, raw material inventory is necessary if the manufacturer is to take advantage of the per-unit price reductions associated with volume purchases. However, when purchased volumes are sufficiently large, purchase contracts are being negotiated based on annual volumes, not the amount purchased on an individual order. Nevertheless, purchased materials have a lower transportation cost per unit if ordered in larger volumes. The reason for this lower per-unit cost is that full truckload and railcar shipments receive lower transportation rates than smaller shipments of less than truckload (LTL) or less than carload (LCL) quantities. When suppliers are located in the same geographic area, it may be possible to consolidate small volumes into one large shipment.

The reasons for holding finished goods inventory are similar to reasons for holding raw material inventory. Transportation economies are possible with large-volume shipments, but for a firm to take advantage of these economical rates, larger quantities of finished goods inventory are required at manufacturing locations and field warehouse locations, or at customers' locations. An alternative to shipping large customer orders only is to consolidate a number of customer orders into one shipment for the long-distance shipment and pay for local delivery in the local market.

Finished goods inventory also makes it possible to realize manufacturing economies. Plant capacity is greater and per-unit manufacturing costs are lower if a firm schedules long production runs with few line changes. Manufacturing in small quantities leads to short production runs and high changeover costs. However, the production of large quantities may require that some of the items be carried in inventory for a significant period of time before they can be sold. The production of large quantities may also prevent timely and responsive recovery on items that experience a stock out, since large production runs mean that items will be produced less frequently. The cost of maintaining this inventory must be compared to the production savings realized. Although frequent production changeovers reduce the quantity of inventory that must be carried, and shorten the lead time that is required in the event of a stock out, they require time that could be used for manufacturing a product. When a plant is operating at or near capacity, frequent line changes may mean that contribution to profit is lost because there are not enough products to meet demand. In such situations, the cost of lost sales plus the changeover costs must be compared to the increase in inventory carrying costs that would result from longer production runs. While these trade-offs exist in the short-term, in the long-term management should invest in manufacturing technology that enables quick changeover and the efficient production of small quantities.

14.1.2 Balancing Supply and Demand

Seasonal supply and/or demand may make it necessary for a firm to hold inventory. For example, a producer of a premium line of boxed chocolates experiences significant increases in sales volume at Christmas, Valentine's Day, Easter and Mother's Day. The cost of establishing production capacity to handle the volume at these peak periods would be substantial. In addition, substantial idle capacity and wide fluctuations in the labour force would result if the company were to produce to demand. The decision to maintain a relatively stable workforce and produce at a somewhat constant level throughout the year creates significant inventory buildup at various times during the year, but at a lower total cost to the firm. The seasonal inventories are stored in a freezer warehouse built adjacent to the plant.

In contrast, demand for a product may be relatively stable throughout the year, but raw materials may be available only at certain times during the year. Such is the case for producers of canned fruits and vegetables. This makes it necessary to manufacture finished products in excess of current demand and hold them in inventory, unless the raw materials can be purchased from parts of the world with different growing seasons. In this case, increased acquisition costs must be compared to the inventory carrying costs associated with local supply.

14.1.3 Specialization

Inventory makes it possible for each of a firm's plants to specialize in the products that it manufactures. The finished products can be shipped to large mixing warehouses, from which customer orders and products for field warehouses can be shipped. The economics that result from the longer production runs, as well as savings in transportation costs, more than offset the costs of additional handling. Companies such as Whirlpool Corporation have found significant cost savings in the operation of consolidation warehouses that allow the firm to specialize manufacturing by plant location. The specialized facilities are known as focused factories.

14.1.4 Protection from Uncertainties

Inventory is also held as protection from uncertainties. Raw material inventories in excess of those required to support production can result from speculative purchases made because management expects either a future price increase or a strike, for example. Other reasons include seasonal availability of supply, such as in the case of fruits or vegetables for canning, or a desire to maintain a source of supply. Regardless of the reason for maintaining a raw materials inventory, the costs of holding the inventory should be compared to the savings realized or costs avoided by holding it.

Work-in process inventory is often maintained between manufacturing operations within a plant to avoid a shutdown if a critical piece of equipment were to break down, and to equalize flow, since not all manufacturing operations produce at the same rate. The stockpiling of work-in-process within the manufacturing complex permits maximum economies of production without work stoppage. Increasingly, management is working to eliminate the manufacturing bottlenecks that led to work-in-process inventories.

Inventory planning is critical to successful manufacturing operations, since shortage of raw materials can shut down the production line or lead to a modification of the production schedule; these events may increase expenses or result in a shortage of finished product. While shortages of raw materials can disrupt normal manufacturing operations, excessive inventories can increase costs and reduce profitability by increasing inventory-carrying costs.

Finally, finished goods inventory can be used as a means of improving customer service levels by reducing the likelihood of a stock out due to unanticipated demand or variability in lead-time. If the inventory is balanced, increased inventory investment will enable the manufacturer to offer higher levels of product availability and less chance of a stock out. A balanced inventory is one that contains items in proportion to expected demand.

14.1.5 A Buffer throughout the Supply Chain

Inventory is held throughout the supply chain to act as a buffer for the following critical interfaces:

- Supplier–procurement (purchasing).
- Procurement–production.
- Production–marketing.
- Marketing–distribution.
- Distribution–intermediary
- Intermediary–consumer/user.

Because members of the supply chain are separated geographically, it is necessary for inventory to be held throughout the supply chain in order to successfully achieve the time and place utility.

Figure 14.1 shows the typical inventory positions in a supplier–manufacturer–retailer–consumer supply chain.

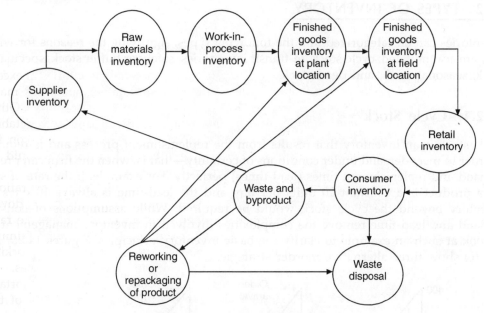

FIGURE 14.1 The logistics flow.

Raw materials must be moved from a source of supply to the manufacturing location, where they will be input into the manufacturing process. In many cases this will require holding work-in-process inventory.

Once the manufacturing process has been completed, product must be moved into finished goods inventory at plant locations. The next step is the strategic deployment of finished goods inventory to field locations, which may include corporate-owned or leased distribution centres, public warehouses, wholesalers' warehouses, and/or retail chain distribution centres. Inventory is then positioned to enable customer purchase. Similarly, the customer maintains an inventory to support individual or institutional consumption.

All of these product flows are the result of a transaction between the manufacturer and the customer, or a decision by the ultimate consumer or user to purchase the product. The entire process depends on a communications network that moves information from the customer to the firm, through the firm back to the customer, and to the firm's suppliers. Clearly, communications is an integral part of managing logistics in the supply chain.

Often it is necessary to move a product backward through the supply chain for a variety of reasons. For example, a customer may return a product because it is damaged, or a manufacturer may need to recall a product because of defects. This is referred to as reverse logistics.

Finally, another aspect that promises to become a bigger factor in the future is waste disposal. As sensitivity to litter from packaging and concern over increase in the use of resources, environmentalists and concerned citizens in states—if not nationally—are likely to push for such laws. To date, these laws have applied only to beer and soft-drink containers, but other packaging materials may become future targets.

14.2 TYPES OF INVENTORY

Inventories can be categorized into the following types, signifying the reasons for which they are accumulated: cycle stock, in-transit inventories, safety or buffer stock, speculative stock, seasonal stock, and dead stock.

14.2.1 Cycle Stock

Cycle stock is an inventory that results from the replenishment process and is required in order to meet demand under conditions of certainty—that is, when the firm can predict demand and replenishment times (lead-times) perfectly. For example, if the rate of sales for a product is a constant 20 units per day and the lead-time is always 10 days, no inventory beyond the cycle stock would be required. While assumptions of constant demand and lead-time remove the complexities involved in inventory management, let us look at such an example to clarify the basic inventory principles. Figures 14.2(a), (b) and (c) show three alternative reorder strategies.

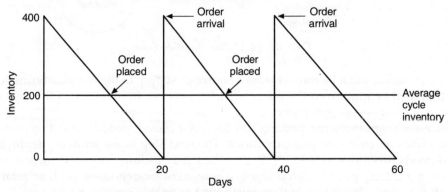

(a) An order of quantity 400 units.

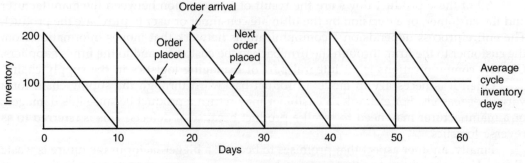

(b) An order of quantity 200 units.

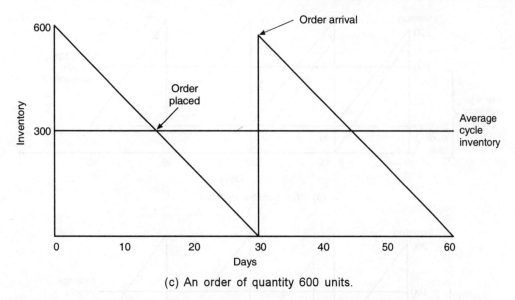

(c) An order of quantity 600 units.

FIGURE 14.2 The effect of reorder quantity on average inventory investment with constant demand and lead-time.

Since demand and lead-time are constant and known, orders are scheduled to arrive just as the last unit is sold. Thus, no inventory beyond the cycle stock is required. The average cycle stock in all the three examples is equal to half of the order quantity. However, the average cycle stock will be 200, 100, or 300 units depending on whether management orders in quantities of 400 (Part a), 200 (Part b), or 600 (Part c), respectively.

14.2.2 In-Transit Inventories

In-transit inventories are items that are enroute from one location to another. They may be considered part of cycle stock even though they are not available for sale and/or shipment until after they arrive at the destination. For the calculation of inventory carrying costs, in-transit inventories should be considered as inventory at the place of shipment origin since the items are not available for use, sale, or subsequent reshipment.

14.2.3 Safety or Buffer Stock

Safety or buffer stock is held in excess of cycle stock because of uncertainty in demand or lead-time. The notion is that a portion of the average inventory should be devoted to cover short-range variations in demand and lead-time. Average inventory at a stock-keeping location that experiences demand or lead-time variability is equal to half the order quantity plus the safety stock, as shown in Figures 14.3(a), (b) and (c).

The average inventory would be 100 units if demand and lead-time were constant. But if demand was actually 25 units per day instead of the predicted 20 units per day

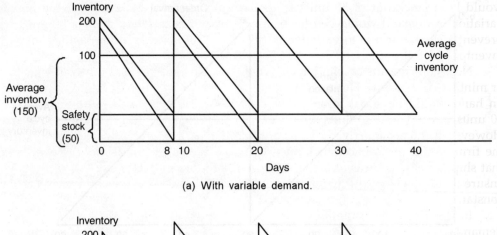

(a) With variable demand.

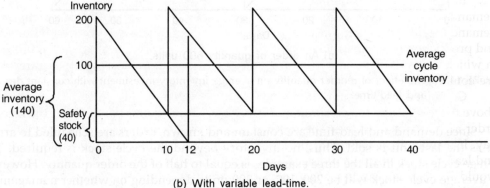

(b) With variable lead-time.

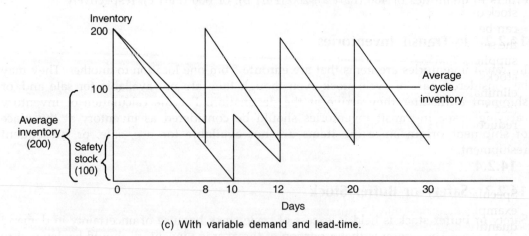

(c) With variable demand and lead-time.

FIGURE 14.3 Average inventory investment under conditions of uncertainty.

with a 10-day lead-time, the inventory would be depleted by the 8th day (200/25). Since the next order would not arrive until the 10th day (order was placed on day zero), the company would experience stockouts for two days. At 25 units of demand per day, this would be a stock out of 50 units in total. If management believed that the maximum variation in demand would be plus or minus five units, a safety stock of 50 units would prevent a stock out due to variation in demand. This would require holding an average inventory of 150 units.

Now consider the case in which demand is constant but lead-time can vary by plus or minus two days (see Figure 14.3(b)). If the order arrives two days early, the inventory on hand would be equal to a 12-day supply, or 240 units, since also are at a rate of 20 units per day and 40 units would remain in inventory when the new order arrived. However, if the order arrived two days late, on day 12—that is a more likely occurrence-the firm would experience stock outs for two days (40 units). If management believed that shipments would never arrive later than two days, a safety stock of 40 units would ensure that a stock out due to variation in lead-time would not occur if demand remained constant.

In most business situations, management must be able to deal with variability in demand and lead-time. Forecasting is rarely accurate enough to predict demand, and demand is seldom, if ever, constant. In addition, transportation delays, along with supplier and production problems, make lead-time variability a fact of life. Consider Figure 14.3(c), in which demand uncertainty (Figure 14.3(a)) and lead-time uncertainty (Figure 14.3(b)) are combined.

Combined uncertainty is the worst of all possible worlds. In this case, demand is above the forecast by the maximum, 25 units instead of 20 units per day, and the incoming order arrives two days late. The result is a stock out period of four days at 25 units per day. If management wanted to protect against the maximum variability in both demand and lead-time, the firm would need a safety stock of 100 units. This policy (no stock outs) would result in an average inventory of 200 units.

In summary, variability in demand and lead-time results in either safety stocks or stock outs. Although it may not be possible to eliminate variability in demand, forecasting can be used to better predict demand, resulting in less safety stock. However, by using the services of transportation companies that deliver consistently on time and by selecting suppliers that have consistent, reliable lead-times, it is possible to eliminate the safety stocks associated with lead-time variability. Referring back to Figure 14.3(c), the elimination of lead-time variability would reduce safety stocks from 100 units to 50 units (see Figure 14.3(a)) and overall inventories from 200 units to 150 units or 25 per cent reduction in total inventory.

14.2.4 Speculative Stock

Speculative stock is inventory held for reasons other than satisfying current demand. For example, materials may be purchased in volumes larger than necessary in order to receive quantity discounts, because of a forecasted price increase or materials shortage, or to protect against the possibility of a strike. Production economics may also lead to the manufacture of products at times other than when they are demanded. Finally, goods may be produced seasonally for consumption throughout the year, or at a constant level in anticipation of seasonal demand in order to maintain a stable workload and labour force.

14.2.5 Seasonal Stock

Seasonal stock is a form of speculative stock that involves the accumulation of inventory before a season begins in order to maintain a stable labour force and stable production runs or, in the case of agricultural products, inventory accumulated as the result of a growing season that limits availability throughout the year.

14.2.6 Dead Stock

Dead stock is a set of items for which no demand has been registered for some specified period of time. Such stock might be obsolete on a total company basis or at just one stock-keeping location. If it is the latter, the items may be either transshipped to another location to avoid the obsolescence penalty or marked down and sold at the current location.

14.3 SYMPTOMS OF POOR INVENTORY MANAGEMENT

(How to Recognize Poor Inventory Management)

This section deals with how to recognize situations where inventories are not being managed properly. Recognition of problem areas is the first step in determining where opportunities exist for improving logistics performance.

The following symptoms may be associated with poor inventory management:

1. Increasing numbers of back orders.
2. Increasing rupee investment in inventory with back orders remaining constant.
3. High customer turnover rate.
4. Increasing number of orders being cancelled.
5. Periodic lack of sufficient storage space.
6. Wide variance in inventory turnover among distribution centres and among major inventory items.
7. Deteriorating relationships with intermediaries, as typified by dealer cancellations and declining orders.
8. Large quantities of obsolete items.

14.4 WAY TO REDUCE INVENTORY LEVELS

1. Multi-echelon inventory planning. ABC analysis is an example of such planning.
2. Lead-time analysis.
3. Delivery-time analysis. This may lead to a change in carriers or negotiations with the existing carriers.
4. Elimination of low turnover and/or obsolete items.
5. Analysis of pack size and discount structure.
6. Examination of returned goods procedures.

7. Encouragement/automation of product substitution.
8. Installations of formal reorder review systems.
9. Measurements of fill rates by stock-keeping unit (SKU).
10. Analysis of customer demand characteristics.
11. Development of a formal sales plan and source demand by a predetermined logic.

14.5   IMPROVING INVENTORY MANAGEMENT

Inventory management can be improved by using one or more of the following techniques: ABC analysis, forecasting, enterprise resource planning (ERP) systems and advanced order processing systems.

14.5.1   ABC Analysis (Pareto Principle)—The 80/20 Rule

In the 18th century, Villefredo Pareto, in a study of the distribution of wealth in Milan, found that 20% of the people controlled 80% of the wealth. This logic of the few having the greatest importance and the many having little importance has been broadened to include many situations and is termed the Pareto Principle. This is true in our everyday lives (such as, most of the decisions we make are relatively unimportant but a few shape our future), and this principle certainly true in inventory systems.

The logic behind ABC analysis is that 20% of a firm's customers or products account for 80% of the sales and perhaps an even larger percentage of profits. The first step in ABC analysis for inventory planning is to rank products by sales, or preferably by contribution to corporate profitability if such data are available. The next step is to check for differences between high-volume and low-volume items that may suggest how certain items should be managed.

Inventory levels increase with the number of stock-keeping locations. By stocking low-volume items at a number of logistics centres, the national demand for these products is divided by the number of locations. Each of these locations must maintain safety stock. If one centralized location had been used for these items, the total safety stock would be much lower. For example, if only one centralized warehouse is used and sales are forecast on a national basis, a sales increase in one city may offset a sales decrease in another city. However, safety stock is required to protect against variability in demand, and there is greater variability in demand when national demand is subdivided into regions. The total system inventory will increase with the number of field warehouse locations, because the variability in demand must be covered at each location; that is, a sales increase in one market area will not be offset by a sales decrease in another market.

When a firm consolidates slow-moving items at a centralized location, transportation costs often increase. However, these costs can be offset by lower inventory carrying costs and fewer stockout penalties. Customer service can be improved through consolidation of low-volume items, thus decreasing the probability of experiencing a stockout. ABC analysis is a method for deciding which items should be considered for centralized warehousing.

14.5.1.1 An example of ABC analysis

Consider an example of ABC analysis. An analysis of sales volume by product revealed that A items accounted for 5% of items and contributed 70% of sales, B items accounted for 10% of items and added an additional 20 per cent of sales, while C items accounted for 65% of the items remaining and contributed only 10% of sales. The last 20% of the items had no sales whatsoever during the past year (see Figure 14.4).

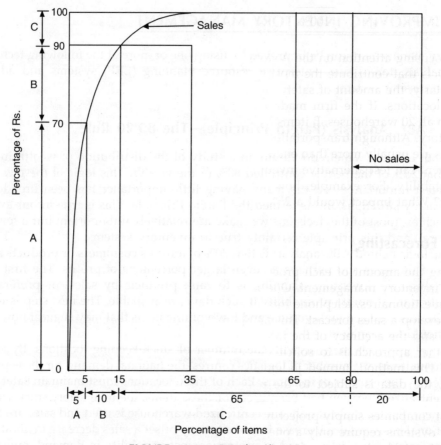

FIGURE 14.4 ABC classification.

This statistical distribution is almost always found in companies' inventories. The "degree of concentration of sales among items will vary by firm, but the shape of the curve will be similar."

For A items, a daily or continuous review of inventory status might be appropriate. B items might be reviewed weekly, while the C items should receive the least attention. Different customer service levels could be established for each category of inventory. An order fill rate of 98% might be set for A items, 90% for B items, and 85% for C items. This policy would result in an overall customer service level of 95%, as shown in Table 14.1.

Table 14.1 Customer service level using ABC analysis

Category service level	Percentage of sales	Customer service level	Weighted customer
A	70%	98%	68.6%
B	20%	90%	18.0%
C	10%	85%	8.5%
	100%	Overall service level: 95.1%	95.1%

By focusing attention on the A items, the management places greater emphasis on the products that contribute the most to sales and profitability.

Similarly, the amount of safety stock is less when lower volume items are stocked in fewer locations. If the firm made use of 20 distribution centres, A items might be stocked in all 20 warehouses, B items in 5 regional warehouses, and C items stocked only at the factory. Although transportation costs for B and C items are greater, the inventory reductions are usually more than enough to make a selective stocking policy worthwhile. Management can test alternative inventory policies for their impact on customer service and profitability. For example, how would the deletion of slow-moving items affect inventory? What impact would a 25% increase in sales have on inventory?

14.5.2 Forecasting

Forecasting the amount of each product that is likely to be purchased is an important aspect of inventory management. One forecasting method is to survey buyer intentions by mail questionnaires, telephone interviews, or personal interviews. These data can be used to develop a sales forecast. This approach is not without problems, however. It can be costly, and the accuracy of the information may be questionable.

Another approach is to solicit the opinions of salespeople or known experts in the field. This method, termed judgment sampling, is relatively fast and inexpensive. However, the data is subject to the personal biases of the individual salespeople or experts.

Most companies simply project future sales based on past sales data. Because most inventory systems require only a one- or two-month forecast, short-term forecasting is therefore acceptable. A number of techniques are available to aid the manager in developing a short-term sales forecast. A method for developing the forecast is shown in Figure 14.5.

Rather than trying to forecast at the stock-keeping unit (SKU) level, which would result in large forecast errors, a management can improve the forecast accuracy significantly by forecasting at a much higher level of aggregation. For example, in Figure 14.5 the forecast is developed at the total company or product line level using a forecasting model. The next step is to break that forecast down by product class and SKU based on sales history. The inventory is then pushed out from the central distribution centre to branch/regional distribution centres using one of the following methods:

- Going rate—the rate of sales that the SKU is experiencing at each location.

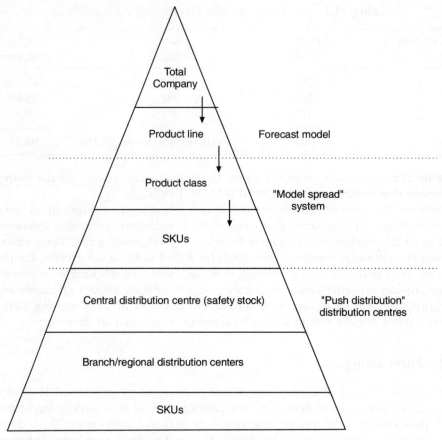

FIGURE 14.5 Building a forecast.

- Weeks/months of supply—the number of weeks/months of sales based on expected future sales that management wishes to hold at each location.
- Available inventory—currently available inventory less back orders.

The only certainty when developing a forecast is that it will not be 100% accurate. For this reason, many firms are developing strategies that focus on reducing the total time from sourcing of materials to delivery of the final product. The shorter this time period can be made, the less critical forecasting becomes, because the firm can respond more quickly to change in demand.

14.5.3   How ERP Systems Contribute to Improved Inventory Management

The German firm SAP AG is the world leader in enterprise resource planning (ERP) software. Although there are many other firms that also provide ERP systems, there is widespread agreement that SAP AG has set new standards in the information technology market with R/3, its client/server application software system. Over 100,000 companies are using R/3 applications worldwide. Leading companies in industries, such as high technology, consumer goods, and chemicals, as well as numerous small and medium-sized firms, have adopted this software. Of the four major modules in R/3, manufacturing and logistics and sales and distribution modules offer significant opportunities to better manage corporate inventories.

The *Manufacturing and Logistics* segment is the largest and most complex of the four modules. It comprises five major components: materials management (MM), plant maintenance (PM), quality management (QM), production planning and control (PPC), and a project management system (PS). Each component is divided into sub-components. Materials management includes consumption-based planning, purchasing, vendor evaluation, and invoice verification. It also includes inventory and warehouse management to manage stock until usage dictates the cycle should begin again. Electronic Kanban/just-in-time delivery is supported by the module.

Production planning and control supports both discrete and process manufacturing processes. Repetitive and configure-to-order approaches are provided. These modules support all phases of manufacturing, providing capacity utilization and requirements planning, material requirements planning, product costing, bills of material explosion and implosion, computer-aided design (CAD) dialogue interface, and engineering change management. The system allows users to link rework orders to production schedules. Orders can be generated from internal sales or from links to a website.

The *Sales and Distribution* module provides customer management, sales order management, configuration management, distribution, export controls, shipping, and transportation management, as well as billing, invoicing, and rebate processing. As with all SAP modules, these can be implemented globally. For example, an order may be received in Hong Kong. If the products are not available locally, they may be internally procured from warehouses in other parts of the world and shipped to arrive together at the Hong Kong customer's site. When implementing the sales and distribution module, the company structure must be represented in the system, for example, R/3 knows where and when to recognize revenue. It is possible to represent the structure of the firm from the point of view of accounting, materials management, or sales and distribution. Also, these structures can be combined.

When a sales order is entered, it automatically includes the correct information on pricing, promotions, availability, and shipping options. Batch order processing is available for specialized industries, such as foods, pharmaceuticals, or chemicals. Users have the ability to reserve inventory for specific customers, request production of subassemblies, or enter orders that are assemble-to-order, build-to-order, or engineer-to-order as well as special customized orders.

The modules are built on what SAP considers industry best practices. The SAP research and development group continually looks for better ways to carry out a particular process or sub-process. System upgrades are designed to reflect the newest best practices.

14.5.4 Order Processing Systems

Many companies have not undertaken comprehensive and ongoing analysis and planning of inventory policy because of lack of time and lack of information. Many times a poor communications system is a contributing factor. A primary goal of inventory management is to achieve an optimum balance between inventory carrying costs and customer service. The essential task of determining the proper balance requires continuous and comprehensive planning. It hinges on to the availability of information. Communications make information available. Linking members of the supply chain with timely and accurate product usage information can reduce the time needed to perform certain elements of the order cycle, including order entry, order processing, and inventory replenishment. Further, variability in the replenishment cycle can be reduced. This way, a firm can gain substantial cost savings by reducing its levels of safety stock as well as the inventories of its customers and suppliers.

In addition, better information systems can reduce message errors and unexpected time delays. This facilitates better decision-making and improves internal coordination in the firm. The result is reduced inventories and faster invoicing, which improves cash flow.

With full, up-to-the-second information on orders, raw materials inventory and production scheduling can be better managed. The distribution centre can meet customer commitments without increasing inventories. More accurate invoices can be prepared, customers can be invoiced sooner, and payments can be received more quickly with fewer reconciliation. When reconciliation is necessary, they can be resolved much more quickly. Reduced inventories and faster invoicing improve cash flow. Inventory management is improved by placing vital information into the hands of decision-makers and by providing them the necessary time to use this information in planning inventory strategies.

14.6 SUMMARY

In this chapter, we examined the basic concepts of inventory management. We described demand and order cycle uncertainty and examined a method for considering both types of uncertainty when calculating safety stock requirements. We also saw that the traditional approach to improving customer service, increasing inventory investment, is costly and inefficient. We described the impact of inventory investment on production scheduling and looked at some symptoms of poor inventory management. The chapter concluded with an explanation of techniques that can be used to improve inventory management.

EXERCISES

1. Explain the reasons for holding inventory.
2. Explain inventory as a buffer throughout the supply chain.
3. Explain the type of inventory stocks.
4. Explain the symptoms of poor inventory management.
5. Explain the techniques used for improving inventory management.
6. Explain how ERP systems contribute to improved inventory management.

15

Managing Material Flow

15.1 INTRODUCTION

Logistics management is that part of the supply chain process that plans, implements, and controls the efficient flow and storage of goods, services, and related information from the point-of-origin to the point-of-consumption in order to meet the customers' require-ments. An integral part of that flow, referred to as materials management, encompasses the administration of raw materials, subassemblies, manufactured parts, packing material, and in-process inventory. Simply, materials management is concerned with those activities related to the physical supply of materials in an organization.

The importance of materials management to the total logistics process cannot be overstated. Although materials management does not directly interface with the final customer, the degree to which raw materials, component parts, and subassemblies are made available to the production process ultimately determines the availability of products to the customer. In essence, the internal customer is just as important as the final customer.

The decisions, good or bad, made in the materials management portion of the logistics process, will have a direct effect on the level of customer service offered, the ability of the firm to compete with other companies, and the level of sales and profits achieved in the market place. Without efficient and effective management of inbound materials flow, the manufacturing process cannot produce products at the desired price and at the time they are required for distribution to the firm's customers. It is essential that the logistics executives understand the role of materials management and its impact on the organization's cost/ service, mix.

Beginning in the 1980s, more firms recognized the importance of materials mana-gement. As business enterprises developed and matured, the role of materials management has expanded to meet the challenges of market-driven, rather than production-driven, economies. Table 15.1 identifies some of the differences between the historical role played by materials management within firms and the present and future environments in which materials are brought into firms' production processes.

While many things such as the need to reduce costs and provide high levels of customer service will continue to remain important, future environments will be characterized by a changing set of priorities and issues. Some of these issues include

Table 15.1 Materials management—past, present and future

	Past	*Present and Future*
Market	Seller's market	Buyer's market
	Low competition	Keen competition
	Restricted export	Global orientation
Products	Small assortment	Wide assortments
	Long life cycle	Short life cycle
	Low technology	High technology
Production	Full capacity load	Full capacity load
	Low flexibility	High flexibility
	Large lot sizes	Low lot sizes
	Long lead times	Short lead times
	Low costs	Low costs
	Make instead of buy	Buy instead of make
Service level	High service level	High service level
	High inventories	Low inventories
	Slow logistics process	Quick logistics process
	Slow transport time	Quick transport time
Information technology	Manual data processing	Electronic data processing
	Paper administration	Paperless factory
Enterprise strategy	Production-oriented	Market-oriented

global orientation, shorter product life cycles, lower levels of inventories, electronic commerce, and a market-oriented focus.

This chapter identifies the various components of materials management and discusses how to effectively manage materials flow within a manufacturing environment. We will examine specific management strategies and techniques used in the planning, implementation, and control of materials flow within organizations.

15.2 SCOPE OF MATERIALS MANAGEMENT ACTIVITIES

Materials management typically comprises of four basic activities:

- Anticipating materials requirements.
- Sourcing and obtaining materials.
- Introducing materials into an organization.
- Monitoring the status of materials as a current asset.

The definition of materials management used in this chapter describes the activity as an organizational system with the various functions as subsystems. The objective of materials management is to solve materials problems from a total company viewpoint by coordinating performance of the various materials functions, providing a communications network, and controlling materials flow.

The specific objectives of materials management are closely dependent on the firm's main objectives of achieving an acceptable level of profitability and/or return on investment, and to remain competitive in a marketplace characterized by increasing competition (see Figure 15.1).

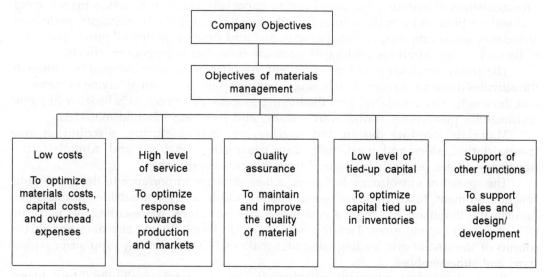

FIGURE 15.1 The objectives of integrated materials management.

Figure 15.1 highlights the major objectives of materials management: low costs, high levels of service, quality assurance, low level of tied-up capital, and support of other functions. Each objective is clearly linked to the overall corporate goals and objectives.

The main objective to make a substantial contribution to profit is reached by optimizing the procurement, management and allocation of material as a productive resource. Hence it is the aim of integrated materials management to achieve optimum supply by reconciling the conflicting goals of low materials costs and overheads, and to achieve a high level of customer service and a very low level of capital tied up in inventories. The optimization of the supply function and, thus, the addition of intangible values, are achieved by totally controlling the flow of materials and information from the supply market through the company and finally to the point of sale.

Materials management encompasses a variety of logistics activities. In a manner similar to the administration of finished goods distribution, the materials manager must be concerned with purchasing and procurement, inventory control, warehousing and storage, order processing, transportation, and almost every other logistics activity. The primary differences between the materials management process and the process that distributes finished goods are that the items being handled in materials management are raw materials, component parts, and subassemblies, and the recipient of the distribution effort is the production or manufacturing group rather than the final customer.

Integral aspects of materials management include purchasing and procurement, production control, inbound traffic and transportation, warehousing and storage, MIS control, inventory planning and control, and salvage and scrap disposal.

15.2.1 Purchasing and Procurement

The acquisition of materials has long been an important aspect of materials management and will continue to be in the future. Rapidly changing supply environments, periods of abundance and shortages, price fluctuations, and lead-time variability all provide ongoing challenges to organizations wishing to optimize materials management efforts.

The terms purchasing and procurement are often used interchangeably, although the activities do differ in scope. Purchasing generally refers to the actual buying of materials and those activities associated with the buying process. Procurement is broader in scope and includes purchasing, traffic, warehousing, and receiving inbound materials.

Materials, product design and engineering, manufacturing, distribution and transportation, sales and marketing, data processing, financial and administrative functions—all are regularly purchased from external suppliers.

The spread of outsourcing has given a new strategic importance to the purchasing function. In many cases, the purchase of goods and services from outside suppliers has become the dominant factor in a company's cost structure, representing up to 70 or 80% of overall expenditures. Two-thirds of the cost of new Boeing airplanes and three-fourths of the cost of one leading computer maker's PCs is spent on supplier-provided parts and subassemblies.

Purchasing and procurement is likely to increase in importance in the future. Many factors will influence this trend, including:

Shorter product life cycles, rapid technological change, and more sophisticated customers have made flexibility and agility increasingly important in the purchasing process.

Emergence of a global economy has forced companies to broaden their sourcing horizons and to locate potential suppliers around the world that can provide low-cost, high-quality goods and services.

Revolution in information technology and telecommunications has provided low-cost, high-speed, automated alternatives to the manual activities that characterize the traditional purchasing department.

Table 15.2 compares the traditional and limited role of purchasing with the innovative and expanded role of procurement. Procurement offers significant potential to organizations in their pursuit of supply chain excellence and optimizing customer service.

15.2.2 Production Control

Production control is an activity traditionally positioned under manufacturing, although a few firms place it under logistics. Its position in the firm's organizational chart is probably not crucial, so long as both manufacturing and logistics have inputs into the production control activity.

The role of production or manufacturing in the logistics process is two-fold.

Table 15.2 Purchasing vs. Procurement

	Traditional Purchasing function	Innovative Procurement function
Organizational positioning	Back-office function	Strategic function
Role	Narrow	Broad
Visibility to top management	Low	High
Staff profiles	Clerical	Professional
Culture	Reactive	Proactive
Buying process	Bureaucratic	Streamlined
Supplier relationships	Adversarial, inflexible	Cooperative, flexible
Performance criterion	Unit price	Overall cost and quality

First, the production activity determines how much and what kinds of finished products are produced. This, in turn, influences when and how products are distributed to the firm's customers.

Second, production directly determines the company's need for raw materials, subassemblies, and component parts that are used in the manufacturing process. Therefore, it is axiomatic that manufacturing and logistics jointly share production control decisions.

15.2.3 Inbound Logistics

Materials management is concerned with product flows into a firm. The first customer of the materials manager is the manufacturing or production department rather than the intermediate or final customer in the marketplace. Much like the firm's target markets, manufacturing requires certain levels of customer service. Manufacturing depends on the ability of materials management to adequately administer a variety of functions, including traffic and transportation, warehousing and storage, and MIS control.

One of the most important activities administered by materials management is the inbound traffic and transportation function. Like their counterparts who are responsible for finished goods movement, materials managers must be aware of the various transport modes and modal combinations available to their companies, any regulations that might affect the transportation carriers their firm uses, the decision of private versus for-hire, leasing, evaluating mode and carrier performance, and the cost/service trade-offs involved in the inbound movement of products. There are basically three major differences between the administration of inbound transportation and outbound transportation.

First, the market demand that generates the need for outbound movement is generally considered to be uncertain and fluctuating. The demand with which the materials manager is concerned originates with the production activity and is much more predictable and stable than market demand. Therefore, transportation decisions made by the materials manager are not subject to the same types of problems his or her counterpart in the outbound traffic area will encounter.

Second, the materials manager is more likely to be concerned with bulk movements of raw materials or large shipments of parts and subassemblies. In addition, raw materials and parts have different handling and loss and/or damage characteristics, which will affect the entire mode/carrier selection and evaluation process.

Third, firms generally exercise less control over their inbound transportation because purchasing procedures tend to look at 'total delivered cost.' A separate analysis of inbound costs is not performed as often or in as much depth.

15.2.4 Warehousing and Storage

Firms must place raw materials, component parts, and subassemblies in storage until they need those items in the manufacturing process. Unlike the warehousing of finished goods, which often occurs in the field, items awaiting use in the production process are usually either stored on-site, that is, at the point of manufacture, or delivered as needed by a Just-In-Time (JIT) supplier.

In firms using a JIT delivery system, the need for inbound warehousing is greatly minimized or eliminated altogether. In other firms, warehouses may be used extensively for the storage of inbound materials and thus the materials manager is usually much more concerned with warehousing and inventory costs because they account for a larger percentage of product value. Generally, finished goods are valued significantly higher than goods-in-process, raw materials, parts, or subassemblies. As a result, warehousing and storage costs are not as important, on a comparative basis, as they would be to the materials manager.

In addition, the warehousing requirements for raw materials and other items are usually quite different. For example, open or outside storage is possible with many raw materials, such as iron ore, sand and gravel, coal, and other unprocessed materials. Also, damage or loss due to weather, spoilage, or theft is minimal with raw materials because of their low value per pound.

15.2.5 Data and Information Systems

The materials manager needs direct access to the firm's information system in order to properly administer materials flow into and within the organization. The types of information often needed by the materials manager include demand forecasts for production, names of suppliers and supplier characteristics, pricing data, inventory levels, production schedules, transportation routing and scheduling data, and various other financial and marketing facts. Additionally, materials management suppliers input into the firm's management information system. Data on inventory levels for materials, delivery schedules, pricing, forward buys, and supplier information are examples of some of the inputs provided by materials management.

Integrated materials management constantly has a multitude of data to process, a task that would not be possible without EDP (Electronic Data Processing)-supported programme systems. Numerous software packages for individual functional elements of integrated materials management have been developed during the last few years, packages that have been tailored for particular branches of industry and particular company sizes. Thus, modern information technology will offer opportunities for the fast and safe transmission and processing of extensive amounts of data, both internally for users within the company and externally for suppliers and customers. Paperless communication is coming to the forefront whereby routine tasks in order processing and scheduling will be decisively facilitated. As a result, new information technology offers great opportunities for linking the planning, controlling and processing functions of materials management that were hitherto performed independently, thereby creating the foundation for the establishment of integrated materials management.

With the proliferation of computerized information systems, including electronic database, this facet of materials management will become more significant in the future.

15.2.6   Inventory Planning and Control

Inventory planning and control of raw materials, component parts, subassemblies, and goods-in-process, are just as important as the management of finished goods inventory. Many of the concepts such as ABC analysis, inventory carrying costs, and economic order quantity (EOQ), are directly applicable to materials management.

Just-in-time (JIT) systems, material requirements planning (MRP I), manufacturing resource planning (MRP II), enterprise resource planning (ERP), distribution requirements planning (DRP I), distribution resource planning (DRP II), and other systems or approaches can also improve the efficiency of inventory planning and control.

15.2.7   Reverse Logistics

One of the most important areas of materials management that a firm often overlooks or considers minor is that of reverse logistics. The disposal or recycling of scrap, surplus, or obsolete materials; the purchasing of remanufactured or refurbished goods; and the handling of product returns and defects are each aspects of a total reverse logistics programme. Such tasks were once considered incidental to other materials management activities, but have become more important because of environment factors and recognition of the revenue aspects of reverse logistics. Many customers now require suppliers to handle these tasks.

15.3   FORECASTING

One aspect of materials management that requires further emphasis is forecasting. Forecasting attempts to predict the future using either quantitative or qualitative methods, or a combination of both. The essence of forecasting is to aid in logistics decision-making.

15.3.1   Why Forecast?

The rationale for forecasting is two-fold.

First, proper control of materials management requires forward planning. Forward planning, in turn, requires good forecasts. The need for forward planning is great if the materials manager wishes to keep operations running smoothly, to adequately prepare for and meet future market conditions, and to minimize potential problems that can occur in materials acquisition.

Second, forecasting is needed if management is to be able to approximate the future with some degree of accuracy. Forecasting can provide an accurate picture of the future and, as such, provides the driving force for all forward-planning activities. In a study of the forecasting practices of a large number of companies, the most widely cited reasons for engaging in forecasting included:

1. Increasing customer satisfaction.
2. Reducing stockouts.
3. Scheduling production more efficiently.
4. Lowering safety stock requirements.
5. Reducing product obsolescence costs.
6. Managing shipping better.
7. Improving pricing and promotion management
8. Negotiating superior terms with suppliers.
9. Making more informed pricing decisions.

15.3.2 Types of Forecasts

Effective and efficient materials management requires many types of forecasts, including:

Demand forecast.   Investigation of the firm's demand for the item, to include current and projected demand, inventory status, and lead-times. Also considered are competing demands, current and projected, by industry and end product use.

Supply forecast.   Collection of data about current producers and suppliers, the aggregate current projected supply situation, and technological and political trends that might affect supply.

Price forecast.   Based on information gathered and analyzed about demand and supply. Provides a prediction of short- and long-term prices and the underlying reasons for those trends.

15.3.3 Forecasting Time Frames

Forecasts can be short-term, midrange, or long-term. The particular time frame most relevant to the firm will be selected:

Long-term forecasts usually cover more than three years and are used for long-range planning and strategic issues. These will naturally be done in broad terms-sales by product line or division, throughput capacity by ton per period, and so on.

Midrange forecasts in the one- to three-year range address budgeting issues and sales plans. Again, these might predict more than demand.

Short-term forecasts are most important for the operational logistics planning process. They project demands into the next several months and, in some cases, more than a year out. These are needed in units, by actual items to be shipped, and for finite periods of time-monthly or perhaps weekly.

Organizations often use a variety of forecasting techniques, ranging from those based on general market information (from suppliers, sales force, customers, and others) to highly sophisticated computer algorithms. The specific technique or approach a firm selects should be appropriate for the unique characteristics of the company and its markets.

15.4 CERTIFYING QUALITY WITH ISO 9000

The terms ISO 9000, Total Quality Management, Quality Assurance, Quality System, Quality Policy, depending upon the individuals you ask, can conjure up many different, and sometimes conflicting, definitions.

Since 1987, one set of standards, the ISO 9000 series, has attempted to define a single definition for "quality" and a "quality system". The ISO 9000 series is a set of five international standards that establish the minimum requirements for an organization's quality system.

The five standards were authored by the International Organization for Standardization, headquartered in Geneva, Switzerland. Contrary to popular belief, ISO is not an acronym for the International Organization for Standardization. ISO is the official nickname, derived from *isos*, a Greek word meaning equal.

The standards themselves are numbered ISO 9000, 9001, 9002, 9003 and 9004. The ISO 9000 series was adopted by the United States as the ANSI/ASQC Q90 series of standards (ANSI is the American National Standards Institute, while ASQC is the American Society for Quality Control).

Each of the five standards has a particular application, explained as follows:

ISO 9000/Q90 specifies the guidelines for selection and use of the other series standards.

ISO 9001/Q91 specifies a quality system model for use by organizations that design/develop, produce, install, and service a product.

ISO 9002/Q92 specifies a quality system model for use by organizations that produce and install a product or service.

ISO 9003/Q93 specifies a quality system model for use by organizations that include final inspection and testing.

ISO 9004/Q94 provides a set of guidelines for an organization to develop and implement a quality system, and interpret the other series standards.

When a firm becomes ISO 9000 certified, they prove to an independent assessor that they meet all the requirements of either ISO 9001/Q91, ISO 9002/Q92, or ISO 9003/Q93. Generally, ISO 9000 certification is given for a period of three years.

15.5 TOTAL QUALITY MANAGEMENT (TQM)

TQM has particular relevance and importance to materials flow within logistics. Many leading authorities have championed the importance of quality in business, including W. Edwards Deming and Philip B. Crosby. Additionally, the Malcolm Baldridge National Quality Award programme of the U.S. Department of Commerce has helped shape corporate thinking on quality issues. Traditional concepts about quality have been modified and enhanced to form the TQM approach outlined in Table 15.3.

Table 15.3 Traditional Management and TQM Comparison

Traditional Management	*Total Quality Management*
Looks for "quick fix"	Adopts a new management philosophy
Fire-fights	Uses structured, disciplined operating methods
Operates the same old way	Advocates "breakthrough" thinking using small innovations
Randomly adopts improvement efforts	Sets an example through management action
Focuses on short-term gains	Stresses long-term, continuous improvement
Inspects for errors	Prevents errors
Throws resources at a task	Uses people to add value
Is motivated by profit	Focuses on the customer
Relies on programmes	Is a new way of life

The TQM approach stresses long-term benefits resulting from continuous improvements to systems, programmes, products, and people. Improvements most often result from a combination of small innovations. A structured, disciplined operating method is used to maximize customer service levels.

15.5.1 Difficulties in Implementing TQM

While TQM has a number of obvious advantages to both organizations and customers, not all firms are successful in implementing it. Many reasons exist for the difficulty or lack of successful implementation, including too much training required, too little focus on human issues, underestimating the time and effort necessary, losing sight of the customer, trying to encompass too many elements, and lack of integration into the firm's core values and competencies. Table 15.4 identifies the relationships between TQM and logistics.

Underlying the specific items listed in the table is the notion that quality is a philosophy of doing business. It is like the marketing concept, cost trade-off analysis, and the systems approach. Each is an orientation or approach to conducting business that influences how individuals, departments, and organizations plan, implement, and control marketing and logistics activities. Therefore, every person involved in logistics must understand his or her role in delivering a level of quality to suppliers, vendors, and final customers.

15.5.2 Keys to TQM Success

Central to TQM success is focus on continuous improvement that leads to higher quality and better customer support whether internal or external to the organization. It normally

Table 15.4 Direct relationships between TQM and logistics

TQM	*Logistics*
Provides a TQM management environment	Uses systematic, integrated, consistent, organization-wide perspective for satisfying the customer
Reduces chronic waste	Emphasizes "doing it right the first time"
Involves everyone and everything	Involves almost every process
Nurtures supplier partnerships and customer relations	Knows the importance of supply and partnership, which are key to customer relations, Customer relations are directly dependent on training, documentation, maintenance, supply support, support equipment, transportation, manpower, computer resources, and facilities
Creates a continuous improvement system	Uses logistics support analysis to continuously improve the system
Includes quality as an element of design	Influences design by emphasizing reliability, maintainability, supportability using the optimum mix of manpower and technology
Provides training constantly	Provides constant technical training for everyone
Leads long-term continuous improvement efforts geared towards prevention	Focuses on reducing life cycle costs by quality improvements geared to prevention
Encourages teamwork	Stresses the integrated efforts of everyone
Satisfies the customer (internal and external)	Places the customer first

requires a cultural change, because most organizations today focus on activities rather than process improvement.

As indicated earlier, TQM is a process. It involves almost every logistics activity and takes a systematic, integrated, consistent, organization-wide perspective for satisfying the customer. And TQM emphasizes continuous improvements. The process begins with a determination of logistics requirements (e.g., customer service levels, inventory levels, transportation strategies). Those requirements are specified as a result of a logistics audit that has examined the materials management and physical distribution aspects of the total logistics system.

After requirements are determined, the processes are continuously reviewed to develop ways to improve. For example, based on historical information, supplier evaluation criteria may be revised, inbound logistics strategies may be modified, or perhaps JIT relationships may be established with selected vendors or suppliers.

15.6 ADMINISTRATION AND CONTROL OF MATERIALS FLOW

Like all of the functions of logistics, materials management activities must be properly administered and controlled. Proper administration and control require some methods to identify a firm's level of performance. Specifically, the firm must be able to *measure, report,* and *improve* performance.

In measuring the performance of materials management, the firm should examine a number of elements, including supplier service levels, inventory, prices paid for materials, quality levels, and operating costs.

Service levels can be measured using several methods, including:

- Order cycle time for each supplier.
- Variability in order cycle time for each supplier.
- Orders fill rate for each supplier.
- Percentage of orders from each supplier that are overdue.
- Percentage of production orders not filled on time.
- Number of stockouts resulting from late deliveries from suppliers.
- Number of production delays caused by materials being out of stock.

Inventory is an important aspect of materials management and can be controlled using the following measures:

- Amount of dead stock.
- Comparison of actual inventory levels with targeted levels.
- Comparison of inventory turnover rates with data from previous time periods.
- Percentage of stockouts caused by improper purchasing decisions.
- Number of production delays caused by improper purchasing decisions.

Materials price level measures include gains and losses resulting from forward buying, a comparison of prices paid for major items over several time periods, and a comparison of actual prices paid for materials with targeted prices.

In the area of **quality control,** measures that can be used are the number of product failures caused by material defects, and the percentage of materials rejected from each shipment of each supplier.

As an overall measure of performance, management can compare the *actual budget* consumed by materials management to the *targeted budget* allocated at the beginning of the operating period.

Once the company has established performance measures for each component of the materials management process, data must be collected and results reported to those executives in decision-making positions. The major operating reports that should be developed by materials management include:

(1) market and economic conditions and price performance,
(2) inventory investment changes,
(3) purchasing operations and effectiveness, and
(4) operations affecting administration and financial activities.

Finally, after performance has been measured and reported, the firm must improve it whenever possible. In order to initiate improvements, the materials manager must address certain key questions. These relate to how the product is produced and how inventories are controlled. Some of the questions to be examined are the following:

1. How many products are to be manufactured? What is the forecasted demand? What is the available capacity?
2. When should the manufacturing plants produce to meet demand? In what amount? At which facility?
3. When are raw materials to be ordered? In what quantities? From which source? With what provisions to remove shortages?
4. How large is the preseason inventory buildup?
5. What are the target inventory levels? Where should inventory be positioned? When should inventory be relocated?
6. How are customers allocated in periods of short supply?
7. How are backlogs managed?
8. What are the information requirements? What types of record keeping and status reporting are needed? What type of cost data must be gathered?
9. When do plans and schedules get revised? What information is used? How far ahead are plans and schedules made?
10. Who sets the management policy for product planning?
11. Who is responsible for planning logistics, sales, and production control?
12. Who is responsible for scheduling?

Computers are also used to improve materials management performance. Systems that have gained acceptance in many firms are Kanban/Just-In-Time (JIT), MRP, ERP, and DRP.

15.7 KANBAN AND JUST-IN-TIME SYSTEMS

Kanban and just-in-time (JIT) systems have become much more important in manufacturing and logistics operations in recent years. Kanban, also known as the Toyota Production System (TPS), was developed by Toyota Motor Company during the 1950s and 1960s. One writer described it as follows: "Kanban is basically the system of supplying parts and materials just at the very moment they are needed in the factory production process so that those parts and materials are instantly put to use. Through reduction of inventories, Toyota identified problems in supply and product quality, because problems were forced into the open. Safety stocks were no longer available to overcome supplier delays and faulty components, thus forcing Toyota to eliminate "hidden" production and supply problems.

Recently, Toyota has computerized its Kanban system and provided it online to suppliers. The data recording technology enables the system to incorporate about 100 times more data than Kanban cards. In addition to increasing the amount of information available to suppliers, the new system will slash times. With the Kanban card process, it is reported that it takes seven to eight hours for the card to reach the production point. Under the new system, parts suppliers receive ordering instructions online, print them out, and attach them to the ordered parts, which are then delivered to Toyota. According to one estimate, if Toyota sent all its transactions to a specific supplier electronically, that supplier would save 2,000 to 3,000 hours per month.

Kanban literally means signboard in Japanese. The system involves the use of cards (called kanbans) that are attached to containers that hold a standard quantity of a single part number. There are two types of kanban cards: move cards and production cards.

When a worker starts to use a container of parts the move card, which is attached to it, is removed and is either sent to or picked up by the preceding, or feeding work centre (in many cases this is the supplier). This is the signal- or "sign" for that work centre to send another container of parts to replace the one now being used. This replacement container has a production card attached to it, which is replaced by the move card before it is sent. The production card then authorizes the producing work centre to make another container full of parts. These cards circulate respectively within or between work centres or between the supplier and the assembly plant.

In order for Kanban to work effectively, these rules must be observed:

There can only be one card attached to a container at any one time.

The using (or following) work centre must initiate the movement of parts from the feeding (or preceding) work centre.

No fabrication of parts is allowed without a Kanban production card.

Never move or produce other than the amount indicated by the Kanban card.

Kanban cards must be handled on a first-in, first-out (FIFO) basis.

Finished parts must be placed at the location point indicated on the Kanban card.

Because each Kanban card represents a standard number of parts being made or used within the production process, the amount of work-in-process inventory can easily be controlled by controlling the number of cards on the plant floor. Japanese managers, by simply removing a card or two, can test or strain the system and reveal bottlenecks. Then they have a problem they can address themselves to an opportunity to improve productivity, the prime goal of Kanban.

15.7.1 JIT

Closely related to Kanban is just-in-time (JIT), introduced in the 1970s, the concept or philosophy of JIT is not new. Many terms are used interchangeably for JIT, although they are not identical. In the food industry, efficient consumer response (ECR) is the preferred term, while in the retail sector, quick response (QR) is commonly used. JIT links purchasing and procurement, manufacturing and logistics. Its primary goals are to minimize inventories, improve product quality, maximize production efficiency, and provide optimal customer service levels. It is basically a philosophy of doing business.

15.7.1.1 JIT defined

JIT has been defined in several ways, including the following:

"A method of inventory control with a focus on waste elimination."

"A programme which seeks to eliminate non-value-added activities from any operation with the objectives of producing high-quality products (i.e. zero defects), high productivity levels, lower levels of inventory, and developing long-term relationships with channel members."

At the heart of the JIT system is the notion that anything over the minimum amount necessary for a task is considered wasteful. This is in direct contrast to the traditional philosophy of 'just-in-case' in which large inventories or safety stocks are held just in case they are needed. In JIT, the ideal lot size or EOQ is one unit, safety stock is considered unnecessary, and inventory should be eliminated.

Many companies in the United States have applied JIT procedures in recent years. Not every component can be handled by the various JIT approaches, but for items that are used repetitively and are not bulky or irregular in shape, the systems work extremely well.

15.7.1.2 Benefits of JIT

There are many benefits of JIT programmes, including the following:

1. Improved inventory turns.
2. Improved customer service.
3. Decreased warehouse space.
4. Improved response time.
5. Reduced logistics costs.
6. Reduced transportation cost.
7. Improved quality of vendor products.
8. Reduced number of vendors.
9. Reduced number of transportation carriers.

15.7.1.3 JIT at Xerox Europe

Xerox Europe realized the following benefits:

1. Its supplier base was reduced from 3,000 to 300.
2. Inbound transportation costs were reduced by 40%.
3. On-time inbound delivery performance was improved by 28%.

Other companies that have successfully introduced JIT into their operations include Cummins Engine, Ford, General Motors, 3M, Textron, and Whirlpool. In sum, organizations that implement JIT is likely to have one or more of the following characteristics:

1. Formalization of performance measurements.
2. Greater reliance on logistics personnel with specialized skills.
3. Delegation of decisions concerning strategic logistics issues down the organizational chart.
4. Greater involvement by senior executives from different functions in the creation of logistics strategy.
5. An increased span of control of senior logistics executives as size of the firm increases.
6. Improved perceptions of the organization's performance relative to the rest of the industry.

15.7.1.4 Problems associated with JIT

While the benefits arising from JIT are many, the approach may not be right for all firms, and the system has some inherent problems. These problems fall into three categories: production scheduling (plant), supplier production schedules, and supplier locations.

When levelling of the production schedule is necessary due to uneven demand, firms will require higher levels of inventory. Items can be produced during slack periods even though they may not be demanded until later, which results in larger inventories of end product. Also, finished goods inventory has a higher value because of its form utility, and thus there is a greater financial risk resulting from product obsolescence, damage, and loss. Smaller, more frequent orders can result in higher ordering costs, which must be taken into account when calculating any cost savings due to reduced inventory levels. Suppliers incur higher production and set-up costs due to the large number of small lot quantities produced. Generally, the result can be an increase in the cost of procuring items from suppliers, unless suppliers are able to perceive the benefits they can receive from being part of a JIT system.

Supplier locations can be a third problem area. As distances between a firm and its suppliers increase, delivery times may become more erratic and less predictable. Transportation costs also increase as small shipments are made. Transit time variability can cause inventory stock outs that disrupt production scheduling. When this factor is combined with higher delivery costs per unit, total cost may be greater than savings in inventory carrying costs.

Other problem areas that can become obstacles to JIT include organizational resistance, lack of systems support, improper definition of service levels, lack of planning, and inventory being shifted to suppliers. Overcoming these and the previously discussed problems or obstacles require cooperation and integration within and between the organizations.

15.7.1.5 Logistics implications of JIT

JIT has numerous implications for logistics executives.

First, proper implementation of JIT requires that the firm fully integrates all the logistics activities. Many trade-offs are required, but without the coordination that integrated logistics management provides, JIT systems cannot be fully implemented.

Second, transportation becomes an even more vital component of logistics under the JIT system. In such an environment, the demands placed on the firm's transportation network are significant, and include a need for shorter, more consistent transit times, more sophisticated communications, use of fewer carriers with long-term relationships, a need for efficiently designed transportation and materials handling equipment, and better transportation decision-making strategies.

Third, warehousing assumes an expanded role in a JIT system. A warehouse becomes a consolidation facility rather than a storage facility. Since many products come into the manufacturing operation at shorter intervals, less space is required for storage, but there must be an increased capability for handling and consolidating items. Different forms of materials handling equipment may be needed to facilitate the movement of many products in smaller quantities. The location decision for warehouses serving inbound material needs may also change because suppliers are often located closer to the manufacturing facility in a JIT system.

15.8 ERP SYSTEMS

Enterprise resource planning (ERP) is a system that includes the core accounting functions of accounts payable, accounts receivable, and general ledger, coupled with logistics functions, to manage the distribution and manufacturing components of an organization. According to one writer, "Integrated inventory handles finished goods, raw materials and source stock, all supported through a requisition system than can be driven from material requirements planning (MRP I) and sales forecasting. ERP becomes the facilitator of the organization, moving data from one function to another and managing the data centrally." In essence, ERP is the newest generation of MRP systems. Other functions that might be supported in ERP can range from fixed assets to a warehouse management system.

ERP systems can interface with supply chain management (SCM) business solutions. For example, Coca-Cola Bottling Co. Consolidated, a North Carolina bottler of soft drinks, combined its ERP system with SCM software to centralize and streamline its planning activities for all of its branches. The combined systems "provide pre-configured business process integration intelligence that is customizable through a point-and-click interface to drive information and decisions through the supply chain.

One particular application of ERP that has become widely used in many companies (e.g., Baxter, Exxon, Kodak, Microsoft) around the world: the suite of software developed by the German firm SAP AG. The SAP R/3 software is server-based, often used on personal computers running Microsoft Windows. The strength of the software is its ability to handle very large databases within four major modules: financial accounting, human resources, manufacturing and logistics, and sales and distribution.

15.9 THE LOGISTICS AND MANUFACTURING INTERFACE

Systems such as Kanban, JIT, MRP, ERP, and DRP require that the logistics and manufacturing activities of a firm work together closely. Without such cooperative effort, the full advantages of such systems can never be realized. Conflicts, both real and perceived, must be minimized. This requires joint planning and decision-making. There are a number of areas in which cooperation is necessary and great improvements can be made. The following actions can be of significant benefit:

Logistics must support manufacturing efforts to increase investment in equipment and computer hardware/software that will increase manufacturing flexibility and reduce replenishment lead-times.

Manufacturing and logistics must work together in the production scheduling area to reduce production planning cycle time. Logistics can provide input into production planning cycle time, production scheduling and system requirements.

Strictly speaking, manufacturing or production orientations must be eliminated. Shortening lead times, set up times, and production run sizes will minimize average inventory levels and stock outs.

Logistics must develop strategies to reduce vendor or supplier lead times for parts and suppliers.

Logistics must adopt the philosophy that slow movers (i.e., products with low inventory turnover ratios) should be produced only after orders are received. Inventories of those items should not be kept.

15.10 SUMMARY

This chapter examined the broad area of materials flow. We discussed the functions of purchasing and procurement, production control, inbound logistics, warehousing and storage, data and information systems, inventory planning and control, and materials disposal. The relationships between materials management and Total Quality Management (TQM) were identified. The TQM process was discussed and some examples of its implementation were presented.

The administration and control of materials flow requires that the firm measure, report, and improve performance. Concepts and approaches being used or developed include Kanban/Just-In-Time, MRP, ERP, and DRP systems. Each system has been implemented by a variety of firms, with significant positive results. Advantages in computer technology have enabled many of the systems to be implemented successfully in manufacturing, retailing, and service firms. The impact on logistics has been substantial.

EXERCISES

1. Explain some of the differences between the historical role played by materials management within firms and the present and future environments in which materials will be brought into firms' production processes.

2. What are the objectives of integrated materials management?

3. Explain the importance of forecasting in inventory management.

4. Explain the relevance and benefits of JIT in inventory management.

16

Forecasting Methods

16.1 FORECASTING

The word forecast means projection of past into the future, for example—demand forecasting, based on past demand, we forecast future demand values.

Importance of forecasting: Based on forecast of the sales volume, we forecast production schedule, raw material purchasing plan and inventory policies. Consequently, poor forecast can result in increased cost to a firm.

Types of forecasting techniques: Two general types of forecasting techniques are used for demand forecasting:

1. Quantitative methods
2. Qualitative methods

Quantitative methods: Quantitative methods use time series analysis and casual methods

1. Time series analysis relies heavily on historical demand data to project the future size of demand.
2. Casual methods use historical data on independent variables, such as advertisements to predict demand.

Time series: Historical sales data form a time series. A time series is a set of observations of a variable measured at successive points in time. The objective is to provide good forecast of the future values of the time series. Alternatively, the objective is to discover a pattern in the historical data and then extrapolate this pattern into the future.

16.2 PATTERNS IN TIME SERIES

1. Random fluctuation
2. Trend projection
3. Seasonal variation

Smoothing methods: The objective is to *smooth out* the random fluctuations in the time series. The methods are: (1) Moving Average, (2) Weighted Moving Average and (3) Exponential Smoothing.

These methods are appropriate for a stable time series, i.e., one that exhibits no significant trend or seasonal effect. Smoothing methods are easy to use and generally provide a high level of accuracy for short range forecast.

Trend component: If the pattern exhibits gradual shifting of time series, regression analysis can be applied to obtain the trend component.

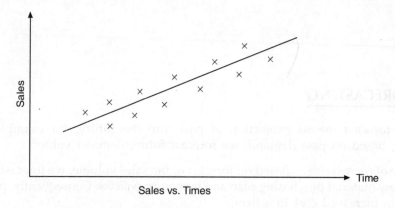

Sales vs. Times

Seasonal Component: Seasonal Component exhibits variability in the data due to seasonal influences.

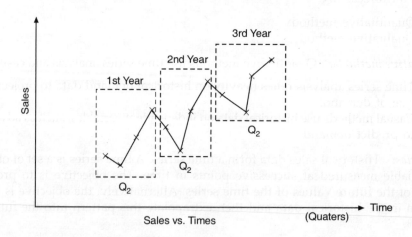

Sales vs. Times

16.3 METHODS OF TIME SERIES

1. Simple average
2. Moving average
3. Weighted moving average

4. Exponential smoothing
5. Trend projection
6. Trend projection adjusted for seasonal influence
7. Casual forecast

16.3.1 Simple Average Method

This method uses the average of the sum of all the data values in the time series as a forecast for the next period. The term simple average is synonymous with arithmetic mean in statistics.

Expressions of simple average method:

$$f_{t+1} = \frac{1}{n}\{d_t + d_{t-1} + d_{t-2} + d_{t-3} + \dots + n \text{ terms} + \dots\}$$

where

f_{t+1} = forecast for period $t+1$

d_t = actual demand for period t

d_{t-1} = actual demand for period $t-1$

16.3.2 Moving Average

This method uses the average of the most recent data values in the time series as a forecast for the next period. The term moving indicates that, as the new observations become available for the time series, it replaces the oldest observation and the new average is computed. As a result, the average will move as the new observations will become available.

Expressions of period moving method:

3 period moving average $f_{t+1} = \frac{1}{3}\{d_t + d_{t-1} + d_{t-2}\}$

$$\text{Sub } t = 3, f_4 = \frac{1}{3}\{d_3 + d_2 + d_1\}$$

$$\text{Sub } t = 4, f_5 = \frac{1}{3}\{d_4 + d_3 + d_2\}$$

4 period moving average $f_{t+1} = \frac{1}{4}\{d_t + d_{t-1} + d_{t-2} + d_{t-3}\}$

$$\text{Sub } t = 4, f_5 = \frac{1}{4}\{d_4 + d_3 + d_2 + d_1\}$$

$$\text{Sub } t = 5, f_6 = \frac{1}{4}\{d_5 + d_4 + d_3 + d_2\}$$

Forecast accuracy: For a particular time series, different lengths of moving averages will affect the accuracy of the forecast. One possible approach to choosing the number of values to be included is to use trial and error to identify the length that minimizes MSE.

Expressions of Forecast Accuracy:

An important consideration in selecting a forecasting method is the accuracy of forecast. Clearly we want the forecast errors to be small.

And we define forecast error as $\equiv e_t = |d_t - f_t|$

The MSE (Mean Squared Error) is an often used measure for the accuracy of a forecasting method.

$$\text{MSE} = \frac{1}{n} \Sigma e_t^2$$

16.3.3 Weighted Moving Average

In the moving average method, each observation in the calculation receives the same weight. One variation known as weighted moving average, involves selecting different weights for different data values and then computing a weighted average of the most recent data. In most cases, the most recent observation receives the maximum weight and the weight decreases for older observations.

Expressions for weighted moving average:

$$f_{t+1} = \alpha_0 d_t + \alpha_1 d_{t-1} + \alpha_2 d_{t-2} + \ldots$$

where

f_{t+1} = forecast for period $t+1$

$\alpha_0, \alpha_1, \alpha_2$ are the weights associated with d_t, d_{t-1} and d_{t-2} respectively such that $\Sigma \alpha_i = 1$ and $\alpha_0 > \alpha_1 > \alpha_2 > \ldots$

d_t = actual demand for period t

d_{t-1} = actual demand for period $t-1$

Expressions period weighted moving average:

3 period weighted moving average $\quad f_{t+1} = \alpha_0 d_t + \alpha_1 d_{t-1} + \alpha_2 d_{t-2}$

$$\text{sub } t = 3, f_4 = \alpha_0 d_3 + \alpha_1 d_2 + \alpha_2 d_1$$

$$\text{sub } t = 4, f_5 = \alpha_0 d_4 + \alpha_1 d_3 + \alpha_2 d_2$$

One set of suggested values of α are:

$$\alpha_0 = \frac{3}{6}; \alpha_1 = \frac{2}{6}; \alpha_2 = \frac{1}{6}$$

use trial and over method to obtain a combination of α that minimizes MSE

16.3.4 Exponential Smoothing

Exponential smoothing is a special case of the weighted moving average method in which we select only one weight, the weight for the most recent observation. The weights of the other data values are automatically compiled, using geometric progression and get smaller and smaller as the observations move further into the past. The basic exponential smoothing model is shown below:

Expressions for exponential smoothing:

$$f_{t+1} = \alpha d_t + (1 - \alpha) f_t$$

where
f_{t+1} = forecast for period $t+1$
α = smoothing constant such that $(0 \leq \alpha \leq 1)$
d_t = actual demand for period t
f_t = forecast for period t

$$f_{t+1} = \alpha d_t + (1 - \alpha) f_t$$

Initialisation of calculation (for a defined value of α, e.g., $\alpha = 0.2$)
We assume that $f_2 = d_1$
Substitute $t = 2$, $f_3 = \alpha d_2 + (1 - \alpha) f_2$
Substitute $t = 3$, $f_4 = \alpha d_3 + (1 - \alpha) f_3$ and so on

16.3.5   Using Trend Projection in Forecasting

The type of time series pattern for which the trend projection method is applicable shows a consistent increase or decrease over time. It is not stable. So the smoothing methods are not applicable. The trend component does not follow each and every up and down movement. Rather the trend component reflects the gradual shifting, for example, growth of the time series values.

Expressions for trend analysis:

$$\hat{Y}_t = \hat{\beta}_1 + \hat{\beta}_2 X_t$$

where
$\hat{Y}_t$ = estimated sales values
$\hat{\beta}_1$ = intercept term
$\hat{\beta}_2$ = slope of the regression line
X_t = time variable (surrogate variable)

$$\hat{\beta}_1 = Y - \hat{\beta}_2 \bar{X}$$

$$\hat{\beta}_2 = \frac{\Sigma xy}{\Sigma x^2}$$

where
$x = X - \bar{X}$ and $y = Y - \bar{Y}$

16.3.6 Seasonal Variation

Many situations in business and economics involve period to period comparisons. Care must be exercised whenever a seasonal influence is present. Removing the seasonal effect from a time series is known as de-seasonalising the time series. The following approach is followed:

1. Compute centred moving average
2. Obtain seasonal index
3. Obtain deseasonalised sales
4. Use deseasonalised sales data to obtain trend using regression analysis
5. Use seasonal index to adjust trend projection

16.3.7 Casual Regression

Casual regression relates to regression analysis applied to two or more variables. If there are two variables under study, it is referred as two variable regression models. However, if there are more than two variables under study then it is referred to as multiple or casual regression analysis.

Expressions for casual regression:
The regression equation of Y on X is expressed as follows:

$$\hat{Y}_i = \hat{\beta}_1 + \hat{\beta}_2 X_i$$

where

$\hat{Y}_i$ = estimation of the dependent variable Y

$\hat{\beta}_1$ = regression coefficient (intercept term)

$\hat{\beta}_2$ = regression coefficient (slope of the line)

X_i = explanatory variable

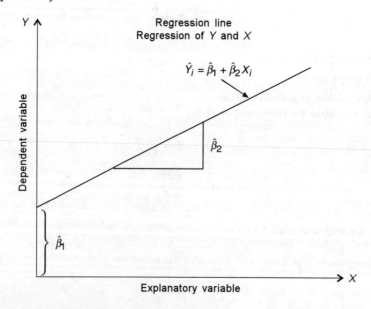

$$\Sigma Y_i = N\hat{\beta}_1 + \hat{\beta}_2 \Sigma X_i$$

$$\Sigma X_i Y_i = \hat{\beta}_1 \Sigma X_i + \hat{\beta}_2 \Sigma X_i^2$$

These equations are usually called the normal equations. In the equations, ΣX_i, ΣY_i, $\Sigma X_i Y_i$, and ΣX_i^2 indicate totals which are computed from the observed pairs of values of two variables X_i and Y_i to which the least squares estimating line is to be fitted and N is the number of observed pairs of values.

If the two normal equations are solved, we obtain the following formulas for the estimators; $\hat{\beta}_1$ and $\hat{\beta}_2$.

$$\hat{\beta}_2 = \frac{\Sigma x_i y_i}{\Sigma x_i^2}$$

where

$$x_i = X_i - \bar{X}$$

$$y_i = Y_i - \bar{Y}$$

$$\hat{\beta}_1 = \bar{Y} - \hat{\beta}_2 \bar{X}$$

$\bar{X}$ and $\bar{Y}$ are the respective arithmetic means

Three-variable regression model

$$\hat{Y}_i = \hat{\beta}_1 + \hat{\beta}_2 X_{2i} + \hat{\beta}_3 X_{3i}$$

$$\Sigma Y_i = N\hat{\beta}_1 + \hat{\beta}_2 \Sigma X_{2i} + \hat{\beta}_3 \Sigma X_{3i}$$

$$\Sigma Y_i X_{2i} = \hat{\beta}_1 \Sigma X_{2i} + \hat{\beta}_2 \Sigma X_{2i}^2 + \hat{\beta}_3 \Sigma X_{2i} X_{3i}$$

$$\Sigma Y_i X_{3i} = \hat{\beta}_1 \Sigma X_{3i} + \hat{\beta}_2 \Sigma X_{2i} X_{3i} + \hat{\beta}_3 \Sigma X_{3i}^2$$

16.4 QUALITATIVE METHODS OF FORECASTING

Qualitative Methods include judgement methods, which translate the opinions of managers, consumer surveys and sales force estimates into Quantitative estimates. In many cases like new product introduction or technology changes, where historical data is not available, judgement methods are the only practical ways to make a forecast. In many other cases where events like heavy discounts or special packages are reflected in the historical data, judgement methods can be used to modify forecast that are generated by quantitative methods. The following are the successful judgement methods.

Sales force estimates: They are forecast compiled from estimates of future demands made periodically by members of a Company Sales force.

Executive opinion: It is a forecasting method in which the opinions, experience and technical knowledge of one or more managers are summarized to arrive at a single forecast.

Market research: It is a systematic approach to determine external consumer interest by creating and testing hypothesis through data gathering surveys

Delphi method: It is a process of gaining consensus from a group of experts who can devote their attention to scientific advances, changes in society, governmental regulations and the competitive environment while maintaining their anonymity.

EXERCISES

1. Define the term Forecast. Explain its importance in business and management.
2. Explain the different possible patterns of past data in time series analysis.
3. Explain the different smoothing methods in forecasting.
4. Explain how to measure the accuracy of the forecasting methods.
5. Explain the use of regression for trend analysis.
6. Explain qualitative methods of forecasting.

PROBLEMS

Problems on use of Forecasting Techniques

PROBLEM 16.1

The accompanying table shows demand for the past 16 months:

Month	1	2	3	4	5	6	7	8
Demand	8.9	9.5	7.9	8.2	8.3	8.9	9.2	8.9
Month	9	10	11	12	13	14	15	16
Demand	9.1	9.6	10.3	9.6	9.0	8.8	9.4	8.9

Predict the demand for the period 17th month using:
  (i) Simple Average Method
  (ii) 3 Months Moving Average
  (iii) 4 Months Moving Average
  (iv) 3 Months Weighted Moving Average
  (v) Exponential smoothing, using constants 0.2 and 0.4

which method of forecasting will you choose for future forecasting? Why?

Solution:

Month	Sales	3-PMA			4-PMA			3-PWMA		
t	dt	ft	et	et²	ft	et	et²	ft	et	et²
1	8.90									
2	9.50									
3	7.90									
4	8.20	8.77	−0.57	0.32				8.60	−0.40	0.16
5	8.30	8.53	−0.23	0.05	8.63	0.32	0.11	8.32	−0.02	0.00
6	8.90	8.13	0.77	0.59	8.48	−0.43	0.18	8.20	0.70	0.49
7	9.20	8.47	0.73	0.54	8.33	−0.87	0.77	8.58	0.62	0.38
8	8.90	8.80	0.10	0.01	8.65	−0.25	0.06	8.95	−0.05	0.00
9	9.10	9.00	0.10	0.01	8.83	−0.27	0.08	9.00	0.10	0.01
10	9.60	9.07	0.53	0.28	9.03	−0.57	0.33	9.05	0.55	0.30
11	10.30	9.20	1.10	1.21	9.20	−1.10	1.21	9.32	0.98	0.97
12	9.60	9.67	−0.07	0.00	9.48	−0.12	0.02	9.87	−0.27	0.07
13	9.00	9.83	−0.83	0.69	9.65	0.65	0.42	9.83	−0.83	0.69
14	8.80	9.63	−0.83	0.69	9.63	0.82	0.68	9.42	−0.62	0.38
15	9.40	9.13	0.27	0.07	9.43	0.03	0.00	9.00	0.40	0.16
16	8.90	9.07	−0.17	0.03	9.20	0.30	0.09	9.13	−0.23	0.05
17		9.0333			9.0250			9.0500		
MSE				0.3468			0.3283			0.2825

		Exponential Smoothing Alpha = 0.2			Exponential Smoothing Alpha = 0.4		
Month	Sales	ft	et	et²	ft	et	et²
t	dt	0.2	0.2	0.2	0.4	0.4	0.4
1	8.90	–	–	–	–	–	
2	9.50	8.90	0.60	0.36	8.90	0.60	0.36
3	7.90	9.02	−1.12	1.25	9.14	−1.24	1.54
4	8.20	8.80	−0.60	0.36	8.64	−0.44	0.20
5	8.30	8.68	−0.38	0.14	8.47	−0.17	0.03
6	8.90	8.60	0.30	0.09	8.40	0.50	0.25
7	9.20	8.66	0.54	0.29	8.60	0.60	0.36
8	8.90	8.77	0.13	0.02	8.84	0.06	0.00
9	9.10	8.80	0.30	0.09	8.BS	0.24	0.06
10	9.60	8.86	0.74	0.55	8.96	0.64	0.41
11	10.30	9.00	1.30	1.68	9.22	1.08	1.18
12	9.60	9.26	0.34	0.11	9.65	−0.05	0.00
13	9.00	9.33	−0.33	0.11	9.63	−0.63	0.40
14	8.80	9.26	−0.46	0.22	9.38	−0.58	0.33
15	9.40	9.17	0.23	0.05	9.15	0.25	0.06
16	8.90	9.22	−0.32	0.10	9.25	−0.35	0.12
17	–	9.1540			9.11		
MSE	–			0.361566			0.353226

Select 3 PWMA because it gives min value of MSE.

PROBLEM 16.2

The accompanying table shows sales for the past 10 years.

Year	1	2	3	4	5	6	7	8	9	10
Sales	21.6	22.9	25.5	21.9	23.9	27.5	31.5	29.7	28.6	31.4

Using Regression Analysis, identify a linear trend?

Solution:

Trend Analysis using Regression (with cell formulas)
Regression of sales on time variable

Year $T(X)$	Sales $S(Y)$	x t	y s	x_2 t_2	y_2 s_2	xy ts
1	21.6	−4.5	−4.85	20.25	23.5225	21.825
2	22.9	−3.5	−3.55	12.25	12.6025	12.425
3	25.5	−2.5	−0.95	6.25	0.9025	2.375
4	21.9	−1.5	−4.55	2.25	20.7025	6.825
5	23.9	−0.5	−2.55	0.25	6.5025	1.275
6	27.5	0.5	1.05	0.25	1.1025	0.525
7	31.5	1.5	5.05	2.25	25.5025	7.575
8	29.7	2.5	3.25	6.25	10.5625	8.125
9	28.6	3.5	2.15	12.25	4.6225	7.525
10	31.4	45	4.95	20.25	24.5025	22.275
55	**264.5**			**82.5**	**130.525**	**90.75**
55	26.45					

Correlation coeff	0.874526167
Regression Coefficients	
Slope B2 cap	1.1
Intrcpt B1 cap	20.4

Regression Trend Equation is:

$$S = 20.4 + 1.1t$$

Forecast using cell formula	32.5

PROBLEM 16.3

A store in Mumbai has used weekend television commercials on ten occasions during the past three months to promote sales at its store. The manager wants to investigate whether a relationship can be demonstrated between the number of commercials shown and the sales at the store during the following week. Sample data for the 10 weeks with sales are shown below:

Week	1	2	3	4	5	6	7	8	9	10
No. of Com.	2	5	1	3	4	1	5	3	4	2
Sales	50	57	41	54	54	38	63	48	59	46

If a relationship exists, estimate the sales corresponding to four commercials planned for the next week.

Solution:

Regression Analysis—Regression of Y on X

Week	No. of comm.	Sales volume						
	X	y	x	y	x_2	y_2	xy	
1	2	50	−1	−1	1	1	1	
2	5	57	2	6	4	36	12	
3	1	41	−2	−10	4	100	20	
4	3	54	a	3	a	9	0	
5	4	54	1	3	1	9	3	
6	1	38	−2	−13	4	169	26	
7	5	63	2	12	4	144	24	
8	3	48	a	−3	a	9	a	
9	4	59	1	8	1	64	8	
10	2	46	−1	−5	1	25	5	
Sum	30	510	0	0	20	566	99	
Mean	3	51						

Regression Coefficients

Slope B2cap   4.95 $\hat{Y}_i = 36.15 + 4.95\,X_i$

Intrcpt B1cap   36.15

PROBLEM 16.4

Fit an appropriate regression model to the the following data {Y Agricultural Production: X_2 Expenditure on Fertilizer; X_3 Expenditure on Irrigation Projects}

Y	6	10	11	19	20	25	30
X_2	1	2	3	7	10	11	13
X_3	20	40	40	51	52	60	60

Solution:

3 Variable Regression Model

Agriculture Production	Expend on Fertilizer	Expend on irrign proj					
Y	X_2	X_3	YX_2	YX_3	X_2X_3	X_2Sq	X_3Sq
6	1	20	6	120	20	1	400
10	2	40	20	400	80	4	1600
11	3	40	33	440	120	9	1600
19	7	51	133	969	357	49	2601
20	10	52	200	1040	520	100	2704
25	11	60	275	1500	660	121	3600
30	13	60	390	1800	780	169	3600
121	**47**	**323**	**1057**	**6269**	**2537**	**453**	**16105**

Solve the Simultaneous Equations

$$121 = 7 B_1 + 47 B_2 + 323 B_3$$
$$1057 = 47 B_1 + 453 B_2 + 2537 B_3$$
$$6269 = 323 B_1 + 2537 B_2 + 16105 B_3$$

Final result (regrn coeff); $B_1 = 1.34, B_2 = 1.39, B_3 = 0.14$

Regression equation $\hat{Y}_i = 1.34 + 1.39X_{2i} + 0.14X_{3i}$

17

Introduction to Operations Research

17.1 THE HISTORICAL DEVELOPMENT

It is generally agreed that Operations Research (OR) came into existence as a discipline during World War II. However, some techniques of OR can be traced back to much earlier. The term Operations Research was coined as a result of research on military operations during World War II. Since the war involved strategic and tactical problems that were so complicated, that to expect adequate solutions from individuals or specialists in a single discipline was unrealistic. Therefore, groups of individuals, who collectively were considered specialists in mathematics, economics, statistics and probability theory, engineering, behavioural and physical science, were formed as special units within the armed forces to deal with strategic and tactical problems of various military operations.

After the war ended, scientists who had been active in the military OR groups made their efforts to apply the operations research approach to civilian problems, related to business, industry, research and development, etc. A key person in the post-War development of OR was George B. Dantzig. In 1947, he developed linear programming and its solution method known as simplex method. Besides linear programming, many other tools of OR, such as statistical quality control, dynamic programming, queuing theory and inventory theory were well developed before the end of the 1950s.

17.2 NATURE AND SIGNIFICANCE OF OPERATIONS RESEARCH

As the term implies, OR involves research on military operations. This indicates the approach as well as the area of its applications. The OR approach is particularly useful in balancing conflicting objectives (goals or interests) where there are many alternative courses of action available to the decision-makers. One such situation is described below:

Consider a large organization with a number of management specialists but not necessarily well-coordinated. For example, consider the basic problem of maintaining stocks of finished goods. To the marketing manager, stocks of a large variety of products are a means of supplying the company's customers with what they want and when they want it. Clearly, according to a marketing manager, a fully stocked warehouse is of prime importance to a company. But the production manager argues for long production runs preferably on a smaller product range, particularly, if significant time is lost when production is switched from one variety to another. The result would again be a tendency to increase the amount of stock carried but it is, of course, vital that the plant should be kept running. On the other hand, the finance manager sees stocks in terms of capital tied up unproductively and argues strongly for their reduction. Finally, there appears the personnel manager for whom a steady level of production is advantageous for having better labour relations. Thus all these people would claim to uphold the interests of their organization, but they do so only from their specialization point of view. They may come up with contradictory solutions—however, they cannot all be right.

In view of the above or of any problem situation involving the whole system, the decision-maker, whatever his specialization, will need help and it is in the attempt to provide this assistance that OR has been developed. Operations Research attempts to resolve the conflict of interests among various sections of an organization and seeks the optimal solution which may not be acceptable to one department but is in the interest of the organization as a whole. Further, OR is concerned with providing the decision-maker with decision aids (or rules) derived from:

(a) A total system orientation.
(b) Scientific methods of investigation, and
(c) Models of reality, generally based on quantitative measurement and techniques.

Thus, successful application of OR techniques for solving a problem must involve:

1. Constructing mathematical, economic and statistical models of the problem under study to treat situations of complexity and uncertainty. This helps to view the problem in its entirety.
2. Analyzing the relationships among different variables and/or parameters associated with the problem so as to determine the consequences of decision alternatives.
3. Suggesting suitable measures of desirability (effectiveness or objective function) in order to evaluate the relative merit of decision alternatives (courses of action, acts or strategies).

17.3 WHAT IS OPERATIONS RESEARCH?

Operations Research or OR is a science which deals with mathematical models and statistical techniques for bettering management decision-making process.

Some of the quantitative decision-making areas are itemized in Table 17.1:

Table 17.1 Quantitative areas in decision-making

Functional area	Certain specific issues and some of the techniques.
Finance, budgeting and investment analysis.	(i) Discounted Cash Flow (DCF) analysis for long-range investments, (ii) Alternative investments' feasibility (Portfolio selection), (iii) Credit policy and dividend policy, (iv) Financial mix that is ratio of equity shares, borrowings, debentures, etc.
Facilities planning	(i) Size and location of plant, (ii) Network analysis in product development, factory construction, installation of equipment and machinery, (iii) Planning other facilities like canteen, housing, transport, etc., (iv) BreakEven Analysis under uncertainty, (v) Rationalization on all company basis.
Exploration, purchase and procurement	(i) Make or buy decisions, (ii) Vendor development through techno commercial survey, (iii) Vendor rating with due weightages to quality and consistency, price, adherence to delivery schedule and after-sales services, (iv) Purchasing with varying prices, (v) Scientific inventory management, (vi) Standardization and variety reduction, (vii) Economic mode of procurement—rail, road, air, waterways.
Personnel	(i) Manpower planning with due consideration to age, skill, wastage and recruitment, using Markovian process, (ii) Recruitment after proper aptitude test and target-oriented training, (iii) Methods study, work measurement, job evaluation, development of incentive plans, wage structuring and negotiating wage and incentive plan with the union.
Manufacturing	(i) Product mix, (ii) Production planning, (iii) Quality control at incoming, inprocess and preshipment stages, (iv) Job sequencing, (v) Optimum run sizes.
Logistics	(i) Number, size and location of warehouses, (ii) Company's transport or hired ones of a mix, (iii) Distribution channel and commission, (iv) Total cost benefit analysis on packaging, insurance etc. with a view to determining the optimum freight structure.
Marketing	(i) Demand forecasting, (ii) Pricing, (iii) Competitive strategies, (iv) Optimum media planning, (v) Sales management, (vi) Market research, market survey and market segmentation.
Maintenance and Replacement	(i) Determination of optimum maintenance crew, (ii) Replacement of items which suddenly fall, (iii) Replacement of items which gradually deteriorate, (iv) Modernization–conveyorisation—link ups etc., (v) Preventive maintenance versus breakdown maintenance.
Research & Development	(i) Product innovations, (ii) Process innovations, (iii) Import substitution.
Others	(i) Plant relocation, expansion, diversification, (ii) Merger and acquisition proposals, (iii) Development of cities and metropolises.

17.4 WHAT ARE OPERATIONS RESEARCH TECHNIQUES?

Not all problems will have one direct solution technique. Some problem areas are, however, amenable to certain treatments through specific techniques. Others will need a combination of several of the quantitative methods. The broad categories of solution techniques in OR, together with a brief outline on them, are brought out in Table 17.2.

Table 17.2 OR techniques and their brief outline

OR Technique	Brief outline
Assignment problem: assignment of jobs to facilities	In assignment problem, one tries to minimize the overall cost or maximize total output, profit, etc. subject to the constraint of only one job per facility, e.g. one machine to an operator or one contract per contractor, etc.
Transportation techniques	The transportation technique deals with minimizing overall transportation cost subject to restrictions on supplies from the sources and demands at the destinations. This technique can equally be used for maximizing profit or sales or productivity etc.
Linear Programming (LP)— Allocation of resources to activities	In LP, one optimizes certain objective functions, like cost minimization, profit maximization, etc. subject to constraints on various resources, like men, machines, material, money, market, etc. For a problem to be resolved through simplex algorithm in LP, its objective function as also the constraints must all be linear. George Dantzig developed simplex method in 1947 whereby any LP problem could be solved, though diet problem and similar other problems were formulated much earlier. Now LP has found extensive applications in business, industry, marketing and administration like product mix, media mix, diet planning, blending problem, manpower planning, optimum bombing pattern, optimum crops rotation plan, wage structuring, etc.
Competitive strategy (Game theory)	Game theory deals with competitive interplay between competing firms. The strategies may consist of advertising, pricing, credit terms, after-sales service, etc. Each participating firm seeks for right mix of its strategies to maximize its own share of market. Game theory is also a part of LP.
Network analysis (PERT/CPM)	Network analysis is a planning and scheduling technique of a project. The project may be erection and commissioning of a boiler, construction of a building for factory expansion, recruitment of personnel or maintenance of a machine It derives its strength from

OR Technique	Brief outline
	the fact that it (a) takes into account the logical sequence of activities and their interdependence; (b) indicates how the failure of performance in any activity affects others and the project as a whole, and (c) shows the possibilities of reducing the time by expediting a limited number of specified activities and thereby aims at project cost trade off. This approach, as an alternative to Gantt chart for planning, was developed around 1958 by the Programmer Evaluation branch of special projects office of the USA navy assisted by Lockheed Missile systems division and a consultant firm. Subsequently, this technique has swept through a number of varying types of organizations in several countries on a variety of application situations.
Decision problems	Decision problems can be under certainty conditions (deterministic) under risk (probabilistic) or under uncertain situations (under uncertainty). Bayesian approach to decision-making tackles uncertainty in terms of risk situation and takes the decision-maker away from hunches and subjectivity.
Queuing theory	Queuing theory attempts to explore, understand and compare various queuing situations, and tries to achieve optimization indirectly. Its application areas in industry are for determining optimum repair crew, allocation of optimum number of machines or machine heads (e.g. spindles) per operator or per setter etc.
Simulation	The word simulation is derived from assumed sequence of occurrences that are apparent rather than real. This technique brings relief to problem areas which cannot be put through formal mathematical or statistical analysis. Waiting line models where arrivals or services do not follow any statistical distribution can only be tackled by simulation technique. In short, simulation is applicable to situations which are too complex for analytical solutions and too difficult, rather infeasible, for actual experimentation. Thus, when all else fails, simulation prevails.
Forecasting models	A number of statistical techniques like regression analysis, time series analysis are used for short term (up to one year) demand forecasting. A better method is exponential smoothing technique which gives more weightage to recent demand and can correct for trends as well.

OR Technique	Brief outline
Inventory control	There are no two opinions regarding the need for controlling inventory. Two basic questions, namely, how much to order and when to order, are answered under varying demand, supply and cost parameters.
Investment decision	Money depreciates over time. Hence for long range investment propositions, discounted expected cash inflows have to be compared with discounted expected cash outflows over a planning period. Net present value of future earnings will, therefore, be a good guide in investment decisions.
Replacement policies	Replacement of a part, an assembly or an equipment is carried out due to various reasons like inadequacy, obsolescence, excessive maintenance, declining efficiency, etc. Replacement policies on items which gradually deteriorate fall in two distinct categories. The problem in the former case is "how many to replace" which involves development of a suitable preventive replacement policy whereas in the latter case the question is "when to replace".
Job sequencing	In a job shop where the processing sequence is well defined, the order in which these jobs should be planned need be determined with the basic objective of completing all the jobs in the shortest possible time. For example, in a printing process changeover from any colour to black colour is very easy but changing over to any colour from black colour is rather difficult. This leads to the problem of sequencing of jobs.

EXERCISES

1. Explain the nature and significance of Operations Research.
2. List down some of the quantitative areas in decision making.
3. List down some of the OR techniques and briefly discuss each of them.

REFERENCES

[1] Quinn, James Brian and Christopher E. Gagnon, Will Services Follow Manufacturing Into Decline?, *Harvard Business Review*, November-December 1986.

[2] Quality is in the Eye of the Customer; *Quality Control Supervisor's Bulletin*, November 25, 1987.

[3] Edwards Deming, W., *Out of the Crisis* (Cambridge: Massachusetts Institute of Technology, 1986).

[4] Rosander, A.C., *Washington Story* (Greeley, CO: Nation Directions, 1985).

[5] Rosander, A.C., *Applications of Quality Control in the Service Industries* (Milkwaukee, WI: ASQC Quality Press, 1986).

[6] Kirby, Eugene, Quality Control in Banking, Administrative Applications Division of ASQC Year Book, 1975.

[7] Latzko, William J., *Quality and Productivity for Bankers and Financial Managers* (Milwaukee, WI: ASQC Quality Press, 11987).

[8] Ryan, John, ASQC/Gallup Survey Results Revealed, *Quality Progress*, November 1985.

[9] Branst, Lee, Disneyland—a Kingdom of Service Quality, *Quality*, February 1984.

[10] Leferve, Henry L., *Quality Service Pays: Six Keys to Success*; Vanity Books International, New Delhi.

[11] Chan, Teng Heng, Nanyang Technological University, Hesan A. Quazi, Nanyang Technological University; Overview of Quality Management Practices in Selected Asian Countries, *ASQ Quality Management Journal*, Vol. 9, Issue 1.

[12] Lulla, Suresh, World-Class Quality: Looking Back, Looking Forward; *BMA Review*, September–October 2002.

[13] Editorial, BMA Review, *A Journal of Bombay Management Association*, Vol. 13, No. 5, September-October 2002.

[14] Rau, R.H.G., Making India World-Class in Quality: How Can We Do It?; *BMA Review*, September-October 2002.

[15] Ramaswamy, V. and S. Namakumary, *Marketing Management*, 3rd ed., Macmillan Business Book.

[16] Patnaik, R.M. and Prof. B Kumar, Productivity Improvement in Electric Utilities by Quality Circle Approach; A Case Study; *Industrial Engineering Journal*, Vol. xxxi, No. 3, March 2002.

[17] Suresh, Lulla, *World-Class Quality: An Executive Handbook.*

[18] Jet Airways: The Service Quality Experience by Steve Forte, CEO, Jet Airways.

[19] Kotler, Philip, *Marketing Management: Analysis, Planning Implementation and Control,* 9th ed., Prentice-Hall of India, New Delhi.

[20] Banerjee, B., TQM to WCM, *BMA Review,* vol. 13, No. 4, July–August 2002.

[21] Stamis, D.H., *Total Quality Service: Principles, Practices, and Implementation,* Vanity Books International, New Delhi.

[22] Lawton, Robin L., Creating a Customer it Centered Culture, ASQC Quality Congress Transactions, May 4–6, 1987.

[23] Puri, Subhash C., A Plan of Excellence for a Regulatory Agency, ASQC Quality Congress Transactions, May 4–6, 1987.

[24] Gupta, P.K., *Services Marketing,* Everest Publishing House Millennium, 2002.

[25] Rosander, A.C., *Applications of Quality Control in the Service Industries,* ASQC Quality Press, Milwaukee, WI, 1985.

[26] Quality Is in the Eye of the Customer, *Quality Control Supervisors, Bulletin,* November 25, 1987.

[27] Levitt, Theodore, Production-Line Approach to Service, *Harvard Business Review,* September-October 1972,

[28] King, Carol A., Service Quality Assurance is Different, Quality Progress, June 1985.

[29] Prasad, C. Gandhi, World-Class Journey—India Incorporated, Total Quality Management, J.S. Ahluwalia (Ed.).

[30] Bennis, Warren and Burt Nanus, *Leaders: The Strategies for Taking Charge,* Harper & Row, New York, 1985.

[31] The inspiration for the phrase "providing a service good enough that people will pay a profit to have it" comes from an Inc. magazine with retailer Stanley Marcus who was quoting the Dayton family in Minneapolis, Dayton-Hudson Corporation.

[32] Drucker, Peter F., Leadership: More Doing than Dash, *Wall Street Journal,* January 6, 1988 published in Valarie A. Zeithaml, A. Parasuraman and Leonard Berry, *Delivering Quality Service—Balancing Customer Perceptions and Expectations,* The Free Press, New York, 1990.

[33] Zeithaml, Valarie A., A. Parasuraman, and Leonard Berry, *Delivering Quality Service—Balancing Customer Perceptions and Expectations,* The Free Press, New York, 1990.

[34] Maruf, Hasan, An investigation of total quality management practices in Australian companies' Ph.D. thesis submitted to University of New South Wales in 1998 published in Research in quality management: Review and Implications, by Himanshu Trivedi, *NMIMS Journal,* January–June 2002.

[35] Total Quality Management: Aspects of Implementation and Performance, Hansson, Jonas, 2003-02-18, Extracted from the Internet in the form of abstract.

[36] Quality Practices and Customer/Supplier Management in Australian Service Organizations, Extracted from the Internet in the form of abstract.

[37] Comparative analysis of cultural, conceptual and practical constraints on quality management implementations—findings from Australian and Korean banking industries, Extracted from the Internet in the form of abstract.

[38] Anders Gustafsson land Lars Nilsson Service Research Center, Sweden; and Michael D Johnson; University of Michigan Business School USA; The role of Quality practices in service organizations; Extracted from the Internet in the form of abstract.

[39] Case Study: Revolutionizing the Service Industry, The Ritz-Carlton Hotel Company Wins Coveted Malcolm Baldrige National Quality Award for the second time; Extracted from the Internet Source: www.ritzcarlton.com/corporate/press_room/releases/mb_award_2time.html–24k–30 Jan. 2004.

[40] Ojha, Abhay, Learning from TQM (TQM—How can we make the implementation effective)", *Vikalpa Journal*, Vol. 25, No. 2, April–June 2000.

[41] Heizer and Nathan, Cases in Total Quality Management, Manufacturing and Services, Thomson South-Western, Curtis P. McLaughlin, University of North Carolina at Chapel Hill, West Florida Regional Medical Center, Case study on Continuous Quality Improvement Process.

[42] Sureshchandar, G.S., Chandrasekharan Rajendran and R.N. Anantharaman, (a) The relationship between management's perception of total quality service and customer perceptions of service quality, *Total Quality Management*, Vol. 13, No. 1, 2002, 69–88 and (b) A conceptual model for Total Quality Management in service organizations, *Total Quality Management*, Vol. 12, No. 3, 2001.

INDEX

'5' S of housekeeping, 96
80/20 rule, 365

ABC analysis (Pareto principle), 365–366
Abnormal distributions, 148
Active planning, 162
ALDEP (Automated Layout Design Planning), 46
American Productivity Centre Model, 186
Annual Plan/Review, 103
Appraisal costs, 96
Assembling, 34
Assignment problem, 404

Benchmarking, 232, 312
    elements, 234
    measurements, 235
    process, 235
    types, 232
Bill of Material (BOM), 255
Break Even Point (BEP), 23–24
Business Intelligence (BI), 69
Business Process Re-engineering (BPR) and
    implementation, 238, 240

C-Chart, 142
CAD/CAM, 191
Capability Maturity Model (CMM), 118
Capacity Requirement Planning (CRP), 68
Casting, 36
Casual forecast, 391
Casual regression, 394
Causal method, 160
Cellular manufacturing, 51–52
Chemical processing, 37
Competitive strategy, 404
Complaint and suggestion systems, 301

Computer Integrated Manufacturing (CIM),
    52, 144, 191
Computer-aided statistical process control
    system, 144
Computerized Relative Allocation of Facilities
    Technique (CRAFT), 46
Concentric growth strategy, 158
Conceptual skills, 19
Confidence limits, 132
Conglomerate growth strategy, 158
Continual improvement, 108
Continuous improvement, 65–66
Continuous sampling inspection, 133
Control phase, 163
Controlled variation, 98
CORELAP (Computerized Relationship Layout
    Planning), 46
Cost of materials, 253–254
Cost of Poor Quality (COQP), 71, 94
CPRF (Collaborative Procurement and
    Replenishment Function), 69
Critical dimensions of TQM (TQS), 333
Critical processes and measures, 102
Crosby, Philip B., 98
CTQ (Critical To Quality), 16
Customer focus, 65–66, 107
Customer Relationship Management (CRM), 49,
    69
Customer satisfaction, 19, 79, 86
Customer satisfaction surveys, 301
Cycle stock, 360

Darsiri method, 225–226
Data and information systems, 376
Dead stock, 364
Decision problems, 405
Decision-making role/Entrepreneurship skills,
    18

Delighted customer, 71
Demand forecast, 378
Demand measurement, 154
Demand technology cycle, 156
Deming, W. Edward, 97
Departmental functions, 29
Dependent demand and Independent demand, 252
Dependent demand items, 52
Dispersion and process capability, 147
Distribution Requirement Planning (DRP), 68, 192, 259
Diversification, 158
DMADV/DMAIC approach, 16
Double sampling plan, 135
Drum–Buffer–Rope Mechanism, 353

E. Goldrat, 98
Economic Batch Quantity (EBQ) and its Graphic representation, 170
Economies of scale, 356
Efficiency/Effectiveness, 86
Energy Conservation Technology (ECT), 192
Enterprise Resource Planning–II, 69
Ergonomics, 194
ERP Systems, 368
Equipments, factors for selection, 58
Esteem values, 218
Explosion, 51, 178
Exponential smoothing, 392
External failure costs, 96

Factual approach to decision-making, 108
Fitness for purpose/use, 78
Flexible Manufacturing System (FMS), 49, 52, 192
Flow diagram, 203
Flow process chart and symbols, 201–202
Ford's Mass Production System (MPS), 49
Forecasting, 377
    judgemental, 159
    long-term, 378
    methods (qualitative), 395
    mid-range, 378
    models, 405
    short-term, 378
    time frames, 378
    types, 378
Forging, 35

Frequency distribution curve, bar chart and histogram, 127
Functional relationship, 28

Game theory, 404
Gantt charts, 175
General Purpose Machines (GPMs), 32
Ghost shopping, 301
Goods and services, differences between, 296
Goods-In-Process (G-I-P), 44
Graphic technique, 165, 168
Group technology, 51, 52, 191
    advantages, 53
    aggregation, 51
    cell, 53, 54
    centre, 54, 55
    disadvantages, 53
    explosion, 51, 178
    flow line, 53, 54
    layout, 52–53
    segregation, 51
Growth matrix, 157

Handling operation analysis, 56
Hard factors of production, 38
Hard standards, 280
Heat treatment and plating, 37
Horizontal quality thinking, 27, 85
Human relations skill, 17

Idle time, 191
Implied need, 19
Informational role/Communication skills, 18
Inspection and quality control, 129
Inter-personal role/Liasoning skills, 18
Internal customer, 27, 85
Internal failure costs, 96
Inventory,
    concepts, 356
    control, 192
    cost, 252
    eight areas, 254
    in-transit, 361
    Inventory Carrying Cost (ICC), 254
    management, 251
    planning and control, 377
    status file, 256
    types, 360
Involvement of people, 107

Ishikawa, Kaoru, 98
Ishikawa diagram, 263
ISO 14001:1996 Environmental Management
    System, 110
ISO 9000:2000, 13, 103, 104

Job
    enlargement, 194
    enrichment, 194
    rotation, 194
Job sequencing, 406
Johnson's rule, 177
Juran, Joseph M., 97
Juran's Quality Improvement Projects (JQIP),
    66, 68, 71
Just In Case Stock (JIC), 262
Just-In-Time (JIT), 261, 384
    benefits, 385
    definition, 384
    enablers, 262
    Japanese practices of JIT, 261
    manufacturing and purchasing, 193
    production, 264
    purchasing, 263
    system, 263
    at Xerox Europe, 385

Kaizen Gemba, 65, 71
Kanban, and flow of two Kanbans, 265
Kanban and Just-in-Time Systems, 383
Key Result Areas (KRA), 194

Labour productivity, 182
Laser technology, 191
Leadership, 107
Learning curve, 194
Less than carload (LCL)/Truckload (LTL), 356
Linear Programming (LP), 167, 404
Loading, 162
Logistics, 250, 381
    flow, 359
    inbound, 375
    management, 192, 250
    reverse, 377
    and supply chain management, 245
Logistics and manufacturing interface, 387
Lost customer analysis, 301
Lucas-TVS Limited, an example, 119

Machine-type Flow Process Chart, 206
Machining, 34
Man type flow process chart, 206
Management by Objectives (MBO), 194
Mangement, concept of, 4
Management Pioneers, 97
Manufacturing processes, types of, 33
Material Flow Management, 371
Manufacturing Resource Planning (MRP–II), 68,
    257, 258
Masaaki Imai, 98
Mass Production System (MPS), 32
Master Production Schedule (MPS), 178, 256
Material control, 162
Material handling, 55, 193
    air transport, 60
    assessment, 58
    animal carrier, 60
    bulk handling, 56
    carrier handling, 56
    cranes, 59
    conveyors, 59
    elevators and hoists, 59
    equipment types, 59
    external equipment, 59
    industrial vahicles, 59
    internal equipment, 59
    marine carrier, 60
    packaging handling, 56, 59, 250
    pipelines, 60
    railways, 60
    rules, 208
    stages, 57
    unit handling, 56
Material Handling Labour (MHL), 58
Material Requirement Planning (MRP–I), 68, 254,
    255
MRP–I & MRP–II combined, 259
Material type flow process chart, 205
Measurement analysis and improvement, 109
Metal forming, 35
Method study, objectives, 195, 200–201
Motion study, 195, 207
    macroscopic motion, 211
    microscopic motion, 211
    motion analysis, 207
Motion economy, principles of, 208
Moving average, 390, 391
Multiple sampling plan, 135
Muther grid, 47

Network analysis (PERT/CPM), 404
Normal distribution curves
    leptokurtic, 129, 131
    multi-model, 131
    platykurtic, 129, 131
    symmetrical, 129–130
    skewed, 129
    triangular, 131

Operation analysis, 203
Operations management functions, 5, 7
Operations Research (OR), 402
    significance, 401
    simulation, 405
    techniques, 404
Order processing systems, 369
    order writing, 161
Organizational mission/vision, 102
Outline process chart, 201

P-D-C-A cycle (Plan-Do-Check-Act), 8, 10, 12, 66
Performance excellence, 72
PEST Analysis (Political, Economic, Social and Technological), 12, 67
Philip Crosby's 14 Steps for quality improvement, 101
    design procedure, 44
Physical Distribution Management (PDM), 22
Plant layout, 43
    design procedure, 44
    fixed position layout, 47–48
    group technology layout, 51
    important factors, 40
    objectives, 44
    process or functional layout, 47, 50
    product or line layout, 47–49
    types, 47
Plant location, 39
Plastic forming, 36
Pokayoke (elimination of mistakes), 66
Poor productivity, causes of, 189
Positioning, weighing and controlling equipment, 59
Prevention costs, 95
Price forecast, 378
Price utility, 247
Priority decision rules, 176
Prior planning, 161
Process
    approach, 108

capability Cp/capability factor Cpk, 15
    planning and routing, 162
Process variation, causes of, 151
Product design, 161
Product design or Redesign, influencing factors, 218
Product Life Cycle (PLC), 155
Product quality, dimensions of, 78
Product quality (small q), 63
Product realization, 109
Product tree concept, 255–256
Product-based productivity technique, 194
Production control, 374
Production indent, 19
Production Planning and Control (PPC), 160
    important features, 164
Production types, 31
    batch production, 32
    continuous production, 32
    job or project production, 32
    mass production, 32
Productivity, 16, 181–182
    index, 182
    partial, 182
    technique applications, 185
Productivity and performance, 182
Program Logic Controller (PLC), 144
Progress reporting, 164
Purchasing and procurement, 374

Quality assurance, 86, 105
Quality, characteristics of, 78
Quality council, 103
Quality management system, 67, 86, 105–106
Quality management, evolution of, 80
Quality movement in Asian countries, 114
    in India, 116
    in Japan, 115
Quality
    concepts and definitions, 76, 85
    control, 70, 86
    improvement, 71, 86
    objective, 86
    plan, 70
    planning, 86
    policy, 85
    record, 86
    system, 86
Quality-related terms, 85
Queuing theory, 405
Q/q or big Q/small q or TQM/product quality, 63

R-A-T-E-R checklist, 282
R-Chart, 137
Resource management, 109
Return On Investment (ROI), 23
    maximization, 72
Reverse logistics, 377
Right
    place, 22, 246
    price, 22
    quality, 20, 245, 246
    quantity, 21
    time, 21
Robotics, 191

Safety or buffer stock, 361
Sales forecast/budget, 154, 158
Sampling, 126
Scheduling, 163, 172
    backward, 174
    factors affecting, 174
    forward, 175
    guidelines, 175
    methodology, 175
    objectives, 173
    types, 175
Scheduling and loading guidelines, 175
Seasonal component, 390
Seasonal stock, 364
Seasonal variation, 393
SEIKETSU, 97
SEIRI, 97
SEISO, 97
SEITON, 97
Sequential sampling plan, 136
Service
    leadership, 306
    provider's point of view, 333
    quality, 268, 285
    quality (customer's perspective), 310
    quality research, 315
    value, 286
Service industry, concept of, 4
Service industries in USA (surveys), 273
Service leaders, characteristics of, 308
Service quality, categories of, 292
Service quality, dimensions of, 330
Service sector definition, 282
Servqual, 311
Seven MUDAS (seven zeros) banner, 92
Sheigo Shingo, 98

Shewart, Walter, 97
Shitsuke, 97
SIMO chart, 211
Simple average method, 390–391
Single criterion rule, 176
Single sampling plan, 134
Six Sigma approach, 14
Skills pyramid, 19
SMART, 67
SMED (Single Minute Exchange of Dies), 226
    examples, 228
    steps, 227
    success stories, 228
Smoothing methods, 390
Soft factors of production, 38
Soft standards, 283
    Indian examples of quality management, 118
SPACECRAFT, 46
Special Purpose Machine (SPM), 49
Specific, Measurable, Attainable, Realistic and
    Time-bound (SMART) vision, 11
Speculative stock, 363
SRM (Supplier Relationship Management), 69
Standard data, 215
Standard time, 214
Stated and implied needs, 79
Statistical process control, 14, 144–145
Strategic quality planning, 65, 67
Style, Fashion and Fad Life Cycles, 157
Sumanth's Five-Pronged Approach to produc-
    tivity improvement, 191
Supplier relationship, mutually beneficial, 108
Supply chain management, 67, 68, 192, 244, 260
    benefits, 248
    objectives, 260
Supply forecast, 378
SWOT analysis, 11
System approach, 108

Taiichi Ohno, 98
Task-based productivity technique, 195
Technical skills, 17
Techniques for determining customer needs, 300
    correspondence, 302
    face-to-face programme, 302
    surveys, 302
    toll free hotlines, 302
Technology-based Productivity Improvement
    techniques (TPI), 191
The Goal (book) by Dr. Eliyahu Goldratt Jeff Cox,
    351

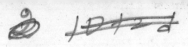

Theory of Constraints (TOC), 351
Therbligs, 211
Three 'F's—Fit, Form and Function, 78
Time series, 389
  analysis, 160
  patterns, 389
Time study (work measurement), 195, 212
Time study form, 216
Tools and manufacturing aids control, 162
Total Employee Involvement (TEI), 11, 68
Total factor productivity, 183
Total labour ratio, 58
Total Organizational Involvement (TOI), 67–68
Total productive maintenance, features, 229–230
Total productivity model, implementation, 196
Total Productivity Model (TPM), 187
  salient features, 188
Total Quality Management (TQM), 65, 379, 380,
    381
  eight building blocks, 90–91
  eleven steps, 102
  keys to success, 380
  process, 70
  reasons for failure, 121
  with reference to Indian industries, 62
  TQM versus traditional management, 380
Total Quality Service (TQS), 286, 323–324
TQM: Definitions, Concepts, Features, 86
TQM and Logistics, 381
Tracking and measuring customer satisfaction,
    tools for, 301
Trend projection in forecasting, 391, 393
Transportation techniques, 404
Transportation management, 250
Trend component, 390
Two-handed process chart, 201

Uncontrolled variation, 98
US quality revolution, 112
Use value, 218

Value addition, 85
Value Analysis (VE) and Value Engineering, 217
Value analysis, 217
  features, 217
  methods, 220
  phases, 223
  steps, 218
Value, concept of, 218
Value engineering, 194, 217
  phases, 223
Value for money, 22
Variance analysis, 133
Vertical chimneys organizational structure, 27
VMI or Vendor Managed Inventory, 69
Voice of the Customer (VOC), 16

Warehouse management, 250
Warehousing and Storage, 56, 376
Water jet machining technology, 192
Weighted moving average, 391, 392
Welding and fabrication, 34
Work study, 198
  advantages/objectives, 199
  application, 199
Work-In-Progress (WIP), 25, 251
Work place layout rules, 208
World-Class Performance, 64

$\bar{X}$-Chart, 136

Zero
  accident, 92
  defect, 92
  delay, 92
  disdain for others, 92
  downtime, 92
  paper, 92
  stock or inventory, 92